T0355330

China's Western Horizon

DANIEL S.
MARKEY

China's Western Horizon

Beijing and the New Geopolitics of Eurasia

OXFORD
UNIVERSITY PRESS

Oxford University Press is a department of the University of Oxford. It furthers
the University's objective of excellence in research, scholarship, and education
by publishing worldwide. Oxford is a registered trade mark of Oxford University
Press in the UK and certain other countries.

Published in the United States of America by Oxford University Press
198 Madison Avenue, New York, NY 10016, United States of America.

Library of Congress Cataloging-in-Publication Data
Names: Markey, Daniel Seth, 1973– author.
Title: China's western horizon : Beijing and the new geopolitics
of Eurasia / Daniel S. Markey.
Description: New York, NY : Oxford University Press, 2020. |
Includes bibliographical references and index. |
Identifiers: LCCN 2019033310 (print) | LCCN 2019033311 (ebook) |
ISBN 9780190680190 (hardback) | ISBN 9780190680213 (epub) |
ISBN 9780190680206 (updf) | ISBN 9780190087883 (online)
Subjects: LCSH: China—Foreign relations—21st century. |
China—Foreign relations—South Asia. | South Asia—Foreign relations—China. |
China—Foreign relations—Asia, Central. | Asia, Central—Foreign relations—China. |
China—Foreign relations—Middle East. | Middle East—Foreign relations—China.
Classification: LCC JZ1734 .M37 2020 (print) | LCC JZ1734 (ebook) | DDC 327.5105—dc23
LC record available at https://lccn.loc.gov/2019033310
LC ebook record available at https://lccn.loc.gov/2019033311

9 8 7 6 5 4 3 2 1

Printed by Sheridan Books, Inc., United States of America

CONTENTS

PREFACE

IN JANUARY 2000, Pakistan's president and army chief, Pervez Musharraf, traveled to Beijing. Just a few months earlier, he had toppled Pakistan's civilian government in a coup, earning Washington's ire and a stiff round of US economic sanctions. During closed-door sessions with Chinese president Jiang Zemin and premier Zhu Rongji, Musharraf pointedly requested China's assistance. He had something very specific in mind: he wanted Beijing's help to construct Gwadar, a new Pakistani deep-water port on the Arabian Sea.[1]

Musharraf needed the trip to China to show that he had Beijing's full confidence and to cement his domestic political legitimacy after the coup. He projected this aim in his comments to the media: "China has stood by Pakistan in difficult times. Our relations have remained strong and steadfast, notwithstanding the cataclysmic changes in the political and security environment at the international, regional or domestic level."[2]

But Musharraf also had a broader geopolitical agenda, one he proudly shared at a small dinner reception in April 2017. "Yes, Gwadar was entirely my idea, not a Chinese idea. I was concerned only about Pakistan's strategic interests," he explained. A Chinese-built port at Gwadar would demonstrate Pakistan's close ties with Beijing and send an obvious signal to India that Pakistan was not to be trifled with. In particular, Musharraf said that he had been concerned India could blockade Pakistan's main port of Karachi. With a functioning port at Gwadar near the gateway to the Persian Gulf, Pakistan could also threaten India's access to Middle Eastern oil. At the very least, a Pakistani base at Gwadar would force India to think twice before launching its own naval operations against Pakistan.[3]

For Musharraf, sending a tough message to India was essential. Just six months earlier, India and Pakistan had come to blows in the Kargil War, a border conflict that Musharraf—then the army chief but not yet president—had advocated and led. A year before that, the two sides had traded nuclear tests. So when Musharraf visited China in 2000, the Indo-Pakistani border was still extremely tense, one of the most likely places in the world to see a nuclear war.

What was most surprising about the story of Musharraf's visit to Beijing, as a Chinese diplomat colleague explained in 2013 over lunch platters of steaming fish and spicy fried shrimp, was that China's top leaders were completely stunned by the Pakistani request to build Gwadar.[4] To Beijing, Gwadar looked like a big waste of money: a white elephant with little commercial necessity, disconnected from Pakistan's transit and communications networks and surrounded by impoverished fishing villages as well as, more menacingly, Baloch separatist groups waging a decades-long insurgency against the state. The Chinese side was so skeptical of Musharraf's proposal that more junior diplomats were immediately sent to ask their Pakistani counterparts whether Pakistan's leader was serious.

He was. In May 2001, on a four-day trip to Pakistan to commemorate the fiftieth anniversary of friendly Sino-Pakistani relations, Premier Zhu Rongji publicly announced China's intention to underwrite Gwadar's construction.[5] And on March 22, 2002, Musharraf hosted Chinese vice premier Wu Bangguo and a thirty-two-member Chinese delegation at Gwadar for a festive, open-air ceremony to commemorate the groundbreaking of the new port. Standing beside his Chinese guests and speaking into a jumble of microphones, Musharraf described Gwadar as a bold infrastructure scheme intended to "end the sense of deprivation among the people of the district and surrounding areas, boost the economic activities and alleviate poverty."[6]

For the next decade, however, Gwadar was plagued by precisely the weaknesses that Chinese diplomats claim they had predicted from the start. Opposition leaders in Balochistan perceived Gwadar more as a scheme to steal their real estate than as a means to strengthen the local economy.[7] In May 2004, the Balochistan Liberation Army blew up a bus carrying Chinese engineers to the port, killing three and injuring nine. That and other deadly attacks stalled the port's construction schedule. High-volume rail and road connections failed to materialize, and neither did commercial demand for diverting Pakistan's shipping from the well-established port of Karachi. In 2013, once it became clear that there would be practically no shipping traffic to or from Gwadar, the Singaporean management company hired to run the port's facilities just gave up.

Yet that was hardly the entire story of Gwadar. Despite the port's practical difficulties, many regional observers perceived Gwadar as a symbol of something much greater: the possibility that China, with its newfound wealth and power, would play an increasingly ambitious role in its western Eurasian neighborhood. Pakistani strategists never gave up on Gwadar's potential and never stopped portraying China as an "all-weather friend." In Indian foreign and defense policy circles, Gwadar fueled long-standing fears about the threat posed by a Sino-Pakistani strategic convergence. And in the United States, some military analysts identified Gwadar as part of a Chinese "string of pearls," by which they meant a series of ports and bases across the Indian Ocean region that would enable China to challenge not merely the Indian navy, but the American one as well.[8] As Robert Kaplan wrote in his influential 2010 book, *Monsoon*, "If there are great place-names of the past—Carthage, Thebes, Troy, Samarkand, Angkor Wat—and of the present—Dubai, Singapore, Teheran, Beijing, Washington—then Gwadar might qualify as a great place-name of the future."[9]

Most of all, Gwadar is a telling example of the complex interplay between China and its neighbors. Gwadar may eventually serve a variety of Chinese goals, but the port was initially the product of a Pakistani effort launched for Pakistani reasons. In this important respect, Gwadar is not unique. To the contrary, it reflects an enduring reality: China is the most powerful actor in its neighborhood, but it cannot simply have its way with the smaller states of the region. Beijing's policies will still be interpreted, constrained, and altered in fundamental ways by its neighbors. Sometimes, the interests of the "weak," or lesser states of the region, will determine political outcomes more than those of the strong.

As a consequence, any attempt to anticipate the emerging shape of Eurasian geopolitics without considering local and sub-regional realities alongside Chinese goals and policies will likely fail. To be sure, we need to better understand what makes Beijing tick, and how Chinese aspirations will play out on the world stage. That effort needs to come hand-in-hand with careful assessment of the politics and economics of Eurasian states themselves, including their domestic and strategic compulsions. What do their leaders, powerful institutions, and people desire, fear, and expect from China? How are they most likely to respond to Chinese investments, diplomatic overtures, or military moves? How do their national histories and popular narratives lead them to perceive the world and China's changing place in it?

With these sorts of questions in mind, this book aims to make sense of the decisive role that China's less powerful neighbors are likely to play as China extends its reach across its western horizon. It then offers guidance about what these developments mean for America's emerging global geopolitical competition with China.

ACKNOWLEDGMENTS

IN A WAY, I have been working on this book for well over a decade. When I started to write my last book on the troubled relationship between the United States and Pakistan, I jumped straight to the chapter on geopolitical relationships between Pakistan, the United States, India, and China. At the time, I was convinced that China's growing power and greater presence in South Asia would influence Pakistan's trajectory, alter the relationship between India and Pakistan, and even transform how US policymakers tended to think about South Asia overall. In the intervening years, many of these initial impressions were reinforced.

Luckily for me, writing this book also expanded my horizons to new regions, including parts of Central Asia and the Middle East. As the years passed, the world—and especially policymakers in Washington—became increasingly fixated on China. The ambitious global initiatives launched by President Xi Jinping first escaped widespread American news coverage, but now even casual news readers will probably have stumbled across stories about the "Belt and Road Initiative" and will, like me, have serious questions about what China is doing around the world, how other states are responding, and what, if anything, the United States should do about it all.

Fortunately, for the past five years I have had the privilege of working at the Johns Hopkins School of Advanced International Studies (SAIS), an institution where these sorts of questions are routinely asked and answered. I am indebted to the faculty for welcoming me and enabling and encouraging my research. My colleagues, starting with deans Vali Nasr and Eliot Cohen, set a high standard for injecting scholarly expertise and policy experience into public debates on international affairs. I continue to learn from their example.

Other SAIS colleagues have shared their wisdom in ways that were directly relevant to this book. Hal Brands, David Bulman, Carla Freeman, and Josh White deserve special thanks for reading and responding to draft text. A number of my students also provided thoughtful and constructive feedback on the manuscript, and several generations of student interns helped with gathering research material. Many other SAIS colleagues, Rebecca Aman above all, have supported this project indirectly by alleviating other professional responsibilities and stresses.

Without the work of outstanding research associates, this book would not exist. I am extremely fortunate that Valerian Sikhuashvili and Noah Reichblum chose to join me at SAIS. I have no doubt that they will go on to greater accomplishments in the future. Valerian helped launch and sustain the initial research for this book. Among other tasks, he organized our memorable research trip to Russia, Kazakhstan, and Georgia. Noah contributed a timely boost of energy and enthusiasm to kick-start drafting and revision. His pace and dedication inspired confidence, and his hard work lightened my load considerably. During the final stages of book production, Jonathon Sine ably picked up where Noah left off.

I am grateful to Dave McBride and his team at Oxford University Press for signing on to this project at the outset and for offering keen suggestions and guidance—all with a light hand—throughout. OUP's external reviewers provided welcome endorsements along with smart suggestions. I would also like to acknowledge the financial support and expert reviews from an external institutional donor that remains committed to fostering policy-relevant book research. I only wish other institutions would follow its lead.

So many colleagues, near and far, have helped me with this book that it would be impossible to name them all. First and foremost, however, thanks to those who shared their experiences and insights in interviews or who helped me connect with other experts. Some are cited in this book's endnotes, but many are not. A handful of stalwarts have taken the time to read drafts and provide invaluable feedback, for which I am particularly grateful: Alexander Cooley, Aaron Friedberg, Paul Heer, Vali Nasr, Rob Nelson, Nadège Rolland, Andrew Small, and Paul Stares. I have learned a great deal from a series of fruitful discussions under the auspices of the SAIS-Peking University dialogue, which benefited from the support of the US Institute of Peace, the Betty Lou Hummel Endowment of the SAIS Foreign Policy Institute, Peking University, and Johns Hopkins SAIS. Other roundtables and conferences that contributed to my understanding of various topics in this book have been generously hosted by Alyssa Ayres, Elizabeth Economy, Sameer Lalwani, Tanvi Madan, Afshin Molavi, Rick Rossow, Barney Rubin, Eugene Rumer, Ori Sela, Jeff Smith, Jennifer Staats, Ashley Tellis, Marvin Weinbaum, Andrew Wilder, and Moeed Yusuf. I also hope that friends and mentors from my time at the Council on Foreign Relations and US State Department will see their intellectual imprint on this book.

Most of all, I would like to thank my family—Robyn, Zachary, and Chloe—for their understanding, patience, and love. This book is dedicated to my parents, Carol and Sanford Markey.

LIST OF ABBREVIATIONS

ADB   Asian Development Bank
AIIB   Asian Infrastructure Investment Bank
ASEAN   Association of Southeast Asian Nations
BLA   Balochistan Liberation Army
BRI   Belt and Road Initiative
CAREC   Central Asia Regional Economic Cooperation program
CGTN   China Global Television Network
CIDCA   China International Development Cooperation Agency
CNPC   China National Petroleum Corporation
CPEC   China-Pakistan Economic Corridor
CSTO   Collective Security Treaty Organization
CUSEF   China–United States Exchange Foundation
EAEU   Eurasian Economic Union
FWO   Frontier Works Organization (Pakistan)
IMF   International Monetary Fund
IRGC   Iranian Revolutionary Guard Corps
JCPOA   Joint Comprehensive Plan of Action
KLP   keeping a low profile, or *taoguang yanghui*
MPS   Ministry of Public Security (China)
NDS   National Defense Strategy (United States)
NIN   National Information Network (Iran)
NSS   National Security Strategy (United States)
OFAC   Office of Foreign Assets Control (United States)
PLA   People's Liberation Army (China)

PML-N   Pakistan Muslim League (Nawaz Sharif faction)
PPP   Pakistan People's Party
QCCM   Quadrilateral Cooperation and Coordination Mechanism
SCO   Shanghai Cooperation Organization
SFA   striving for achievement, or *fenfa youwei*
TTP   Tehrik-i-Taliban Pakistan

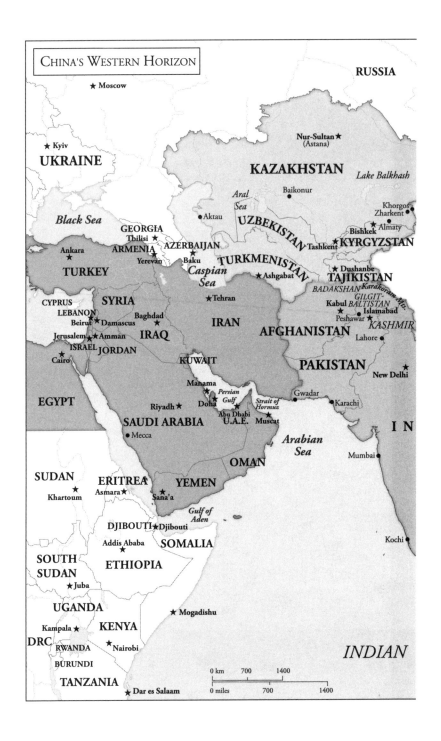

MAP China's Western Horizon

CHAPTER 1 | China and the New Geopolitics
of Eurasia

THE NEXT CHAPTER of the Gwadar story began on September 8, 2013, in far-off Nur-Sultan (Astana), Kazakhstan. Chinese president Xi Jinping stood in an auditorium behind a mahogany lectern emblazoned with the crest of Nazarbayev University. Flanked by a row of alternating flags, the bright red of China and the pale blue and sunny yellow of Kazakhstan, Xi described how imperial Chinese envoys had traveled through Central Asia more than two millennia earlier, claiming that their mission was to open the transcontinental Silk Road that linked Asia to Europe.[1] The president's plans unveiled that day were similarly ambitious: to build a "New Silk Road Economic Belt" that would knit together modern continental Eurasia.

In the years since his speech in Kazakhstan, Xi's vision has matured and expanded to become the "Belt and Road Initiative," or BRI for short, for which China has built new multilateral institutions, devoted high-level diplomatic attention, and directed hundreds of billions of dollars in financing. Even if only partly realized, the effort would constitute a breathtaking feat with the potential to transform economic and political conditions across a vast region of 4.4 billion people and an economy comprising a third of the world's GDP.[2]

China is pursuing the BRI for a wide variety of reasons, not all of which are publicly acknowledged by Beijing. China's official justification was spelled out in March 2015 by a document jointly issued by the National Development and Reform Commission, Ministry of Foreign Affairs, and Ministry of Commerce. Entitled "Vision and Actions on Jointly Building Silk Road Economic Belt and 21st-Century Maritime Silk Road," the report presents the BRI as China's noble attempt to "promote the economic prosperity of the countries along the Belt and Road and regional economic cooperation, strengthen exchanges and mutual learning between different civilizations, and promote world peace and development. It is a great undertaking that will benefit people around the world."[3]

During China's 2015 Boao Forum for Asia, a homegrown attempt to replicate the gathering of global elites at the World Economic Forum in Davos, Switzerland, President Xi spoke of "China's firm commitment to building friendship and partnership with its neighbors to foster an amicable, secure and prosperous neighborhood. Under the principle of amity, sincerity, mutual benefit and inclusiveness, China is working actively to deepen win-win cooperation and connectivity with its neighbors to bring them even more benefit with its own development."[4]

Notwithstanding these altruistic claims, self-interested motives also lie behind Beijing's generosity. Massive infrastructure investments benefit China's own economy, and not merely in a "rising tide floats all boats" sort of way. After decades of spectacular growth at home, China has—at least temporarily—over-built its domestic infrastructure. Empty roads, airports, high-speed trains, and entire ghost cities litter the Chinese landscape.[5]

Chinese industrial enterprises with the capacity to build more will sit idle unless they can be set loose on projects outside China.[6] As He Yafei, then a vice minister in China's State Council, wrote in January 2014, the challenge of Chinese overcapacity for producing iron, steel, cement, aluminum, and other building materials is best turned "into an opportunity by 'moving out' this overcapacity on the basis of [China's] development strategy abroad and foreign policy."[7]

Chinese loans to neighbors like Pakistan quickly cycle back into Chinese pockets when Chinese firms win construction contract bids. In the best-case scenario, Chinese companies are kept afloat by doing business in China's neighbors. Even if loans are slowly or incompletely repaid, the entire effort amounts to China subsidizing its own firms. This is hardly unusual in China's state-dominated (and still nominally communist) system.[8]

A political rationale reinforces this economic logic. China's ruling Communist Party has largely traded its ideological claims of legitimacy for claims founded in economic growth and effective governance.[9] China's leaders know that a recession or depression would pose the single greatest threat to their hold on power. The BRI is thus part of a wider set of initiatives intended to reform China's economic model from the one that produced several decades of torrid growth—and permitted hundreds of millions of people to work their way out of poverty and into the global middle class—to one that can cement China's place as a developed economy over the long haul.

Domestic economic and political concerns explain much of President Xi's agenda in Eurasia, but it would be a mistake to overlook the role of Beijing's territorial aspirations and security fears. Prior to the modern era, China's western frontier was the source of wars, conquest, and the dissolution of imperial dynasties. Today, Beijing is extremely sensitive about its hold over China's western territories because they are home to the largest groups of non-Han minorities. Xinjiang's Uighurs, with their Turkic ethnic roots, Muslim faith, and cultural ties to Central Asia, have chafed under the rule of the People's Republic.

Uighur riots in the provincial capital of Urumqi left hundreds dead in 2009 and convinced Beijing of the urgent need to respond. Since then, as detailed in chapter 2, the full force of the Chinese police state—armed with old-fashioned and high-tech tools of political repression—has been imposed in Xinjiang. There are good reasons to anticipate that China's repressive tactics will only worsen Uighur resentment, alienation, and political violence over time, but little evidence that Beijing is inclined to take a softer touch or reassess its strategy in Xinjiang altogether.

Beijing's domestic security concerns also motivate some of China's counterterror cooperation with neighboring Pakistan and the states of Central Asia under the auspices of the Shanghai Cooperation Organization. More recently, China's security officials have turned their attention to Syria as well, where hundreds, possibly thousands, of Uighurs have joined ISIS and other terrorist organizations.[10]

Finally, China's new initiatives in Eurasia are driven by the expansive global ambitions of President Xi Jinping. Unlike his predecessors, Xi has deviated from the famous twenty-four-character dictum established in 1990 by Deng Xiaoping: that China should "Observe calmly; secure our position; cope with affairs calmly; hide our capacities and bide our time; be good at maintaining a low profile; and never claim leadership," so as to avoid conflict and continue along the path of rapid economic development during a post–Cold War era defined by global upheaval. To the contrary, President Xi has eagerly asserted China's leadership and pressed China's interests in dealing with neighbors throughout Asia and increasingly on the global stage as well. Xi's China is also loosening its adherence to the principle of "non-interference" in the internal affairs of other states, even as Beijing zealously defends its own sovereign claims.

To be influential, China's involvement in other states does not need to take the shape of old-fashioned empire or even modern investments in roads, railways, or ports. In this century, information and telecommunications networks—and their supporting hardware, software, and standards—are also potent sources of power. In much of the world, China is already a leading provider of these technologies. As state-supported companies like Huawei undercut their Western competitors, China has the potential to cement its global dominance. The implications are not merely economic, but touch politics and security. China's exports of tools that enable censorship and surveillance offer Beijing new opportunities to influence other states and, in some cases, gain access to their information.

The details of Xi's initiatives are not set in stone, and when Beijing has experienced setbacks, it appears open to new tactics. That said, China remains steadfast in its commitment to extending its access and influence in ways that would make it not merely the most dominant state in east Asia, but a full-fledged Eurasian superpower and rival to the United States. In tandem with the BRI are other Chinese initiatives, including efforts to extend the reach of China's military, energized forays into high diplomacy, and the construction of new multilateral political and economic institutions. All of these are discussed in greater detail in chapter 2.

Winners . . . and Losers

Pakistan found itself at the leading edge of the BRI in April 2015, when President Xi launched the China-Pakistan Economic Corridor (CPEC) during a trip to Islamabad. The two sides unveiled fifty-one memoranda of understanding and plans for $46 billion in Chinese investments and concessional loans for new power plants, industrial zones, and the transportation infrastructure to link all of them to ports of entry on land and sea. The effort was framed as a transformative opportunity. Pakistan would become, in time, a veritable freeway for commerce between China's western provinces and the Arabian Sea. Once again, fifteen years after Musharraf's surprising request to finance Gwadar, the deep-sea port was touted as a centerpiece of Sino-Pakistani cooperation. This time, however, it would also serve as a pilot project for the vastly more ambitious BRI as a whole.

David Ricardo's classic theory of comparative advantage teaches that two states will always gain from opening trade with each other. On reflection, however, while states are likely to experience overall gains from trade, those gains will be distributed unevenly. Within each state some sectors will win, others will win less, and some will be outright losers. Politicians instinctively recognize that distributional consequences are politically salient; winners and losers will mobilize for or against trade policies that suit their purposes without necessarily caring about how they affect the national economy.

In that context, Gwadar highlighted the political challenges facing Beijing as China projects its influence into continental Eurasia. China's investment will create local winners and losers, even if China claims its goals are purely benign. Baloch politicians were, on the whole, no less skeptical about Gwadar port in 2015 than when the project was first announced in 2002. They continued to view the project as a new chapter of exploitation by outsiders, this time the Punjabi-dominated government and military backed by the Chinese state, financed with Chinese capital, and built by Chinese engineers. In November 2017, Pakistan's federal minister for ports and fisheries, Hasil Bizenjo, briefed the Senate that 91 percent of profits from Gwadar port would flow to China over the next forty years. The other 9 percent would go to Pakistan's federal government, leaving provincial and local authorities empty-handed.[11]

Not surprisingly, Balochistan's provincial leaders are less motivated by Pakistan's national goals than by concerns about what the port's development will mean for themselves and their constituents. In tangible terms, a ballooning real estate market around Gwadar port could displace locals from their homes. New jobs could be snapped up by outsiders. Traditional livelihoods, like fishing, could be lost forever. Early signs suggest that all of these steps are already underway. Prime real estate near Gwadar has been purchased by big private investors and the Pakistani navy, while fishing communities suffer limited access to traditional waters and some are being forcibly relocated away from the port.[12]

If Beijing and Islamabad fail to prove the value of Gwadar in terms that matter to locals, the Baloch insurgency will be taken up by the next generation. The violence that follows will make it far less likely that Gwadar ever achieves its promise for Pakistan or China.[13]

On the morning of November 23, 2018, three men calmly walked up to the security gate of the Chinese consulate in Karachi. Then, without warning, they opened fire with submachine guns and threw hand grenades into the compound in an attempt to storm the building.[14] Within forty-five minutes all three attackers were dead, but not before they killed two policemen and two civilians.[15] The Balochistan Liberation Army (BLA) immediately claimed responsibility via Twitter, posting a photo of the three attackers. Subsequently, BLA leader Jihand Baloch proclaimed that "The objective of this attack is clear: we will not tolerate any Chinese military expansionist endeavours on Baloch soil."[16]

The consulate attack came just a few months after another BLA member blew himself up alongside a busload of Chinese engineers, injuring five.[17] And the next May, three BLA gunmen struck Gwadar's Pearl Continental hotel, targeting a group of visiting Chinese and Pakistani investors. In an English-language message to the media, the group's intent was clear: "We warn China to stop her exploitative projects in Balochistan and do not support Pakistan in the genocide of Baloch people, otherwise, we would respond with more attacks."[18] There is little reason to anticipate that the BLA will soon relent in its violent campaign against Chinese workers in Pakistan.

Balochistan's politics are unusually violent, but they are not unique. Similar localized challenges await China at other points along the new Silk Road. Wary provincial politicians across Eurasia will judge the value of Chinese investments by whether they advance their own parochial interests, and in some cases, by whether they benefit relatively more or less than their nearby neighbors. Throughout the region, local identities—and jealousies—often run deeper than any sense of national unity.

In short, the multifarious forces of domestic politics within states across Eurasia, from separatist movements and special interest groups to opposition political parties, constitute the ground realities within which Chinese initiatives like BRI must operate. Much will remain outside China's control, although Beijing is exporting tools of political repression throughout its neighborhood. Even so, China will find some circumstances fraught with hazard, while others prove more welcoming. All will also be susceptible to dramatic, even unpredictable change through democratic elections or other more violent turns of events.

Chapters 3, 4, and 5 of this book examine the domestic political contexts and consequences of Chinese involvement along its western horizon. Rather than attempting to deliver an encyclopedic account of developments across a vast and complex territory, this book trains its attention on prominent states with special strategic significance to China. In South Asia, the subject of chapter 3, Pakistan is the focal state. In the fourth chapter, on Central Asia, it is Kazakhstan. And in the fifth chapter, on the Middle East, Iran takes center stage. Each of these three states lies along a swath of continental Eurasia with a deep and consequential history of connections to China. Today, each is also experiencing a historically unprecedented level of interaction with Beijing. Looking ahead, these ties show every sign of tightening.

Exacerbating Regional Rivalries

Chinese initiatives will not merely affect the domestic political and economic storylines of its neighbors. They will also play into many of Eurasia's defining interstate relationships, such as the hostility between Pakistan and India, the historical dominance of Russia in Kazakhstan, and the sectarian-tinged competition between Iran and Saudi Arabia. These interstate relationships and China's evolving place in them are also assessed in greater detail through chapters 3, 4, and 5.

Returning to the Gwadar example, the significance of a port development scheme in Pakistan cannot be understood without considering the dominant geopolitics of South Asia. Ever since 1947, those have been defined by Indo-Pakistani hostilities. As a consequence, when Pakistan and China trumpet Gwadar's benefits for commerce and economic development, India perceives a nefarious strategic gambit. From New Delhi's perspective, Gwadar strengthens a frustrating and often hostile Pakistan and opens a new beachhead for China on the Arabian Sea. No matter what China's true or original intentions might have been, Gwadar now has the potential to exacerbate Indo-Pakistani tensions.

Chapter 3 picks up this story and offers a fuller account of China's role in relations between India and Pakistan. Of course, this general pattern is not unique to South Asia. Across the region, heads of state will perceive the costs and benefits of China's activities through the prism of their own geopolitical circumstances. They will nearly always care more about how China is tipping the scales in competitions close to home than about whether the region as a whole stands to benefit. Wherever possible, they will harness China's wealth, power, and influence to serve their own agendas.

In Central Asia, Kazakhstan's closer ties with China have the potential to unsettle Russia, which has long been the region's dominant neighbor. Looking to the future, China's increasing role is likely to heighten Sino-Russian tensions, possibly also spurring greater geopolitical turmoil. In the Middle East, Iran and Saudi Arabia both see China as the single most important market for their oil and gas. Rather than quelling tensions between Tehran and Riyadh, revenues from sales to China provide essential fuel for their conflicts. Beijing's backing facilitates Iran's quest to buck international pressures, especially from the United States.

Across these three cases, China's involvement is, on balance, likely to exacerbate existing geopolitical and political-economic patterns that favor conflict, competition, and instability. This is true despite China's claim that its primary motive for expanding its investments and presence in Eurasia is the desire to foster economic growth and, by extension, to enhance security.

That China's initiatives could turn out to be so counterproductive might surprise some readers. Many scholars of international relations, however, begin with the core assumption that all states rationally pursue their self-interests, and more than that, tend to care about how they fare relative to other states more than they care about their gains in absolute terms.[19] By this logic, Eurasian states should be expected to behave competitively in their interactions with each other and to seek advantage from their dealings with China.

This reminder of the self-interested nature of states is necessary mainly because China has been so eager to portray BRI and its other activities in the region as ways to generate mutual economic gain and to downplay or ignore geostrategic consequences. According to Beijing, the BRI is a manifestation of the "Silk Road Spirit," described as "Peace and cooperation, openness and inclusiveness, mutual learning and mutual benefit."[20] Chinese commentators frequently characterize the BRI in similar terms, and while some may simply be starry-eyed optimists, others are undoubtedly part of a concerted propaganda campaign surrounding China's overseas initiatives.

One extreme case of the latter was Patrick Ho, a Chinese propagandist who headed a Hong Kong–based think tank until 2018 when he was arrested in the United States and charged with money laundering and violations of the Foreign Corrupt Practices Act.[21] Before assembled guests at a December 2016 BRI conference in Washington, DC, Ho declared: "The Belt and Road is a vision rather than a project, and a vision which is constantly expanding and may always do so. It is a connection of hearts and minds connecting souls, connecting the Chinese Dream with the American Dream and other dreams, freedom from want, freedom from fear, harmony with nature, and peace."[22] However noble-sounding these goals may be, they should not obstruct clear thinking about the geopolitical motives and likely consequences of China's policies.

The Consequences for America

Across continental Eurasia, China is "pushing" itself into new territory, led by economic and commercial activity, if often with diplomatic and military initiatives not far behind. At times, China will benefit from greater influence and access, and many of its initiatives are likely to advance Chinese commercial or strategic interests. China has much to gain from Eurasian markets, natural resources, arms deals, transit corridors, ports, and security partnerships.

Yet China is also being "pulled" by the leaders of Eurasian states who seek new means to advance their own domestic and regional agendas. As a consequence, China's proclamations of benign intent, whether of "win-win" projects or of the exciting dreams of regional interconnectivity, need not be entirely suspect to be largely beside the point. What China says it wants is not irrelevant, but it is an incomplete guide to likely outcomes because those outcomes will be so heavily contingent on the choices made by and for Eurasians. In South Asia, Central Asia, and the Middle East, China already feels the tug from the sorts of no-win geopolitical predicaments that other great powers—including the United States—have faced elsewhere throughout history. China will at times pay a price for overseas entanglements in a part of the world known for messy politics within states and long-standing hostilities between them.

All of this means that Eurasia will present a tricky set of strategic challenges for the United States. US policymakers will need to factor China into their specific policy calculations in the region, often in ways that would have seemed unnecessary only a few years ago. It is now blindingly obvious, for instance, that US nuclear sanctions on Iran or diplomatic pressure on Pakistan will prove far less effective if actively opposed by Beijing. China's capacity to stymie or remake American policy initiatives in Eurasia is only likely to grow. More and more, asking the question "Where does China stand on this issue?" will become second nature to American diplomats in the region.

At the same time, the evolution of China's role along its western horizon will have a direct bearing on its own aspirations for global leadership and, as a consequence, on its geopolitical competition with the United States. How Washington and Beijing relate to each other in Eurasia will often reflect the tone of their dealings on other vital issues, from bilateral trade negotiations to military buildups in east Asia and the Pacific. Yet even if continental Eurasia is not likely to be the primary theater for US-China competition, what happens there has the potential to influence the evolution of that competition in important ways. For its part, Washington has a wide spectrum of policy options in Eurasia, running from "benign neglect" at one extreme, to "militarized competition" at the other. Each of these is discussed at greater length in chapter 6.

In contemplating America's geopolitical competition with China, some of Washington's foreign policy hands will nostalgically recall the Cold War, when America's plentiful resources conferred advantages over its Soviet adversary and the dividing lines between East and West often seemed simpler. Others may think back to the immediate post–Cold War period as the "end of history," when US ideals seemed the envy of the world.[23]

Now, however, and for the foreseeable future, the character of the global order will be more fluid, the United States' sway less dominant. In this new environment, and especially along China's western horizon, US policymakers would be wise to implement a strategy defined by selective and differentiated competition with China rather than attempting a reflexive, one-size-fits-all effort to beat China at its own games. Along the way, as this book argues, gaining a firm understanding of how Eurasians perceive China in the context of their own interests will be essential to America's success.

CHAPTER 2 | Beijing's Global Aspirations

O N July 18, 2014, Beijing appointed Ambassador Sun Yuxi to serve as China's first special envoy to Afghanistan.[1] American policymakers working the "Af-Pak" portfolio at the time saw Beijing's move as a milestone in the expansion of China's regional activity and ambition. The Obama administration had encouraged the move for several years and welcomed it when China finally named Sun to the post.[2] For Dan Feldman, who was promoted to serve as the US Special Representative for Afghanistan and Pakistan just a few weeks later, Sun's appointment represented a "significant upgrading of the Chinese engagement in Afghanistan."[3] He hoped China's formalized diplomatic presence would lend additional heft to a variety of cooperative ventures in the region, including peace talks with the Taliban.[4]

On a visit to Washington a month after his appointment, Ambassador Sun held forth in one of the cavernous conference rooms of the Chinese embassy.[5] His informal, chatty manner distinguished him. Equally memorable was his desire to share some of the sensitive details of his past experiences in Afghanistan. He casually dropped names of US policymakers he worked with in the 1980s, like then-CIA officer Joseph DeTrani, who later rose to senior policy positions in the US intelligence community and Department of State. DeTrani recalls that Sun was personally responsible for delivering thousands of donkeys to the Afghan mujahidin fighting against Soviet forces. The donkeys served as cheap, reliable porters for arms, ammunition, and other supplies across the difficult terrain into Afghanistan.[6]

Sun's colorful history did not end in the 1980s. In 1999, Beijing rushed him to Serbia in the immediate aftermath of the US bombing of China's embassy in Belgrade. In 2002, Sun was dispatched to Kabul as China's first ambassador to Afghanistan since 1979. While there, he grappled with the hardships of reestablishing China's embassy in the midst of a devastated and still highly volatile situation. In between travels to landmine-infested Chinese construction sites, he found the time and resources to outfit the embassy grounds with tennis courts, a sauna, and gymnasium for Chinese staff and diplomats from other embassies.[7]

To explain his own perspective on the practice of diplomacy, Sun cites Zhou Enlai, the first premier and foreign minister of the People's Republic. Zhou defined Chinese diplomats as members of a "culturally armed People's Liberation Army." He said they should be "soft on the outside and hard on the inside, armed with [an understanding of] culture and possessing loyalty to the country as well as absolute discipline."[8]

In 2006, Sun made waves when as China's ambassador to India he announced that the whole of the Indian northeastern state of Arunachal Pradesh belonged to China. His statement, a direct and apparently unnecessary slap against New Delhi's official position, came just days before President Hu Jintao visited New Delhi. Sun may have paid a price for that move, as his next postings were to Italy and Poland. In our August 2014 exchange he clearly relished a return to South Asia. He also exuded the confidence and energy of a senior diplomat with an exciting portfolio and the bureaucratic freedom to stretch his wings. He explained to American colleagues that he had accepted the new job with several conditions, one of them being that he would not be shackled to normal office hours or forced to fight Beijing's notorious rush-hour traffic.[9] He was, according to Feldman, a "breath of fresh air."[10]

Sun Yuxi's appointment as special envoy came at a time when Beijing was nervous about potential instability stemming from the Obama administration's plan to reduce the US military footprint in Afghanistan. Sun was charged with keeping an open channel to American diplomats and met with them routinely, if without fanfare, in various settings around the world.[11] Sun's activism was also consistent with a broader shift in Beijing's strategy for its Eurasian periphery in the year after President Xi announced his new Belt and Road Initiative (BRI). China had previously shied away from attracting attention with bold or formal diplomatic forays. Now it had sent an adventurous and outspoken diplomat to pursue a variety of talks: with Kabul, Islamabad, Washington, and the Taliban insurgents themselves.

China's moves were quickly noticed and appreciated in Afghanistan. After winning a protracted election battle, Afghan president Ashraf Ghani chose to take his first overseas trip to Beijing (rather than Washington) in October 2014. Then, several months later, China followed up with the unprecedented step of hosting talks between the Afghan government and Taliban representatives in Urumqi.[12] Although these particular talks faltered in mid-2015, Ambassador Sun's initiatives paved the way for subsequent rounds of Taliban "reconciliation" dialogues in different configurations, including with representatives of the United States and Pakistan.[13]

Beijing and the "Greater Middle East"

Beijing's enhanced diplomacy in Afghanistan reflected China's interests and growing ambition along its western horizon. Afghanistan is but one treacherous patch in the grand sweep of land that American policymakers and scholars rather artificially divide into the sub-regions of South Asia, Central Asia, and the Middle East. Geopolitically, and certainly in the popular American mind, much of this region seems peripheral: distant, exotic, and resting on often bloody fault lines between the world's major powers.

This was not always true. In *The Silk Roads*, Oxford historian Peter Frankopan describes how he "found out about an important medieval Turkish map in Istanbul that had at its heart a city called Balasaghun, which I had never even heard of."[14] Balasaghun, or Quz Ordu, was a Uighur city located in present-day Kyrgyzstan, and Frankopan remarks with wonder that it "was once considered the centre of the world."[15]

To their credit, some prominent Chinese analysts have started to refer to this swathe of Eurasian territory as the "Greater Middle East (*Da Zhong Dong*)," showing an appreciation of the geopolitical significance and increasing interconnectedness of the region.[16] Their appreciation stems, in part, from China's long-standing self-perception as a continental power more than a maritime one, a nation more attuned throughout its history to looking west than east. Until the rise of European imperial fleets, the threats that most often dictated Chinese security strategies, like the Mongols, tended to sweep in over land.[17] Overland commerce, Buddhist networks, maritime trade, and Western colonial expansion have all linked China to its western neighbors in various ways at different stages in its recorded history.

Looking to the future, there are good reasons to anticipate that China will again focus greater attention westward, both to address perceived threats and to capitalize on opportunities.[18] As noted in the previous chapter, Beijing's renewed interest in China's overland periphery has been driven above all by immediate security concerns related to the restive Xinjiang province.

There the stakes for Beijing are high. The Xinjiang Uighur Autonomous Region alone comprises one-sixth of China's landmass, about a fifth of the national oil reserves, 40 percent of high quality coal reserves, and only 1.5 percent of the population.[19]

China has a long history of waxing and waning control over these vast western lands inhabited mainly, if sparsely, by Turkic peoples.[20] The Uighurs converted to Islam between the tenth and fifteenth centuries, and for much of their history have hardly considered themselves "Chinese" at all.[21] Contrary to Beijing's official histories, in which Xinjiang is depicted as an ever-present part of China, the lands were for centuries "culturally intertwined with the Middle East" and governed by non-Chinese kingdoms.[22] Moreover, the present-day dividing lines that separate Xinjiang from Central Asia have little basis in local political distinctions. They were mainly the product of a nineteenth-century settlement between imperial Russia and China.[23]

Today's Uighur political alienation, radicalization, and violence is thus a predictable consequence of Beijing's often colonial-style rule and ethnic persecution. In the face of Beijing's overwhelming power, Uighur extremists have adopted terrorist tactics similar to other anti-state groups around the world. To date, the biggest international headline-grabbing attack took place in October 2013. Three Uighur suicide terrorists managed to steer their SUV into Beijing's heavily guarded Tiananmen Square, where they rammed into crowds before eventually bursting into flames. The audacious but unsophisticated suicide assault killed two tourists and sent up plumes of black smoke just outside the main gates of Beijing's Forbidden City.[24] Other attacks, including a 2014 spate of combined knife stabbings and bombings in Kunming and Urumqi, received less international coverage but were far deadlier. They clearly embarrassed China's leadership and signaled the depth of the political and security challenge facing Beijing.

Beijing has responded to these threats with an iron-fisted crackdown on Uighur communities. In 2018, researcher Adrian Zenz shocked the world with revelations of a "sprawling network of secretive political reeducation camps" housing up to one million Muslims, where internees are "subject to intense indoctrination procedures that force them to proclaim 'faith' in the Chinese Communist Party while denigrating large parts of their own religion and culture."[25] In addition to these camps, Urumqi and other parts of Xinjiang have become "the most closely surveilled places on earth," where Chinese security measures include facial scanners, smartphone searches, and ubiquitous identification card checks.[26]

For decades, Beijing has also pursued a resettlement and development campaign intended to transform conditions inside Xinjiang. The resettlement scheme has probably yielded the most dramatic change. State-led infrastructure investment and business opportunities have enticed waves of new, ethnically Han settlers.[27] Whereas in 1953 ethnic Uighurs accounted for 75 percent of the region's people and ethnic Han only 6 percent, by 2011 the figures stood at roughly 40 percent each.[28]

China's involvement in western Asia is at least partly driven by a desire to add a third prong to its Xinjiang strategy: to tackle the ideological and logistical roots of terrorism beyond China's own borders. Chinese investments in Pakistan are, for instance, intended to create jobs, reduce anti-state sentiment, and generate public resources for additional improvements in law and order. China has also used its influence with Islamabad to compel the Pakistani military to target Uighur terrorist cells and the larger—usually Central Asian—jihadist groups that train and host them. Similarly, China has invested time and resources in regional counter-terror cooperation initiatives with Central Asian states like Uzbekistan, Kazakhstan, and Tajikistan.[29]

To a lesser extent, Beijing also appreciates that links between Xinjiang and the rest of continental Eurasia offer natural opportunities for economic development and growth. According to the 2015 BRI "Vision and Actions Plan," Xinjiang's location makes it a "window of westward opening-up" and a "key transportation, trade, logistics, culture, science and education center."[30] China's aspirations for the lands to the west of Xinjiang thus have important defensive, and even potentially constructive, motivations.

It would be naïve, however, to overlook the region's potential geostrategic value. Nadège Rolland, a former policymaker in the French Defense Ministry and now an analyst at an American think tank, the National Bureau of Asian Research, has written the most comprehensive assessment of Chinese goals behind the BRI, based on a wide and systematic survey of expert Chinese views. In *China's Eurasian Century?* Rolland concludes that Beijing's aims in continental Eurasia are intimately tied to China's ambition to achieve the status of a global great power.[31] Rolland instructively cites the work of two Chinese geographers, who write that "only vast lands can cradle great powers. Eurasia has always been the stage for the rise of new international orders: Vienna, Versailles, Yalta."[32]

For China, the potential benefits of power projection into its Eurasian hinterlands are twofold. First, the area offers a territorial scale that would place China on par with current (and former) continental superpowers.[33] Second, overland westward expansion would provide China with a means to escape the confines of East Asia and the Pacific without directly confronting the United States and its Asian allies.[34]

To be clear, this does not necessarily mean China is involved in an old-fashioned project of imperial conquest along Western European lines. Simply by building and expanding overland routes—via Pakistan to the Arabian Sea, Central Asia and Iran to the Persian Gulf, or Turkey to the Mediterranean—and incentivizing states to permit relatively unfettered commercial flows along them, China would have alternative ways to access global centers of energy production, natural resources, and economic markets.

Historical Wellsprings and Broader Context

President Xi's BRI and the extraordinary propaganda campaign surrounding it could easily obscure the fact that China is not the only force pulling together the states of continental Eurasia. Nor is today's regional integration properly framed as a reinvigoration of the ancient Silk Road that once tied East to West.[35] That history undoubtedly provides a romantic narrative for new Chinese initiatives, but the overland routes of the Silk Road were centuries ago severed by empires and rendered irrelevant by new, mainly maritime pathways for trade.

The current reintegration of the region actually finds its wellsprings in the late twentieth-century industrialization of east Asia and the breakdown of Cold War barriers.[36] When the Cold War's iron curtain lifted, the path was opened for new links between West and East. Trade in energy led the way, tying the hydrocarbon-rich Middle East and Central Asia to the new and spectacularly productive factories of east and southeast Asia.[37]

Today's Eurasian integration is therefore a thoroughly modern development. It is also part of a trend that started decades before President Xi came to power in China. The story began with energy flows, whether by tanker trade or pipelines. Those ties were complemented by, and contributed to, other flows of people and ideas. Efforts to accelerate the pace of regional integration, mainly by improving transportation networks, also predated Xi's BRI. Different initiatives have popped up repeatedly throughout the post–Cold War era, spearheaded by the United Nations, European Union, Asian Development Bank, South Korea, Japan, and the United States.[38]

It would not even be accurate to attribute Beijing's own plans in continental Eurasia to President Xi in 2013. To the contrary, much of what now counts as the BRI was already in the works before then, and nearly all the rest is best appreciated within the broader context of China's expanding power, influence, and ambition around the world. That power is most obvious on the economic front, as China's nominal GDP of over $13 trillion in 2018 was ranked

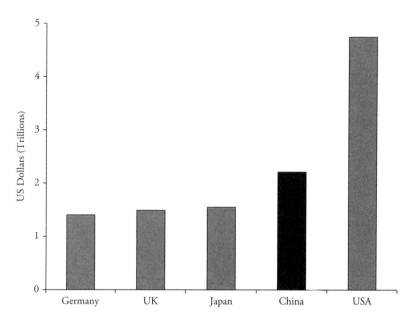

FIGURE 1 Outward Foreign Direct Investment, 1999–2017
Created by author using data from the UN Conference on Trade and Development.

second only to that of the United States (over $20 trillion). When economists attempt to take relative purchasing power into account, they already rank China's economy as about 25 percent larger than that of the United States.[39]

The first driver for BRI is found in China's long-standing domestic economic development agenda, which has for decades stressed the need to extend growth and prosperity to the nation's western provinces.[40] And, dating to 1999, when President Jiang Zemin encouraged Chinese companies to "go out" into the world to compete and invest, China has been a more significant commercial presence not just in Eurasia, but nearly everywhere across the globe.[41] Between 1999 and 2017, Chinese outward Foreign Direct Investment (FDI) totaled $2.2 trillion, second only to the United States (see fig. 1).[42] Some analysts predict that China's overall FDI will surpass that of the United States as early as 2027.[43] From 2005 to 2018, China's direct investments in South Asia, Central Asia, and the Middle East were each less than its regional spending totals in east Asia or the West. Collectively, however, China's investments in continental Eurasia totaled more than in East Asia but less than Europe and the United States (see fig. 2).[44]

Chinese trade spreads well across Eurasia, where China is the largest trading partner for sixteen Asian countries and has become the EU's second largest trading partner.[45] This story of China's skyrocketing trade has repeated

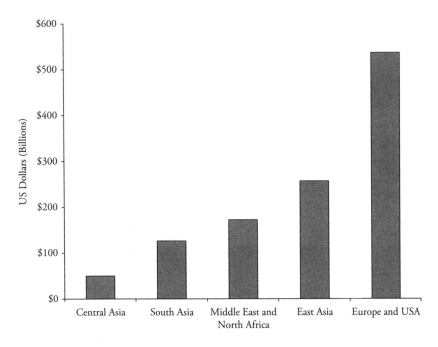

FIGURE 2 Chinese Investments, 2005–2018
Created by author using data from the American Enterprise Institute.

again and again, if over slightly different periods, around the world.[46] By 2020, 200 million Chinese, a number that would rank as the seventh largest country in the world, will travel outside of China each year for business.[47] In 2017, 600,000 Chinese students traveled abroad.[48] To expand and defend its interests in global commerce and finance, Beijing has pursued new trade regimes like the Regional Comprehensive Economic Partnership and Free Trade Area of the Asia-Pacific, and has played a more active role in old multilateral institutions, like the Group of Twenty and the International Monetary Fund.

China's emphasis on infrastructure investment overseas should also be appreciated in context. As noted in chapter 1, China's overcapacity in building materials, like steel, aluminum, and cement, can be put to productive use outside China, employing Chinese companies that would otherwise lack sufficient demand.[49] Chinese leaders clearly recognize the vital importance of maintaining economic growth as a means to retain political legitimacy.[50] A spike in unemployment and social unrest would put the regime in a terrible bind.

Any new initiatives that Beijing undertakes in Eurasia must be appreciated in the context of China's growing hard-power capabilities as well. The practical consequences of China's growing military have been relatively easy to spot, especially in the crowded and contested seas along its eastern seaboard, but China's new weapons, technologies, and know-how will also be directed westward.

Many of the biggest changes have come at sea. In the early 1990s, the United States held such a decisive naval advantage over China that Beijing could not credibly threaten to invade Taiwan across the 110-mile strait separating it from the mainland. A decade later, China was clearly "putting into place the pieces of what Pentagon planners refer to as an 'anti-access' or 'area denial' capability aimed squarely at the United States," that would not merely enable such an invasion, but would effectively keep American forces at bay.[51]

Since then, China has busily built out a wide array of new weapons, including ballistic, cruise, and antisatellite missiles, submarines, nuclear warheads, unmanned aerial vehicles (UAVs), and offensive cyber forces.[52] In 2018, China spent an estimated $239.2 billion on its military. Although that was less than half the $633.6 billion spent by the United States, it represented a sixfold increase from 2000, when Chinese expenditures were $41.3 billion. It also made China the world's second largest spender. Russia, by comparison, spent $64.2 billion in 2018.[53] China also maintains the world's largest standing army and contributes over 2,500 personnel to United Nations Peacekeeping missions.[54] The People's Liberation Army has undertaken several rounds of modernization and strategic review since the early 1990s, reflecting changes in China's overall power as well as the changing nature of warfare, especially the role of new technologies.[55]

China has escalated its scuffles with neighboring claimants to offshore territories with, among other moves, a remarkable island-building campaign in the South China Sea and the declaration of an Air Defense Identification Zone (ADIZ) in the East China Sea.[56] Although they came as a surprise to China's neighbors, these steps did not come all of a sudden or out of the blue. To the contrary, they were set in motion by prior incidents. Plans for the ADIZ, for instance, were formulated after the midair collision between a US reconnaissance plane and a Chinese fighter jet over Hainan Island back in 2001.[57] A dozen years later, China had built sufficient military capacity to back its policy shift.

As early as the 2000s, some American defense analysts started to anticipate that China would aim to project its power farther from its shores. One widely cited 2004 report by consultants with the defense contractor Booz Allen Hamilton kicked off a debate over whether Beijing would build a "string of pearls" across the Indian Ocean, by which they meant a series of military bases or dual-use ports suited to the People's Liberation Army (PLA) Navy that would enable Chinese ships and submarines to reach the Persian Gulf, the coast of Africa, and beyond.[58] String of pearls or no, in February 2011 China made history when it evacuated 35,000 of its citizens from a collapsing Libya. For China, the mission was unprecedented in its scale and marked the military's first operational deployment to North Africa and the Mediterranean.[59]

For decades, China has also busied itself with the project of building foundations for regional and global diplomatic influence commensurate with its economic and commercial presence. In the mid-1990s, for instance, China convened a meeting of leaders from Russia and three Central Asian states (Kazakhstan, Kyrgyzstan, and Tajikistan) in Shanghai, ostensibly to discuss border issues. After several additional meetings, that group, plus Uzbekistan, formally launched the Shanghai Cooperation Organization as a vehicle for addressing regional security issues, especially counter-terrorism. Similarly, in October 2000 China hosted a ministerial-level conference with dozens of African states and regional organizations to discuss economic development issues. Six years later, the initiative evolved into the Forum on China-Africa Cooperation.

To promote its image and state-censored version of the news, Beijing is also buying its way into global media. For China (as well as Russia, Iran, and numerous other illiberal states), the foray into worldwide news broadcasting reflects frustration with the way dominant, largely Western, private media networks portray them. China Central Television (CCTV), the state's largest network, began its process of international expansion in the early 1990s, but in 2009 announced plans to grow overseas CCTV staff tenfold by 2016 as part of China's $6.6 billion in new, global media investments.[60] In 2016, CCTV's international operations were rebranded as "China Global Television Network," with production facilities in Beijing, Nairobi, and Washington, and bureaus in over seventy locations around the world.[61]

In sum, as China "marches westwards" into Eurasia, it follows a twenty-first-century path toward continental economic integration. China carries with it the experience of prior overseas involvements that have nearly always started with investment and trade but then informed political and diplomatic outcomes. Now Beijing acts not as a bit player, but as an economic giant and increasingly a top military power too.

The Xi Jinping Era

Appreciating the important points of continuity in China's foreign and defense policies highlights the reality that not every development in China under

President Xi is novel.[62] That said, these are not ordinary times in China. Xi is actively consolidating political power over the world's most populous state with a ruthlessness unseen since the era of Mao Zedong.[63] Xi has sidelined rivals, emphasized the ideological and political centrality of the Communist Party, and stamped his personal impression on major new undertakings like the BRI.[64] He hammered the last nail into the coffin of a decades-old system of collective leadership in October 2017. That move came at the start of his second term as China's supreme leader when the 19th National Congress of the Communist Party of China voted to incorporate "Xi Jinping Thought on Socialism with Chinese Characteristics for a New Era" into the party's constitution.

In January 2018, law professor Jiang Shigong of China's Peking University (often called China's Harvard) penned a lengthy essay in the Guangzhou journal *Open Times*.[65] In it, Jiang undertook a close reading of President Xi's report to the 19th Party Congress and wrote that China is entering a new age, "labeled the 'Xi Jinping era' by perceptive scholars in China and abroad."[66] Jiang explained that the post-revolutionary Mao Zedong era could be characterized by China "standing up," while during the Deng Xiaoping era of the 1980s China focused on "getting rich." Now, during the Xi Jinping era, China would turn its attention to "becoming powerful."[67]

Jiang's essay is an exercise in interpreting political narratives, not objective historical analysis. China's history since 1949 is hardly a straightforward story of three evolutionary eras, nor does China's current policy conform strictly to the "thought" of one man.[68] That said, Jiang's work is revealing because it so clearly emphasizes the ways in which China is breaking with past patterns in new ways. The state is building new institutions and undertaking new initiatives in the service of grander ambitions at home and abroad. China's Communist Party has justified all of these moves, and the innumerable other initiatives that it is undertaking on the home front (which will not be explored here), as essential building blocks in the effort to achieve Xi's "Chinese Dream" of becoming a "rich and strong socialist country" by 2049, the hundredth anniversary of the People's Republic.

From the perspective of China's international affairs, the Xi Jinping era is marked by two major strategic shifts, the first more widely recognized than the second. In combination with China's wealth, military power, and diplomatic influence, these changes signal an unprecedented new chapter in China's relations with the world.

That first shift is captured in shorthand by China-watchers as the move from "KLP" to "SFA." KLP stands for "keeping a low profile," and SFA refers to "striving for achievement." Further unpacking the meaning of these catchphrases, KLP reflects the strategic outlook prescribed by Deng Xiaoping in 1990, whereby China should "hide its capabilities and bide its time," focusing its attention on economic development and avoiding moves that would unnecessarily provoke an international backlash to its growing power. That perspective held sway as a rough guide to Chinese foreign policy for the subsequent twenty years.[69]

October 24, 2013, marked the death of KLP, at least according to Professor Yan Xuetong of China's Tsinghua University (China's "MIT"). That day, President Xi spoke to the "highest level conference on diplomatic work in China since the beginning of communist leadership in 1949," where he formally presented the strategy of *fenfa youwei*, or striving for achievement (SFA).[70] President Xi reaffirmed China's shift in late November 2014 in his first keynote address to the Central Foreign Affairs Work Conference of the Communist Party, a formal and exceedingly rare gathering of top Chinese officials.[71] Three years later, by the time of the 19th Party Congress in October 2017, China had unambiguously adopted a strategy to demonstrate its leadership and power on the world stage.[72]

From Yan's perspective, the shift to SFA was motivated in large part by a new reality facing China. In 2010, China surpassed Japan as the world's second largest economy. The global financial crisis of 2008 had already highlighted China's central role in international markets and convinced Beijing that the time had come to assert greater leadership. By that point, and probably years earlier, the notion of "hiding" China's wealth and power no longer made much sense. Neither other powerful states (above all, the United States) nor smaller neighbors could be appeased by Chinese professions of remaining a mere developing country. The Obama administration implemented its "pivot" or "rebalance" to Asia as a means to deal with China as a great power. Ready or not, China needed to think more politically and strategically, not just economically, about its relations with other states.[73]

Reflecting official reasoning as well as his own interpretation, Yan did not equate this shift with a Chinese move to accept pure realpolitik or power-based politics. Instead, he stressed that China would aim to convince other states of the possibility of *gongying*, or "win-win" for all.[74] Strategically, the initial Chinese goal under SFA would be to encourage states through economic and other incentives to "choose a neutral stance between China and the United States." Then, over time, China could convince them of the value of a Beijing-led "community of common destiny" that would involve some sort of military cooperation.[75]

Yan recognized that China's neighbors, especially historical adversaries like Japan, might very well perceive SFA as threatening. He suggested that "China needs to implement the SFA very delicately to avoid being regarded as an aggressive power."[76] In practice, the balance between "striving for achievement" in ways that win friends and flexing new muscles in ways that evoke trepidation seems a difficult one to strike.

Central to that balancing act will be the question of how China chooses to exercise influence with other states. One of the ways that Beijing has historically attempted to appear less threatening is by claiming to adhere to the principle of "non-interference" in the internal affairs of other states. In the new Xi Jinping era, however, a second strategic debate is taking place over whether China should relax its actual and rhetorical adherence to that principle or even abandon it altogether.

The People's Republic of China adopted a strict interpretation of the international principle of non-interference at its founding in 1949. The sprawling but weak state that had suffered a "century of humiliation" at the hands of foreign powers was run by a communist, one-party regime that craved the ability to exclude external influences. Beijing has enshrined the principle in the preamble of the Chinese constitution as well as numerous treaties, including the 1954 agreement with India on the "Five Principles of Peaceful Coexistence," or *Panchsheel*.

China's impulse to stave off foreign influences was again reinforced by the experience of Tiananmen Square in 1989.[77] Today, although China is no longer weak or poor, nothing about Beijing's recent policies suggests any desire to take a softer line on issues of territorial sovereignty. To the contrary, Xi's China has redoubled its efforts to control everything that happens within its borders, including the information available to Chinese citizens and, it would seem, the ideas inside their minds.

Over the same period, China has also claimed to adhere reciprocally to the non-interference principle. In other words, it has pledged to stay out of the internal affairs of other states. But China has been inconsistent in its adherence to non-interference. For instance, the radical policies of Mao Zedong never actually stopped at China's borders; Beijing's goal was to advance its proletarian revolution throughout Asia, Africa, and beyond.[78] But for decades, China only rarely had the ability or desire to project its influence very far beyond its borders, especially if it was not welcome. Then, during the twenty years of "hide and bide," non-interference provided a convenient logic for Chinese officials seeking to eschew foreign overreach by their own increasingly powerful state (or at least to be selective about it), as well as an appealing mantra intended to mollify nervous sovereigns in other states.

In short, it is fair to conclude that Beijing adhered to the norm of non-interference when it suited China's strategic and ideological interests. China is by no means alone in this hypocrisy.[79] The operative question now is how a rich, strong China with a much wider array of overseas interests and points of influence will behave if those interests are at risk. As early as 2014, outside analysts found evidence that China was "slowly moving away from a strict interpretation of non-interference."[80] New concepts like "creative involvement" offer Beijing more flexibility overseas and have gained acceptance among scholars and policymakers alike.[81]

When it comes to non-interference, it looks as if China would like to have its cake and eat it too. On the one hand, the non-interference principle helps Beijing fend off external criticism of Chinese policies, especially its repressive human rights practices. Non-interference also remains a useful talking point for Chinese diplomats who seek to reassure other countries that China would never intrude in their internal affairs. In this, China aims to draw a contrast with the United States and other similarly meddlesome Western, liberal powers.

On the other hand, when it comes to protecting overseas Chinese businesses, workers, and investments, Beijing increasingly feels it needs to play a more intrusive role. And as China has become more powerful, other states have even demanded that Beijing "make more 'contributions' to, and shoulder bigger 'responsibilities' in global issues" especially when it is commercially involved in war-torn and fragile parts of the world like Sudan or Myanmar.[82]

As a consequence of these potentially contradictory ends, the meaning of terms like "creative involvement" or "constructive involvement" remains hazy, defined as much by what they are not as what they are.[83] As a practical matter, however, China is undoubtedly finding itself deeply enmeshed in the affairs of other states. Huge Chinese overseas investments can give Beijing undue influence over political outcomes in other states—at least an indirect form of interference—and also invite more extensive Chinese involvement. This is especially likely in smaller, poorer investment partners.

The case of Sri Lanka has attracted global attention for precisely this reason. In 2007, the Mahinda Rajapaksa government eagerly opened the door to Chinese developers in its ports.[84] When 2015 elections ushered a new president, Maithripala Sirisena, into office, the change initially brought Chinese activities to a halt. Sirisena's election manifesto had specifically attacked the Chinese for its corrupt relations with the Rajapaksa government, declaring that "the land that the White Man took away by means of military strength is now being obtained by foreigners by paying ransom to a handful of persons. . . . If this trend continues for another six years our country would become a colony and we would become slaves."[85]

Once in office, however, the Sirisena government changed its tune. Indeed, "after a few months the island nation's rising foreign debt due to Chinese investment had almost crippled the economy, forcing Colombo to repair its relations with China and resume the infrastructure projects."[86] In 2017, desperate to escape from the burden of hundreds of millions of dollars in Chinese loans, the Sri Lankan government decided to grant a ninety-nine-year lease to China Merchants Port Holdings for its new Hambantota port. "We had to take a decision to get out of this debt trap," explained Mahinda Samarasinghe, Sri Lanka's ports and shipping minister.[87]

Sri Lanka's complicated mix of local and Chinese interests thus produced a contentious outcome and more than enough blame to go around. There is little evidence that China originally approached its relations with Sri Lanka specifically as a means to trap it into a port lease with undue debt burdens.[88] Then again, to suggest that China has strictly avoided intervention in Sri Lanka's internal affairs would be equally misleading. And to perceive China as entirely lacking political and diplomatic motives for its overseas investment decisions would be naïve.

A similar story played out along the island chain of the Maldives to Sri Lanka's southwest, where in 2014 Xi Jinping became the first Chinese president to visit since the country's independence in 1965. Chinese vacationers and investments have flooded the islands over the past decade, and China even leased one of the nation's uninhabited islands for fifty years to use as a tourist destination. Opposition politicians claimed that nearly 10 percent of the national budget was spent on debt repayments to China.[89] In February 2018, when President Abdulla Yameen declared a state of emergency and jailed top opposition figures, one of his first acts was to send his economic development minister to China to make sure he still had Beijing's support.

The Maldives' previous president, Mohamed Nasheed, whom Yameen had ousted and sent into exile in 2013, accused China of a "land grab" of "islands, key infrastructure, and even essential utilities."[90] In 2018, Nasheed wrote, "I fear that, piece by piece, island by island, the Maldives is being sold off to China," and begged for India to lead "the international community in forcing President Yameen to comply" with the Supreme Court and pave the way for new elections.[91] Chinese officials called Nasheed's land grab claims "absolute nonsense," declared—despite all evidence to the contrary—that "China will not interfere in the internal affairs of the Maldives," and then subtly warned India to stay out.[92]

China failed, at least temporarily, to distance the Maldives from Indian influence, and in September 2018, opposition candidate Ibrahim Solih won a shocking victory at the polls over President Yameen. In November, Indian prime minister Narendra Modi attended Solih's inauguration and pledged Indian financial support to the Maldives. Solih reciprocated by promising an "India first" foreign policy.[93] China's reversal of fortune notwithstanding, it is difficult not to perceive that Beijing (and New Delhi) had strayed well beyond "non-interference."[94]

Although China may remain reluctant to disown "non-interference" outright, there can be no mistaking the fact that President Xi's foreign policies represent a clear break from those of his immediate predecessors. President Xi's China shows no sign of pulling back from its ambitious overseas agenda. To the contrary, in August 2018 meetings to mark the five-year anniversary of the BRI and again at the second international BRI Forum in April 2019, Xi congratulated assembled officials on their progress to date, then urged them onward with new vigor. Xi's 2019 speech took on critics of the BRI (including the United States) and reflected a slight shift in tone, but not overall direction.[95] He declared that, "going ahead, we should focus on priorities and project execution, move forward with results-oriented implementation, just like an architect refining the blueprint, and jointly promote the high-quality BRI cooperation."[96]

To support these broad foreign policy shifts, China is also breaking new ground in (1) its use of economic statecraft, (2) its projection of military power and defense diplomacy, and (3) its leadership and overseas diplomatic engagement. Each of these three developments builds upon prior Chinese efforts, but with new vigor, important modifications, and more plentiful resources. They are discussed in the following sections in turn.

China's New Toolkit for Economic Statecraft

President Xi's BRI provides the quintessential example of how Beijing is engaging in new forms of economic statecraft that simultaneously serve Chinese commercial interests and advance Beijing's political agenda.[97] Economic tools have always been a part of the games states play, but the BRI is taking China's game to a new level.

Even though aspects of the BRI are more evolutionary than revolutionary, the scale, hype, and ambition of the effort set it apart. Originally conceived around six main "corridors" of economic integration across Eurasia, the BRI has been depicted in a profusion of stylized maps as a spider's web of connections stretching from Beijing to Western Europe, with hub cities and ports linked by various modes of transportation and telecommunication.[98] Beijing has dubbed its land-based corridors as the "Silk Road Economic Belt," while sea-based routes fall under the "21st Century Maritime Silk Road." The "Digital Silk Road" covers the Internet as well as its associated networks of fiber optic cables and satellites. In January 2018, China even extended the BRI to the Arctic with the "Polar Silk Road," publishing plans to exploit new shipping routes made possible by global warming.

Some of the BRI's links and hubs are well established, while others are only barely conceived. The sum total of Xi's scheme has an eye-popping (and imprecise) price tag of somewhere between $1 and 8 trillion.[99] As the former president of China's Foreign Affairs University, Wu Jianmin, put it in 2015, the BRI is "the most significant and far-reaching initiative that China has ever put forward."[100]

By harnessing principally economic means to achieve a range of economic, developmental, and geopolitical ends, the BRI offers an ingenious blueprint for China to expand its global influence without relying as much on military power. China's focus on regional connectivity and infrastructure investment offers a positive vision and addresses some legitimate needs. A 2017 Asian Development Bank study calculated that Asia will require $26 trillion in infrastructure investment from 2016 to 2030. At 2015 investment levels, this leaves an annual gap of over $800 billion.[101] The point is not that Beijing can or will fill this gap with its own investment, nor even that Beijing's initial plans for BRI will prove sustainable over the long run, but only that there is plenty of demand for what China is offering in the way of funds, construction capacity, and technical know-how.

In its official 2015 policy paper on the BRI, Beijing stressed that the initiative would embrace "the trend towards a multipolar world, economic globalization, cultural diversity and greater IT application," and would "uphold the global free trade regime and the open world economy in the spirit of open regional cooperation."[102] Champions of a liberal, capitalist world order will find these sentiments hard to fault. Yet Beijing's emphasis on "multi-polarity" also carries an implied dig at the United States (for its unilateral tendencies) that finds a number of receptive audiences in parts of Eurasia. It shows how even a seemingly innocuous economic agenda can be turned to a broader strategic purpose. The BRI is full of similar examples.

To finance the BRI, China has mobilized its policy banks and created entirely new funding mechanisms.[103] Beijing is thus armed with policy capabilities unmatched by other capitals, including Washington. For example, President Xi announced a new "Silk Road Fund" in 2014 with $40 billion to spend on BRI projects pulled together from China's State Administration of Foreign Exchange, China's sovereign wealth fund (the China Investment Corporation), the Export-Import Bank of China, and the China Development Bank.[104] These latter two Chinese "policy banks" have announced their intentions to bank-roll even larger projects, to the tune of hundreds of billions of dollars, without necessarily being bound by the commercial restrictions inherent in the private sector or multilateral lenders.[105] In other words, Beijing can take on riskier projects that it judges to hold political or strategic utility, even if the financial payoff may never materialize.

For top-quality infrastructure investments, China has also built a new in-stitution: the Asian Infrastructure Investment Bank (AIIB). The bank was for-mally established in late 2015 with $100 billion in capital, 50 percent of which was contributed by China and the rest from fifty-six other countries.[106] By the end of 2018, the AIIB had grown its membership to ninety-three countries.[107]

The AIIB has already paid off for China in several ways, some more obvious than others. To start, the bank serves, in itself, as a critique of the existing col-lection of multilateral development banks, such as the International Monetary Fund (IMF), that offered China and the rest of the developing world less influ-ence over policy than their share of the global economy would warrant. In the IMF, for instance, voting rules give the United States a veto over major policy decisions. It took five years for the United States Congress to approve a reform measure that extended China's voting share from 3.8 percent to 6 percent in 2015. In the AIIB, China has a voting share of 28.7 percent, which is signifi-cantly greater than any other state, but no single state holds veto power.

In addition, the AIIB adheres to a narrower set of conditions related to cor-porate governance, environmental impact, and commercial integrity.[108] This is in contrast to the IMF, which imposes conditions on borrowers grounded in liberal free-market practices. Such IMF conditions are often politically painful for recipient nations and not high on China's own list of priorities.

Furthermore, by launching an entirely new bank focused on infrastruc-ture, China demonstrated leadership and skilled diplomacy. China's victory was all the sweeter because Washington actively opposed the bank and asked friends and allies to refuse membership. Aside from Japan, however, most of the world—including some of America's closest allies like Australia, Britain, Germany, Italy, and South Korea—took China's side.[109] China had flexed its financial and diplomatic muscles to great effect.

The AIIB has chalked up at least two other important successes. First, winning plaudits from many outside observers, it appointed a known quan-tity, Jin Liqun, as director. Jin had previously served as China's vice minister of finance, Chinese sovereign wealth fund chairman, and vice president of the Asian Development Bank. In addition, the AIIB has consistently followed in-ternationally recognized norms and procedures common to other multilateral development banks (MDBs). As Natalie Lichtenstein, a thirty-year veteran of the World Bank and the AIIB's first chief counsel who helped draft the AIIB's charter explains, "The considerable overlap with the Charters of other MDBs is apparent to those who peruse the AIIB Charter."[110] The choice was deliberate, she adds, because "starting with something workable, known and respected would offer something reliable to governments, financial markets, potential recipients and contractors."[111]

These moves generally convinced member states with lingering skepticism about Beijing's plans that the decision to join the AIIB and to participate in its governance had been the correct move. It also convinced some of those states of the wisdom of participating in future Chinese initiatives such as the BRI Forum. That summit brought representatives from 130 countries, including twenty-nine heads of state, to Beijing in May 2017. By then even the United States appeared to have learned a lesson about the futility of opposing Chinese initiatives alone. The Trump administration sent a senior White House staffer rather than boycotting the meeting altogether.[112]

Second, the AIIB complements China's financing tools and gives policymakers appropriate alternatives for nearly any circumstance. The best, most financially viable projects go to the AIIB or even to other multilateral lenders in which China has influence, like the Asian Development Bank's Central Asia Regional Economic Cooperation (CAREC) program. Risky but strategically important projects can be financed by China's policy banks. Mid-grade projects with particular appeal to China can go to the Silk Road Fund. And if foreign leaders seek funding for pet projects that hold neither financial nor strategic appeal to China, Beijing can politely avoid saying "no" by sending them to the AIIB, where they are likely to be rejected by the bank's board of directors.[113]

Many of China's overseas projects fall at least partly into the category of "aid" or "assistance" rather than investment. Oftentimes the line is hazy, such as when China offers concessionary loans with below-market rates and long repayment terms to finance projects that neither Beijing nor recipient nations are entirely sure will ever be repaid. Many Pakistani observers have speculated that some of China's investments in their country, such as the Lahore Orange Line Metro, could end up in this category.[114]

China has a long history of assistance to developing countries, especially in Africa and Asia.[115] Data collected from 2000 to 2014 show, however, that only about one-fifth of China's global financial contributions qualified as "official development assistance" (ODA), while the rest came as export credits or market-rate loans. To qualify as ODA, at least 25 percent of the value of a project has to be delivered as a grant.[116] By contrast, over 90 percent of global financial contributions by the United States qualified as ODA. Total ODA during this period from the United States came to $366.4 billion, while China delivered only $81.1 billion.[117] In other words, China's assistance was less "generous" than America's, at least by the most commonly used measures.

Until recently, Beijing has also lacked an agency specifically dedicated to the task of delivering grant aid.[118] Instead, a jumble of different agencies were involved, creating obvious problems in policy coordination and implementation.[119] President Xi himself explained in February 2017 that China needed to "improve management over foreign aid funds and projects, reform the foreign aid administration system and improve the overall results of foreign aid."[120]

One month after Xi's comments, Beijing unveiled plans for a new China International Development Cooperation Agency, or CIDCA, as part of a broader ministerial shakeup during China's 13th National People's Congress.[121] State Councilor Wang Yong told the parliament that CIDCA would report directly to China's State Council, chaired by the premier. He explained that CIDCA would be responsible for forming policies on foreign aid, as well as granting aid and overseeing its implementation. He went on to note that CIDCA would "allow aid to fully play its important role in great power diplomacy . . . and will better serve the building of the 'Belt and Road.' "[122]

The next spring, Yang Jiechi, one of China's top foreign policy officials and former foreign minister, was on hand to open the new agency. With the foreign minister Wang Yi in attendance, he reiterated State Councilor Wang Yong's themes and declared grandly that CIDCA would "safeguard world peace and promote common development."[123] Because little about Yang's statements clarified precisely how the new agency would be run or answered questions about its personnel, resources, or authorities, expert observers prognosticated on the basis of who had been appointed to CIDCA's senior leadership.[124]

Wang Xiaotao, a former deputy in China's macro-economic planning department, the National Development and Reform Commission, took CIDCA's reins. Just below him, two vice-chairs hailed from the Ministry of Commerce and Foreign Affairs. Together, these appointments suggested that the new agency would not be beholden to any one of China's ministries, but would coordinate among them.[125] At fifty-seven, CIDCA Director Wang Xiaotao had logged decades at National Development and Reform Commission (NDRC) on domestic economic planning. In recent years, however, his focus turned outward. He played a central role in a range of bilateral negotiations, including on transportation and power projects in a wide range of BRI partner countries.[126] By most accounts, that made Wang well-suited to the role of aid planning.[127]

To support Wang's efforts, Chinese ambassadors around the world were instructed to report additional development-related information to CIDCA. In addition, by early 2018 the agency had assumed responsibility for managing at least some concessionary loans previously handled by the Ministry of Commerce, and it is possible that other Commerce offices will be transferred into the new aid agency wholesale.[128] Yet until CIDCA is fully established, with personnel and institutional structures in place, many Beijing-based observers will remain skeptical about how effective it is likely to be. Some fear, in particular, that the agency could struggle to hire sufficient numbers of expert staff and could be strangled in its infancy by bureaucratic competitors in more powerful ministries.[129]

Finally, as a number of analysts have started to appreciate, Beijing appears increasingly willing to seek political leverage from controlling overseas investment decisions, playing gatekeeper to foreign firms seeking access to China's burgeoning consumer market, and building a dominant advantage in strategic industries.[130] One of China's most blatant attempts to use economic leverage for political purposes came in 2017, when Beijing pressured Seoul to remove an American missile defense system (the Terminal High-Altitude Area Defense, or THAAD) from South Korean territory.[131] Chinese pressure tactics took multiple forms, including a ban on Chinese tourist travel to South Korea that targeted Korea's airlines and tourist industry to the tune of nearly $7 billion in lost revenues.[132] In addition, Beijing encouraged unofficial Chinese boycotts of Korean products, and Korean popular music and movie stars found themselves less welcome in China. China also turned its regulatory inspections process on Korean businesses in China, citing minor code violations on the way to shutting down 80 percent of the supermarkets in the Korean-owned Lotte chain. Although Seoul did not submit to Chinese demands on THAAD, South Korea bore significant economic costs, and it is easy to imagine China utilizing similar pressure tactics in the future.

In addition to the buying power of its consumers, China can also leverage the power of its suppliers. In 2010, China temporarily suspended sales of "rare earth" minerals to Japan in the middle of a maritime dispute in an attempt to place greater pressure on Tokyo.[133] The minerals are essential components for manufacturing a variety of high-tech items, like the glass for solar panels, and although they are not in fact terribly rare, China had built a nearly complete monopoly over their processing facilities. Beijing threatened to take similar actions against the United States in 2019. Although Chinese export bans of this sort can backfire over time by leading states to seek alternative, more reliable sources of supply, Beijing clearly considers them as a tool of commercial coercion and influence.

Huawei offers another example of how China could translate commercial and industrial capacity into political and diplomatic advantage. Since its founding in 1987 by a former Chinese military officer, Ren Zhenfei, Huawei has grown into the world's largest telecommunications equipment manufacturer in the world. Its low prices and advanced technologies, especially 5G wireless networks, have enabled Huawei to gain a clear competitive advantage over Western companies that once dominated the cellular market. Huawei's services and products are cheap in part because it enjoys direct and indirect support from the Chinese state, including guaranteed access to a share of China's huge domestic market, low-interest loans, and subsidies.[134]

US officials fear that Huawei's dominance will allow it to set future technological standards, continue to outpace other communication technology providers, and even offer Chinese intelligence services "backdoor" access to networks installed overseas.[135]

Huawei's place at the core of vital national communications networks across the world could conceivably be exploited for political leverage in other ways as well. These concerns led the Trump administration to try to convince other allies and partner nations not to buy Huawei equipment, and in May 2019, Washington took the extraordinary step of banning Huawei equipment from US networks and barring US companies from selling to Huawei.[136]

In sum, with the BRI, AIIB, and CIDCA, Xi's China has built several new and noteworthy tools for global economic statecraft. The BRI provides a broad conceptual vision and opens the door to a vast array of new Chinese projects across the planet. The AIIB is a practical implement, but one that demonstrated China's convening power and diplomatic muscle. CIDCA is still in its infancy, but already suggests ways in which Beijing is adapting its institutions to grapple with global demands. When combined with China's enormous market power, investments, and dominance over strategic industries, these types of tools have the potential to pack a punch.

Safeguarding "Overseas Interests"

As in the economic sphere, Xi's China has also taken important steps to develop new security tools. These too do not spring from a vacuum; they are evolutionary steps consistent with the decades-long trend of China's growing wealth and military strength discussed earlier in this chapter.[137] Not all of these steps would be required, however, if China were aiming merely to defend its territorial sovereignty against external aggression. Beijing's security policies under President Xi clearly have more ambitious aims, among them extending the reach of China's military and other security and intelligence agencies in order to better defend China's increasingly far-flung interests, such as an estimated 30,000 Chinese overseas businesses.[138]

In 2014, the PLA began a major organizational overhaul.[139] By December 2017, when Senior Colonel Ding Hao met with a small group of visiting American analysts at the PLA Academy of Military Science in Beijing, the initial phases of that overhaul were just wrapping up.[140] His soft voice aided by a microphone to reach across an oversized table in an even more massive conference room, Colonel Ding described how these military reforms included the reconfiguration of the national command structure. The shift regrouped China's forces into an American-style set of five "theater commands" with an eye to improving joint coordination among the armed services.[141]

After Colonel Ding's overview, his colleague, Colonel Wang Guifang, took on the challenge of explaining how China had recently revised its definition of "overseas interests," and what that new definition would mean in terms of defense policy.[142] The subject, she said, had spurred considerable debate among Chinese analysts, but the bottom line was simple and significant: Chinese enterprises, investments, and personnel operating outside China needed more protection.[143] This was especially true because China is becoming more deeply involved in developing and war-torn parts of the world that often lack strong local governments and are infested with terrorists, criminal networks, and insurgents.[144]

The obvious next question for Colonel Wang was what specific steps the PLA was preparing to better defend China's overseas interests. Her response was revealing, if unsatisfying. She observed that China would depend, above all, on close security cooperation with other states. Later, she added that since so many of the security threats facing China's overseas interests were "nonconventional," relating to personal security, or piracy, or criminal violence, they would not necessarily require PLA involvement, and they would be extremely unlikely to necessitate unilateral military action by China. Her point, as I took it, was that nothing about the PLA's plans should be interpreted by outside observers as aggressive or hostile.

Despite Colonel Wang's emphasis on cooperative, non-military means to defend China's overseas interests, other evidence suggests that the PLA is taking harder-edged measures as well. In particular, the same 2014 strategic guidelines that spurred broad organizational reforms within the PLA also officially elevated the importance of "preparations for maritime military struggle."[145]

Many of China's security concerns at sea are focused on "offshore waters defense," by which Chinese strategists refer to the area from China's eastern coast through the Philippine Sea. Yet some US experts believe that China is also working hard to build a navy with global reach, or "far seas protection" capabilities, by investing in military technologies like aircraft carriers, modern destroyers, and amphibious forces.[146] In part to develop capabilities and train for these sorts of "far seas" missions, China's navy has sent ships to participate in counter-piracy missions in the Gulf of Aden since 2009.[147]

In what qualifies as perhaps the most unanticipated military breakthrough of all, in November 2015 China publicly acknowledged that it was building its first overseas military base. The facility is in Djibouti—already home to other Chinese commercial investments—on the Horn of Africa at the mouth of the Red Sea, where it is well placed to extend the navy's reach for counter-piracy, intelligence collection, non-combat evacuation, peacekeeping, counter-terrorism, and sea-lane protection operations.[148] It includes a dedicated berth at the nearby Doraleh Port built to accommodate all but the largest ships in China's fleet, and the base itself is large enough to house thousands of Chinese personnel.[149]

It is important not to overstate the strategic significance of a single over-seas military base, especially when compared to America's global network of bases and alliances. That said, Beijing's move broke with decades of Chinese policy and represented a major change from past practice.[150] In 2000, a Chinese Defense White Paper had declared that "China does not seek military expan-sion, nor does it station troops or set up military bases in any foreign country."[151] As late as 2010, China's Ministry of National Defense website claimed that reports of overseas Chinese bases were groundless.[152] Moreover, now that the taboo of base-building has been broken, Beijing presumably faces one fewer obstacle to building others.[153]

To complement new naval investments and base-building, some Chinese military analysts have called for a wider range of expeditionary capabilities, including lighter, more mobile ground forces, as well as special operations and army aviation units.[154] The PLA marines are a top target for expansion, and a sizable detachment is likely to be based at Djibouti.[155]

The protection of overseas interests also implicates other parts of China's se-curity establishment. Units from the People's Armed Police, officially charged with internal security, have participated in overseas exercises and appear to have operated without fanfare in counter-terror missions in Afghanistan and Iraq.[156] A new Chinese Anti-Terrorism Law went into effect on January 1, 2016, authorizing these sorts of overseas anti-terror missions.[157]

In addition, the powerful Ministry of Public Security (MPS), responsible for China's internal security and law enforcement, extended its reach by placing more police liaison officers in China's embassies. By 2017, sixty-four officers were deployed to thirty-one embassies.[158] Ministry officers have worked with local host forces in some of the neighborhood's least safe environments, in-cluding in Afghanistan, Pakistan, Laos, and Thailand. Beyond that, the MPS has assumed responsibility for a number of counter-narcotics and counter-terrorism missions. In 2013, its leaders even contemplated launching a drone strike against a drug lord in Myanmar.[159]

MPS's continued interest in safeguarding China's growing number of overseas interests was plain during my December 2017 trip to Beijing, when officials from the China Association for Friendship hosted a small dinner discussion.[160] The multi-course meal was memorable not merely for our conversation about security threats in South Asia, especially Afghanistan, but because of the location. We dined inside the ornate and recently renovated Tang-era Hanlin Yuan, imperial China's royal scholarly academy, now incongruously situated behind the walls of the imposing MPS compound on Beijing's East Chang'an Avenue. Association officials, including a former MPS vice-minister, used the meeting to explain how they routinely host counterparts from throughout Eurasia and discuss law enforcement, cyber, and counter-terrorism matters.[161]

China's new overseas investments in locations plagued by crime, terrorism, and political instability have also ignited demand for private security contractors "with Chinese characteristics."[162] President Xi publicly blessed the still-nascent industry in 2015 after three Chinese nationals were killed in the terrorist attack on the Radisson Blu hotel in Bamako, Mali.[163] That same year, the Chinese market for overseas security forces grew to over $10 billion.[164] By 2017, about twenty Chinese private security companies provided international protective services.[165] Calling China's security firms "private" is not entirely accurate, however, as most are run by active-duty or former MPS officials.[166]

Assuming Chinese private security contractors can overcome China's legal barriers to carrying guns, they could begin to fill the yawning gap between the often low-quality defenses that host nations offer and any PLA "boots on the ground" that Chinese forces would provide only in the most extraordinary circumstances.[167] Some are already pushing the envelope; in 2018, the Pakistan branch of China Overseas Security Group provided live-fire training exercises for managers and security guards in China's diplomatic mission in Pakistan as well as Chinese-funded enterprises based there.[168]

Over the past decade, China has developed another military tool with the potential to play a major role in overseas security as well as defense ties with other states: the drone. Like the United States and Israel, China has developed both armed and unarmed variants. Although China has yet to use armed drones in combat, it has deployed them for potential reconnaissance and strike missions at sea, as well as for surveillance within Tibet, Xinjiang, and Yunnan.[169] Drones would appear to offer China an irresistible means to improve the physical security of its overseas facilities at a relatively low cost and without large numbers of personnel engaged in intrusive operations on the ground.

Until 2018, US regulations restricted armed drone sales to a handful of America's closest allies, but China has entered the global drone market with abandon.[170] China has exploited the drone industry as a means to build defense ties with states that purchase most of their other weapons from America, like Saudi Arabia. The drone is thus turning into an important commercial, military, and diplomatic tool for Beijing.

Chinese drones tend to be marginally less capable than their US-made counterparts, but they also cost about half as much. In dollar terms, Chinese military sales still lag behind the American and Israeli competition, but by 2017 China enjoyed a commanding lead in commercial sales.[171] Chinese companies controlled nearly 80 percent of that market worldwide, and the Chinese company DJI alone had a 72 percent share.[172]

Over time, China's success in the commercial drone market will likely translate into technological breakthroughs with important military applications. Chinese military drones could become both cheaper and better than their competitors. For now, they still appeal to bargain-hunters. Pakistan, Egypt, and Myanmar topped China's list of military-grade drone buyers in 2017. Between 2008 and 2017, over three quarters of China's drone sales were of the strike-capable variety.[173]

In sum, new Chinese military capabilities for overseas missions including the unprecedented base in Djibouti, more extensive foreign activities by other Chinese security services like the MPS and "private" security contractors, and Chinese successes with game-changing military technologies like the drone will gradually enable Beijing to project power far beyond China's borders. When it goes abroad, China usually puts its commercial and economic foot first, but the security boot is following not far behind.[174]

Experiments in Global Influence

In its efforts at global diplomatic outreach, President Xi's China has taken a huge leap into the future. As we have seen in the economic and security arenas, Beijing is wielding a variety of new tools and breaking with past practices.

Once again, the BRI is an instructive place to start. When President Xi chaired the BRI Forum in May 2017, Foreign Minister Wang Yi described it as "the most extensively attended and most highly represented multilateral diplomatic event that China had initiated and hosted."[175] Although it built on the experience of earlier Chinese initiatives, like the Shanghai Cooperation Forum and the Forum on China-Africa Cooperation, the 2017 BRI Forum was clearly intended to demonstrate an even greater global ambition. Wang Yi waxed euphoric about the new era for Chinese diplomacy, concluding his speech with a poem: "With the rising tide and favorable wind, it is time to sail the ship and ride the waves." He added, "In a great era that is unfolding before our eyes, let us follow the leadership of the CPC Central Committee with Comrade Xi Jinping at its core, keep our mission firmly in mind, live up to the trust placed in us, and scale new heights in our major-country diplomacy with Chinese characteristics."[176]

As the leader of a state that historically preferred to conduct its diplomacy quietly and bilaterally, and still frequently sticks to less-risky roles in multilateral settings, Xi has stepped out of character.[177] He opportunistically leapt into the global limelight of the 2017 World Economic Forum in Davos, Switzerland, where he declared Chinese leadership in promoting free trade, a clean environment, and global cooperation. It was the first time a top Chinese leader had addressed the group. Although Xi's speech was arguably less effective at convincing skeptics that the Communist Party–led China is actually the world's defender of a liberal, capitalist order, his tone and ambition were stunning, as was the stark contrast of his global message with the inward turn by newly elected President Trump.

Xi has not shied from similar opportunities in other international forums, old or new.[178] By 2015, only three years into his rule, Xi Jinping had become the most-traveled communist leader of China. That year, he visited fourteen countries, outpacing President Obama's eleven.[179] And China's president is not alone. Other top Chinese officials sing from the same sheet about China's desire and capacity to assume a global leadership role.[180]

Xi's China is also experimenting with other tools of diplomatic influence, from hosting showy international conferences to expanding its educational and cultural exchange programs.[181] Naturally, some initiatives have been more effective than others.

Building on the prior expansion of China Global Television Network, in 2018 Beijing announced plans to merge its overseas radio and television networks into a single entity, the "Voice of China," with a transparent propaganda agenda.[182] State-run news agency Xinhua explained that the new media platform's goal would be to "guide hot social issues, strengthen and improve public opinion, push multimedia integration, strengthen international communication and tell good China stories."[183] Hardly "All the News That's Fit to Print"! Reflecting American concerns, in early 2019 the US Justice Department pressured the Chinese television network to register as a foreign agent of the Chinese government.[184]

One atypical experiment in Chinese public outreach is on display in Pakistan, where by mid-2019 the embassy's deputy chief of mission, Zhao Lijian, had attracted over 180,000 followers to his Twitter feed (compared to only 47,000 followers for the official Chinese embassy feed). The entire phenomenon of Zhao's Twitter presence is slightly peculiar, starting with the fact that the use of Twitter is banned inside China. In addition, although nearly all of Zhao's tweets are dedicated to promoting a positive narrative of China-Pakistan relations and playing up the benefits of the China-Pakistan Economic Corridor, his commentary is anything but the standard boilerplate typically associated with staid diplomats. To the contrary, Zhao has zealously dived into Twitter wars with Pakistani critics, both prominent and unknown.

In December 2016, Zhao castigated liberal journalist Cyril Almeida (who maintained a Twitter following of nearly 190,000 by 2019) for alleging that Chinese prisoners were working as construction workers on Pakistani projects. Zhao wrote, "It is really unfortunate that senior journalists believe in this kind of stories of Chinese prisoners in CPEC projects. Are they out of mind [sic]." Clearly taken aback by Zhao's tone, Almeida replied: "Much that is unfortunate here and several out of their minds, but surely not a reasonable (diplomatic?) response. . . ."[185] Zhao's use of Twitter is edgy and unprecedented, but cannot conceivably represent a solo or unauthorized act. It must be appreciated as an unusually nimble part of a broader Chinese media strategy to promote Beijing's perspective inside Pakistan.

Another very different experiment was on exhibit in December 2016 during a visit to China's northwest city of Yinchuan, just south of Inner Mongolia. After attending one of China's innumerable workshops on the BRI, a half-dozen American attendees were packed aboard a bus to visit the China Hui Culture Park. The Hui are a group of roughly 10 million Chinese Muslims, distinguished by their cultural practices that include adhering to Islamic dietary laws. Far more thoroughly integrated into Han society than the Uighurs, and consequently less ruthlessly persecuted by the state, the Hui live all over China. More concentrated Hui communities are found in the northwest, including Ningxia, which Beijing designated as the Hui Autonomous Region in 1958.

The day was cold and clear, and from the distance we could spot an enormous structure resembling the Taj Mahal. On closer inspection, the edifice was actually a 125-foot-high domed entryway to the park, behind which lay open plazas and several other monumental scale buildings. One, the "golden palace," is meant to look and feel like a mosque, but it is not actually a place of worship. Another in the distance looked like a spaceship on stilts rising from an artificial lake, and was apparently the set for an elaborate $30 million light show and pageant entitled "A Dream Back into Tales from the Thousand and One Nights."[186]

The park was almost entirely deserted aside from our small group and a guide. We made our way into the "mosque" where we were instructed to remove our shoes, then free to wander the carpeted floor and gaze at the vast ceiling painted with arabesque designs in gold and blue. After that, we were guided through a makeshift museum on Chinese and Hui history replete with oversized maps of the ancient Silk Road and depicting an imperial China that covered much of northern India, Central Asia, and all of the Russian Far East.

The visit left me and my American colleagues slightly befuddled, and it was only after additional reading that I appreciated the park's purpose to serve as a "Sino-Arab cultural bridge" that would "promote all aspects of Sino-Arab exchange and cooperation."[187] Opened in 2005, the park would present an "acceptable face" of Islam to the rest of China and to visitors from the Arab world, one clearly differentiated from the politically radioactive story of Xinjiang's Uighurs.[188] In preparation, Yinchuan's airport started a 900,000-square-foot expansion project and Emirates Airlines began direct flights from Dubai.[189] Even though the Muslim theme park has yet to prove itself as a tourist attraction, it isn't difficult to imagine that it could be used as a set for televised international galas that project Beijing's preferred self-image to the world.

Other Chinese outreach efforts have proven even more controversial. China's Confucius Institute program started in 2004, but by 2018, Beijing had bankrolled over 500 institutes in 138 countries.[190] Ostensibly, these institutes were founded to teach Chinese language and culture. Over time, however, Beijing has attempted to turn its financial support to foreign academic institutions into a means to influence overseas debates and silence critics.

One professor who heads a Confucius Institute outside the United States explained in June 2018 that his university felt it had to negotiate the terms of the arrangement carefully in order to avoid Chinese influence over faculty appointments or activities beyond the bounds of language and culture. Even so, Chinese embassy officials attempted to pressure university administrators to deny platforms to speakers critical of Beijing. Although that university rejected Chinese demands, another professor at the same school told of how he had met Confucius Institute directors from poorer universities. Desperate to hire and retain faculty, they were far more vulnerable to Chinese leverage.

My own school, Johns Hopkins SAIS, found itself enmeshed in a mini-scandal in November 2017, when *Foreign Policy* magazine reported that a new professorship was being funded by the China–United States Exchange

Foundation (CUSEF), a Hong Kong–based nonprofit led by former Hong Kong chief executive Tung Chee-hwa. The magazine article asserted that SAIS was being targeted for Chinese influence operations intended to extend China's global reach and reshape overseas perceptions of China.

Tung's ties to Beijing are undoubtedly strong, and *Foreign Policy* suggested (over CUSEF's denials) that he was indirectly linked to the Communist Party's "United Front Work Department."[191] The United Front has been described by Mao Zedong (and more recently by Xi Jinping) as one of China's "magic weapons" for propaganda. The organ of the Chinese Communist Party has always been charged with the duty of winning over non-party members, and in recent years it has specifically targeted "ethnic Chinese overseas and students studying abroad."[192]

In defense of the school's decision to accept the gift from CUSEF, SAIS's then-director of the China Studies program, Professor David Lampton, explained that it would impose "absolutely no conditions or limitations" on SAIS faculty or scholarship. The claim was reasonable; SAIS is not so cash-strapped that it could be forced to toe Beijing's line in order to pay its professors, and the faculty contract in question specifically stipulated that its funding would persist even if CUSEF pulled its support.

The issue of outsized donor influence is hardly new in academia, and well-endowed schools clearly have greater latitude to restrict the influence of donors or to reject their funds altogether. Along these lines, in 2017 the University of Texas at Austin came under fire from Senator Ted Cruz for considering funding from CUSEF. After a lengthy internal discussion, university president Gregory Fenves announced that his school would turn down the cash.[193]

Debates over the appropriate role for Chinese (or any foreign) funding in American educational and research institutions will likely continue to rage, and it is important to distinguish between traditional, overt public diplomacy and more nefarious influence operations. There are also tough questions to be asked about how American universities are managing a large influx of Chinese students, whether those students are empowered to adopt American-style practices of free speech and thought during their stays in the United States, and how overseas educational experiences tend to inform their perspectives and actions when they return to China.

In any case, Beijing does not appear to be playing a short-term game when it comes to projecting political influence abroad, and its initiatives are likely to range from subtle relationship-building to active bribery and coercion. In 2017, a series of revelations about the United Front's influence-buying activities in Australia set off alarm bells.[194] Prime Minister Malcolm Turnbull observed that "media reports have suggested that the Chinese Communist

Party has been working to covertly interfere with our media, our universities and even the decisions of elected representatives."[195] In response, the prime minister announced a "Counter Foreign Interference Strategy" in December 2017 and introduced legislation that required foreign lobbyists to register their affiliations, beefed up espionage laws, and established a consolidated Department of Home Affairs.

Australia's reaction suggests that perhaps China's muscular diplomacy will set off an equally forceful counter-reaction in some of the world's wealthiest liberal democracies, where Chinese communist propaganda will have more trouble finding fertile ground. Elsewhere, however, Chinese tools for political repression at home are finding eager authoritarian copycats.

China's so-called Great Firewall, whose algorithms block entire websites, specific webpages, and politically sensitive search terms from China's 500 million Internet users, is just one piece of the censorship puzzle. In 2013, an estimated 2 million Chinese were employed in positions responsible for monitoring and censoring Internet content.[196] Direct and indirect pressure from the state forces self-censorship of content, and if that does not work, China has shown a willingness to deploy cyber-attacks against businesses and political activists.[197] Beijing is not merely able to monitor and manipulate old-fashioned print and mass media, but to drive or curtail social media and modern communications. State censorship appears to prioritize "attempting to forestall collective activities" that could conceivably result in anti-state political mobilization.[198] Even when citizens find temporary ways to circumvent state controls, such as by using virtual private networks (VPNs), an overall culture of fear exists. The result is that the world's single largest Internet population cannot access content the Chinese state deems politically sensitive.[199]

In addition to leading by example, Chinese officials are not shy about sharing their technical skills with other regimes aspiring to shut down political dissent. For instance, they have sponsored a series of training workshops in Beijing for foreign officials on topics like "big data public-opinion management systems," and a "positive energy public-opinion guidance system."[200] Major Chinese technology companies have already sold other sophisticated digital tools useful for repressing populations, like facial-recognition and network monitoring software. Unlike the United States, China has no export controls on such technologies.[201]

In short, Beijing's experiments in global outreach, backed with vast human and financial capital, are certain to prove politically influential around the world, especially when combined with China's other new tools of economic statecraft and hard-power projection.

Global Consequences

Most American policymakers and foreign policy scholars are only just now waking up to the new realities of China's global game.[202] Washington is, as a consequence, reacting to Beijing's moves rather than anticipating or moving out ahead of them. Moreover, many of those American policymakers who now accept that "prevailing policies toward China have failed and that an alternative approach is now urgently required" remain focused on familiar (and still critically important) topics like trade, North Korea, or the various maritime disputes off China's eastern seaboard.[203]

To be fair, Beijing's broad strategic shift outlined in this chapter—away from "hide and bide" and toward a more selective adherence to the principle of non-interference—is gaining wider attention. So are China's wide array of new economic, military, and diplomatic tools for projecting and protecting its overseas interests, many of which have been explored in some detail earlier in this chapter.

Least-well appreciated among most American experts is the extent to which China is casting its gaze westward to continental Eurasia, or the "Greater Middle East." But as this chapter argues, there are significant economic and strategic reasons for China to push in that direction. In historical terms, China's "natural" focus is to its north and west. Contemporary security fears compel Beijing to worry about threats of Islamist radicalization and terrorism. Geopolitical aspirations lead Chinese strategists to recast the space as an overland bridge to energy supplies and markets as well as a zone of influence befitting a global superpower.[204]

To be clear, this does not mean that Beijing will forsake other interests and march exclusively westwards. There is no doubt, for instance, that China's military remains fixated on perceived threats to the east, including that posed by the United States and its Asian allies. But it does suggest that a greater premium should be placed on understanding what China is up to in Eurasia and what the implications of its activities are likely to be. More to the point, Washington needs to develop its own strategy for the region that takes Chinese activities into account.

Analytically, this is challenging in part because China's increasingly ambitious overseas policies, including the BRI, are still works in progress.[205] Equally important, much is out of Beijing's hands.[206] No matter what visions are dreamed up in Beijing, outcomes on the ground will depend in large part on the political reactions of other states in China's western periphery. Small states are often politically unstable, especially fragile democracies and autocracies with old leaders. Local grievances and disputes could spark resistance to Chinese efforts. Other great powers, including Russia and the United

States, will also have a role in parts of the region where their influence may be waning in relative terms but is still more entrenched than China's.

All of these factors require more attention than Western (and likely even Chinese) analysts have given them to date. The following three chapters take up these issues in much greater detail. They describe China's historical and contemporary relations with South Asia, Central Asia, and the Middle East, in turn. More than that, each chapter explains how the domestic political and economic realities of important Eurasian states actually shape the economic, political, and strategic opportunities open to Beijing. They depict how local groups tend to perceive China in terms of their own, often parochial, agendas. While some locals eagerly anticipate the financial and political gains they can accrue from closer Chinese ties, others warily fear potential losses.

Finally, each of the next three chapters explores how different Eurasian statesmen factor China into their strategic calculations. Some see China's potential as a supportive outside partner, enabling their states to compete with or resist pressure from other states, while others view China as an irritant or threat to their geopolitical aspirations. The heterogeneity of perspectives about China across Eurasia is itself instructive. It helps to inform a number of the recommendations for US strategy and policy contained in this book's final chapter.

| South Asian Conflicts

D ESPITE THE FORMIDABLE mountain ranges and seas that naturally
insulate the Indian subcontinent from the rest of Asia, human ties between China and South Asia date back millennia.

In 1976, Chinese archeologists unearthed the tomb of Lady Fu Hao, near
Anyang in the Yellow River Valley. Fu Hao lived over three thousand years
ago; her life story was recounted in bone inscriptions also discovered in nearby
digs. As the favorite wife of King Wu Ding, a prominent ruler of the Shang
Dynasty period, Fu Hao was said to have led 13,000 soldiers into battle against
warring tribes. Her tomb yielded a remarkable collection of roughly two thou-
sand artifacts, including weapons, jade animal statues, and precious stones.
Not least among the treasures were vast piles of cowrie shells, over 6,800 in
all. The shells, according to historians, were used as a form of money in early
China. The shells also provide the earliest evidence of ties between China and
South Asia, because the sea snails that originally called them home lived in the
Indian Ocean, near the Maldives and Sri Lanka.[1]

Precisely how the cowries made their way to ancient China is less well
understood, as the earliest historical record of Chinese relations with South
Asia is dated a thousand years later. In 138 BCE, the Han emperor Wu sent an
emissary, Zhang Qian, to Central Asia. Zhang Qian's mission was to explore
the possibility of a military alliance against a warring adversary on the edges
of China's expanding empire. This is the same emissary that President Xi
Jinping mentioned in his 2013 speech at Nazarbayev University, misleadingly

describing him as merely seeking friendly ties with Central Asia and paving the way for the overland Silk Road that would famously connect China to Rome.[2]

Present-day distortions aside, during his travels in Central Asia, Zhang Qian came across cloth and bamboo sticks in a market that were said to come from southern China via "Shendu." What seemed like a minor or passing observation was in fact an historical landmark. Professor Tansen Sen, a historian of China-India relations, explains that "this was the first mention in Chinese records of a name that for the subsequent centuries remains associated with India."[3] China extended its reach into (and trading ties with) Central Asia over the next two centuries, and dynastic histories of the period record missions arriving to the Han court in Xi'an from a region located in contemporary Pakistan and Afghanistan.[4]

For much of the first millennium CE, however, the main driver of relations between China and India was Buddhism. Monks from South Asia traveled to China and vice versa. The Chinese monk Faxian recorded his travels through the Buddhist holy sites of South Asia starting in 399 CE. He completed a wide loop, starting overland from present-day Xi'an in China and passing through Xinjiang on his way to Buddhist sites in Pakistan, Afghanistan, and eventually northern India and Nepal. For his return to China, he went by ship from Bengal to Sri Lanka, then through the Strait of Malacca and South China Sea.[5] Another of the most famous Chinese monks, Xuanzang, studied in northern India at the Nalanda seminary and returned to the Tang dynasty capital in 645 CE. As Sen observes, Xuanzang's letters to former teachers and classmates on doctrinal and other issues offer clear evidence of the active and important linkages that existed between the two societies at the time.[6]

In addition to religious concepts, rituals, and relics, Buddhist networks of the era also conveyed other ideas and material goods between South Asia and China. South Asian astronomy, mathematics, and medicine were all brought to China, as was the process of making sugar. Chinese paper likely came to South Asia through similar networks, with gunpowder arriving later.[7] By the end of the first millennium, however, regional trading networks had shifted away from the overland routes that connected Buddhist points of interest to coastal centers of maritime trade that also extended farther westward to the Muslim world.[8] Still, the links between China and various parts of present-day India persisted through flows of trade and tribute.

Six hundred years ago, the newly installed Ming "Yongle" emperor sent his own trusted emissary on a series of celebrated overseas voyages. The Muslim eunuch, Admiral Zheng He, is still relatively unknown in the West, but celebrated in contemporary China as a symbol of China's global reach and overseas initiatives. Zheng He's fleet established Ming Dynasty China's "hegemonic power over much of the Indian Ocean world" by controlling its most important ports, including those of Sri Lanka and along India's southwestern Malabar coast.[9] In Cochin (India's present-day city of Kochi), Zheng He delivered a stone tablet inscribed by the Ming emperor signifying the region's great importance as a source of spices (especially pepper) and as a staging point for westward exploration to Arabia and Africa.[10]

Again, contrary to the narrative often purveyed by Beijing today, Zheng He's voyages were not merely peaceful exploratory missions.[11] His armadas of mighty warships carried over 26,000 men, mostly well-armed soldiers, and Zheng He was himself an experienced soldier, not a sailor.[12] Historian Geoff Wade summarizes his missions as intended to demonstrate the might and legitimacy of the Ming emperor, forcibly asserting a *"pax Ming* throughout the known world."[13] To this end, Wade catalogues a history of coercive violence involving Zheng He in present-day Indonesia, Myanmar, Thailand, Somalia, Sri Lanka, and India.[14]

Historians Sen and Wade are both inclined to see this Ming period of Chinese maritime dominance as an important precursor to the centuries of European imperialism that followed shortly thereafter.[15] Facing mounting financial and political challenges at home and overland security threats from the north, China's maritime ambition collapsed shortly after the apogee of Zheng He's missions. That collapse opened the door to the Portuguese, then the Dutch, and finally the British.[16]

All three colonial powers presided over vast trading empires based in part on passing highly prized goods between China and India, starting with spices, textiles, and porcelain, then shifting to tea. The British thirst for tea created a trade imbalance that flooded China with silver currency. But when British traders started selling Indian-grown opium to China, the imbalance was reversed. By the mid-nineteenth century, millions of Chinese were addicted to the narcotic. Qing rulers tried to curtail the opium trade, but Britain's gunboat diplomacy forcibly reopened access to Chinese markets. Thousands of Indian troops served under British command in the Opium Wars of the mid-nineteenth century, and 30,000 Indian troops fought for the British during China's Boxer Rebellion of 1900.[17]

India was freed from European imperialism only in 1947 after World War II, but immediately traumatized by the subcontinent's partition and war with Pakistan. India's fiercely anti-imperialist prime minister Jawaharlal Nehru initially found a degree of common cause with Mao Zedong's communist China in an embrace of Pan-Asian solidarity.[18] Pakistan, for its part, was momentarily left to the side and quickly jumped into an alliance with the United States as a means to address its own urgent sense of insecurity.[19] Pakistan's Cold War alignment did not, however, lead it to a break with China. To the contrary, Pakistan's leaders assured their Chinese counterparts that they would not participate in any US-led move against China, and they had reached a "mutual understanding" of nonaggression by the time of the Bandung Conference in 1955.[20]

The Sino-Indian honeymoon was not built to last. The modern nation states quickly began to spar over China's repression in Tibet and their (still) unresolved land boundary disputes.[21] Historian John Garver sees their "protracted contest" as rooted in competing nationalist narratives and, likely more important, a "classic security dilemma," in which each tends to see the other's strength as a potential threat.[22] Modern India has proudly claimed a traditional sphere of influence based on cultural and linguistic ties that extends through southeast and Central Asia, where it clearly overlaps with China's own modern, if historically derived, claims of regional hegemony.[23] In Tibet and along their shared land border, Sino-Indian tensions have run especially high.

These differences erupted into the open in 1962, when China fought a brief, victorious war against India. Since then, Beijing has clearly privileged its strategic ties with Pakistan, considered a reliably anti-Indian partner perched atop India's northwest shoulder.[24] Despite their striking ideological, religious, and cultural differences, China continues to see Pakistan as one of its few true "friends" in the world. That friendship is hailed at nearly every opportunity with a standard paean: "Pak-China friendship is higher than the Himalayas, deeper than the ocean, sweeter than honey, and stronger than steel."

Other romanticized depictions of the modern Sino-Pakistani relationship stress how the once-insular Communist China used Pakistan as a diplomatic conduit to the outside world. Most spectacularly, Pakistan played a leading role in the Nixon administration's opening to China. After two years of Sino-American diplomacy via Islamabad, Henry Kissinger made a secret trip to Beijing in early July 1971. While visiting Pakistan, Kissinger feigned an illness and hopped on a Pakistan International Airlines jet to Beijing. Even the US embassy's political counselor in Islamabad fell for the ruse.[25] President Nixon only broke the news of Kissinger's talks with Mao Zedong two weeks later.

In sum, whether in modern or ancient times, the relationships between China and South Asia have been consequential for both sides, yet still somewhat distant. Ideas, goods, and people have moved in both directions, leaving important historical legacies. The China–South Asia relationship is also difficult to assess as an exclusive or closed loop; it has always been part of a wider regional or even global geopolitical space, whether defined by the overland pilgrimage routes of Buddhist monks that extended into central, north, and southeast Asia; the active networks of maritime trade that fed into the Middle

East and Africa; the far-flung colonial empires of Western European powers; or the global competition of the Cold War.

Finally, although outright violent conflict between China and South Asia has been relatively infrequent, that fact is more convincingly explained by geography than by any special cultural or ideological affinity. During periods when the two sides have come into more routine contact, such as when Zheng He sailed the high seas or Jawaharlal Nehru held forth in New Delhi, they have shown little sign of escaping normal patterns of geopolitical competition or conflict.

China's New Push into South Asia

In South Asia today, China pursues multiple, overlapping interests. At the most basic level, China would benefit from stable trade and commercial relations with India—by far the region's largest market—and with Pakistan, where China enjoys a deeper level of trust and friendship. China's leaders have engaged in high-level summitry with their Indian and Pakistani counterparts. China has included India and Pakistan in new regional and other multilateral initiatives, such as the Shanghai Cooperation Organization and the Asian Infrastructure Investment Bank. Chinese companies are active in both markets, both as traders and as investors. Reflecting these interests, China has played a vigorous diplomatic role on several occasions to help avert wars between India and Pakistan.

Yet China's regional interests have not uniformly led Beijing to neutral policies in South Asia. Today, a powerful China no longer requires Pakistan's services in most of the ways it did during the Cold War, but Beijing still perceives strategic utility in the relationship. Above all, Chinese concerns about Uighur unrest in Xinjiang—discussed in chapter 2—lead Beijing to see neighboring Pakistan in a new light: as an essential security partner against the small but violent Uighur opposition groups that have found refuge in Pakistan and Afghanistan.

It is through this lens of internal security that Chinese officials initially perceived the greatest utility in the China-Pakistan Economic Corridor (CPEC). From their perspective, CPEC was an economic development initiative intended to create conditions inside Pakistan that would reduce the appeal of violent, anti-state ideas and stem their flow into China. Accordingly, China has shown little interest in encouraging greater movement of people (with potentially dangerous perspectives) across its border with Pakistan. To the contrary, the "corridor" aspect of CPEC has mainly meant improving transportation within Pakistan itself as a means to create opportunities and efficiencies for trade and production.[26]

As observed in the first chapter of this book, China's interests in Gwadar port were initially marginal, reflected in the skeptical response of Chinese officials to Pakistani president Musharraf's proposal. As the years passed, however, Gwadar's strategic potential to the Chinese navy has become increasingly clear. Unlike the new naval facility at Djibouti, Gwadar would offer an overland route directly to China's western provinces. To be sure, this is not an easy route (over the Karakoram Mountains!), and that terrain imposes severe limitations on its viability as a commercial thoroughfare. Yet as a hub on the Arabian Sea overlooking India and the Persian Gulf, Gwadar could one day provide an excellent naval complement to Djibouti.

Similarly, the Chinese perspective on CPEC has also evolved and expanded. Chinese officials have often portrayed CPEC as an essential part of BRI, dubbing it the "flagship" of the overall enterprise.[27] In this context, China's interests in CPEC echo those of the BRI as a whole: to export industrial overcapacity, use trade and infrastructure investment to extend Beijing's global diplomatic influence, and gradually carve out a continental-sized zone of China-led economic integration.

According to a 2015 report published by Pakistan's Ministry of Planning, Development, and Reform loftily entitled "Ascending the Saga of National Progress," CPEC was envisioned as nothing less than a "fate-changer for Pakistan" comprising a "comprehensive package of cooperative initiatives and projects, which covers key areas including connectivity, information and network infrastructure, energy cooperation, industries and industrial parks, agricultural development, poverty alleviation, tourism, financial cooperation as well as livelihood improvement including municipal infrastructure, education, public health and people-to-people communication."[28] The report went on to detail a suitably extensive list of CPEC projects, from roads and ports to power plants, schools, and a hospital, all with estimated costs and dates of completion.

Two years later, the Pakistani government followed up with a "long term plan" for CPEC.[29] No less ambitious, the plan envisioned that by 2030 CPEC would yield an "endogenous mechanism for sustainable economic growth . . . and South Asia shall grow into an international economic zone with global influence."[30] The plan did stress that CPEC initiatives were identified through a joint consultative and planning process between China's National Development and Reform Commission and Pakistan's Ministry of Planning, Development, and Reform. The two sides agreed to prioritize "Gwadar, Energy, Transport Infrastructure and Industrial Cooperation."[31]

China has been eager to tout CPEC's successes. In late October 2018, the Chinese embassy in Pakistan released a set of briefing slides on CPEC, evidently intended to demonstrate that Chinese initiatives were on track, beneficial to Pakistan, and very much in line with the goals of Pakistan's then-newly elected government under Prime Minister Imran Khan. A summary slide counted ten "early harvest" projects completed and twelve more "under smooth construction," amounting to a contract total of $19 billion. The list reflected CPEC's emphasis on energy and transportation infrastructure, which both Islamabad and Beijing had believed would be crucial to national economic development.[32]

Not surprisingly, India finds little to like in China's initiatives in South Asia. As it has since independence from the British empire, New Delhi perceives itself as the rightful regional hegemon on the subcontinent and China as an external interloper. A growing economy feeds India's own global ambitions, against which China looks like a long-term strategic competitor.[33]

India's material differences with China begin with disputed land boundaries, as they have for decades.[34] Talks since the 1962 war have failed to establish a mutually acceptable international border. Military patrols in the area often stray into territory claimed by the other side, sparking mini-standoffs and diplomatic flaps.

The potential dangers posed by territorial disputes were highlighted in the summer of 2017. Over seventy-three days, Indian and Chinese armies faced off in Doklam, a remote territory at the trisection of India, China, and the mountain kingdom of Bhutan. There Indian troops moved into disputed territory to cut off Chinese road-building crews. Although the details quickly get complicated, India almost certainly acted out of fear that Chinese forces were constructing a new road that would enable them to threaten the nearby Siliguri land corridor that links the main territory of India to the seven states of its North Eastern Region. At its narrowest, the passage is only 17 miles wide.[35] By summer's end, however, Beijing and New Delhi managed to negotiate their way out of the crisis, with both sides agreeing to pull forces from the contested area.[36]

The Doklam incident demonstrated that, on the one hand, China and India are highly motivated to avoid outright violence, not least because it would profoundly disrupt their mutually beneficial economic ties. On the other hand, the incident showed that both sides are unwilling to make territorial concessions or back away from confrontations in ways that could avert similar confrontations in the future.[37] Beijing and New Delhi are investing in new border forces and facilities that will bring them into more routine contact.[38] Within the next decade, analysts anticipate that the two sides could amass roughly a half-million forces along the mountainous border within weeks if a crisis were to erupt.[39]

Now and for the foreseeable future, however, China perceives India as a lesser player. And by all measures other than population, the Chinese are right. India is at least decades away from rivaling China in terms of hard power or influence. Even by 2050, India is projected to account for only about 7 percent of global GDP, as compared to China's projected 20 percent.[40]

That said, from the mid-2000s, Beijing has been forced to grapple with an unanticipated development: India's tilt toward the United States. New Delhi's landmark civil nuclear deal with Washington during the Bush administration and subsequent follow-on agreements with the Obama and Trump administrations hardly qualify as the stuff of treaty alliances. Even so, Beijing has had to recalculate India's potential now that New Delhi enjoys easier access to American military technologies and the clear diplomatic support of a bipartisan consensus in Washington.

China appears less concerned about India's independent clout than about India's contribution to counterbalancing groups of states in Asia.[41] One telling indicator came during my December 2017 trip to Beijing. Along with a half-dozen other American scholars, I was repeatedly peppered with questions about a recent meeting of the "Quad," a security dialogue between American, Japanese, Indian, and Australian diplomats.[42] Judging by the intensity of that interrogation, one would have assumed that the Quad was the equivalent of a new anti-Chinese NATO (and that comparison was even framed as a question once). In reality, however, the Quad remains a relatively minor affair. It met again in June 2018 but to that point had failed to accomplish much other than rekindle a series of consultations that had fallen dormant a decade earlier.[43]

In any event, to the extent that China can prevent India from aligning firmly with the United States (or with Japan, for that matter), Beijing appears eager to do so. Beijing's courtship of New Delhi was on full display when President Xi and Prime Minister Modi met in Wuhan, China, in late April 2018. The principal aim on both sides of that summit was to "reset" the China-India relationship from its low point during the Doklam crisis of the previous summer.[44] But China also arrived with a second goal: to induce "greater caution and reluctance on India's part to challenge, or gang up against, China."[45]

All in all, China's aims in South Asia do not add up entirely neatly. Beijing appears to seek a variety of (possibly mutually incompatible) ends and walks a vanishingly fine line between India and Pakistan. More than that, however, new Chinese initiatives are likely to run headlong into two sorts of ground realities: first, Pakistan's messy domestic political economy, and second, the toxic conflict between India and Pakistan.

China Meets Pakistan's Domestic Realities

Baloch fears about the China-backed development of Gwadar were noted in this book's introduction. When outside investments benefit some Pakistanis relatively more than others, they raise the potential for disputes and conflict. Similar points can be made for the rest of China's involvement in Pakistan.

Even if we assume that Pakistan as a whole stands to benefit from closer ties with Beijing, starting with the tens of billions of dollars China is devoting to CPEC, some Pakistanis will gain more than others, and some will lose outright. In a competitive political environment, especially one as riven by ethnic, socioeconomic, sectarian, and ideological cleavages as Pakistan's, distributional consequences are all-important. They will influence the way that Pakistan responds to China in ways large and small. They are likely to determine the fate of grand initiatives like CPEC.

Indeed, many of the initial questions that Pakistanis raised about CPEC revolved around how Chinese infrastructure investments should be spread across each of Pakistan's provinces, at what scale, and in what order. Of particular concern was the extent to which CPEC's eastern corridor (running through Punjab) would be prioritized over its western corridor (running through Khyber-Pakhtunkhwa and Balochistan).[46] As the largest, wealthiest, most secure, and often best-organized province, Punjab has huge advantages when it comes to working with outside partners to attract aid, investment, and know-how. Punjab is also the most developed province; it is relatively easy for CPEC projects to build upon existing infrastructure.

It was no surprise, then, that the government initially focused on CPEC's eastern corridor. In 2015–2016, Pakistan's National Highway Authority allocated 110 billion rupees to the eastern route and only 20 billion to the western.[47] A series of "All Parties Conferences" in 2015 and 2016 temporarily soothed tensions once the government promised to devote more attention to the western corridor and to allow provinces more of a say in CPEC decision-making and oversight.[48] Government officials even claimed that Balochistan would receive more funding than Punjab for energy projects, but the issue continued to surface as the government made plans for construction projects, such as for new fiber optic lines.[49]

Such political tussles show no signs of abating. Prime Minister Imran Khan's government again found itself facing new rounds of political skirmishing in December 2018, when the chief minister of Balochistan refused to attend a CPEC coordination meeting in Beijing. Bolstering the chief minister's demands for greater CPEC transparency and frustration that his province had never received its fair share, the Balochistan provincial assembly adopted a "resolution demanding the formation of a national commission to show that there has been an 'injudicious distribution of projects and funds under the China-Pakistan Economic Corridor.' "[50]

When it comes to CPEC, Balochistan is not the only aggrieved territory. A 2018 report from the International Crisis Group outlines how residents of Pakistan's mountainous Gilgit-Baltistan region bordering China are disappointed by how few tangible benefits CPEC has produced. Rather than welcoming local input, Pakistani authorities have quashed dissent and routinely implied "that dissidents and protesters are Indian spies" as a means to delegitimize them and justify additional crackdowns. The report adds that "hasty, flawed reforms, with limited local buy-in, have aggravated longstanding grievances in Gilgit-Baltistan, [and] anti-Chinese sentiment is also on the rise."[51]

Elsewhere too, CPEC plans have the potential to spark significant political backlash. One especially important sector is agriculture, which still accounts for nearly a quarter of GDP and half of Pakistan's jobs.[52] As in any traditional society, land rights are contentious and freighted with economic significance as well as political baggage. Many Pakistani farms are small holdings, although larger tracts are owned by feudal landlords and worked by tenant farmers. In some important instances, tenants lack property rights, making them vulnerable to displacement.[53]

In this context, the 2017 CPEC "Long Term Plan" quickly sparked debate with its ambition to "promote the systematic, large-scale, standardized and intensified construction of agricultural industry . . . [and] promote the transition from traditional agriculture to modern agriculture."[54] Since the release of that plan, core questions about the nature of China's involvement in the Pakistani agricultural sector have not been resolved, including the most basic question of all: whether Chinese firms have already been allowed to operate.

In December 2018, Dr. Vaqar Ahmed, a researcher from Pakistan's Sustainable Development Policy Institute, catalogued concerns from a survey of Pakistani farmers, mainly centered on fears that "they will not have a level playing field in competing with their Chinese counterparts."[55] He concluded that "to sell agricultural cooperation under CPEC and also remain politically safe, the PTI [ruling party] government may have to provide some safeguards at least during the short and medium term to local farmers who are already facing a host of supply-side constraints."[56]

Chinese land acquisitions are not a hypothetical or distant issue. In July 2017, one landlord with family holdings in Punjab explained that he and his neighbors had already been approached by Chinese companies seeking long-term leases.[57] He had rejected the offer, but neighboring families were considering it more seriously. It is easy to imagine CPEC initiatives to modernize Pakistani farms could feed public suspicions, anxieties, and protests.[58]

The other major challenge facing China in Pakistan is the sheer uncertainty of national elections. As an illiberal and authoritarian state, China is not inherently comfortable navigating the disorderly politics of a developing democracy.

Pakistan's 2018 campaign swept a new party into national power, led by a former cricket star and longtime opposition politician, Imran Khan. It clearly caught China off-guard. Having invested heavily in forging close ties to the Sharif government under the assumption that it was likely to win another term, Beijing indirectly found itself on the receiving end of Khan's harsh criticism.[59] For several years, Khan had blasted the Sharifs for their opaque deals with China that appeared to benefit their home province of Punjab over Pakistan's other three provinces.[60]

On assuming office in mid-August 2018, Khan's government attempted to reopen negotiations on all CPEC projects.[61] Beijing rebuffed the move, rejecting any review of projects that had already begun.[62] In addition, Pakistan's army sent a clear message on the need for CPEC to stay on course, as Army Chief Qamar Javed Bajwa rushed to China in September 2018 to reassure Beijing that "the Belt and Road initiative with CPEC as its flagship is destined to succeed despite all odds and Pak army shall ensure security of CPEC at all costs."[63]

Still, China scrambled to mend fences with the new party in power and address Imran Khan's substantive concerns about CPEC.[64] The Chinese embassy announced plans to emphasize job creation, industrial cooperation, and broad socioeconomic uplift in future CPEC rounds, all priority areas for Khan.[65] It touted the 75,000 jobs already created by CPEC and cited research reports suggesting that CPEC would create over 700,000 jobs by 2030. In an attempt to absolve China of responsibility for Pakistan's desperate financial straits, the embassy argued that the vast majority of CPEC projects were financed entirely through commercial loans to Chinese firms, not loans to Pakistan itself.[66] China also rolled out the red carpet to Imran Khan personally, inviting him to China to meet with President Xi and participate in China's International Import Expo as chief guest. While there, the two sides discussed CPEC as well as Pakistan's broader economic woes.[67]

Imran Khan's critiques of CPEC could amount to little more than the ephemera of political campaigns, quickly overshadowed by the needs of a government facing severe financial pressures, or they could assume a lasting resonance. In either case, Khan will almost certainly follow a pattern set by his predecessors, who clearly used the relationship with China as a tool to serve their own ends. The recent history of that pattern, and its consequences for both Pakistan and China, follows.

Politicians and the Establishment

Central to this story are the Sharif brothers of Punjab. In 2013, the elder of the brothers, Nawaz Sharif, led his party to win an outright majority of seats in the national assembly. The victory returned him to the prime minister's seat for a third time. It marked a triumphant return to Islamabad, as Sharif's second term had ended in 1999 with General Pervez Musharraf's military coup and a bitter decade of exile in Saudi Arabia and London.

Sharif's 2013 triumph was tempered by the fact that his government inherited an economy with GDP growth still stuck below pre–financial crisis levels. The combination of high fiscal deficits and low FDI had depleted Pakistan's reserves, forcing the country to seek an emergency $6.6 billion loan from the IMF.[68] In that context, Beijing offered an essential shot of confidence by stepping in with important investments. Between 2013 and January 2017, China plowed $1.8 billion into Pakistan, well above America's $505 million.[69] From 2013 to 2017, China vaulted from seventh in net FDI to first, accounting for 44 percent of the total in 2016–2017 and 35 percent in 2017–2018.[70] With China's encouragement, foreign investments in Pakistan reached an all-time high in 2016.[71]

Chinese investments in the country's largest province of Punjab directly benefited the prime minister's party, the PML-N, which enjoyed its strongest base of support in that province. There Nawaz Sharif's brother and closest political partner, Shehbaz Sharif, served as chief minister from 2013 to 2018 and enjoyed a strong reputation for management of the provincial bureaucracy. Well before any CPEC announcement, Shehbaz Sharif courted Chinese backers for high-profile infrastructure projects in Lahore, the provincial capital. His pet project was the Orange Line—slated to be Pakistan's first commuter metro rail system—financed with Chinese soft loans, operated by Chinese companies, and stocked with Chinese cars.

As the managing director of the Punjab Mass Transit Authority, Sibtain Fazal Haleem, explained in a conference room at his headquarters in early 2016, discussions about the Orange Line predated CPEC.[72] The original project plans had been on the books for decades, but it was only after the Chinese committed financing in 2014–2015 that the effort became viable.[73] Fazal Haleem then walked down the hall for an introduction to the city's previous, less costly mass-transit venture: Lahore's elevated bus system. Closed-circuit feeds from stations throughout the city could be monitored on the many flat-panel displays spread across a massive wall.

For a sprawling city of over 11 million people, it was clear Lahore's top politicians, from Shehbaz Sharif down, expected that a safe, modern, and efficient transit system would pay both practical and political dividends. Opposition politicians like Imran Khan also appreciated the stakes. In May 2018, Khan launched a social media assault on the Orange Line, claiming via Twitter that "the real reason for building these loss-making mega projects has always been massive kickbacks."[74]

Whichever of the Orange Line's benefits were more prized, the Sharif brothers were hardly the first Pakistani politicians to court China as a cash cow. For the five years before Nawaz Sharif won power, President Asif Ali Zardari and other leaders from his Pakistan Peoples Party (PPP) made multiple trips each year to China to seek material and moral support.[75] Despite a reported twenty-nine visits to China during his tenure, Zardari failed to win the confidence of potential benefactors in Beijing, however, because the Chinese perceived his administration as overly corrupt and incompetent.[76] Having won the nickname "Mr. Ten Percent" for skimming from the public purse in the 1990s during the tenure of his wife, Prime Minister Benazir Bhutto, Zardari did little to clean up his act when he assumed power in 2008 after her assassination. Yet it was the Zardari government's incompetence, not its corruption, that most upset Chinese counterparts.

The Sharif family also undeniably enriched itself from public office. Prime Minister Sharif was booted from office and barred from 2018 elections in a corruption scandal.[77] However, unlike Zardari, the Sharif brothers and their cronies often got rich in the process of building motorways and other public works projects. Sweetheart land deals, well-timed acquisitions, and kickbacks were standard practices for the Sharifs' political party.[78] Despite this pattern of cronyism, claims of good governance and pro-growth policies framed stump speeches by party leaders. Ahsan Iqbal, promoted to interior minister in the shakeup after Prime Minister Sharif left office in 2017, routinely cited the transformative economic effects of CPEC as a reason Pakistanis should vote his party back into office.[79]

Pakistan's political families have turned to China for handouts and bailouts for decades. Shahid Javed Burki, who served as Pakistan's interim finance minister in 1996, recounts that on his watch Beijing stepped in with a $500 million emergency loan at generous rates to stave off a looming bankruptcy.[80] In this respect, Imran Khan's government was no exception. Imran Khan's first trip to Beijing in November 2018 forced him into the role of supplicant, principally as a means to reduce the scale and urgency of another IMF bailout. To add insult to injury, the Pakistani national broadcaster, PTV, mistakenly ran the title "Begging" rather than "Beijing" in the top corner of the screen during its live broadcast of Khan's speech in China.[81]

Political leaders aside, an important segment of Pakistani society will benefit from closer ties to China no matter who nominally holds power in Islamabad. Keen observers of Pakistani politics, like the historian Christophe Jaffrelot, appreciate that even as different governments come and go, an elite core maintains its privileged position of status, wealth, and influence.[82] Pakistan's "establishment" forges alliances of convenience with the army and political parties so as to protect its interests. Its persistence over decades is a part of what makes Pakistan resistant to revolutionary political change.

There are many reasons to anticipate that this establishment will continue to benefit from Pakistan's ties with China. Indeed, many political analysts perceive Imran Khan's party itself as a creation of the establishment, backed by the military and not likely to rock the national boat despite Khan's sometimes fiery rhetoric. The main difference between Khan and his predecessors is that whereas the Sharif government favored Punjabi tycoons, Khan appears more firmly backed by Karachi-based business houses that felt excluded during the Sharif years.[83] So while some of the names are different, establishment figures have assumed important roles in Khan's political party, and many others are neatly positioned to connect Chinese businesses with Pakistani partners in government and the private sector. In the process, they will profit at multiple levels in deals negotiated between Islamabad and Beijing.

The Pakistan-China Institute provides an excellent example of the role that well-placed Pakistanis play. Situated within the cavernous Pakistan-China Friendship Center building that occupies a swath of green space adjacent to Islamabad's main sports complex, the institute is the pet project of a prominent father-son team, Senator Mushahid Hussain and Mustafa Hyder Sayed. The senator has had a long career in journalism and politics, where he has—aside from a stint in jail at the outset of the Musharraf regime—navigated his fortunes so as to always remain near the center of Pakistan's power elite.

The senator's son manages the day-to-day operations of the institute as its executive director. There I met him one afternoon in February 2016, just before he ushered me into a conference room to deliver a presentation to a small audience of former Pakistani government officials, members of the diplomatic community, and assorted policy analysts. I casually remarked on the institute's plush digs and glossy newsletter and quickly came to appreciate that in addition to its research and convening activities, the operation provides a platform for cultivating lucrative ties with the Chinese, a one-stop shop for helping Chinese businesses negotiate and influence the labyrinthine Pakistani bureaucracy, link up with other Pakistani partners, get deals done, and evangelize the benefits of closer Sino-Pakistani relations.

Strictly speaking, the business model is not entirely different from many of the lobbying and consulting groups that populate Washington, DC, or other capitals around the world. Each case is illustrative of the old adage, "it's not what you know, but *who* you know, that matters."

Bolstering a Broken System

When crony capitalism goes too far, it stymies real competition and discourages the entrepreneurship required to produce economic growth. Pakistani advocates of CPEC have suggested that Chinese investments have the potential to encourage reforms that would unlock Pakistan's economic potential.[84] In a rosy scenario, the practice of dealing with outside investors on major projects would naturally translate into more effective and accountable government institutions and more competitive private enterprises.[85] With so much work to be done, streamlined processes and simplified regulations should be the shared interest of investors, banks, politicians, and tens of millions of common Pakistanis alike. Those improvements would encourage a virtuous cycle of investment, reform, and growth.

However, even before Imran Khan's party voiced its critique of CPEC, some of Pakistan's economists feared that a very different pattern was emerging.[86] They worried that rather than creating opportunities and incentives for reform and private sector growth, windfall Chinese investments and loans could enable a continuation of past practices: in short, another short-term bail out of a broken, corrupt system.

Backing this view, analyst Arif Rafiq observed in November 2018 that although CPEC increased overall foreign investment in Pakistan, "the country actually fell on the World Bank's ease of doing business rankings." Chinese investments failed to attract others to Pakistan because they could not receive the same preferential treatment and "still face the legal and political risks that have deterred them for decades."[87] The real losers from Pakistan's failure to reform will be the tens of millions of Pakistanis who need more open markets and less corruption at all levels of government bureaucracy in order to enjoy the fruits of their own labors.

Pakistan's energy sector is a prime example of a broken system in need of reform. Reflecting its centrality during the first phase of CPEC, of the total $46 billion initially projected by Pakistani officials, $34 billion was slated for power projects.[88] This focus on energy was not surprising. Not only were average Pakistanis suffering routine brown-outs and blackouts (called "load shedding"), making life in a hot climate nearly unbearable for parts of the year, but erratic power supply was also crippling Pakistan's industrial base, particularly in textiles, which accounts for half of Pakistan's exports. Recognizing the effect of power outages on production times and efficiency, foreign investors had turned to competitors such as Bangladesh to produce finished goods for Western consumers. Pakistan was left to export unfinished goods, which require fewer workers and generate less profit.[89]

On the surface, Pakistan's power outages appeared to be a problem of too much demand for electricity and too little supply. By this logic, bringing more power plants and distribution lines online would solve the problem. In reality, however, Pakistan's power shortage is as much the consequence of political and bureaucratic dysfunction as simple supply and demand. The dysfunction goes by the name of "circular debt."

To understand circular debt, it is important to understand the interconnected web of Pakistan's energy sector. Simply put, refiners sell fuel to power producers, who sell power to distribution companies, who then sell electricity to consumers of various types. The problem begins when consumers pay artificially low prices for electricity, thanks to Pakistani's political leadership, or steal it outright. Theft accounts for as much as 30 percent of total electricity production in parts of the country.[90] As a consequence, and despite government subsidies, distribution companies often face revenue shortfalls and pile up enormous debt. By 2009, for instance, they owed $10.5 billion, nearly as much as the outstanding credit to Pakistan's largest sector of the economy, textiles.[91] Eventually, the debt burden forces distributors to stop paying power producers. In turn, producers stop paying for fuel.[92] Under those circumstances, cash-strapped companies along the supply chain begin to cut back on services. Lacking fuel, power plants operate below capacity and generate less electricity, forcing distributors to "load shed" their consumers.

By 2012, circular debt had climbed to a whopping 4 percent of GDP.[93] In 2018, even after the government's China-backed investments in power plants and pledges to solve Pakistan's energy problem, the debt stood at $9 billion, roughly 3 percent of GDP.[94] Solving the circular debt problem, rather than merely bringing new power plants online, is the prerequisite to a well-functioning energy sector.[95]

This is not to suggest that Pakistan has no need for additional energy supplies. To the contrary, if Pakistan's consumers and industry had a steady flow of relatively inexpensive power, demand would almost certainly grow, and with it, the national economy would expand. The point is that addressing

Pakistan's supply problem without tackling circular debt could prolong, and even exacerbate, the inefficiencies and counterproductive incentives of the system. From the perspective of reform-minded Pakistanis, this would be an enormous missed opportunity and a net loss, likely to leave Pakistan with an even larger, less tractable version of an old problem.

Similarly, unless Pakistan's leaders take firm and decisive action, Chinese investment is likely to worsen patterns of political and bureaucratic corruption. New cash flows will enrich and empower corrupt officials, discouraging other potential investors in the process. As one Pakistani expert explained in March 2016, if the nation's leaders were primarily interested in opening markets and enhancing infrastructure, they would begin with a series of investor-friendly reforms, welcome non-Chinese competitors, and make the entire process as transparent as possible, thereby making sure that Pakistan would get the best foreign technologies and negotiated terms.[96]

So far, however, Pakistan actually seems more interested in tilting the playing field in China's favor. One tangible example presented itself at Lahore's airport in March 2018. There, just outside the baggage claim area, was a "Chinese Security Desk," manned by a Pakistani guard and clearly intended to help apprehensive Chinese visitors. Although official numbers are unavailable, at any given time there may be as many as 70,000 Chinese workers in Pakistan.[97] Roughly 30,000 Chinese requested visa extensions in 2016, a 41 percent increase on 2015.[98] Unfortunately, there are no "American" or "International" security desks to encourage non-Chinese investors in ways that could plausibly build upon business-friendly foundations laid by CPEC.

In a further effort to offer preferential security arrangements for Chinese workers and firms, the Pakistani military raised a special CPEC division of over 15,000 troops (9,000 from the army and 6,000 paramilitaries).[99] Each of Pakistan's four provinces has also raised thousands of additional police to protect CPEC personnel and projects.[100] No other state's citizens or commercial interests enjoy such a privileged position in Pakistan. In September 2017, China's ambassador to Pakistan publicly pledged close cooperation to "improve the professional capacity of civil armed forces of Pakistan."[101] Even so, Chinese analysts and officials continue to raise concern about the safety of their workers and investments.[102]

Imran Khan's campaign against the ruling party's management of CPEC in 2018 raised questions about China's privileged position. In addition to special treatment on the ground, critics complained that Chinese deals were being hatched behind closed doors, reducing competition as well as the likelihood of healthy institutional reforms. Pakistan was also assuming billions of dollars in new debt and other liabilities to China and Chinese investors.[103] Pakistanis wondered whether Pakistan was actually benefiting from the relationship.

With Chinese workers a more common sight in Pakistan's major cities, as well as widespread (although likely false) rumors of Chinese prison labor camps in more remote locations, popular Pakistani opposition to CPEC appears to have grown.[104] Local tensions between Chinese workers and Pakistani officials hit the headlines in April 2018. By Pakistani accounts, the Chinese attacked police units because they were barred from leaving their construction camp to visit a nearby "red light" district. Video on social media showed Chinese jumping on police vans and attacking officers.[105] That specific incident in southern Punjab was one minor indication of the broader challenges associated with managing Chinese labor in Pakistan.

Finally, Pakistani critics of CPEC raise questions about whether they have fallen into a Beijing-sponsored "debt trap." In the early stages of CPEC, most concerned Pakistanis simply had no way of judging whether CPEC deals with China were likely to bankrupt the state over time, as the Sharif-led government—and even opposition members of parliament—kept a lid on the details.[106] Outside analysts have, however, identified Pakistan as a state at "particular risk of debt distress" based on its plans for CPEC projects.[107] As information gradually trickled out, analysts stressed that Pakistan would have trouble meeting its repayment obligations to Chinese firms if profits from power producers and toll roads fail to live up to (very rosy) projections.[108] In late 2018, documents from Pakistan's Ministry of Planning and Development showed that the state had accrued obligations to China of nearly $40 billion, scheduled to be repaid over twenty years. Annual repayments would begin in 2019–2020 at $1 billion and grow to over $3 billion in 2025–2026.[109]

At this writing, it remains unclear whether the current government led by Imran Khan will actually manage CPEC much differently than its predecessors have. Khan's party slogan, Naya ("New") Pakistan, sounds revolutionary, but Imran Khan's party—like Khan himself—is a complicated amalgam of figures representing both establishment and reform. Most likely, his party will simply seek new, marginally different ways to harness China—and its vast resources—to its own political purposes. Critics will undoubtedly slam the government for a lack of follow-through on its promised transparency and reforms, but Pakistan's long history of government mismanagement, corruption, and general incompetence would be difficult to overcome under even the best of circumstances.

The Army

In any case, Imran Khan will not be the only actor to play the China game. He is not even the most important. In Pakistan, the army chief usually calls the shots, even during periods of nominal civilian rule. Aqil Shah, a professor and author of *The Army and Democracy: Military Politics in Pakistan*, trenchantly observes that "despite passing the two-turnover test of democratic consolidation, the country's political system may be most accurately classified as a pseudodemocratic façade covering the reality of continued military tutelage. As the military constricts the civic space for opposition and dissent, it expects Khan to do its bidding if he wants to remain prime minister."[110]

Pakistan's army, like its politicians and elite families, perceives significant value in its relations with China. Above all, Pakistan's generals see in China a partial solution to their most important strategic dilemma: how to deal with India. For Pakistan, China is the quintessential "external balancer," both because it threatens India directly and because it has provided Pakistan a steady stream of military technologies and materiel over decades. Pakistan's nuclear and missile programs—the nation's guarantees against India—were assisted and accelerated by China from the start.[111]

The Pakistani military benefits from a strong China relationship in at least two ways. First, China sells decent arms at cut-rate prices. Pakistan's Al-Khalid battle tanks, Zulfiqar-class frigates, and JF-17 Thunder aircraft all have Chinese origins.[112] From 2011 to 2018 (the last year for which we have data), China was Pakistan's top arms supplier.[113]

Fully indigenous development of new, high-tech weapon systems such as jets, drones, and missiles would overtax Pakistan's defense complex, and purchasing these items from the United States or Europe is often prohibitively expensive or legally difficult. As noted in the previous chapter, the United States has refused to sell Pakistan lethal drones because of its interpretation of the Missile Technology Control Regime guidelines.[114] And the on-again, off-again history of US sales of F-16 fighter jets to Pakistan has been a critical bone of contention ever since the early 1990s.

China, however, has no such limitations.[115] In December 2018, the *New York Times* revealed that the Pakistani air force was in discussions with China about producing "a new generation of fighter jets," for which "navigation systems, radar systems and onboard weapons would be built jointly by the countries at factories in Pakistan."[116] As the *Times* story explains, those jets—and perhaps the rest of Pakistan's high-tech weaponry as well—will presumably rely on China's Beidou Navigation System, with Pakistan-based satellite stations built by China, as an alternative to the American Global Positioning System (GPS).

On the drone front, Beijing sold 20 Caihong-3 (CH-3) armed drones in 2009.[117] Those models appear to be less reliable than the roughly equivalent US drones (the Predator), but they are also 75 percent cheaper.[118] The CH-3s provided a blueprint for Pakistan to build its own knockoff, the Burraq, that Pakistani forces used to conduct strikes starting in September 2015.[119] In October 2018, Chinese officials announced plans to sell Pakistan 48 Wing Loong II (CH-4) drones in a co-production deal that would be China's single largest drone sale to date.[120] The Wing Loong IIs are similar to, but again much less expensive than, America's MQ-9 Reaper armed drones.

In addition, Pakistani officers benefit personally from major defense deals, either directly—through various means of skimming off the top—or indirectly by membership in a national institution that effectively dictates its own budget without interference from the elected government, negotiates its own contracts, and provides a separate system of schools, healthcare, housing, and pensions. As Pakistani defense analyst Ayesha Siddiqua famously pointed out, Pakistan's military is an active economic interest group in its own right.[121] She estimated that in the mid-2000s the army held over $130 billion of assets in listed companies.[122]

One example of the army's place in Pakistan's economy is the Fouji Foundation, formed as a charitable trust for ex-servicemen in 1945. Over the decades, the foundation grew into one of Pakistan's largest business conglomerates, with interests in cereals, gas, fertilizer, petroleum, banking, cement, and power. As such, it benefits directly and indirectly from China's investments in Pakistani infrastructure.

Similarly, the Pakistani army's construction unit, the Frontier Works Organization (FWO), benefits financially from CPEC projects. The unit's ties to China run deep; founded in 1966, the unit's first mission was to help build the high-altitude ribbon of highway that links Pakistan across the Karakoram Mountains to China. Today the FWO has a wide portfolio of projects in the infrastructure, power, oil, real estate, mining, and railway sectors.[123] In recent years, the FWO has been busy building the roads that link Gwadar Port to the rest of Pakistan's highway network. No private Pakistani firm could operate there, as according to the FWO's chief executive officer, construction crews were routinely attacked by Baloch militants during the earliest stages of construction.[124] The FWO thus enjoys a monopoly-like status when competing for CPEC projects in territories of Pakistan considered insecure by the army.

The army also tends to see at least one additional benefit to working with China: Pakistan's generals can rest assured that China would never hold them to account for undermining civilian-led democratic institutions. In contrast, the United States has frequently freighted its assistance to Pakistan with a variety of politically directed conditions, including some related to democracy promotion and the maintenance of civilian rule.

Pakistani liberals often complain that they too rarely found adequate champions of their cause in Washington, DC.[125] The Bush administration, for instance, never seemed to apply its vaunted "Freedom Agenda" to dealings with Pakistan's military dictator, Pervez Musharraf. To the contrary, as S. Akbar Zaidi points out, "with George Bush in the White House backing his 'buddy' in Islamabad fighting the War on Terror, Musharraf could get away with a great deal at home. And he did."[126] Such critics are right that the US record on this score has been spotty, at times thoroughly hypocritical, and appears to be getting worse.[127] But Pakistani liberals will lack even an audience for such complaints against China; they are almost certainly fated to be losers the closer Islamabad draws to Beijing and the more its leaders learn from their Chinese counterparts.

Nothing about Pakistan's tightening relationship with China suggests that liberals or democrats will soon find greater room for dissent. To the contrary, as discussed in chapter 2, authoritarian China can offer the repressive Pakistani state a wealth of expertise—both technical and institutional—for controlling the media and political opposition.

Pakistan would not even need to implement its own "Great Firewall" or retreat to a single-party political system in order to witness a steady, Chinese-assisted weakening of individual rights and the expansion of state powers in the name of national security. For instance, assuming Pakistani civilians make greater use of Beidou, China's alternative to GPS, their movements and activities will be more easily tracked by state authorities.[128]

Beijing and Islamabad have completed the first stages of a new Chinese-built fiber optic network that connects China and Pakistan overland, services all of Pakistan, and then links to new undersea cables at Gwadar.[129] According to unconfirmed Pakistani media reports, those plans include targets for delivering digital television to Pakistani homes to serve as "a cultural transmission carrier" from China. The digital infrastructure would also host Pakistani government data and facilitate the development of Pakistani "safe cities," whose security forces would be armed with "sophisticated monitoring, smart alert systems and visual command and dispatch."[130]

Pakistan has already taken low-tech steps toward greater political repression without China's help. For example, recognizing that Pakistan's troubled and overburdened courts were unable to deal with the flood of arrests related to the army's campaign against anti-state insurgents in Pakistan's northwest, the state opened a separate system of military tribunals in 2015. Undoubtedly more efficient, these courts also afford less protection to the accused and circumvent normal civilian institutions without strengthening their capacity over time. From 2015 to 2019, the courts sentenced 310 people to death. Fifty-six were executed. Suspects likely confessed to crimes under pressure.[131] In over one hundred cases, the military did not release any information.[132] According to the army, by the end of 2018, fifty-six individuals convicted by the courts had been executed.[133] In late December 2018, Pakistan's new government declared that it would extend the tenure of the courts for another two years.[134]

Over the past decade, Pakistan has also taken steps to expel a variety of international nongovernmental organizations (NGOs) from the country. In 2015, Islamabad started a new registration regime for all international NGOs and forced fifteen to shut down operations.[135] In October 2018, Imran Khan's government banned another eighteen NGOs.[136] Many of these groups were devoted to promoting human rights and civil society. Pakistani officials have since raised suspicions that other NGOs might also be linked to Western intelligence agencies.[137] Such moves are not unique to Pakistan but now constitute a familiar playbook for authoritarian and authoritarian-leaning states around the world.

It is hard to miss the sad reality that Pakistan's crackdown on dissent, often justified in national security terms, has targeted journalists, human rights advocates, academics, and nonviolent opposition figures. American researchers have found it increasingly difficult to travel to Pakistan, and once there, have suffered from tighter constraints on where they can go and what they can see. Gwadar port, for instance, is virtually off-limits unless the state offers a specific invitation.[138]

At the same time as the state has quashed liberal political dissent, some of Pakistan's most dangerous extremist organizations continue to organize, hold rallies, and preach hateful speech under the noses of state authorities. Hafiz Saeed is almost literally the "poster child" of this problem. The founder of the Pakistani terrorist group Lashkar-e-Taiba responsible for the deadly 2008 attacks in Mumbai, among other atrocities, Saeed lives in the open and runs the organization's charitable foundation despite having a $10 million US bounty on his head. In 2017, he founded the Milli Muslim League, and during the 2018 national election contest his face graced the party's campaign posters.[139]

All in all, China's foray into Pakistan suits certain very powerful Pakistani interest groups. The "establishment" and army are especially well positioned to gain financially and politically from the relationship. On the whole, Pakistan's "winners" will keep winning. More than that, they will have important incentives to keep the game running without political or economic reforms that might dislodge them from power.

Lots of questions remain, however. Beijing could lose patience with Pakistan's fiscal profligacy, and China might shift CPEC into a lower gear. The Pakistani army could grow increasingly nervous about Chinese military ambitions on its soil, starting at Gwadar. And the Pakistani public could tire of stories about Chinese-fueled economic growth if they do not quickly yield jobs and other tangible benefits.

Amid these and other critical uncertainties, what is clear is that China is not yet contributing to Pakistan's political or economic reform in ways that are likely to produce long-term stability. To the contrary, the Sino-Pakistani relationship is reinforcing unhealthy political and economic patterns and worsening domestic strains. As the June 2018 International Crisis Group report on CPEC concludes, "as currently rolled out, the corridor risks aggravating political tension, widening social divides and generating new sources of conflict in Pakistan."[140]

South Asia's Toxic Brew

Not all of these tensions will stay bottled up inside Pakistan. To be sure, Baloch militant attacks on Chinese projects, including the November 2018 Balochistan Liberation Army attack on the Chinese consulate in Karachi described in this book's introduction, must be understood first and foremost as cases of CPEC "have-nots" directing their ire at Beijing. Yet those attacks are freighted with wider geopolitical implications, in part because Pakistani authorities have always been quick to blame external Indian sponsorship for incidents of domestic terrorism.

Pakistani investigators claimed that the Karachi consulate attack was plotted by a Balochistan Liberation Army commander from his hospital bed in New Delhi, where he had fled after being wounded by Pakistani security forces eighteen months earlier.[141] The clear insinuation was that India had supported the attack to undermine CPEC. Even Prime Minister Imran Khan got into the act, claiming the violence as part of a broader conspiracy and suggesting that "terrorists are being fed from outside to destabilize this country."[142]

On March 25, 2016, Pakistani authorities announced the arrest of a man by the name of Kulbhushan Jadhav. They claimed he was an Indian spy caught several weeks earlier when he attempted to enter Pakistani territory by way of Iran.[143] To back their claims, Islamabad released a confession video featuring a clean-shaven Jadhav wearing an open-collared white dress shirt and, for the most part, a stare that suggests he may have been reading from a teleprompter script. Planted on a leather couch in an empty room, Jadhav recounted his role in "directing various activities in Balochistan and Karachi at the behest of RAW [the Research and Analysis Wing, India's intelligence service]." "My purpose," he appeared to say, "was to hold meetings with Baloch insurgents and carry out activities with their collaboration. . . . These activities have been of criminal nature, leading to killing of or maiming of Pakistani citizens."[144]

Pakistani officials claim that Jadhav was a serving commander in the Indian Navy while he worked for RAW from 2013 to 2016.[145] During that time, they say he was involved in the planning of insurgent attacks on Pakistani army and other security posts as well as consulates in neighboring Iran. Speaking to an April 2016 conference on CPEC in Gwadar, Pakistan's chief of army staff, Raheel Sharif, claimed that "India, our immediate neighbor, has openly challenged this [Chinese-sponsored] development initiative. . . . I would like to make a special reference to Indian intelligence agency RAW that is blatantly involved in destabilizing Pakistan."[146]

Indian officials, on the other hand, claim Pakistan was using the Jadhav case to establish a rough moral equivalence between the dirty games played by intelligence agencies on both sides of the border. They argued that Pakistan was bidding for sympathy outside the region and deflecting from the Inter-Services Intelligence (ISI)'s far more extensive support for anti-Indian, anti-Western, and anti-Afghan militants and terrorists.[147] Most American analysts and policymakers tended to share this perspective.

The details of the Jadhav case remain contested, and will almost certainly stay that way. As one former Indian diplomat with direct knowledge of the case explained, Jadhav will likely rot in his Pakistani jail.[148] Whatever Jadhav's fate, his case hints at the ways in which China finds itself increasingly enmeshed in the murky, often bloody relationship between India and Pakistan.

Ever since 1947, when India and Pakistan declared independence from the British empire, their relationship has run from hot war to cold truce without coming close to lasting peace. The two fought conventional wars in 1948, 1965, and 1971.[149] Then, in 1999, only a year after they stunned the world with tit-for-tat underground nuclear tests, India and Pakistan fought a brief border war and raised worldwide fears that their conflict would cross the atomic threshold for the first time since Nagasaki. Fortunately, the two pulled back from the abyss. Yet both continue to prepare for conflict, racing ahead with efforts to build nuclear warheads as well as an ever wider array of delivery systems.[150]

In South Asia, borders tend to be porous and politics fractious. Tanks, missiles, and even fast-growing nuclear arsenals do little to secure against such vulnerabilities. Over the past decade, Pakistan's army has been more bloodied by battles against homegrown militants than by skirmishes with Indian troops. India's history has also been marred by domestic militancy, if not at levels that usually posed an existential threat.

Such internal divisions make good fodder for exploitation by foreign adversaries. Over the decades, each side has accused the other of supporting separatist movements on its soil. Major attacks by Pakistan-based terrorist groups sparked Indo-Pakistani crises in 2001–2002 and again in 2008. If India and Pakistan fight a war in the near future, it will most likely have been triggered by another Pakistan-sourced terrorist outrage.

Perhaps not surprisingly, it is Pakistan—the smaller, weaker, and in recent years more economically disadvantaged side of South Asia's defining Indo-Pakistani conflict—that has made more extensive use of unconventional warfare. The Inter-Services Intelligence directorate, Pakistan's spy agency, has cultivated a wide variety of terrorist groups as proxy forces, including the Taliban in Afghanistan and Lashkar-e-Taiba and Jaish-e-Mohammed in India. In theory, if not always in practice, proxies offer states the benefit of plausible deniability, reducing the costs of violence and risk of escalation, at least in comparison to conventional military operations.

Pakistan runs these risks mainly because it rejects India's regional hegemony and has never been content with the way that the region's borders were drawn at partition, especially around the former princely state of Jammu and Kashmir. Pakistan's national psyche remains scarred by the loss of half the nation in 1971, when East Pakistan seceded and declared independence as the new state of Bangladesh. Pakistan's sense of victimhood and susceptibility to ethnic fragmentation persists, both among members of the Punjabi majority as well as the nation's principal minorities in the smaller provinces of Sindh, Balochistan, and Khyber Pakhtunkhwa. Movements for greater autonomy, if not outright secession, simmer in each of these three provinces, informing political opposition to the national government and at times boiling over into insurgency.

Indian prime minister Narendra Modi has undoubtedly taken a tougher stance toward Pakistan. On September 18, 2016, India suffered another cross-border attack on an army base in Uri, just across the "Line of Control" that serves as a de facto border between Indian and Pakistan-administered parts of Kashmir. Nineteen Indian soldiers were killed. This time, India struck back militarily, but perhaps even more important, with a public relations campaign intended to signal that New Delhi would be playing a new and different game with Islamabad.

Eleven days after the Uri attack, India's director general of military operations, Lieutenant General Ranbir Singh, called a press conference to announce that "the Indian army conducted surgical strikes last night" against terrorist "launch pads" across the Line of Control.[151] Subsequent news accounts in the Indian media, clearly informed by official sources, portrayed the strikes as helicopter-borne commando raids as far as several kilometers across the border.[152] Pakistan rejected these claims, arguing that the strikes were nothing more than the too-familiar artillery shelling. Such disputes aside, India's leaders clearly intended a finite, calculated escalation to demonstrate they were no longer willing to take a purely defensive approach with Pakistan, but also not eager to push relations down an uncertain spiral of violence.

The Uri episode was not the only evidence of a new Indian attitude toward Pakistan. In a fiery speech before Indian party leaders in early August 2016, Prime Minister Modi caught his audience off guard by including Balochistan in his condemnation of Pakistani atrocities. Until that speech, Modi's standard litany had focused only on Pakistan's actions within the disputed territories of Kashmir, not other parts of Pakistan.

That shift was no one-time gaffe. Modi repeated the new formulation from the ramparts of New Delhi's famous Red Fort on August 15, as the Indian online news magazine *Quartz* reported, "Narendra Modi's speech at India's 70th Independence Day celebration was unremarkable, except for one explosive word: Balochistan."[153] Modi's inclusion of Balochistan could only be interpreted as a thinly veiled threat, echoing, if not entirely endorsing, his national security adviser's statement from a couple of years earlier: "You can do one Mumbai; you may lose Balochistan."[154]

Modi's reference to Balochistan set off alarm bells in Islamabad, of course, but also in Beijing. As Dr. Hu Shisheng, one of China's most knowledgeable experts on South Asia, commented to one Indian journalist, Chinese scholars were "deeply disturbed by the reference."[155] Coming from the director of the South Asia program within the China Institute of Contemporary International Relations, Dr. Hu's words carried more than merely academic weight in Beijing. His institute is the research arm of China's principal intelligence agency, the Ministry of State Security. Researchers like Hu can play an influential, if indirect, role in Beijing's foreign policy making process.

Dr. Hu drew a direct connection between China's new infrastructure investments in Pakistan and Modi's remarks. He explained that "if India is adamant and if [the] Indian factor is found by China or Pakistan [to be] disrupting the process of CPEC . . . it will really become a disturbance to China-India relations. . . . If that happens China and Pakistan could have no other way but take united steps. . . . The Pakistan factor could surge again to become the most disturbing factor in China-India relations."[156]

Dr. Hu's remarks help to situate Indo-Pakistani conflict within a newly emergent geopolitical context. Twenty years ago, the shockwaves of Prime

Minister Modi's mention of Balochistan would have resonated only very faintly in Beijing. By 2016, however, Chinese analysts were far more inclined to view Indian actions through the lens of China's own regional ambitions.

Roughly two and a half years after India's "surgical strikes," India and Pakistan again came to blows when a terrorist attack killed forty Indian paramilitaries in Kashmir. For the first time since their 1971 war, Indian fighter aircraft struck inside Pakistani territory. In retaliatory air skirmishes, Pakistan downed an Indian jet, and Islamabad's decision to return the Indian pilot offered both sides a quick way to declare victory and end the immediate crisis.[157] The sharp escalation demonstrated that despite decades of stalemate, Indo-Pakistani war remains a realistic possibility.

In addition, the crisis highlighted Beijing's increasingly central role in South Asia. China publicly urged restraint by both sides, and both Indian and Pakistani foreign ministers conspicuously reached out to Beijing to seek its backing. Precisely what role Beijing may have played behind the scenes was not immediately evident, but the *Guardian* mused that while American influence in the heat of the crisis was likely more limited than in years past, "China may yet prove to be the more decisive diplomatic influence in enforcing restraint."[158]

China as a Regional Stabilizer?

One starting point for assessing all of these issues is to ask whether, on balance, China's increasing role in South Asia will stabilize or destabilize relations between India and Pakistan. A stabilizing Chinese role would improve prospects for Indo-Pakistani normalization and see smooth sailing in China-India relations as well. If destabilizing, not only would Indo-Pakistani relations suffer, but China-India relations would face even stiffer headwinds.

There are reasons to hope that China could play a stabilizing role in South Asia. First and foremost, China's interest in regional economic integration extends well beyond the China-Pakistan Economic Corridor and even the BRI as a whole. China-India bilateral trade was $84 billion in 2017, well above $17 billion in China-Pakistan trade.[159] And although China ranked only eighteenth in terms of FDI into India over the period from 2000 to 2018, India is a growing destination for Chinese funds.[160] Between 2014 and 2016, Chinese investments more than doubled, and then tripled between 2016 and 2017.[161] A May 2017 Credit Suisse report predicted that India would likely be the world's greatest beneficiary of Chinese investments over the subsequent five years, at between $84 and $126 billion.[162] In meetings between President Xi and Prime Minister Modi the two have discussed plans to do more, including President Xi's promise of $20 billion in infrastructure investments at a 2014 summit.[163] The incentives are obvious; India is the world's largest recipient of capital investment, and China is Asia's top capital investor.[164]

Second, along with economic investments in Pakistan, China has helped Islamabad prosecute its war against internal anti-state militant groups. Beginning in the early 2000s, largely at the behest of the United States, the Pakistani military reluctantly took up arms against a variety of armed groups based in the tribal areas along the Afghan border. Those campaigns were not considered very effective in Washington or Kabul, where US and Afghan officials continued to believe that Pakistan offered safe haven and often even training, equipment, and financial support to Afghan insurgents. Nevertheless, Pakistani military campaigns inside the Federally Administered Tribal Areas along the Afghan border sparked local resentments, especially among radicalized young tribal leaders.

These resentments metastasized into a full-blown anti-state insurgency in 2007 with the formation of the Tehreek-e-Taliban Pakistan (TTP). Violent jihadists from other regions of Pakistan joined the cause after the military crushed a minor uprising at Islamabad's Red Mosque (Lal Masjid) in July of that year.[165] The Pakistani Taliban unleashed several waves of violence against the Pakistani military, intelligence services, and ordinary citizens, from bombings in markets to devastating commando-style attacks on schools.

In December 2014, terrorists murdered 132 innocent school children at the Army Public School in Peshawar. Pakistani forces retaliated with extensive military campaigns in the rugged terrain of the country's northwest as well as security crackdowns in major urban centers like Karachi.[166] Over time, Pakistan's response paid off, reducing terrorist attacks by 45 percent from 2014 to 2015 and by 27 percent from 2015 to 2016.[167]

Along the way, Pakistan could count on China's moral and material support as the two sides both perceived TTP as a threat. Beijing appreciated the need to attack insurgents who would threaten its investments and its workers inside Pakistan. Moreover, Chinese officials believed that Uighur anti-Beijing terrorists, such as the East Turkistan Islamic Movement, (renamed the Turkestan Islamic Party), were aligned with the TTP. After the 2014 Peshawar school attack, China pledged that it would "stand firmly with the Pakistani government and people in their unremitting efforts to fight against terrorism and safeguard stability of the country and security of the people."[168] Beijing voiced support for Pakistan's subsequent counterinsurgency campaigns, such as operation Zarb-e-Azb in North Waziristan, both to back Pakistan's own internal security and to advance its own agenda against Uighur groups.[169]

China's arms sales, including CH-3 drones, strengthened Pakistani military efforts in ways that Washington was unwilling to match, and the two held joint counterterrorism exercises in 2014, 2015, 2016, and 2018.[170] At the regional level, China and Pakistan formed the Quadrilateral Cooperation and Coordination Mechanism with Afghanistan and Tajikistan in 2016. The mechanism's purpose, according to China's defense ministry, was to share intelligence to support "the unremitting efforts made by the militaries of the four countries on fighting against terrorist and extremist forces."[171] Pakistan's security services will likely continue to benefit from China's partnership as they confront anti-state militants like the TTP.

Third, China's support to Pakistan could conceivably introduce a new and positive dynamic into the region: an increasingly self-confident Pakistan with something valuable to lose. Pakistan's confidence could cut in different ways (more on this later), but a wealthier Pakistan might have less to prove in its status competition with India and possibly also less insecurity about the prospect of loosening cross-border restrictions on commerce and trade. Building business ties has repeatedly been identified by analysts in both India and Pakistan as one of the best means for enhancing trust and nurturing "constituencies for peace," or lobbying groups that would have something very tangible to lose from violent conflict.[172]

Fourth, as historian John Garver observes, since the late 1980s China has consistently taken a more balanced approach in South Asia, especially with respect to issues like Kashmir that have demonstrated the potential to spark conflict.[173] To be sure, Garver is careful to point out that China never dropped its core commitments to Pakistan or stopped supporting Islamabad quietly and in important ways. One of the biggest was military assistance. China helped Pakistan rebuild its army after the 1971 war, modernize its air force in the 1980s, build up a missile arsenal in the 1990s, and develop nuclear warheads.[174] On the whole, however, Garver concludes that over the decades China has gradually leavened its commitment to Pakistan with a strong preference for avoiding Indo-Pakistani war.

It is even possible to argue that by enhancing Pakistan's conventional military capabilities, China could—at least theoretically—give Pakistan the tools it needs to secure itself against the threat of Indian hegemony without relying on sub-conventional militant forces and a first-strike nuclear doctrine, both of which are very dangerous when it comes to sparking and escalating a crisis. In other words, a Pakistan secured by Chinese aid might make less risky moves against India. A beefed-up defensive capability could permit Pakistan to sit peacefully on its side, confident that any Indian strike could be batted back. Moreover, a Pakistan filled with Chinese investments and advisers as well as close military-to-military ties could count on Beijing to come to its defense. Or, at the very least, India would have to think twice about that prospect before picking a fight. This logic holds if Pakistan's attachment to anti-Indian militants and nuclear weapons is, in fact, driven by insecurity.

When it comes to Indo-Pakistani crisis management, China has already shown its willingness to play a role in calming tempers in New Delhi and Islamabad. Analysts Michael Krepon and Polly Nayak have observed China's crucial role on several occasions, including when Beijing helped Washington defuse India-Pakistan tensions in 2001–2002 and pressured Islamabad to arrest terrorists after the 2008 Mumbai attacks.[175] In their analysis of the 2008 crisis, Krepon and Nayak suggested that in the future China's role could become more important, while the United States would have less sway with the South Asian antagonists.[176]

Fifth, despite their many differences, China and India cooperate in a variety of regional and international forums, including in ways that are likely to help mitigate tensions. India and China (along with Brazil, Russia, and South Africa) are members of the BRICS grouping. Together, they have started a development bank conceived by India and located in China. The Indian government is also a member of the China-led AIIB despite New Delhi's misgivings about China's broader BRI. It is worth noting that two of the AIIB's first new projects were located in Pakistan, suggesting another indirect means by which China could play a stabilizing role in South Asia.[177] Regular diplomatic cooperation between China and India provides opportunities to sort out differences. Among these, the 2017 Doklam standoff was quietly resolved in the lead-up to the BRICS summit. By some accounts, India had threatened to boycott the summit if China did not agree to concessions.[178]

In sum, by investing in the region beyond Pakistan, supporting Pakistan's internal security operations, bolstering regional "constituencies for peace," aiming to mitigate Indo-Pakistani conflict, and partnering with India in a range of global forums, China could conceivably play a stabilizing role in South Asia.

How China Fuels Indo-Pakistani Tensions

It is more likely, however, that China will worsen the tenor of India-Pakistan relations. From the start of its relationship with Pakistan, China perceived Pakistan's strategic value as an easy means to distract and undermine India.

For starters, China goes out of its way to shield the Pakistani state from international condemnation for supporting and utilizing anti-Indian militant groups, like Lashkar-e-Taiba and Jaish-e-Muhammad.[179] For decades, Pakistan's leaders have had good reasons to be confident that China would accept its strategic use of militant proxies in neighboring India and Afghanistan, at least to a point. Beginning with the 1962 Sino-Indian War, China's own tensions with India led Beijing to sympathize with Islamabad.[180] And in Afghanistan during the 1980s, China—like the United States—worked with Pakistan's intelligence services to funnel arms and cash to some of the most extreme groups of Afghan mujahedeen.[181]

For the United States, the 9/11 attacks brought into sharp relief the shortcomings of Pakistan's armed proxy policy. Yet America's about-face was never fully imitated by Pakistan or China. To the contrary, China continued to (at least tacitly) back Pakistan's approach. Beijing's diplomats repeatedly protected groups like Lashkar-e-Taiba, including their members, affiliates, and official patrons, from international sanctions at the United Nations.[182] Hamid Gul, a former chief of Pakistan's ISI and ardent supporter of the Taliban as well as other anti-Western terrorist groups, proudly claimed that his own name was kept from UN sanctions lists only because of China's intervention.[183]

Small cracks in the foundation of China's support for Pakistan on this issue may be forming. Well-placed Chinese experts, previously unwilling to share their concerns about the Pakistani army's ties to extremists and terrorists, are now marginally more willing to discuss them quietly with American counterparts. In a nutshell, they fear that Pakistan's army may not be able to control the social and political forces represented by the extremists. Similar concerns appear to be affecting China's diplomacy, if only at the margins. The September 2017 BRICS summit in Xiamen saw Chinese hosts joining India in a joint declaration condemning terrorists based in Pakistan, to include the Haqqani Network, Jaish-e-Muhammad, and Lashkar-e-Taiba.[184]

Although that single declaration may have been little more than a Chinese diplomatic misstep, it was not the only step.[185] The next one came in February 2018, when China chose not to take Pakistan's side in a dispute at a meeting of the Financial Action Task Force, an intergovernmental body established to combat financial crimes. As a consequence of US pressure and China's vote, the group placed Pakistan on its "grey list" for its insufficient effort to combat money laundering and terror financing.[186] Once again, China may have had additional reasons for its vote.[187] Nonetheless, Pakistan could not miss the message: Beijing might not always have Islamabad's back in international settings, especially on counterterror matters. And the Task Force vote had tangible consequences: it complicated Pakistan's ability to access commercial loans as the country stared into a looming balance-of-payments crisis.[188]

China's decision in the Financial Action Task Force set off a further firestorm in Pakistan several months later, when Pakistani journalist Cyril Almeida published an interview with recently ousted Prime Minister Nawaz Sharif.[189] In the interview, Sharif lamented that Pakistan risked international isolation—including by China—because of its failure to crack down on militant organizations. Sharif added, "it's absolutely unacceptable. This is exactly what we are struggling for. President Putin has said it. President Xi has said it."[190]

So far, however, the ties between the Pakistani state and the country's notorious terrorist organizations have outlasted their critics. Prime Minister Sharif, barred from contesting elections in 2018, has cycled in and out of jail. For his role in the affair, journalist Almeida has also faced charges of treason. He was forced to suspend his regular Sunday column for the English-language *Dawn* newspaper in January 2019. Several months later, the International Press Institute, a media watchdog organization, named Almeida its "World Press Freedom Hero" of the year.[191] Whatever pressure Pakistan might face from China over the issue of hosting terrorist organizations appears to have led Islamabad's military and intelligence officials to silence those who might share embarrassing stories more than to go after the terrorists themselves.

Since 9/11, whenever American officials pressed Pakistan to "do more" in the fight against Pakistan-based terrorist groups, the response was the same. Pakistani leaders informed their American counterparts that they simply lacked the means to tackle these entrenched groups quickly or effectively, but with sufficient time (not to mention billions of dollars in US assistance), Washington could eventually expect to see progress. Judging from conversations with Chinese analysts, it would appear that Pakistanis are now deploying similar talking points in Beijing.

The lingering question is whether Beijing, like Washington, will eventually lose its patience with Islamabad, and if so, how long that might take. Indeed, in March 2019, just weeks after terrorist attacks in Indian Kashmir yet again brought India and Pakistan to the brink of war, Beijing shielded the founder of Jaish-e-Muhammad, Masood Azhar, from being blacklisted by the UN Security Council.[192] By late April, however, once diplomatic pressure mounted from Washington and other capitals, Beijing relented on the listing but still insisted that it not specifically mention Azhar's connection with the most recent attack or refer to Kashmir in general.[193] China's patience is being tested by Pakistan, but it is not fully exhausted. It could take a while: China has a great deal invested in Pakistan, and many US officials also gave Islamabad the benefit of the doubt for years after 9/11.

For now, Pakistan's terrorists pose an enormous threat to regional stability that China has not yet seen fit to address. Along with these steps, Beijing has carried Pakistan's water in other international forums, such as the Nuclear Suppliers Group, where Chinese diplomats have assiduously worked to block Indian membership.[194] In such cases, it can be difficult to tell the difference between Chinese actions intended to help Pakistan or steps meant to box-in India, but of course this is precisely the point. From New Delhi's perspective, too often these are two sides of the same coin.

Pakistan's use of China to balance India has not been strictly defensive. That is, Pakistan has aimed to use China as a cudgel against India as well as a shield for defense or deterrence. The issue is complicated, but it begins with the fact that Pakistan rejects Indian hegemony and the region's territorial status quo.

One symptom of that aversion is Pakistan's strenuous rejection of India's right to the former princely state of Jammu and Kashmir. The consensus among Pakistani leaders is that the British partition of India unfolded in a way that left Pakistan in an unfair and unsatisfactory position.[195] Over the more than seven decades since, Pakistan has never given up this grievance, despite shocking defeats in war, the loss of East Pakistan, and the many other sacrifices associated with being locked in permanent hostility with what would otherwise be its closest and most natural neighbor. Given this context, it is harder to envision that Pakistan would suddenly appreciate the benefits of normalizing relations with India under a security umbrella held by Beijing.

To the contrary, Islamabad is more likely to perceive improved links with Beijing, including new weapons and implicit security guarantees, as a license for aggressive revisionism. The experience of Pakistan's nuclear program bolsters this argument further.

Pakistan has used its ties with China to threaten India with a first nuclear punch. Pakistan's arsenal is larger than India's and includes tactical, artillery-launched warheads. China has provided critical help at multiple stages of Pakistan's nuclear program: scientific delegations (1974), technology cooperation (1976), enriched uranium and blueprints for a warhead (1983), designs for research reactors (1989), and nuclear-ready missiles (late 1980s and 1990s).[196] Beyond the simple transfer of equipment, Chinese assistance was an essential ingredient in Pakistan's development of the know-how and institutional structures needed to build and field nuclear warheads and ballistic missiles.[197]

Throughout this period, China also stood up as Pakistan's shield against international pressure to halt the program or increase transparency. After China signed the Nuclear Nonproliferation Treaty in 1992, it shifted tactics to assist Pakistan's nuclear civil program. In moves that angered India as well as the United States, China "grandfathered in" two new nuclear plants for Pakistan in 2010 and again in 2013, thereby bypassing Nuclear Suppliers Group restrictions against assisting Pakistan's program.[198]

Pakistan's arsenal of nuclear warheads is now estimated to be slightly larger than India's, and growing.[199] By providing an effective deterrent against existential threats posed by India, Pakistan's nuclear weapons could have been a justification for Islamabad to reduce other military expenditures and to step away from conflict. Instead, Pakistan appears to have been emboldened, particularly in its use of militant proxies, believing that nuclear weapons would deter India from undertaking a major conventional war.[200]

Nor has Pakistan been content to develop a "credible minimum nuclear deterrent." This would have meant building an arsenal just large enough to guarantee Pakistan's ability to inflict unacceptable punishment on India, but no larger. Instead, Pakistan has aimed for a far costlier capability, one that would permit it to threaten nuclear retaliation at lower levels of conflict.[201] Exhibit A of this approach is Pakistan's development of tactical nuclear weapons. These short-range weapons were explicitly designed to deter rapid punitive strikes by India in retaliation for another attack on Indian soil by Pakistan-based terrorists.

All signs point to a continuation and expansion of this nuclear arms race between India and Pakistan. In January 2017, Pakistan announced a successful test of a nuclear-capable submarine-launched cruise missile, the Babur-3, officially extending the tit-for-tat competition to sea.[202] In short, Pakistan has developed costly nuclear tools that permit it to continue a fight against India rather than to back away from one.

Shifting now to an Indian perspective, New Delhi tends to view China as Pakistan's protector. China is also an increasingly dominant regional and global power. India will need to cooperate with China when beneficial, but must also prepare for competition and even outright conflict.[203] A jealous rising power, India keeps a watchful eye on China's activities across Asia and beyond. Little about CPEC or BRI has escaped New Delhi's gaze.

Indian officials have voiced concerns about China's BRI from its inception, immediately perceiving it as a "national Chinese initiative" and one that was almost certainly driven by geopolitical motivations.[204] New Delhi has publicly expressed reservations about CPEC because portions of the corridor run through territory India claims as its own. In February 2017, India's foreign secretary Subrahmanyam Jaishankar bluntly stated, "CPEC violates Indian sovereignty because it runs through Pakistan-occupied Kashmir. . . . We were very frank with them [China] in sharing what our concerns were and we share it in public. But the issue for us is a sovereignty issue."[205] Subsequently, India issued a thoroughgoing critique of BRI, asking whether the initiative was sufficiently inclusive, transparent, environmentally friendly, or sensitive to the debt burdens it would place on participating nations.[206]

Mainly, however, India worries about the strategic implications of a greater Chinese footprint in the region. As David Brewster, a top Australian expert on Sino-Indian relations, argues, India sees itself as the rightful leader in South Asia and "takes a somewhat proprietorial attitude towards the Indian Ocean, perceiving the presence of extra-regional powers, particularly China, as essentially illegitimate."[207] Brewster notes that India's first prime minister, Jawaharlal Nehru, even went so far as to declare an Indian "Monroe Doctrine" to rid its region of colonial intrusions.[208] Subsequent Indian prime ministers have taken more nuanced approaches to claims of regional hegemony. Nevertheless, because China shows no sign of honoring India's self-defined prerogatives, Brewster anticipates "an ever-sharper and long-running contest between India and China in the Indian Ocean."[209]

Brewster also correctly notes that, for now at least, much of India's concern about China is defensive. Indian strategists frequently express concerns about the virtual Chinese "encirclement" that would result from China's presence in Pakistan and along the Arabian Sea at Gwadar. Similarly, New Delhi perceives Djibouti, where China is building a naval base, or other lesser Chinese-backed port projects in Sri Lanka and Bangladesh, as Chinese incursions into India's maritime surrounds.[210] Elsewhere in India's neighborhood, like Myanmar and the Maldives, India has been troubled by China's apparent bids for political and economic influence.[211]

In the maritime context, India jealously aims to defend its place as a leading Indo-Pacific naval power.[212] New Delhi has responded with what amounts to a three-pronged strategy, but one with only mixed success to date.

First, India is investing in its own military capabilities. As a 2015 *Jane's Intelligence Review* report catalogues, "by 2027, India aims to spend around $150–200 billion to modernize its military. This includes inducting power projection platforms such as aircraft carriers, mid-air refuellers, dock landing ships, strategic lift aircraft, and six nuclear-powered attack submarines. . . . [These] will supplement four 6,000-tonne nuclear-powered ballistic missile submarines."[213]

Second, India is attempting to improve relations with several of its closest neighbors, especially Sri Lanka, Myanmar, and Bangladesh in ways that are intended to counterbalance Chinese influence. For a time, it seemed that India was falling hopelessly behind China in each of these theaters, but various missteps by Beijing and local political upheavals have played to New Delhi's advantage.[214] Even so, India has its work cut out for it.[215]

Third, India aims to tighten its ties with states farther afield, especially Vietnam, Indonesia, Japan, and the United States, each of which holds a common interest and can field naval capabilities of its own. India participates in training exercises and coordinated patrols with members of ASEAN and is a regular participant in multilateral summits devoted to topics of regional defense. In its 2016 outreach to Vietnam, New Delhi offered $500 million in credit to Hanoi for military equipment purchases.[216] As a part of its broader effort to improve its regional standing, India has taken a firmer stance on the South China Sea dispute, supporting freedom of navigation in ways that tend to contradict the Chinese position.[217]

Similar Indian concerns extend to issues beyond maritime competition. In Afghanistan, Nepal, Burma, and Bangladesh, Indian diplomats perceive China's influence as coming at a cost. In some instances, such as Nepal, the cost is in terms of losing traditional influence over a smaller regional actor.[218] In other cases, like Afghanistan, New Delhi perceives that China's policy positions (for instance, in supporting a political reconciliation with the Taliban) may contradict Indian preferences or advance Pakistan's agenda.

As a consequence, policymakers in New Delhi cannot help seeing China's actions, starting with CPEC, as ominous signs for Indian interests. All told, Indians tend to perceive China's involvement in Pakistan as more threatening than stabilizing. They read China's influence as unlikely to encourage a constructive strategic shift by Pakistan. They doubt a Pakistan confident of China's backing would be more inclined to sever ties with militant proxies or engage in a serious process of diplomatic normalization.[219]

All this Indian wariness is problematic. India has direct concerns about competition with China, about conflict with Pakistan, and about the possibility that China's support of Pakistan will make Pakistan even more aggressive. As a consequence, India appears to perceive the need for a more hawkish line of its own. India's "surgical strikes" and air attacks across Pakistan's border foreshadow a future of greater regional tension, arms racing, and violence. That, in turn, could lead to an even tighter bond between Beijing and Islamabad, as all sides join in a downward spiral of mistrust and insecurity.

A Net Assessment

China's connections to South Asia date back millennia, but Beijing's energetic new push into the region lacks obvious historical precedent. China now aims to extend its strategic reach to the Arabian Sea and to promote a stable zone to its west on the way to meeting security goals for Xinjiang, fostering regional economic integration, and in time, consolidating China's strategic influence along its western horizon. In particular, Chinese officials have tended to portray the China-Pakistan Economic Corridor as the leading edge of President Xi's BRI. China's investments there are touted by both sides as likely to spur "win-win" economic growth throughout the region, but as this chapter shows, China's relations with Pakistan run wider and deeper than CPEC alone.

This chapter also shows that by plunging headlong into a zone of long-standing and bloody feuds, China is likely to exacerbate political and economic disputes within Pakistan and heighten tensions between Pakistan and India. This is not because Beijing intends such outcomes. It almost certainly does not. But the complicated interplay between Chinese actions and regional realities will ultimately determine outcomes.

China will find it nearly impossible to avoid being sucked into Pakistan's domestic politics. Worse, although Chinese investments in Pakistan have the potential to spur economic growth, they have already come at the expense of contentious politics. Within Pakistan, powerful interest groups, such as politicians and the army, are best positioned to play China to their advantage. They profit disproportionately from Chinese investments and will use Chinese assistance to avoid difficult political or economic reforms. Pakistan is already veering in the direction of greater political repression, with autocratic Beijing playing an enabling role.

At the same time, the evidence suggests that Pakistan will harness Chinese resources and support to extend its competition with India. India, for its part, will find China's regional activities increasingly threatening, whether because of China's support to Pakistani adventurism or its encroachment on India's traditional sphere of influence. The result will be greater regional tensions and competitive arms buildups, even if China may objectively have strong reasons to prefer stability in South Asia.

In sum, it is plausible to imagine a future in which China succeeds in extending its economic, political, and military influence into South Asia, and especially through Pakistan to the Arabian Sea. But that extension would not necessarily bring with it peace, prosperity, or security within Pakistan, much less political or economic reform. At the same time, China's more extensive regional presence would exacerbate tensions with India, worsening prospects for Indo-Pakistani normalization and increasing the potential for Sino-Indian conflict. For the United States, this would amount to the "worst of all possible worlds" in which China extends its strategic reach without contributing to regional peace.

Unfortunately, broadly similar outcomes appear likely in Central Asia and the Middle East, the subjects of the next two chapters.

| Central Asian Insecurities

THE CAPITAL OF Kazakhstan is a sort of architectural laboratory in the Central Asian steppe, where grandiose visions are realized in concrete and steel. While much of the rest of the country's landscape is flat and empty, the city surges upward in a collection of massive, whimsical structures, from the leaning yurt-shaped shopping mall and prone headlamp that houses the national library, to the futuristic pyramidal "Palace of Peace and Reconciliation." The towering skyscrapers and their brightly lit nighttime façades could have been plucked from Dubai or Shanghai.[1]

Oil and gas revenues, combined with an extraordinarily long period of one-man rule, have made Kazakhstan the postmodern oddity it is. In March 2019, the capital's name was abruptly changed from Astana to Nur-Sultan, in honor of the country's aging dictator, Nursultan Nazarbayev. The name change is not the only transition facing Kazakhstan. The country's future continues to hinge disproportionately on Nazarbayev's choices: how he manages politics at home, and how he balances relations with Kazakhstan's two enormous neighbors, Russia and China. Indeed, the interplay between Nazarbayev, Vladimir Putin, and Xi Jinping will have lasting and significant consequences for Kazakhstan, continental Eurasia, and the world.

Today, China's involvement in Kazakhstan and the rest of Central Asia is expanding rapidly. As in Pakistan and South Asia, China is injecting itself into challenging national political economies and a complicated set of deeply rooted geopolitical relationships. China is the one making headlines, but the context of Chinese actions will also be shaped by local actors. On the whole, China's intensified presence in Central Asia is likely to prove politically contentious, even if that is not what Beijing seeks. Eventually, Russia will awaken to the cruel consequences of China's regional preeminence, although by then there may be little Moscow can do to respond.

The Blurred Borders of Eurasia's Crossroads

When today's officials at the US State Department refer to Central Asia, they mean the five "Stans": Kazakhstan, Kyrgyzstan, Tajikistan, Turkmenistan, and Uzbekistan, all of which are former Soviet republics. Yet the boundaries of the region are not easily delimited because the ethnic, linguistic, and historical commonalities of its people extend southward into Afghanistan, eastward into Mongolia, Xinjiang, and Manchuria, and northward into parts of Russian Siberia.[2] For S. Frederick Starr, a scholar of Central Asia and its history, the core of Central Asia was "assuredly a 'crossroads of civilizations,' it was, even more, a *crossroads civilization*, with its own distinctive features."[3]

For thousands of years, the forbidding geography of Eurasia funneled intrepid traders and pilgrims—as well as great invading armies—through Central Asia as they slowly made their way between the continent's settlements, markets, oasis cities, and religious sites. In 1877, the German geographer Baron Ferdinand von Richthofen plotted a single overland east-west route across a detailed map of the region and labeled it the "*Seidenstraße*," or "Silk Road." The name is not without merit; ancient Rome was indeed inundated by the scandalously exotic silks that traveled along this route, and bolts of the material long served as a form of currency for trade in other commodities.[4] Yet as Silk Road historian Valerie Hansen argues, the Baron's single road was actually a collection of many different routes that "became one of the most transformative super highways in human history—one that transmitted ideas, technologies, and artistic motifs, not simply trade goods."[5]

Archeological digs in Xinjiang have unearthed evidence of east-west overland trade into China through Central Asia dating back at least three thousand years. Some of the precious items found in Lady Fu Hao's tomb, described in chapter 2, almost certainly traversed this route to her home in China's Yellow River Valley.[6] A thousand years later, when the second-century BCE Chinese emissary Zhang Qian described his travels in Central Asia to Han emperor Wu, he was only formalizing the imperial court's knowledge of Central Asia and describing long-standing patterns of trade.

Historically, the demarcation between imperial China and Central Asia has been a fluid one. In the period after Zhang Qian's travels, the Han dynasty extended its military reach westward in part as a means to satisfy its inexhaustible demand for the region's famed war horses.[7] The "heavenly" horses of Central Asia were an essential component of Chinese military might, and throughout its history China never found an adequate home-grown substitute. In 101 BCE, Chinese forces defeated an opposing confederation of Central Asian tribes and pushed all the way into Ferghana, in present-day Uzbekistan.

China's military presence waned with the collapse of the Han in 220 CE, and it was not until the early eighth century's Tang dynasty that a new power vacuum in Central Asia opened the way for Chinese forces to assert themselves in territories of present-day Xinjiang as well as parts of Kazakhstan, Kyrgyzstan, and Uzbekistan. But Tang advances would be relatively short-lived. From 755 to 763, China was engulfed in a bloody civil struggle, the An Lushan rebellion, that forced Tang rulers to pull their armies from the west and focus on the home front. For roughly the next thousand years, "no power based in China would again rule Xinjiang."[8] Over that millennium, Xinjiang saw the ebb and flow of numerous other empires, including Turkic rulers who introduced Islam to the area in the tenth century.[9]

China's inward turn and Arab conquests in Central Asia created auspicious conditions for an intellectual and cultural flowering in the region's cities like Bukhara, in Uzbekistan, and Merv, once a magnificent oasis city that now lies in ruin in the sands of Turkmenistan. In his book *Lost Enlightenment*, Starr describes how Central Asia's intelligentsia were full members of the vibrant Islamic civilization radiating from Baghdad. Indeed, many of the world's greatest and most famed "Arab" scholars of that period, like Avicenna, Al-Biruni, Al-Khwarizmi, Al-Farabi, and Al-Ghazali, actually hailed from Central Asia.[10] These remarkable polymaths advanced human understanding of science, philosophy, the arts, and many other fields.

Starr celebrates Central Asia's golden age, but also recognizes that it was in decline even before the dawn of the thirteenth century, when Eurasia's greatest conqueror, Chinggis Khan, unified the nomadic tribes of the Mongolian steppe under his command.[11] His fearsome Mongol horseback army swept into northern China, then westward through Central Asia and Persia to the Caspian Sea. His grandson, Kublai Khan, whose fame spread to Europe by way of Venetian explorer Marco Polo's travelogue, ruled China as the first Yuan emperor. Historians credit his reign with deepening China's links with Central Asia. This time, however, "the current . . . flowed in the other direction, and Central Asian administrators, merchants, technicians, and craftsmen . . . flooded the Middle Kingdom under the aegis of the Mongols."[12]

A century later, China's early Ming dynasty, which had tossed out the Mongols and their Central Asian administrators and sent Zheng He's fleets to India and Africa, also launched significant overland trade missions to Central Asia and the Middle East. Ming emperors were clearly no less interested than their predecessors in acquiring the region's valuable horses.[13] But the Ming soon turned inward as well. In Central Asia a new conqueror, Timur, or Tamerlane as he became known in Europe, forged a new empire that ran to Syria in the west and Delhi in the south. Had he not died unexpectedly in 1405, he would have fought to extend his conquests eastward across China, thereby rebuilding a Eurasian empire to rival that of Chinggis Khan.[14]

Had Timur succeeded, perhaps his conquest of Eurasia would have restored a free flow of people and goods across much of the continent from west to east. Instead, the political turmoil and insecurity along the overland routes encouraged the rise of maritime trade. When Vasco da Gama's fleet rounded the southern tip of Africa and then made its way across the Arabian Sea to India's west coast port of Calicut in 1498, the Portuguese explorer further tipped the scales. The European race for global trade and imperial expansion was officially on, and nearly all of it would bypass Central Asia.

Starved of the wealth from east-west overland trade, for the next several hundred years, Central Asia would find itself "a contested borderland sandwiched between expanding Russian and Chinese imperial states."[15] Ivan IV, "the Terrible," of Moscow led the charge out of the west in the mid-sixteenth century. His father (Ivan III, "the Great") had been the first Russian ruler to successfully stand against his Mongol overlords and live to tell the tale.[16] Ivan IV pressed the advantage and gobbled up vast swaths of Mongol territory, starting a process of imperial conquest that would last four centuries. Historian Peter Golden recounts that "from 1500 to 1900, Russia, one of the most rapidly expanding states in the world, acquired approximately 50 square miles a day."[17] Russian armies fought their way across the steppe and reached the Pacific coast in 1638.[18]

To the southeast, the Russians contended with the Chinese Qing dynasty. The Qing were themselves invaders, of a sort. In the early seventeenth century, the minor Manchurian chieftain Nurhaci unified northwestern clans into a military coalition and, in time, laid the foundations for what would become a solid, centralized ruling regime.[19] His improbable rebellion caught the Ming dynasty at a moment of weakness and civil strife. Nurhaci's descendants and their allies, including Han Chinese and Mongolians, consolidated their control over Ming China, assumed most of its bureaucratic apparatus, and harnessed the huge agricultural production of southern China to fund extensive military campaigns.[20] Qing emperors then quickly turned their attention westward toward expansion into Tibet and Xinjiang.

In Tibet, Xinjiang, and Kazakhstan, the Russians and Chinese faced the Zunghars, the last of Central Asia's major nomadic Mongol empires. In the mid-seventeenth century, Zunghar rulers managed to find favor with Tibet's Dalai Lama and establish a capital city in what is now the northwest of Xinjiang. The Zunghar state minted coins, collected taxes, and manufactured weapons, including Russian-style cannons that could be transported by camels. This was "not an ephemeral steppe structure, but a state with imperial ambitions."[21]

Russians, Manchus, and Zunghars negotiated and traded extensively, but eventually fell into an outright contest for power. The foremost Western historian of the Qing dynasty's westward march, Peter C. Perdue, writes that during that contest, "distances were vast, communications slow, military campaigns extended and costly, and cultural alienation was huge. By the end of this epic confrontation [which lasted until the mid-eighteenth century] . . . only two empires were left standing. The Qing and the Russians faced each other along an extended border. They had become two of the largest empires in world history. The Zunghars had vanished."[22] The end of the Zunghar empire marked the closing of Central Asia's great frontier, an event "more important in world history than the renowned closing of the North American frontier."[23]

In subsequent centuries, Beijing and Moscow would continue their own imperial competition while asserting varying levels of control over these conquered regions. One persistent challenge was that of drawing permanent boundaries between Chinese and Russian domains. Perdue finds that, as with previous empire builders of Eurasia, the "greatest problem [has always been] to define their stopping point, and, once they had stopped, to make provisions for security along their frontier. Basic natural features such as rivers, mountains, and settlements did not define well-enclosed spaces, but tended to create centrifugal patterns. . . . Empires and their borders shifted constantly across the region because no natural boundaries existed."[24]

Beijing's efforts to "Sinicize" western territories have always fallen incomplete. During the nineteenth century, Beijing contended with numerous revolts in former Zunghar lands but eventually managed to assert its direct rule over the region and named it the province of Xinjiang, meaning "New Dominion," in 1884.[25] However, as China became increasingly enfeebled and divided during the early twentieth century, local Uighur leaders reasserted their autonomy. When the communist forces of the People's Republic of China overwhelmed the nationalists and consolidated political control over China, the western territories were officially designated the "Xinjiang Uygur

Autonomous Region" in a nod to its distinctive ethnic identity. Since then, as noted in chapter 2, millions of Han Chinese have settled in Xinjiang, and Beijing has undertaken a brutal, repressive campaign to silence Uighur dissent.

Similarly, Russia's colonization eventually brought millions of ethnic Russian settlers and their political, educational, and other institutions to the conquered territories in Central Asia. Yet local ethnic and religious (Muslim) identities were never fully wiped away. They burst into the open at the time of Russia's revolution and civil war, when Central Asian leaders tended to view the struggle through the lens of local concerns and grievances.[26] After the Bolsheviks won and established the Soviet Union, they divided Central Asia into republics that would, at the Soviet Union's collapse seven decades later, become today's independent states. Soviet policies intentionally highlighted the linguistic and ethnic differences across the Central Asian republics as a "massive—and largely successful—project of social and ethnic engineering," with the political consequence of undermining "Pan-Turkist" aspirations that might have unified the region.[27]

It should be no surprise, then, that the modern national borders of Central Asia and the neighboring parts of Russia and China provide an incomplete and even misleading guide to the region's history of ethnic, religious, and cultural connection. This is not to discount the significance of such borders; the region's history is filled with the tales of the millions who fought and died to defend or erase them. But persistent border-spanning affinities, such as those between Chinese Uighurs and their Kazakhstani neighbors, also offer important insights about the future, especially in a period that looks primed for significant change.[28]

A Vision of New Roads, Rails, and Cities

Kazakhstan is enormous. By landmass, it is the ninth largest country in the world. End to end, it runs over 1,800 miles, roughly the distance from Washington, DC, to Albuquerque, New Mexico. Almaty, Kazakhstan's former capital and still the country's main commercial hub, lies in the southeast, close to the border with Kyrgyzstan and roughly 200 miles from the crossing into China.

Our late April 2017 drive from Almaty to the Chinese border started as it would have for decades. A bumpy city road opened up to the suburbs and then to a more rural scene, with pockets of corrugated metal-roofed homes, shops, schools, and gas stations crowding either side. Eventually, the landscape began to resemble the big-sky plains of the American West, with horses grazing in the distance and the snow-capped peaks of the Tian Shan range that forms Kazakhstan's border with Kyrgyzstan looming farther off to the south. At that point, our driver carefully guided the Toyota through a small unpaved patch of a construction zone and onto a partly completed concrete highway. Our two lanes were separated by a low metal median fence from two on the other side, still under construction, so the rather few vehicles plying the stretch from there to the Chinese border shared one side of the strikingly flat, new pavement. Just to the highway's north ran a new companion railway line.

A couple hours later, we turned off the highway after seeing the sign to Zharkent, a small border town with a spare but very clean inn and a kebab house incongruously decorated with wall murals of American cultural icons like Rocky Balboa and Marilyn Monroe. As we slowed to navigate the rutted two-lane strip ahead, our driver, in his clipped English, chuckled as he informed us, "China road end. Now Kazakhstan road."

Of course, lonely Zharkent was neither our main destination nor the reason for impressive new road and rail lines. The main draw was the new free trade zone and dry port at the nearby Khorgos crossing into China. If Presidents Nazarbayev and Xi have their way, in twenty years Khorgos will be a bustling new city, a binational hub in the New Silk Road from East Asia to Europe, noteworthy for offering a route that circumvents Russian territory as well as the straits of Malacca by traversing Kazakhstan overland, then crossing the Caspian Sea to Azerbaijan, and heading onward to Georgia, Turkey, and Western Europe. It represents the coming together of Kazakhstan's own national infrastructure plan, the Nurly Zhol ("way of light"), and China's BRI. To date, however, this transit path has suffered from numerous delays—some even suggest that Russia has had a hand in them—and in early 2017, Khorgos still looked like a rather speculative venture.[29]

We visited the dry port first. Having read *Forbes* dispatches by intrepid adventure reporter Wade Shepard, I was prepared for the sight of the enormous yellow gantry cranes rising from the otherwise empty steppe, surrounded by piles of shipping containers.[30] Although I was there on a holiday when the gates were locked and the facility practically deserted, it was pretty easy to imagine that each month the containers from sixty-five freight trains could be shifted from cars outfitted for narrower Chinese gauge rails to the wider Russian tracks that would head westward along Kazakhstan's network.[31] In 2017, Khorgos handled more than 100,000 containers, double the number in all of 2016, and the goal is to increase that volume fivefold by 2020.[32] Although that number would still represent only 1 percent of the total volume of container traffic that flows westward from Asia by sea, it would still be a stunning development for a spot seemingly in the middle of nowhere, not far from the "Eurasian Pole of Inaccessibility," or the most distant point from the sea in continental Eurasia.[33]

The Khorgos free trade zone, by comparison, was livelier. We waited on the Kazakhstani side in one of about six long lines for nearly an hour before finally being ushered through an airport-style security check. The others in line were mainly Kazakhstani small traders looking to buy Chinese goods to sell in Kazakhstani cities, or individual bargain hunters seeking retail items that were either less expensive or more plentiful than could be found in Almaty.[34] Roughly 4,500 Kazakhstanis cross the border there daily.[35] When I seemed puzzled by the plethora of shops specializing in furs and phones, our driver explained that in today's Kazakhstan, a bride-to-be always wants two things from her groom: a fur coat and an iPhone.

Once past security, we boarded a bus for the short ride across the border. For a free trade zone, it was tightly secured with fences and walls: little chance of an illegal crossing there. Most impressive, however, were the many construction cranes and new high-rise buildings dotting the horizon, already housing a population of about 100,000 Chinese. Back on the Kazakhstani side were oversized posters with colorful plans of all that the new city would eventually include, from an amusement park to a conference center, apartment complexes, hotels, and shopping malls.[36]

If not for having witnessed the spectacle of Astana (now Nur-Sultan) and for seeing the ongoing construction in person, all of this would have seemed little more than a fantasy. And for some of the merchants, the reality was not yet living up to its billing. One Chinese shopkeeper bemoaned the lack of foot traffic, and especially missed the well-heeled buyers who could conceivably pay global retail prices for his Omega brand watches. That morning as he chatted with me in his otherwise empty store, he wasn't entirely sure whether his move to chilly Khorgos had been a smart one. But perhaps his luck would shift, and as one gregarious Kazakhstani gushed about his brand-new restaurant, he couldn't hide his enthusiasm for the new commercial opportunities. The month before, he explained, there had been a well-attended mixed martial arts competition at the new sports arena down the road, and more events were on the way.

China's Expanding Role

It seems everyone is taking a bet on Khorgos, not just the governments of Kazakhstan and China. The new "China road" that had sped our drive from

Almaty was actually financed by the Asian Development Bank (ADB) as part of its broader commitment to promoting Central Asia trade through improved connectivity. China's contributions to the bank are less than half those of Japan or the United States, and its voting share is only about 5.5 percent of the total. Yet for well over a decade, Chinese officials have shrewdly steered the bank's CAREC working groups to build projects that support its own schemes, including the connecting roads and rails between Khorgos and Almaty.[37] As of 2019, China had directly backed at least twenty-three CAREC projects and funded separate projects that connect into CAREC's transport corridors in Kazakhstan.[38]

Of course, the Chinese have also put their own resources and technical expertise into Central Asian transportation and communications infrastructure.[39] In 2015, Nur-Sultan (Astana) and Beijing announced that they would jointly refurbish and construct a "Khorgos-Aktau railway" connecting Khorgos to the Caspian Sea. From there, cargo would cross to Azerbaijan, Georgia, and Turkey on the way to Western Europe.[40]

When it comes to transcontinental routes that could link China with Europe, Kazakhstan represents an important alternative to Russia. Whether through Iran or by ferry across the Caspian Sea, containers can now be shipped overland in as little as fifteen days, as compared to thirty-plus days by cargo ship.[41] The obstacle, however, is cost. In 2017, one Astana–based expert quoted a more than tenfold differential between the two, making sea freight the prohibitive favorite for trade in anything that is not time-sensitive.[42] In the best-case scenario, the cost differential would be reduced to the point that it would prove worthwhile for a wider category of goods, but for the foreseeable future it will remain a niche option between cheaper and slower sea freight and faster but even more expensive air freight.[43]

In thinking through China's interests in Kazakhstan, however, it would be wrong to focus solely—or even primarily—on transportation infrastructure. China's investments in Kazakhstan really kicked off in the 1990s with Kazakhstan's energy sector. To meet its vast energy needs, China has invested heavily in Kazakhstani oil and gas production as well as in the pipelines needed to deliver those resources to Chinese markets.

In the oil sector, China's largest national oil company, China National Petroleum Corporation (CNPC), entered the market in 1997 when it bought a 60 percent share in Kazakhstan's fourth-largest oil and gas company, AktobeMunaiGas. From 2002 to 2009, the Chinese worked methodically with Kazakhstani partners to build a series of oil pipelines spanning the country from west to east, and by 2017 the China-Kazakhstan pipeline accounted for 5 percent of Kazakhstan's total oil exports.[44] In 2013, China paid $5 billion for just over 8 percent in Kazakhstan's giant Kashagan oil project, marking its first entry in a major multinational consortium.[45] By 2017, Chinese firms were responsible for one-fourth of Kazakhstan's oil output.[46]

In the gas sector, China uses Kazakhstani pipelines to transport gas extracted from Turkmenistan by way of CNPC pipelines.[47] By 2014, the Central Asia–China gas pipeline through Kazakhstan accounted for a whopping 44 percent of China's overall gas imports.[48] In 2017, it made up 15 percent of China's gas consumption overall (much of which is domestically produced).[49] Kazakhstan started shipping its own gas to China through the pipeline in October 2017, bypassing Russian lines.[50] The next year, Kazakhstan's national gas company announced plans to double its exports to China, at levels expected to generate $2 billion in annual revenue.[51] Newswires reported that the pipeline hit maximum capacity in preparation for China's winter.[52]

Not only does Kazakhstan now meet an important and growing share of China's energy needs, but its overland supplies are secure from piracy or blockade in ways that seaborne supplies from the Middle East, Latin America, or Africa are not.[53] More important than physical security, however, is the value to Beijing of energy supply diversification. The more supply options China has, the less vulnerable it is to any single source. As China energy expert Erica Downs noted in her 2015 testimony to the US-China Economic and Security Review Commission, "China appears to have successfully used the price it pays for Turkmen gas to drive a hard bargain with Russia for the price of the gas it will import through the Power of Siberia pipeline."[54]

Strategically, China's investment in the China–Central Asia Gas Pipeline broke the effective control that Russian giant Gazprom enjoyed over export routes. The significance of this shift is hard to overstate, because until the 1990s, all energy pipelines (as well as transportation and communication networks) of Central Asia ran to and through Russia.[55] This legacy of Russian and Soviet colonial rule gave Moscow overwhelming advantages in negotiations with former Central Asian republics for years after the breakup of the Soviet Union. Western and Iranian firms chipped away at the monopoly, but the most significant investors in Central Asian pipelines have been the Chinese.

Kazakhstan is also an important source of fuel for China's nuclear program. Home to over 10 percent of the world's uranium reserves and currently the world's largest producer of unenriched uranium, in 2014 Kazakhstan shipped 55 percent of its exports to China.[56] In 2017, a joint venture between China General Nuclear Power Group and Kazatomprom began building an enrichment facility that would enable Kazakhstan to export enriched uranium to

China in 2020.[57] The commercial deal will allow Kazakhstan to produce ready-to-use nuclear fuel, a first for the country.[58]

Although China is principally involved in Kazakhstan's energy sector, Beijing has pledged to invest in other industries as part of a broader development agenda. In 2016, Kazakhstani officials announced that China would invest in fifty-one different projects across sectors, from ore smelting to petrochemistry.[59] Thus far, however, these efforts have come up relatively dry, likely reflecting China's limited economic stakes and Kazakhstan's troubled business environment. As of December 2017, only twenty-five out of sixty-three total BRI projects in Kazakhstan had investors.[60] A 2018 study found that only four out of fifty-one joint industrial projects were underway.[61]

Despite limited progress in terms of direct Chinese investment, trade between China and Kazakhstan—like trade between China and the other states of Central Asia—has grown by leaps and bounds. China is now by most measures the most important external economic partner to all of the Central Asian states. From 2000 to 2015, the value of Kazakhstan's imports from China increased over thirty-two-fold.[62] Across the region, total trade flows climbed from $1.3 billion in 1999 to $30 billion in 2016.[63] In 2017 and 2018, China was the region's largest trading partner.[64]

The real turning point came in 2008 and 2009. Carla Freeman, a scholar at Johns Hopkins SAIS, has chronicled how the downturn in global energy markets simultaneously lessened Russia's ability to throw its weight (and cash) around Central Asia, created a serious economic crisis among Central Asian states, including Kazakhstan, and opened the door to a hungry and still cash-rich China, which swept in with massive loans to the region.[65] In 2009 alone, the Development Bank of Kazakhstan took a $5 billion loan from China's Ex-Im Bank, KazMunaiGas received a $5 billion loan from CNPC, and the mining company Kazakhmys took a $2.7 billion loan from China Development Bank.[66] In addition to these blockbusters, China came through with other loans amounting to at least another $1 billion and increased its direct investment in Kazakhstan by 290 percent, from $439.1 million in 2007 to $1.7 billion in 2010.[67]

With these investments, China secured greater influence in Astana.[68] Not only did China buy up major Kazakhstani assets, such as oil producer MangistauMunaiGaz, to guarantee long-term access, but it also bought sway with Kazakhstan's leaders by making sure that they profited personally and politically from Chinese deals. Political scientist Daniel O'Neill even goes so far as to argue that "during the recent [2008] global economic crisis, Chinese resources were particularly crucial for Kazakh leaders to maintain stability and their rule in that period."[69]

Kazakhstan is not alone in this respect. The other states of Central Asia have fallen into similar debtor relationships with China that have the potential to translate into vulnerability to Bejing's influence.[70] China's Ex-Im bank is the largest external creditor to Kyrgyzstan and Tajikistan.[71] Both states feature prominently on a list of states "significantly or highly vulnerable to debt distress" compiled by researchers at the Center for Global Development. One noteworthy episode suggesting China's ability to turn debt into negotiating leverage took place in 2011, when Tajikistan had trouble repaying Chinese loans. In response, Beijing wrote down "an unknown amount of debt owed by Tajikistan in exchange for some 1,158 square kilometers of disputed territory."[72]

The region's most repressive and autocratic state, Turkmenistan, temporarily found itself in an especially compromised relationship with China. Ashgabat's ties to Beijing deepened during the 2009 financial crisis, when it received $8 billion in Chinese loans. Then, in 2017, when Turkmenistan's ties to Russia and Iran deteriorated, China became its only gas buyer.[73] For a country with the world's fourth-largest proven gas reserves, Turkmenistan held practically no negotiating leverage. The dip in gas revenues threatened what the regime most valued: self-preservation.[74] Desperate to gain another customer, in April 2019 Turkmengaz announced renewed sales to Russia, reportedly at "embarrassingly low" prices.[75]

In short, China's wealth and successful energy diversification strategy means that Beijing holds most of the cards in its economic dealings with Central Asian states. But parts of China are more dependent on the region. China's trade with Central Asia is a tiny fraction of the state's overall global trade, but it accounts for a much more significant share of Xinjiang's economy. Over the long run, Chinese officials believe that Xinjiang's growth and political stability will depend at least in part on its being embedded in a stable and economically vibrant region. Kazakhstan already accounted for 40 percent of Xinjiang's foreign trade by 2016.[76] Thus, improved connectivity through Xinjiang to Central Asia offers two potential benefits for Beijing: localized development inside Xinjiang and transcontinental linkages between the rest of China all the way to Europe.[77]

Beijing's fight against Uighur opposition groups and Islamist terrorists has dominated its security policies in Central Asia.[78] Above all, Beijing has been eager to stem what it clearly perceives as a threatening flow of people, resources, and ideologies from South and Central Asia. An estimated 300,000 ethnic Uighurs live in Central Asia, where they share a common Turkic heritage and Muslim religion. Although the overwhelming majority of these people are no threat to China, hundreds, and possibly thousands, of Chinese do appear to have fought with the Islamic State, and there is no doubt that Beijing is worried about their possible return to China.[79]

China, Russia, and the states of Central Asia first began to appreciate the value of greater counter-terror and security cooperation with the rise of the Islamic Movement of Uzbekistan in Afghanistan in the late 1990s. Together, they also faced the more general scourges of violence, criminality, and narcotics spilling over from the Afghan war.[80] Starting in 1996, China, Russia, Kazakhstan, Kyrgyzstan, and Tajikistan joined together as the "Shanghai Five" in an effort to build stronger intelligence and security ties. In 2001, they added Uzbekistan and formed the Shanghai Cooperation Organization (SCO).

Beijing has not fully achieved its security goals in Central Asia through the SCO, in part because the organization remains weak and has been frequently hamstrung by poor relations among its members.[81] It has mainly served as little more than a clearinghouse for terrorist "watch lists" used by member states' security agencies.[82] Consequently, China has also expanded its bilateral security cooperation with the states of Central Asia. Beijing and the undemocratic leaders of the region share an interest in cracking down on dissent, and often find it convenient to label opposition groups as terrorists. To advance this agenda, China has concluded border security and extradition agreements with Kazakhstan and Kyrgyzstan. While the agreements are more bark than bite, the countries now share intelligence and equipment and conduct the occasional bilateral training exercise outside of SCO, and therefore Russian, control.[83]

In addition to Beijing's specific Xinjiang-related concerns, China benefits strategically from having a relatively quiet backyard in Central Asia. This has been especially true as China's relations on its eastern front have become more acrimonious. Disputes in the South and East China Seas, North Korea, and Taiwan have been more easily managed during a period of calm with Russia and Central Asia. As a consequence, Beijing has—with some important exceptions—worked to keep a relatively low profile and friendly, accommodating posture in Central Asia.

China's accommodating posture was on display soon after the dissolution of the Soviet Union, when Beijing resolved territorial disputes inherited by the newly independent Central Asian states. China managed this feat over a decade through territorial concessions that generally left its smaller and weaker neighbors satisfied. That said, many Central Asians hold lingering concerns that China may someday seek to revisit its border treaties from a position of greater strength.[84]

China places special emphasis on its relationship with Kazakhstan. Kazakhstan's combination of abundant energy resources and vast territory traversing much of continental Eurasia puts it in a special class among the post-Soviet states of the region. China actively works to cultivate better and deeper ties. It routinely sends expert delegations to Kazakhstan's academic institutions and think tanks as part of a systematic effort to gain a deeper understanding of the country and its region and to pave the way for more extensive involvement over time.[85]

One especially friendly face of Chinese influence in Kazakhstan is that of Adil Kaukenov, director of the Center for China Studies.[86] In downtown Almaty, Kaukenov's institute occupies a small storefront, the front of which is a retail space devoted to tea, teapots, souvenirs, and other traditional knickknacks sourced from China. Proudly wearing what resembled a Peking University letterman's jacket, Kaukenov greeted us in the rear of the shop, where he served tea in a room fashioned for that purpose, with pillows and carpets on the floor. His institute, he explained, is dedicated to teaching Chinese language and culture. It also conducts research projects for businesses seeking opportunities with Chinese counterparts.

Kaukenov's enthusiasm for China is palpable, not unlike that of the thousands of American students who have studied there. For him, the goal of promoting greater common understanding is indisputably good, not least because Kazakhstan's economy is desperate for Chinese investment. Whereas the West appears narrowly focused on extracting Kazakhstan's energy and Russia is too cash poor, China offers new opportunities. Kazakhstan, he explained, should harness Chinese resources for economic growth and learn from Chinese technology and culture to improve productivity and reduce corruption.

Kaukenov noted that after President Xi's 2013 speech in Astana, China announced 25,000 scholarships for Kazakhstani students in China, and observed that officially there are 10,000 Kazakhstani students in China and four Confucius centers in Kazakhstan.[87] Kazakhstan is not alone; between 2014 and 2016, the number of students in China from BRI participant countries grew eightfold.[88] Similar investments in education and people-to-people ties will, he believes, build a more welcoming environment in Kazakhstan for new Chinese ventures. That change is likely to take root more quickly in Kazakhstan's south and east, closer to the border with China.

Others, however, see China differently. Greater Chinese presence, no matter the intention, raises warning flags. As Kazakhstani analyst Daniyar Kosnazarov, co-founder of SINOPSIS, an organization focused on China–Central Asia relations, puts it, China could be more of a "panda or a dragon," depending on how Beijing chooses to exert its influence.[89] Either way, how Kazakhstan responds to that influence will ultimately shape the nature of China's growing presence in Central Asia.

Central Asia's "Local Rules"

Alexander Cooley, one of America's foremost scholars of Central Asia, has written extensively about the "local rules" that confront outside powers like the United States when they attempt to use the region for their own purposes.[90] For Washington in the post-9/11 era, Cooley's story revolved around the challenge of supplying the war effort in landlocked Afghanistan. The principal route ran from the port of Karachi overland through Pakistan, but because Islamabad was an on-again, off-again partner, US planners sought alternatives through Turkey and the Caspian Sea to a "Northern Distribution Network" that linked to rail lines and airports in Central Asia. To maintain these alternatives, Washington gradually learned to ignore the corrupt and repressive practices of its Central Asian partners.

Cooley's research shows that Washington was not the only one to learn this lesson about "local rules" in Central Asia. Beijing and Moscow have also accommodated themselves to dealing with the region's ground realities. The story is similar to that of Pakistan, as discussed in chapter 3. The domestic political economy is likely to shape the consequences of Chinese investment at least as much as Beijing's own aspirations.

Because domestic conditions vary, precisely how this story plays out will differ from state to state. Still, similar questions are worth asking. Which actors within a state and society are best positioned to benefit from outside involvement? And how they are likely to turn new resources to their own advantage? In Kazakhstan, as in Pakistan, there are good reasons to anticipate that the injection of new resources—no matter Beijing's intent—are likely to reinforce past practices.[91]

At one level, Kazakhstan's domestic political economy couldn't be more different from that of Pakistan. Rather than a history of tumultuous democratic politics or squabbles between military and civilians, Kazakhstan has been better defined as a stable, patronage-based, authoritarian "developmental state." Severe limits on free speech, political opposition, and labor organizing have been justified in the name of tightly managed political, social, and economic reform.[92]

Nursultan Nazarbayev has ruled, more or less singlehandedly, since independence in 1991. He assumed the presidency after having led the Kazakh Soviet Socialist Republic as its first secretary and, before that, its prime minister. On March 19, 2019, when he voluntarily resigned from office and promoted the Senate Speaker, Kassym-Jomart Tokayev, to the presidency, Nazarbayev retained the title of "Elbasy," or Leader of the Nation. By most accounts, the resignation left Nazarbayev with pretty much the same degree of political control over Kazakhstan as he had enjoyed the day before.

As Tokayev announced during his swearing-in ceremony, "Elbasy's word will have a priority in the strategic decision-making in the country."[93] He followed up with a pledge to rename Kazakhstan's capital "Nur-Sultan" in Nazarbayev's honor. Dmitri Trenin, director of the Carnegie Endowment for International Peace's Moscow Center, concluded that with the move, Nazarbayev was "not stepping down; he is stepping up . . . a version of this model of 'president mentor' copyrighted in Singapore by Lee Kwan Yew."[94] In June 2019, Tokayev won a stage-managed national election with 71 percent of the vote.[95] Thousands of protesters were arrested prior to the polls, and no serious opposition was permitted in the contest.[96]

President or otherwise, Nazarbayev dominates the political and economic life of Kazakhstan. Journalist Joanna Lillis, who has lived and worked in Kazakhstan for years, writes that "for his fans, he has presided over years of political stability and petrodollar-fueled prosperity, and forged a coherent nation state out of a melting pot of peoples inherited from the USSR. For his critics, he has created a repressive get-rich-quick kleptocracy, clinging on to power by rigging elections, crushing dissent and nourishing a creeping—and creepy—cult of personality."[97]

In Nazarbayev's 2015 election, the state reported he won 97.7 percent of the vote.[98] His party, more "an extension of his rule than a platform for political discourse," controls the parliament.[99] All ministries and other state agencies are run directly by the president or his trusted deputies, and these loyalists are shuffled between different roles so that they cannot accumulate too much power.[100] Nazarbayev and his family have their hands in every pie, so to speak.

Most of the nation's biggest businesses across the private sector, including the banks, are managed by the president's family or inner circle.[101] These leaders enrich themselves, their families, and their own subsidiary networks of loyalists. Their corruption is enabled by the protection of the president, which also leaves them vulnerable to prosecution should he find them disloyal. Among his other points of leverage, the president controls the state's intelligence and law enforcement agencies.[102] In short, a seamless web of ties links all nodes of political and commercial power, with Nazarbayev sitting, spider-like, at the center of it all.

Judging from present practice, Kazakhstan's leaders will generally aim to harness Chinese resources to cement their own hold over domestic power, extract better deals from other competing powers, and maintain sovereign independence.[103] Nazarbayev has skillfully crafted and assiduously tried to maintain a "multi-vector" foreign policy, one that enables him to cut deals with the West, Russia, China, and anyone else willing to play by his rules.

Not only does that provide him bargaining leverage, but it keeps Kazakhstan less vulnerable to the predations of its larger neighbors. So far, Kazakhstan has done well in its energy deals with China, and it is likely to play a similar game in trade and transit. Indeed, analyst Kosnazarov suggests that the country's oil barons could also become transit tycoons, as that industry also offers the opportunity for tiny numbers of oligarchs to control vast resources.[104]

Kazakhstan's post-independence relations with China are aptly summarized by Sebastien Peyrouse, a French-trained scholar of Central Asia, as running through four stages.[105] First, China resolved territorial disputes. Second, it built the SCO as a counter-terrorism mechanism. Third, China bought access to the Central Asian hydrocarbon market, and fourth, it began the process of extending its "soft power" through education and cultural exchange. It is noteworthy that the first three stages all quietly connected Beijing only to Kazakhstan's top echelon of leaders, and even a great deal of China's cultural diplomacy is aimed at Central Asia's well-educated elite, people like proud Peking University graduate Adil Kaukenov.

At the popular level, Kazakhstan suffers from serious Sinophobia. For anyone unfamiliar with Kazakhstan, the intensity of that anti-China sentiment is surprising. One might have assumed that a nation emerging from the yoke of Russia's colonial and communist rule would direct its greatest animus toward Moscow, but Kazakhstanis—both ethnic Kazakhs and Russians—tend to harbor deeper suspicions about the Chinese. As Peyrouse finds, these views can be traced to decades of Soviet propaganda, which played on "an old Central Asian tradition, handed down through centuries-old oral epics," that "presents China as a distant but recurrent enemy of Turkic peoples and as an historical opponent of Islam."[106]

Today, that history is reinforced by modern Sinophobic narratives that trade on vague fears of a "yellow peril," the theft of Kazakhstani women by Chinese men seeking wives, and Chinese land grabs.[107] Surveys suggest that, if anything, Kazakhstanis became more anti-Chinese during the period 2007–2012.[108] Central Asians are, as Peyrouse recognizes, widely inclined to play up the cultural, even "civilizational" barriers between themselves and China, discounting the possibility of a peaceful Sinicization of the region.[109] Reflecting this fear of being swamped by China's vast population and resources, one policy professional in Astana shared a common Kazakhstani saying: "if every Chinese simply threw his hat across the border, the entire country would be buried."[110]

More seriously, in the spring of 2016 thousands of Kazakhstanis flocked to the streets to protest land reforms that would have permitted the Chinese to hold twenty-five-year land leases, up from the ten-year leases that were already permitted. In the end, the protests forced the resignation of two government ministers and Nazarbayev chose to shelve the land reform plan for at least five years. For Kazakhstan, where all anti-government protests are harshly suppressed, even these relatively small public outbursts were extraordinary. The demonstrators were motivated by both pocketbook and nationalistic fears. Farmers worried that the reforms would raise their own land costs. Their concerns were reinforced by the popular feeling that cracking open the door to more Chinese landholders could unleash a flood of migrants.[111]

In the summer of 2018, Sayragul Sauytbay became the new face of popular Kazakhstani fears of China.[112] That July, in the town of Zharkent near the Khorgos crossing into China, the former elementary school teacher testified in court. She explained how she had been forced by Chinese officials to teach in a Uighur "re-education camp" in Xinjiang. Sauytbay managed to escape the camp and to cross the border into Kazakhstan where she reunited with her Kazakhstani husband and children. Her testimony made global headlines, as it confirmed stories about abuse and indoctrination that Beijing had denied.

Beijing sought to silence Sauytbay by extraditing her to China. Her fight to win asylum in Kazakhstan mobilized Kazakhstani activists concerned about the fate of ethnic Kazakhs and Uighurs in China. More broadly, it exposed Astana's difficult balancing act in managing ties with Beijing, especially after the 2017 crackdown in Xinjiang introduced deeply unpopular constraints on the traditional movement of ethnic Kazakhs across the China-Kazakhstan border and landed some in re-education camps.[113] In January 2019, Astana negotiated the release from China of over 2,000 ethnic Kazakhs in what looked like an effort mainly to defuse public tensions.[114] Then, in March, the pendulum swung the other way: Kazakhstani authorities arrested Serikzhan Bilash, a Chinese-born Kazakhstani activist who had collected and shared information about the camps in Xinjiang, accusing him of "inciting racial strife" against Han Chinese.[115]

Land protests and the cases against Sauytbay and Bilash highlight the way that perceptions of China differ across Kazakhstan's socioeconomic lines. Where farmers and common Kazakhstanis worry about being exploited or barred from seeing their families in China, Kazakhstan's most powerful are busy profiting from megadeals with Chinese firms. Peyrouse correctly observes that this need not signal positive views of China among the rich, but merely a hard-nosed recognition that there is huge money to be made, at least for those well-positioned enough to benefit from Kazakhstan's patronage networks.

As a consequence, Kazakhstan's leaders have taken steps to keep China's presence under the radar. Kazakhstan has effectively enacted an anti-Chinese visa regime. Whereas much of the rest of the world can enter the country visa-free, Chinese passport holders cannot obtain an individual tourist visa and Chinese tour group visas were not granted until 2016.[116] In an unusual online outburst in May 2016, China's ambassador to Astana complained about visa restrictions on diplomats' families.[117] In 2017, to bolster attendance at the Astana Expo, Kazakhstan began to allow Chinese visitors seventy-two hours of visa-free transit as long as they had booked onward travel to a third country. By comparison, this is well short of the ninety-day, visa-free regime for Russians or the thirty-day regime for Americans and Europeans.[118]

Chinese companies also appear to have kept a low profile. As Raffaelo Pantucci, an expert and regular traveler to the region, reports, CNPC workers in Aktobe are intentionally housed outside the city in a compound that used to be a sanatorium and China's presence in Aktobe's city limits remains "minimal."[119] Chinese energy companies are mainly employing local Kazakhstanis, and when Chinese construction workers do come into the country, they stay away from locals, often residing in temporary camps.[120]

Together, the countervailing forces of commercial incentives and widespread Sinophobia mean that Nur-Sultan (Astana) and Beijing will find it ever more challenging to manage the dissonance between the cooperation that serves elite interests and the distrust that permeates Kazakhstani public opinion.

Succession Scenarios

One vulnerability common to all dictatorships, even relatively benevolent ones, is the period of succession. Eventually all dictators die, and Nazarbayev, born in 1940, knows he will be no exception. In 2016, he traveled to Samarkand for the funeral of Uzbekistan's dictator, Islam Karimov, and witnessed first-hand the unfortunate fates that can befall a dictator's family when he fails to implement a dynastic succession plan before dying.[121] Nazarbayev would prefer to control the terms of his transition from power and, to the greatest extent possible, even to wield influence from his grave. To that end, in 2010 Kazakhstan adopted the "Law on the Leader of the Nation," which granted Nazarbayev the right to shape national policies after leaving the presidency.[122]

Even so, Nazarbayev's 2019 presidential resignation at age seventy-eight marked a milestone in Kazakhstan's history. It was one step in a longer process, and an initial test of Nazarbayev's effort to script the political transition that will inevitably come when he dies, if not a day sooner. The looming, as yet unanswered, question is whether the dictator can achieve his aim of a smooth, orderly transition that enables his family and close allies to remain on top.

Nargis Kassanova, a professor at KIMEP University in Almaty whose office is plastered floor to ceiling with boldfaced posters of recent lectures from visiting internationally acclaimed specialists on Eurasia, believes that the transition process in Kazakhstan has been handled in ways that reinforce a political system defined by networks of personal patronage rather than strengthening modern, impersonal institutions of state.[123] As a consequence, she has worried that a messy period of jockeying for political power could follow Nazarbayev's demise.

Kazakhstan's succession will be historically important in its own right. In addition, it offers a window into the deeper problems that plague the nation's domestic political culture. Whatever happens upon Nazarbayev's political demise, until the state builds stronger and more representative institutions, it will remain vulnerable to similar disruptions.

Patronage politics is not unique to Central Asia, and it follows a pattern familiar to many other parts of the world. Leaders like Nazarbayev distribute state resources to their associates and receive political loyalty in return. In such systems, corruption and nepotism constitute core operating principles, not aberrations, rendering them incompatible with basic liberal commitments to individual rights and the "rule of law." Henry Hale, a scholar who has written extensively about what he terms "patronal politics" throughout post-Soviet Eurasia, finds that there, "politics is first and foremost a struggle among extended networks of personal acquaintances, not among formal institutions such as 'parties,' 'parliament,' 'firms,' or even 'the presidency' or 'the state.' "[124]

Kazakhstan's patronage networks are deeply rooted in history. Domestic power alignments overlap only partially with tribal or clan-based groups, even though modern Kazakhstani society does bear the hallmarks of these networks as well in the form of "hordes" that trace their histories back to the Mongol period before Russian colonial rule.[125] Kazakhstan's patronage networks were altered and also reinforced during the Soviet era by the influx of ethnic Russians, Stalin's collectivization and purges of the 1930s, an extensive modernization campaign, and ultimately, Moscow's decision to entrust the region to local strongmen in exchange, as Alexander Cooley puts it, for "guaranteeing political stability and ensuring unwavering allegiance to the center."[126]

Soviet-era patronage patterns were so deeply entrenched that they persisted throughout much of the region even after the collapse of the Soviet Union. As the last standing Soviet holdover in Central Asia, Nazarbayev manages a dynasty that is quintessentially patrimonial in character. Indeed, "Nazarbayev's stunning oil wealth . . . has allowed him to maintain the Soviet social contract while ensuring the continued passivity of the Kazakh population."[127]

The debate over post-Nazarbayev futures is a serious one, not least because so many people (including major foreign investors) have a stake in its outcome. Some experts expect that Kazakhstan will navigate a succession smoothly, more or less as neighboring Turkmenistan and Uzbekistan appear to have done in recent years. University of Toronto professor Edward Schatz writes, "there is no doubt that succession is in the air, and it is likely to be orderly. All of the globe's geopolitical winds, including Western ones, are blowing in the same direction: for political stability and continuity, above all."[128]

In a narrow sense, Schatz's logic is undoubtedly correct: if given a simple choice between continuity and change, today's power players in Kazakhstan would pick the former. However, the process of decision might not be nearly so simple. The many uncertainties of a transition could alone create coordination problems among disparate domestic groups, even if their interests were basically aligned.

In a closed, patronage-based system it is especially difficult to know which potential successor would be best placed to assemble a winning coalition, and Kazakhstan is big and complicated enough that the financial and industrial interests cannot simply crowd into a single room to hammer out a compromise. Professor Kassanova is not alone in seeing an opening for "intra-elite power struggles" and observing that Kazakhstan's "elites are more diverse, empowered, and consequently less disciplined than their Uzbek and Turkmen counterparts."[129] It is reasonable to expect that even if political jockeying does not destroy the system, it could be protracted and yield unexpected outcomes.[130]

Kazakhstan's elites can be loosely identified as falling into at least a dozen or so "financial-industrial groups" that represent the main units of national political competition.[131] Each group competes for favor and fortune by winning the ear of the president, as "decisions over who is allowed to become a player in Kazakhstan's big business are ultimately the president's prerogative."[132] A post-Nazarbayev succession could involve a bitter competition between these groups, each with "the political and economic resources to stake their claim once the president exits centre stage."[133] That competition would be all the more cutthroat if it happens at a time of an economic downturn or crisis of the sort Kazakhstan faced in the post-2008 period and the subsequent era of low global energy prices.[134]

For pessimistic analysts, Kazakhstan looks like a political disaster waiting to happen. As one Astana-based observer put it, "Nazarbayev is like the sun around which the planets circle. What happens when the sun goes out?"[135] The persistent lack of a succession plan raises the possibility that several decades of political stasis could erode or even come crashing down in a more dramatic fashion. There is, as that same expert put it, "less stability than meets the eye."[136]

Among the pessimists, some analysts fear that political competition could extend beyond Kazakhstan's elite in ways that threaten the state's unity. Sultan Akimbekov, the author of a comprehensive history of Afghanistan, fears that the weakening of the Kazakhstani state after Nazarbayev's death would open the door to other destabilizing influences, including the Islamists, a group that has been relatively small and marginalized to date.[137] To Akimbekov, today's Kazakhstan has too many unsettling similarities to Afghanistan of the 1960s, where the weakening of the state marked the beginning of a slide into civil war.

If Kazakhstan begins to unravel, uncertainty and turmoil could render its domestic politics more susceptible to foreign influence. The new question is whether China's growing role in Kazakhstan would also play into a succession scenario in any meaningful sense.

On the one hand, China could play a calming role, as its core economic interests would best be served by political continuity. The CNPC, in particular, would presumably aim to ensure that its Kazakhstani partners, like KazMunayGas, would honor their commitments and that domestic political conditions would permit the smooth functioning of major pipelines.

On the other hand, China's influence could be destabilizing even if Beijing has no particular intent to play such a role and is only narrowly concerned with defending its energy-related investments. China's efforts to secure its interests could lead it to take sides in a competition among Kazakhstan's financial-industrial groups. China's influence has nearly always come behind closed doors, but Beijing has on occasion pressed Kazakhstan's top leaders hard. In the late 1990s, for instance, Beijing successfully demanded the closure of all pro-autonomy Uighur associations in Kazakhstan.[138]

Several of Kazakhstan's most prominent figures—political leaders and business magnates who have been a part of Nazarbayev's inner circle—are also perceived as more "pro-China" than others. One example is former prime minister Karim Massimov, an ethnic Uighur who speaks fluent Chinese and "is considered by some experts to be *the* representative of the Chinese lobby."[139] Massimov was Kazakhstan's trade representative in China, facilitated huge Chinese investments in Kazakhstan, and has headed the sovereign wealth fund Samruk-Kazyna that owns, among its many other holdings, KazMunayGas, the major CNPC partner. In 2016, Nazarbayev appointed him chairman of the National Security Committee, Kazakhstan's powerful intelligence agency, and in the days before Nazarbayev's 2019 resignation from the presidency, Massimov was promoted to the military rank of major general.[140] Someone like Massimov could appeal to Beijing in a succession scenario, as would other leaders of financial-industrial groups with extensive connections to China.[141]

For Beijing, the potential perils of picking sides are obvious. Chinese officials might nonetheless run the risk if they believe they are backing a winning horse, desperate to ensure that Chinese interests are being adequately defended, or believe that Kazakhstan is in danger of unraveling in a more dramatic way. China's turn to a diplomacy of "creative engagement," as discussed in chapter 2, props open the door to all of these possibilities in a way that strict adherence to "non-interference" might not.

Even if it is more likely that China adopts a more passive stance, it could still be swept up by Kazakhstan's domestic conflicts and used as a way for opposition forces to sling mud on their adversaries. Although Kazakhstan's business elite have come to appreciate the benefits of working with China, public Sinophobia makes this an appealing tactic. As one Moscow-based expert explained, even Nazarbayev has been labeled a "Chinese agent" by his political opponents. The sin of accepting Chinese bribes is considered especially powerful "kompromat" in Kazakhstan, even though many other forms of corruption are rampant.[142]

Nazarbayev has proven himself an especially skilled operator, particularly with respect to dealing with external political pressures. One of his greatest assets has been his ability to find a balance between passively accepting Russia's unusual penetration of Kazakhstani sovereignty and credibly building an independent, post-Soviet national identity. A successor, especially one lacking Nazarbayev's personal experience with and ties to Moscow and the Soviet system, could have trouble striking a similar balance.

Moscow would almost certainly aim to influence Kazakhstani succession politics. Its history of involvement in Kazakhstan and strong ties to the country give it the greatest sway. Nazarbayev and his closest allies are likely to confide in Moscow as they plot any political transition. It was widely reported, for instance, that Nazarbayev called Putin shortly before he publicly announced his resignation from the presidency in 2019. Nothing about contemporary Russian foreign policy suggests any reluctance to interfere in the political developments of other states, as Ukrainians, Georgians, and others are quick to point out.

At the very least, Russia would likely take steps to soothe the anxieties of Russian-ethnic Kazakhstanis, who feel they have already suffered from pro-Kazakh reforms, fear political instability, and favor closer ties with Moscow.[143] Post-independence language policies, in particular, tended to favor Kazakh over Russian, a shift for which the Russians found themselves unprepared and largely unwilling to accept. In another move unpopular with Russians (both in Kazakhstan and in Russia proper), Nazarbayev has pushed plans to use the

Latin, rather than Cyrillic, alphabet for written Kazakh. Political sensitivities have repeatedly delayed implementation of that policy, but in 2017 the president announced a gradual phase-in of the change to be fully implemented by 2025.[144]

Many Russian-ethnic Kazakhstanis have already voted with their feet. At the time of independence, ethnic Kazakhs and Russians each comprised about 40 percent of the national population. By 1999, however, Kazakhs were in the majority, and Russians fell to only 30 percent. The trend continued, and by 2016 Kazakhs were roughly 70 percent of the total and Russians only 20 percent.[145]

These demographic trends have not been uniform across Kazakhstan's geography, however, as there is now an uneven distribution of ethnic Russians. Most live in pockets along the Kazakhstan-Russia border, such as the cities of Kustanay and Petropavlovsk or Ust-Kamenogorsk.[146] At least part of the reason that Nazarbayev moved the nation's capital north to Astana from Almaty was to encourage ethnic Kazakhs to resettle the north and address this new demographic imbalance.[147]

After Russia's 2014 intervention in Ukraine and forceful annexation of Crimea, a region with an ethnic Russian majority and Russia's vital Black Sea Fleet base at Sevastopol, Kazakhstani fears of a similar scenario unfolding in its own northern territories spiked.[148] Indeed, the reaffirmation of "the independence, territorial integrity, and sovereignty of Kazakhstan," at the outset of the January 2018 US-Kazakhstan joint statement was almost certainly motivated by Nazarbayev's concern that Moscow could violate Kazakhstan's borders with impunity.[149]

Many Russian experts, like Sergei Karaganov, dean of the Faculty of World Economy and International Affairs at Moscow's Higher School of Economics, discount this possibility, observing that northern Kazakhstan is not nearly as important to Russia, and adding that Russian actions in Crimea were a response to political provocation.[150] These points may be narrowly true; northern Kazakhstan does not hold the historic or strategic significance for Russia that Crimea does.

Then again, Kazakhstanis can be forgiven for worrying that Moscow could view northern Kazakhstan as a natural extension of Russian territory similar to parts of Ukraine or Georgia.[151] A Ukraine-like "provocation" in Kazakhstan could rather easily emerge in the turmoil of a post-Nazarbayev succession, when ethnic anxieties might also spike.[152]

Russia need not actually undertake military or paramilitary operations in Kazakhstan in order to exert influence. The threat of force combined with a media and subversion campaign could be sufficient to advance Moscow's aim of installing a pro-Russian leader in Nur-Sultan (Astana), for instance by backing and facilitating a coalition of Kazakhstan's financial-industrial groups.[153] In short, even if Russia is not likely to invade Kazakhstan, Moscow's involvement could easily influence, and possibly exacerbate, a post-Nazarbayev power struggle.

Putting all the pieces together, the purely economic logic of post-Nazarbayev succession politics points to a quick and painless replacement so that gas and oil keep flowing and everyone gets paid. Nazarbayev's own succession planning also transparently aims for a similar outcome. However, the political and social reality could end up being much messier than planned. Whether Beijing likes it or not, China could get sucked into an ugly succession fight. Worse, China's involvement in Kazakhstan increases the likelihood of a tumultuous outcome because it exacerbates interethnic rivalries and heightens Moscow's anxieties about maintaining a dominant political influence in Nur-Sultan (Astana).

Russian Rules

All of these domestic political intrigues relate in important ways to the broader issue of Russia's strategic aims in Central Asia. If Russia were content to see China's political, economic, and military influence grow, the prospects for a competitive struggle over Nazarbayev's succession would be reduced. But Russia is keen to maintain a dominant sphere of influence in Central Asia.[154] As recounted at the outset of this chapter, Russia fought to assert and maintain its imperial sway over Central Asia for centuries. Moscow's direct hold over the five Central Asian republics was broken only after the collapse of the Soviet Union. President Vladimir Putin and many other Russians perceive that disruption as a temporary tragedy that ought, in time, to be rectified as Moscow reasserts its influence, if not outright dominion, over the region.[155]

Security ties continue to bind Russia to Kazakhstan and the rest of Central Asia. The Russian-led Collective Security Treaty Organization (CSTO) counts Tajikistan, Kyrgyzstan, and Kazakhstan as members. The CSTO Collective Rapid Reaction Force is composed of about 15,000 troops. Of that total, 10,000 are Russian and 3,000–4,000 are Kazakhstani.[156] Unlike the SCO, Russia dominates the CSTO and excludes China. As Konstantin Syroezhkin, one of Kazakhstan's top experts on China, observed in early 2017, "the CSTO is the region's only mechanism for raising troops in an emergency."[157] It is Russia's "multilateral instrument of influence" in the region.[158]

Russia also stations border guards in Tajikistan and shares information with most of the region's intelligence services. Many Central Asian military and intelligence officers are trained in Russia. Professional links between the Kazakhstani and Russian militaries run especially deep; from 1993 to 2006, Kazakhstan sent 2,475 officers to Russia, as compared to 220 sent to the United States.[159] Russian instructors routinely teach courses at Kazakhstan's National Defense University.[160]

When the Soviet Union launched Sputnik and sent Yuri Gagarin into space, or more recently, whenever Russia flies American astronauts to the International Space Station, it does so from Baikonur Cosmodrome. The facility is in Kazakhstan, where Russian military facilities occupy roughly 9 million hectares of leased land, a territory slightly smaller than the size of South Korea.[161] The Cosmodrome is leased until 2050. Russian forces routinely test new missiles, ammunition, and jets in Kazakhstan.[162] Similarly, Russia's radar node based at Lake Balkhash provides crucial data for Moscow's ballistic missile defense system, and Kazakhstan's own air defenses are tightly intertwined with Russia's.[163]

Bearing the full burden of defending its lengthy border with Russia would be inconceivable for Kazakhstan. Nur-Sultan (Astana) spends only 1 percent of GDP on defense, so it cannot afford to have significant external enemies of any sort.[164] Russia allows Kazakhstan to purchase arms at discount prices, with few limitations.[165] From 2000 to 2018, Kazakhstan bought 80 percent of its arms from Russia, including aircraft and missile defense systems.[166] A 2015 deal sent four Sukhoi Su-30SM fighter jets to Kazakhstan, the same model used by the Russian Air Force, and in 2017 Russia and Kazakhstan announced that Astana would purchase twelve more.[167]

Kazakhstan was the last of the Central Asian states to announce its independence from the Soviet Union, and Russia still enjoys stronger cultural and "soft power" ties to Kazakhstan than to other Central Asian states. In Kazakhstan's tightly controlled media environment, pro-Russian media dominates the airwaves to the point that it worries nationalistic Kazakhstanis.[168] Russia's "soft power" overtures show signs of success: a 2015 poll found that 84 percent of Kazakhstanis put Russia at the top of the list of states most friendly to Kazakhstan.[169] Among Central Asians, Kazakhstan is frequently depicted as a Russian tool, less independent and more controlled by Moscow.[170] Over 70 percent of all ethnic Russians in Central Asia reside in Kazakhstan.[171]

Kazakhstan's economic ties to Russia remain strong as well. In 2018, Kazakhstan imported over 38 percent of its goods from Russia and sent roughly 8 percent of its exports there.[172] Slumping oil prices in the late 2000s forced Russia to retreat economically, but Russians still own roughly one-third of all foreign businesses in Kazakhstan.[173] Even China's initial entry into Kazakhstan's gas market served Russian interests. At that time, the oversupply of gas was Moscow's main problem, and Chinese purchases temporarily propped up prices.[174]

Soon enough, however, China's forays into the Kazakhstani energy game started to worry Moscow. When CNPC edged Russia's Gazprom from its place as a controlling player in the Central Asian gas market, it also freed China from the Russian stranglehold over Central Asian gas supplies and gave Central Asian states more market leverage.[175] Subsequently, Chinese financing and joint ventures with Kazakhstani firms also enabled the construction of gas pipelines to serve consumers inside Kazakhstan.[176] In the process, China extended its reach into Central Asia's domestic distribution market.

As part of its effort to reassert Russia's regional influence, Moscow has launched new multilateral institutions designed to bind its neighbors in exclusive ties.[177] Kazakhstani insiders report, for instance, that Moscow framed the Eurasian Economic Union (EAEU) and the CSTO as "with us or against us" choices for Kazakhstan.[178] A loose version of the EAEU was originally Nazarbayev's brainchild, but at every step along the way Moscow has attempted to make it more exclusive and political. Russia's first draft of the EAEU treaty included plans for political integration and currency sharing. Kazakhstani negotiators rejected it.[179] Over time, Astana succeeded in making the EAEU more economically oriented.[180] In the end, however, Kazakhstan's EAEU membership still binds it to Russia by granting tariff-free access to Russian goods and requiring Kazakhstan to enforce the organization's common external tariff against non-EAEU imports, including those from China.[181]

Central Asia expert Niklas Swanström finds that all of the major Russian-led multilateral groupings in Central Asia "were designed to promote specifically Russian interests and have effectively circumvented any involvement from other significant actors such as China and the United States."[182] Not only that, Swanström finds that Russia has even used the SCO as a means to monitor and constrain China's role in the region, rather than to promote it.[183] Supporting that logic, Moscow has resisted all moves to turn the SCO into a multilateral economic institution in ways that might privilege Chinese influence or detract from the significance of the EAEU.[184]

Looking back, throughout most of the 1990s and early 2000s Moscow perceived that the main threat to its free hand in Central Asia came from an encroaching American, or at least Western, influence. Washington did pay greater attention to Central Asia throughout the period. In the immediate post–Cold War era, US policy focused on assisting the region's transition to democracy and capitalism. After 9/11, the focus shifted to supplying Afghanistan's battlefields through Central Asian transit links.

Now, however, Russia has little to fear from American involvement in the region. Washington's military footprint in Afghanistan has shrunk, and neither the Obama nor the Trump administration ever showed much interest in promoting democracy (or much else) in the states of Central Asia. Moscow arguably has more reason for concern about the potential for an abrupt American withdrawal from Afghanistan than a prolonged US military presence in Central Asia.

With the acme of American involvement in Central Asia in the rearview mirror, the greatest conceivable threat to Russian dominance in Central Asia is China.

China versus Russia?

In June 2017, President Nazarbayev hosted the annual summit of the SCO, just days before opening the much-anticipated (by Kazakhstanis, at least) EXPO 2017 in Astana. Photos from the conference show Nazarbayev wedged between Xi and Putin, a symbolic reflection of his country's geographic and geopolitical place in the world.[185]

In many ways other than geography, Kazakhstan has spent at least the past decade edging closer to China. Yet nearly all sides—Russia, China, and many of the Central Asians themselves—avert their eyes from that reality and speak of a China-Russia "division of labor" in the region. In a nutshell, that division leaves Russia in a dominant role on regional diplomatic and security issues, while China expends its energies and resources on economic development.

As a sign of their cooperative approach in Central Asia, in May 2015, during President Xi's visit to Moscow, China and Russia jointly pledged to tie China's Silk Road Economic Belt together with Russia's EAEU. Putin hailed the effort "to form a Common Economic Space spanning the entire Eurasian continent," or a "Greater Eurasian Partnership."[186] Both sides made similar pledges the subsequent two years.[187] These moves likely reflected Russian preferences more than those of the Chinese, but Beijing played along.[188]

As one top Kazakhstani expert quipped in 2017, echoing a widely held view in Central Asia, "Russia is a rifle and China a purse."[189] Perhaps as important as any material consideration, the division of labor confers upon Moscow a superior geopolitical status in the region, with Beijing accepting a secondary role. Thus far, China's deferential approach has eased geopolitical friction with Russia.

Among seasoned analysts of Sino-Russian relations, the common interests, tensions, and vulnerabilities of Beijing and Moscow are judged to stack up in slightly different ways.[190] By and large, outright Sino-Russian conflict is deemed highly improbable in the near term.[191] Similarly, few anticipate or advocate a full alliance.[192] The more debated question is precisely how China and Russia will manage their current modus vivendi and the likelihood that they might slip into a more rivalrous competition or tight-knit partnership over time.

First things first, it is essential to recognize that developments in Central Asia are only one piece in the global-sized puzzle of bilateral relations between China and Russia. Strikingly, those relations are now as good as or better than they have been at any time in modern history.[193] Ahead of his June 2019 state visit to Moscow, President Xi was effusive in his praise for President Putin, telling Russian media, "I have had closer interactions with President Putin than with any other foreign colleagues. He is my best and bosom friend. I cherish dearly our deep friendship." He added that "we share a high degree of consensus on the strategic significance of the China-Russia relationship and therefore the same resolve and desire to deepen and sustain its growth."[194] As described earlier in this chapter, the current state of play represents an historical anomaly; the two continental powers of Eurasia have more often than not had a tense, competitive relationship that played out along the edges of their empires.

The present-day Sino-Russian rapprochement cannot be explained without reference to their mutual dissatisfaction with the American-led world order that prevailed in the aftermath of the Cold War. In the decades since the collapse of the Soviet Union, that dissatisfaction went unresolved. For different reasons, some related to American policies and others to the interests and aspirations of Moscow and Beijing, Russia and China bridled at the implications of American leadership in the world.[195]

In 2008, this effect of negative "repulsion" from the United States was appreciated by Australian analyst and diplomat Bobo Lo, who memorably described the improved Sino-Russian relationship as an "axis of convenience."[196] At the time, Lo argued that while the Sino-Russian axis was not immediately under threat, it would be wrong to see it as an enduring equilibrium that would foster closer partnership. The relationship looked "tactical and instrumental," because the two sides "share neither a long-term vision of the world nor a common understanding of their respective places in it."[197] Lo concluded that China and Russia were more likely heading toward "strategic tension" than "strategic convergence," by which he meant a relationship "mistrustful and unsatisfactory in many respects, but also relatively predictable and useful."[198]

Ten years later, Alexander Lukin, the head of the international relations department at Russia's National Research University Higher School of Economics, took issue with Lo's characterization of the Sino-Russian relationship.[199] In his 2018 book *China and Russia: The New Rapprochement*, Lukin claimed that Moscow and Beijing are not merely repelled toward one another by their negative reactions to the United States. He effectively flips the negative repulsion into a positive attraction, arguing that both China and Russia embrace the vision of a multipolar world in which sovereign states are free to choose their forms of government without American meddling.[200] Making extensive use of official Russian and Chinese source material as well as Russian and Chinese commentary, he argues that this shared worldview offers a stable foundation for the steady strengthening of bilateral relations across Eurasia.

Lukin is right not to underestimate the ways in which Chinese and Russian leaders perceive the world similarly. His own castigation of the United States for what he describes as bullying and a hypocritically self-serving democracy-promotion agenda undoubtedly resonates with leaders in Moscow and Beijing (and elsewhere as well).[201] This attention to state sovereignty is an obsession that exposes the core of what animates Putin and Xi: regime survival.[202] Clearly united in their anti-democratic preferences, the regimes in Moscow and Beijing are not merely on the defensive, however. It is no secret that Putin's Russia has undermined democratic practices in other nations, but Xi's China appears increasingly willing to play similar games.[203]

Russia and China are linked by other important material interests as well. Their most critical area of cooperation has been energy. In 2013, Rosneft and CNPC closed a monster $270 billion, twenty-five-year oil deal, and by 2016 Russia was China's top oil supplier.[204] Turning to the gas sector, by the end of 2018, Gazprom had completed most of the "Power of Siberia" pipeline that travels 3,000 kilometers across Siberia, linking huge Russian gas fields to Chinese consumers. Upon completion, it is expected to bring 38 billion cubic meters of gas into China annually for thirty years.[205] That should meet roughly 12 percent of China's total anticipated demand.[206] Beyond oil and gas investments, China has pledged billions of dollars for nonhydrocarbon projects in the Russian Far East, including at the free port of Vladivostok and in the mining and chemical sectors.[207]

On the security front, Russia has overcome its reticence to selling major weapons systems to China, a breakthrough that opened the door to deeper cooperation. Russian manufacturers had feared the long-run consequences of Chinese reverse engineering and competition, but arms deals are now justified as Russia's only way to make money for reinvestment into the defense industry.[208] Accordingly, Moscow has sold some of Russia's highest-quality arms, like the S-400 air defense system and Su-35 aircraft.[209] China now buys roughly 80 percent of its foreign weapons from Russia, and roughly 15 percent of Russia's arms sales from 2015 to 2018 were to China.[210]

The two are also more actively engaged in military exercises than ever, including an annual series of small naval drills that started in 2014.[211] In the summer of 2017, Russian and Chinese defense ministers met in Astana to sign a "roadmap" on military cooperation for 2017–2020, signifying their intention to build even closer defense ties.[212] Perhaps most significant to date, when Russia staged its enormous Vostok 2018 conventional military exercises that included nearly 300,000 personnel, China sent 3,200 troops of its own. The move was intended to signal a higher degree of cooperation and trust.[213]

In Central Asia as well, China and Russia share multiple common aims. Above all, they prefer the sort of political stability born of secular, authoritarian rule. Russia expert Eugene Rumer succinctly concludes that "the key factor from Moscow's point of view is that Beijing—unlike Washington—does not promote political reform in the region or threaten its stability."[214] This is particularly true in Central Asia, where Moscow and Beijing fear the rise of political Islam and its potential to contribute to violence, whether through terrorism or mass popular movements.[215] These aims motivated the formation of the SCO.

China and Russia also have some shared interests on the economic front. Chinese investments in Central Asia often indirectly benefit Russia. For instance, Russia appreciates China's financial bailouts and development projects that help to prop up pliant Central Asian autocrats. In addition, parts of the new Chinese-backed infrastructure connecting Eurasia from east to west tie into Russian networks at some point along the way.[216]

In this context of unusually warm Sino-Russian relations, most of Central Asia's leaders continue to seek ties with a variety of outside players, thus avoiding dependence on any single external patron. Having several outside suitors helps Central Asian states drive harder bargains on energy deals and other negotiations. To a certain degree, it insulates their less powerful regimes from coercion and intrusion and preserves their own ability to dictate domestic conditions.[217]

Along these lines, Nazarbayev's "multi-vector" strategy was initially born as "a means of circumventing the hegemony of Russia . . . and establishing at least a semi-independent path for Kazakhstan's foreign policy, especially at a time when relations with Russia were frequently tense."[218] Over the years it has also helped Kazakhstan remain "an authoritarian regime that nevertheless has integrated itself into multiple security and economic relationships" in the

West, such as the Organization for Security and Cooperation in Europe.[219] The strategy enables Kazakhstan to pursue a wide range of economic and political ties without becoming entirely "Finlandized" by either Russia or China.

All of these points tend to reinforce Moscow's confidence about the resilience of Russian dominance in Central Asia and its ability to avoid serious friction with Beijing. In October 2017, over a formal banquet in Moscow's historic Hotel Metropol, famous to Americans as the setting of the best-selling novel *A Gentleman in Moscow*, I quizzed a Russian colleague about the stability of the Sino-Russian balance in Central Asia. She, an expert steeped in regional security affairs, pulled all the moving parts together into a cohesive whole.

She reasoned that China would be smart enough to steer clear of trouble with Russia because the Chinese would benefit from economic opportunities without shouldering costly security burdens. The Central Asian states, for their part, would also have strong incentives to build economic ties with China while maintaining closer political and strategic links with Russia. Russia, she added, was not terribly threatened by China's growing economic clout and had not experienced any of the over-hyped problem of Chinese population flows into its Far East. In conclusion, Moscow could readily keep the game going for the foreseeable future.[220]

Boosters of Sino-Russian rapprochement like Alexander Lukin stress many of these same points. The logic is compelling in the short run, but tends to downplay areas of friction and the potential for future conflict.[221] Russia's current anger with the West generates a near-blind acceptance of the spectacular rise of Chinese wealth, power, and influence on Russia's eastern doorstep. It motivates the belief that Beijing's acceptance of Moscow's traditional sphere of influence in Central Asia is durable, not ephemeral.[222]

Yet the sheer scale of the imbalance in wealth and trade between China and Russia cannot be so blithely dismissed. Russia's 2018 GDP measured less than 12 percent of China's.[223] In 2018, Russia's trade with China—both imports and exports—was greater than its trade with any other state.[224] Russia, however, accounted for a tiny 1.9 percent of China's overall exports in 2017.[225] Over time, these asymmetries would seem to leave Russia vulnerable to China in potentially uncomfortable ways, not least by chipping away at Russia's remaining military and technological advantages that underpin Moscow's influence in Central Asia.

To be sure, power disparities need not ruin ties between like-minded states. Lukin correctly notes that the United States and Canada, for instance, are generally on excellent terms despite obvious asymmetries.[226] This is true enough, but it assumes that Russians and Chinese are as satisfied with the emerging terms of their relationship as the Americans and Canadians have been for the past two centuries.[227] There are a number of important reasons to question that assumption.

The glaring vulnerability of Russia's relationship with Central Asia is already apparent when it comes to economics. As described in earlier sections of this chapter, China has dislodged Russia's stranglehold over regional commerce by buying and constructing pipelines and transit routes that skirt Russian territory. China dominates the region's trade and commerce, even if it does so relatively quietly. That China could translate that economic dominance into political influence to rival Russia's cannot be dismissed, even if Beijing has so far been quite careful to avoid giving that impression.

In addition, Russians have long worried about Chinese encroachment in the Russian Far East, where Russia's mixture of blatant anti-Chinese racism and desire to defend national territorial sovereignty combine in unhealthy ways with the reality of vast, underpopulated land, a record of local government mismanagement, and Chinese citizens seeking economic opportunity.[228] Although Moscow clearly prefers to keep a lid on popular Russian anxieties, it also courts Chinese investment as an essential component for developing the region. The balancing act is difficult to maintain. Local suspicions about the influx of Chinese businesses and workers came to the fore in 2015, when large demonstrations erupted in Russia's Baikal region north of Mongolia in response to a forty-nine-year land lease to a Chinese company.[229]

Other Russian security anxieties were stirred in 2006 and 2009 when Chinese military exercises along the Russian border were perceived by at least some analysts in Moscow as demonstrations of China's "readiness to launch a potential large-scale land offensive against Russia."[230] Analysts Paul Stronski and Nicole Ng point out that in 2017, Russia deployed new S-400 air defense systems in the Far East, and that even though the chance of militarized border tensions is currently near zero, "as it is not clear what China's long-term intentions are with Russia, the Kremlin's insecurity in Northeast Asia could increase if the Far East remains underdeveloped."[231]

A series of new military initiatives by Beijing suggest how China could further upset the division of labor in Central Asia that Russia favors. These include new forms of institutionalized security cooperation, arms sales, and investments in new military capabilities. Russia will find these moves increasingly irritating, or worse. Irina Zvyagelskaya, a well-connected Russian professor of international relations, adamantly declared in 2017 that "Russia will not accept a major Chinese security role" in Central Asia, even though China and Russia do have a common interest in fighting terrorism and instability.[232]

Chinese moves in nearby Afghanistan suggest how China's regional security posture could evolve. On February 29, 2016, Chinese general Fang Fenghui made an unannounced and unprecedented visit to Kabul, where he met with Afghan president Ashraf Ghani, his national security adviser, and other top officials.[233] The meeting was unusual because of the seniority of the visitor; it was the Chief of Joint Staff's first visit to Afghanistan since the beginning of his tenure in 2012. It was also noteworthy for the Chinese pledge to deliver $73 million in military aid to Afghanistan, also a first, which Afghan officials hoped would come in the form of transport and logistics aircraft, mobile radars, and uniforms.[234] Last, the Chinese proposed to launch a Quadrilateral Cooperation and Coordination Mechanism (QCCM).

All three steps demonstrated a growing Chinese focus on Afghanistan, but the last piece—the QCCM—was the one that most caught Moscow's eye. As proposed, the QCCM would bring together China, Afghanistan, Pakistan, and Tajikistan to promote counter-terror information sharing. In itself, the move was not earth-shattering. China and Tajikistan were already counterterror partners through the SCO, Pakistan has been a close Chinese friend for decades, and Afghanistan is clearly happy to partner with any of its powerful neighbors if it holds a prospect of strengthening the fight against terrorism.

Officially, Russia responded with nonchalance, as Russia's special envoy to Afghanistan, Zamir Kabulov, announced: "There's no reason for us to join. We have our own plans in the framework of the CSTO. Moreover, we discuss these issues with China in the framework of the SCO."[235] Indeed, it is under SCO auspices that the most routine "Peace Mission" series of regional counter-terror exercises have been held, with participation from China, Russia, Kazakhstan, Kyrgyzstan, Tajikistan, and Uzbekistan.[236]

Yet the QCCM move actually prompted a sharp response from some of Russia's prominent regional and security experts. As one observed, "it appears that in this 'Central Asian NATO' under the Chinese umbrella, Russia may be the odd one out."[237] Another quipped that the Chinese initiative could "de facto reject the antiterror component of the Shanghai Cooperation Organization."[238]

Chinese defense officials clearly felt a need to temper Russian discomfort. They quickly downplayed the QCCM and rejected its characterization as a "Central Asian NATO."[239] But even Chinese analysts perceived something new and important in the QCCM, as one wrote in the English-language official paper of the Chinese Communist Party, the *Global Times*, that the QCCM "shows that China eyes a bigger role in maintaining security in Central Asia."[240]

In his analysis of the situation, journalist Joshua Kucera concluded that, "the fact that this proposed alliance would include Tajikistan, and exclude Russia, has raised alarm bells in Moscow. Russia has, until now, seen itself either as the primary security provider in Central Asia or, at times, a partner with China. But that may be changing."[241]

In addition to the QCCM, China and Tajikistan conducted a joint counter-terror exercise in October 2016 with a combined 10,000 troops.[242] More dramatic, however, were early 2018 reports that Chinese forces had established a military base in Badakshan, Afghanistan.[243] That region, a narrow panhandle in Afghanistan's remote northeast, is most accessible from China through Tajikistan, and Chinese forces appear to have sent their patrols along that route. Locals in the remote region confirm that "there are quite a lot of Chinese soldiers here," but they generally aim to keep a low profile.[244]

Although Beijing officially rejected reports of any counter-terrorism base, Afghan officials contradicted their Chinese counterparts.[245] At least one Tajik official claimed that "China in 2015 or 2016 signed secret agreements with authorities that gave Beijing rights to refurbish or build up to 30 to 40 guard posts on the Tajik side of the country's border with Afghanistan."[246] At the very least, the two sides appear to have expanded their cooperation in ways designed to stem any flow of militants directly from Afghanistan into China, as one facet of China's intensifying overseas anti-terrorism efforts noted in chapter 2.

Kucera has also tracked major Chinese arms sales to Central Asia, most of which have gone to Turkmenistan and Uzbekistan.[247] These include drones, missiles, and—most important—air defense systems.[248] To date, China has sold only three orders of drones to Kazakhstan, both Pterodactyl-1, or Wing Loong, models with the capacity—like US-made Predators—to be outfitted with small missiles or bombs.[249] However, Kazakhstan was also in discussions with the drones' manufacturer, Aviation Industry Corporation of China, about building an aircraft maintenance and service center, and in 2016 Astana signed an agreement with China's Norinco Corporation to buy technology and equipment, including large caliber ammunition.[250]

As with the QCCM, China has not come anywhere close to pushing Russia from its perch as the top security provider or arms merchant in Central Asia, and especially not in Kazakhstan. To the contrary, there are still big obstacles in the way of China-Kazakhstan defense partnership, from linguistic differences to the fact that most of Kazakhstan's arsenal and doctrine have been Russian imports.[251] The point is that Beijing is taking incremental steps toward greater involvement in this sector in ways that are liable to grow and to rankle Moscow.[252]

The inability of Central Asian states to quash anti-Chinese terrorists on their territory is the most likely reason that China would send its own security forces further into the region. On August 30, 2016, a suicide bomber rammed his small Mitsubishi van into the gates of the Chinese embassy in Bishkek,

Kyrgyzstan.[253] Several Kyrgyz personnel were wounded, and the embassy compound was damaged. Beijing urged Kyrgyz authorities to investigate the attack, which was subsequently traced to Uighur militants based in Syria and connected with the Nusra Front.[254]

The question comes if and when Beijing judges that its Central Asian partners lack the capacity to adequately secure Chinese interests in their countries. At that point, or if Beijing judges that its energy investments are under threat, it is possible to imagine China beginning to take matters into its own hands.[255] As described in chapter 2, Chinese private security contractors are proliferating, the Ministry of Public Security (MPS) is expanding liaison relationships outside China, and units from the People's Armed Police, a paramilitary force trained to quell civil unrest, have participated in anti-terror operations overseas.[256]

As part of its broader military modernization, China has invested in capabilities that could enable an intervention in Central Asia. Analyst Richard Weitz pulls the story together in Central Asia, noting that while the transformation of China's military from a "static, region-based defense force into a rapid reaction force" was mainly focused on Taiwan contingencies, it would also be relevant "in anticipation of an intervention in Central Asia."[257] China has upgraded its air, road, and especially rail transportation to cross western China. For the Peace Mission 2010 military exercises, China moved an expeditionary force of 1,000 troops and vehicles from eastern China to Kazakhstan, using a combination of air and rail.

China and Russia also find themselves at odds with respect to how they perceive their relationships with other important regional powers, such as India and Vietnam. Moreover, even if Russia and China do tend to perceive the United States in similar terms, they approach relations with Washington differently. Putin's Russia boldly contests American leadership head-on, but even Xi's China is usually more inclined to pursue indirect, subtle, or passive tactics.[258]

Finally, Russia simply cannot fathom a reality in which China outranks it, status-wise, on the global chessboard. As China continues to grow, it threatens to leave Russia "at the margins of international decision-making."[259] In time, Russia could find itself a mere "raw materials appendage" or "vassal" state to China.[260] This fate would pose problems for any state with pretensions of global influence, but especially so for Putin's Russia, which places a disproportionate emphasis on asserting its status on the world stage. Angela Stent, a Georgetown University professor and renowned expert on Russia, astutely characterizes Putin's animating project since he assumed power in 2000 as "the return of Russia to the world stage as a great power to be respected, feared, and . . . liked and even admired."[261]

This combination of Russian interests, anxieties, and ambitions would seem to rub uncomfortably against accepting the role of "junior partner" to China, especially in Central Asia, where Russia has played a dominant role for so long. Perhaps Lukin and his Russian fellow-travelers will be right to judge that China's ambitions in Central Asia will only ever impinge on Russian economic interests, not political or security ones. More likely, however, they place too much emphasis on Chinese words, and too little on Chinese actions.[262]

In this respect, China's "charm offensive" in East Asia and the Pacific during the early 2000s offers an instructive lesson. During that period, many East Asian leaders were spellbound by Beijing's apparently single-minded focus on economic "win-win" opportunities. The mood was not entirely dissimilar from present-day Central Asia: enthusiasm for China's trade and investment and relatively little concern about Beijing's geopolitical agenda.[263] At that time, east Asians perceived the United States as decidedly out of touch, fixated on the global war against terrorism and, to a lesser extent, geopolitical competition with China.

However, by 2010, Beijing had turned more aggressive in the South and East China Seas as well as in other regional diplomatic forums. At the normally staid ASEAN Regional Forum in July 2010, Chinese foreign minister Yang Jiechi lost his temper and walked out of the room during Secretary of State Hillary Clinton's speech as she endorsed freedom of navigation in the South China Sea. When he returned, he angrily expressed China's sense of place in the region, declaring that "China is a big country and other countries are small countries, and that's just a fact."[264] The smaller states of east Asia quickly woke up to the reality that China's huge economic advantages gave Beijing threatening tools of geopolitical leverage. Since then, the operative question in the region has been whether the United States and these smaller countries have the capacity, interest, and will to stick together in ways that balance a more aggressive Chinese posture.

A similar pattern could play out in Central Asia, with China gradually and quietly consolidating its position with economic incentives, then pressing its strategic advantage at a time of its choosing. Unlike in east Asia, however, that time could come long after Russia and the weaker states of Central Asia have lost any serious capacity to resist.

Of course, none of this demonstrates that a Sino-Russian spat over Central Asia is inevitable. Even if it does come, it could take a long time, even a decade or longer.[265] Because Russia and China are playing a global game not confined to Central Asia, leaders in Beijing, Moscow, and each of the Central Asian states have strong incentives to downplay the potential for deteriorating ties, even as they are underway.[266] Hypothetically, if either Beijing or Moscow were somehow to improve ties with Washington, their own relations would probably suffer. But such about-faces with Washington are improbable, at least as long as the current Russian and Chinese regimes stay in power.

In short, although China's activities are, on balance, irritants in Sino-Russian relations, they are unlikely to force a near-term rupture between Moscow and Beijing.[267] Still, greater Chinese involvement in Central Asia comes at a cost to Russia's traditional dominance and is almost certain to worsen over time. If Moscow and Beijing continue to develop their rapprochement into a deeper strategic partnership, it will be in spite of their interests in Central Asia, not because of them.

A Forecast for Central Asia

When compared to South Asia, where China's greater involvement exacerbates the competitive dynamic between Pakistan and India and reinforces troubling trends within Pakistan itself, Central Asia looks as if it is on firmer footing. In the short run, at least, China's involvement in Kazakhstan and across the region has been less disruptive domestically and geopolitically. The ongoing, if historically anomalous, Sino-Russian modus vivendi could persist a great deal longer than one would expect. This is because Putin's Moscow is blinded by anti-Americanism, China is skillful at playing to Russia's pride and has not blundered terribly in its management of sensitive sovereignty issues, and the two sides have other narrowly complementary but important political and economic interests.

That said, Kazakhstan—Central Asia's most important player in terms of energy and geography—is heading into the storm of an uncertain and potentially divisive political transition that is a direct consequence of its "patronal" politics.[268] When Nazarbayev leaves the scene, and again at subsequent points of political turmoil, Chinese interests, including substantial energy investments as well as long-term geopolitical aims, will be at stake. China's non-interference strategy will be tested. Even if Beijing tries to stick to the sidelines, it will likely find it hard to avoid being sucked into a nasty political scramble in ways that upset relations with Nur-Sultan (Astana), Moscow, or both at the same time.

Political instability in Kazakhstan is not the only scenario for a future of more intrusive Chinese involvement in Central Asia. Other security threats to Chinese investments—and the inability of Central Asians to deal with them— could invite a Chinese security presence that riles Moscow and redefines their regional division of labor. Change could come gradually, as it has thus far, blanketed in Chinese pledges of mutual respect and nonintervention to avoid immediate friction with Moscow or among Central Asians.

Nonetheless, massive economic shifts have already taken place, through which China has already gained a measure of political influence, and even relatively minor moves on the security front like the QCCM will accumulate over time. Less clear is how long Moscow will choose to whistle past the graveyard of China's growing influence and presence in the region, to maintain its obsessive focus on threats posed by America and the West, even as Beijing has taken surprisingly muscular steps to assert itself elsewhere around the world, from the South China Sea to Sri Lanka and Djibouti.

Finally, although Central Asia's response to China is quite different from South Asia's, certain similarities can be identified across both cases. First, in Kazakhstan as in Pakistan, the domestic political economic consequences of China's growing involvement are mixed but show far greater potential to contribute to corrupt and anti-democratic outcomes than to liberalizing economic or political reforms.[269] Both also show signs of a cleavage between popular and elite views of China, as the wealthy and powerful are best positioned to benefit from Chinese commercial opportunities while others are excluded and alienated. These are not solid foundations for economic and political development over the long run.

Second, although India and Russia have so far responded very differently to China's increasing presence in their traditional spheres of influence (whether in Pakistan or Kazakhstan), New Delhi and Moscow actually face comparable balancing acts as they weigh emerging opportunities and threats. China is a significant investor and trade partner as well as a competitor. Indian and Russian leaders each consider regional changes within the context of global geopolitical developments, not least their (starkly different) relationships with the United States. To date, India's response reflects a wariness and competition with China that is more apparent than Russia's, but it is difficult to envision a future in which Moscow is not increasingly vexed by the expanding scope of Chinese activities in Central Asia.

The comparison of South and Central Asia highlights the ways in which local circumstances are likely to condition the consequences of Chinese involvement. These comparisons invite new questions. What, for instance, is likely to happen when China becomes more deeply involved in a state with a political economy similar to energy-rich, authoritarian Kazakhstan, but is also engaged in regional geopolitical hostilities similar to those between India and Pakistan? The answer is found in the Middle East, the topic of the next chapter.

| Middle Eastern Entanglements

TRAVELING WESTWARD ALONG Eurasia's Silk Road from Central Asia takes us to the Middle East, a region whose immense energy reserves are matched only by its unrelenting political conflict. More than Central or South Asia, the modern Middle East has been an active zone of great power competition. The Middle East's "local rules" have ensnared and bedeviled outside powers for generations. Today American and Russian militaries are again engaged in the region's hot wars.

China's ties to the Middle East have ancient origins, but since the end of the Cold War, China's regional presence has mainly been motivated and defined by energy-related trade and investment. Owing to their vast stores of hydrocarbons, two states in the Middle East have tended to occupy the lion's share of China's attention: Iran and Saudi Arabia. The two are also strategically important powers and today represent two poles in the region's defining geopolitical contest. Beijing is well aware of all this, and generally eager to steer clear of trouble with either Tehran or Riyadh (or, for that matter, to tangle with Washington or Moscow). That said, Xi Jinping's China has grander ambitions of its own, and China's connections with Iran and Saudi Arabia have deepened over the past two decades even as the Iran–Saudi Arabia competition has heated up.[1]

Iran and Saudi Arabia have vital stakes in ensuring that China's activities serve their own domestic and geopolitical purposes. As illiberal states themselves, their leaders see in Beijing an appealing model of growth without political freedom. They have already demonstrated that they know how to harness Chinese resources to their advantage in ways both obvious and subtle. They will continue to do so. Tehran and Riyadh are eager to court Beijing and to cultivate greater Chinese investment and involvement in their countries.

The competition for China's affections between Iran and Saudi Arabia is unlikely to yield a single winner, but it will yield important advantages that neither side can afford to go without. To contemplate how China is likely to play into the Middle East's future, this chapter first turns to explore the past.

China in the Middle East, Ancient and Modern

The emissary Zhang Qian, remembered in the Han dynasty annals for his travels through Central Asia in the second century BCE and for mentioning the existence of "Shendu" (India), is also credited for opening China's imperial relations with Parthia. The Parthians were successors to the mighty Persian empire founded in the sixth century BCE by Cyrus the Great. The ancient Greek historian Xenophon would later write admiringly that Cyrus had started with only a "little band of Persians," and built an empire of lands so vast that "it is a difficult matter even to travel to them all, in whatever direction the east or the west, toward the north or the south."[2] By Zhang Qian's time, the Parthian empire was only a shell of Cyrus's, but still stretched across much of modern-day Iran and Turkey.

Today, when top Chinese and Iranian leaders invoke 2,000 years of peaceful civilizational ties at practically every summit meeting, they refer to this history.[3] Of course, ancient China's unrecorded links to the Middle East reach to the mists of time, with archeological evidence supporting connections in the fourth millennium BCE. In the centuries of recorded history after Zhang Qian's travels, however, we can be sure that the connections between Persia and China intensified, as the two were linked by the aforementioned caravan routes of the Silk Road.[4]

By the rise of China's expansionist Tang dynasty in the seventh century CE, another great kingdom had risen in the Middle East: the Sasanian Empire. Sasanians coined the name "Iran" during this period to denote a common identity that would unify diverse peoples within their domain.[5] At the height of their powers, Sasanian armies moved west and laid siege to Constantinople, the seat of the Byzantine Romans. Although that invasion was repelled, the Sasanians claimed much of the territory of modern-day Egypt, the Levant, Turkey, Iran, large swaths of Central Asia, Afghanistan, and Pakistan. Along with the Tang Chinese and the Byzantine Romans, the Sasanians were one of "three interlocking empires [that] dominated the earth" in late antiquity.[6]

Because the Sasanian empire had reached such heights of power and wealth, its collapse in the mid-seventh century marked a traumatic turning point in world history. It came at the hands of conquering Arabs, fueled by their zealous conversion to the new religion of Islam and a series of snowballing battlefield victories that had started in Arabia during the lifetime of their prophet and leader, Muhammad.[7] The Sasanian empire's rapid and unanticipated demise was likely also enabled by its own civil strife and costly wars with the Byzantine Romans. The new Islamic caliphates built after Muhammad's death were founded on Sasanian foundations, as Arab victories in Persia brought with them vast stores of wealth and knowledge that quickly helped to transform the young religious movement into a sprawling and powerful empire.[8]

Just prior to the Arab conquest of the Sasanian Empire, official Chinese annals recorded regular and increasingly frequent Sasanian embassies to the Tang court and the popularity of Persian "food, fashions, and entertainments."[9] Persian settlements in China were large enough that the Chinese wrote special laws to segregate and govern the terms of their commercial and social exchanges.[10] China's Hui, whose "Culture Park" is described in chapter 2, are the putative descendants of Muslim traders who began to arrive in China during this period.[11]

The Tang dynasty also chronicled several unusual events that unfolded during the final days of the Sasanians. In the year 638, Sasanian emperor Yazdgard III, desperate for allies to ward off his Arab invaders, sent an urgent appeal for military assistance all the way to the Tang court in Xi'an. But Emperor Gaozong refused the plea, and although we can only guess at his precise reasoning, it is clear that such an adventure beyond the already extended western reaches of China's empire would have been extraordinarily difficult.[12]

Soon after Gaozong's refusal, a second even more remarkable visitor arrived at the Tang court: none other than Prince Firuz, Yazdgard III's son. The Chinese welcomed Firuz, who then made multiple unsuccessful attempts to reconstitute his armies and fight his way back into Persia. In failure, Firuz and his entourage eventually settled in the Tang capital of Xi'an where the emperor granted him and his successors a hollow honorific and permitted them to reside in the style of a permanent foreign embassy.[13] Today, in Gaozong's monumental underground tomb not far from Xi'an, a statue of Firuz can be found among those of sixty-one other foreign emissaries. It bears the inscription, "King of Persia, Grand General of the Right Courageous Guard and Commander-in-chief of Persia."[14]

Chinese links to the wider Islamic world waxed and waned over the subsequent centuries. The Mongol armies of the thirteenth century that swept across much of Eurasia and installed China's Yuan dynasty never actually created a single administrative empire across the continent, although they did at times ease the flow of people and goods between Turkey and Iran in the west and China in the east. In any event, as noted in prior chapters, maritime trade had already surpassed overland Silk Road trade by the end of the first millennium. Many of the sea routes linking Africa, the Middle East, India, and east Asia were plied by Persian and Arab sailors.

During the era of the Ming dynasty's eunuch admiral Zheng He, Chinese fleets dominated the far eastern routes and brought them into direct contact with Persia and Arabia. On the fourth voyage of his famed treasure fleet in the fall of 1413, Zheng He made his way across the Arabian Sea to Hormuz, at the mouth of the Persian Gulf. Subsequent voyages also landed in Hormuz and traveled along the southern end of the Arabian Peninsula to Aden, then proceeded south to Africa's east coast before returning home to China.[15] Unlike his father and grandfather, Zheng He never made a pilgrimage to Mecca, but other Chinese Muslims on his expeditions detached from the main fleet to complete the hajj.[16]

As noted in earlier chapters, China's seafaring ways did not last, and with the rise of European global exploration and colonization, China and the Middle East shared in the humiliations of Western imperialism. The post–World War II period finally reopened direct ties between an independent (and by 1949, Communist) China and the major states of the Middle East. Owing to their vast oil reserves, Iran and Saudi Arabia have since assumed prominent regional roles for China, but Egypt, Turkey, Iraq, Israel, Gulf states, and others have built significant connections with Beijing over the years as well.[17]

China's modern ties with Iran took root only in the 1970s, once Beijing had already broken with the Soviet Union and pursued an opening with Nixon's United States, which was then Iran's Cold War ally. China briefly found tactical utility in relations with the American-backed Mohammad Reza Shah's Iran, which served as a bulwark against Soviet expansion in the Middle East.

The 1979 Islamic Revolution that deposed the Shah caught Beijing by surprise.[18] Although Iran's new Islamist politics and China's communist ideology were fundamentally opposed in many respects, both remained revolutionary, illiberal states. Their shared worldviews quickly opened the door to mutually beneficial collaboration, if not trust. With the outbreak of the Iran-Iraq War in 1980, Tehran could no longer buy weapons from Western suppliers and desperately turned to Beijing. Chinese manufacturers were more than happy to supply both sides in the war. Over the subsequent decades, as detailed later in this chapter, China began to sell Iran more sophisticated weaponry, including nuclear and missile technologies. Also over time, Iran's tremendous energy supplies became a more important means for China to satisfy its burgeoning demand.

For modern Saudi Arabia, the initial barriers to relations with communist China were ideological and geopolitical.[19] The Saudi Kingdom owed its eighteenth-century origins to an alliance between Saudi monarchs and "Wahhabi" preachers and was deeply suspicious of the anti-religious Chinese.[20] The exile of thousands of Chinese Muslims to Saudi Arabia and other Middle Eastern states after the Chinese Communist Party took power in 1949 further soured Riyadh's view of the ruling regime in Beijing.[21] China's early Cold War support to other revolutionary movements in the Middle East also unnerved conservative Riyadh.[22]

But Beijing's opening to Washington in the early 1970s scrambled the Cold War map, as did Riyadh's leadership in the 1973 oil embargo. By then, China and Saudi Arabia each perceived the Soviet Union as a significant threat, especially after its invasion of Afghanistan in 1980. The two gradually expanded their trade and formally established diplomatic ties in 1990.

In sum, even a cursory review of the long sweep of China's ancient and modern history of relations with the Middle East suggests that Beijing has wide latitude for building its future with the region. Unlike, say, China's relations with Japan or Vietnam, geographic and cultural distance from the Middle East generally prevented the development of deeply rooted or painful memories of conflict. For all of the rise and fall of mighty land empires, none but the Mongols briefly—and even then, only nominally—brought the eastern and western edges of Eurasia under a common reign.

Also missing, however, are deep bonds of friendship or cooperation between China and the Middle East. The story of Sasanian pleas for Tang military assistance evokes a hypothetical history of direct Chinese involvement that "might have been," and yet never actually was. Zheng He's voyages similarly raise questions about how China could conceivably have entrenched itself more firmly in the Middle East, as the Europeans did in subsequent generations.

This is not to say that China's history in the Middle East provides a blank slate. Ancient cultural familiarity through the intermingling of peoples, ideas, goods, religions, and technologies from China to the region and back again runs deeper than a purely modern history would show. The Hui Muslim community is an obvious demographic manifestation of that past. Perhaps even more important, the shared experience of European imperialism and the Cold War has shaped current Chinese, Iranian, and Saudi worldviews and relationships. Looking to the future, the pressing interests and geopolitical ambitions of these states will be motivated, framed, and pursued in ways that echo this history, even if they are not always tightly bound by it.

China's Interests in the Middle East

Professor Yitzhak Shichor started studying China in the early 1970s and is still the rare sinologist in Israel, as he explained in the living room of his Jerusalem apartment on a sunny June morning in 2017. There he lamented the relative dearth of Israeli expertise on contemporary China and shared a few of his hopes and plans for building up a stronger cadre of scholars in top Israeli universities.[23]

Shichor's 1979 book, *The Middle East in China's Foreign Policy, 1949–1977*, remains a classic. It lucidly demonstrates that "if we try to evaluate Chinese achievements [over the first three decades of Communist Party rule] in the Middle East in traditional terms of power politics, then China's Middle East policy must be admitted a complete failure. Yet, if we bear in mind that Peking has never sought direct involvement and presence in the Middle East, nor economic or other gains, the conclusion would be somewhat different."[24]

Shichor stressed that during the early Cold War, China's influence in the Middle East was constrained by four main factors: distance, lack of cultural affinity, China's objectively limited power and resources, and the dominating presence of the Cold War superpowers.[25] The Cold War is well over, but there is little doubt that Beijing continues to take a back seat to Washington (and even Moscow) when it comes to the major feuds of today's Middle East. That said, in the post–Cold War period Beijing's objective interests and capacity to project its influence into the region have been transformed by China's economic growth, and especially its voracious consumption of energy.[26]

In 1959, China struck oil at the massive Daqing field in the country's northeast. The find temporarily turned China into an oil exporter, but by the mid-1980s growing domestic demand led Beijing to shift gears and shed the goal of oil self-sufficiency. Market reforms and rapid economic growth turned China into a net oil importer by 1993.[27] Since then, China has become only more reliant on imports, and policymakers in Beijing have come up with various strategies, such as direct investment in overseas production facilities, pipelines, a strategic reserve, and new refineries to alleviate their fears about losing reliable energy supplies.[28]

It was only natural that China should seek a significant portion of these imports from hydrocarbon-rich Iran and Saudi Arabia. Iran's vast oil reserves were initially tapped by the British, when "in 1909, the Anglo-Persian Oil

Company (APOC) quickly emerged as a significant oil producer, permanently altering Iran's economy and its relations with the rest of the world."[29] Iran became a vital gas station for the British empire and the United States, at least until the 1979 revolution. Similarly, in 1938 American surveyors discovered a practically inexhaustible supply of oil in eastern Saudi sands along the Persian Gulf. The kingdom opened its doors to the Arabia American Oil Company (Aramco), and by 1949 it was producing over 500,000 barrels of crude per day.[30]

China went from importing approximately 38 billion kilograms of oil from all Middle Eastern sources in 2000 to roughly 187 billion kilograms in 2017, catapulting China from minor consumer to one of the region's top buyers (see Figure 3).[31] The Middle East has provided China with 50 percent of its total oil imports since 2000.[32] And the growth of imports is likely to continue; experts project that by 2040, 80 percent of the oil China consumes will come from abroad.[33]

As the world's factory, China benefits from cheap energy. In the period after 2014, slumping global energy prices saved China an equivalent of 1.4 percent of GDP.[34] Yet China has been more concerned about securing its energy

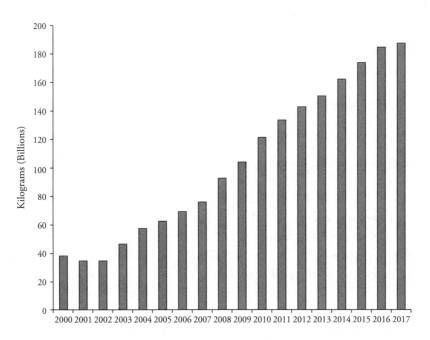

FIGURE 3 Chinese Imports of Middle East Petroleum
Created by the author using data from UN Comtrade Database.

supplies than saving cash. Rather than cutting purchases, Beijing took advantage of the buyers' market to stockpile oil reserves at a rate of 1.7 million barrels a day.[35]

Many analysts anticipate a long future of cheap oil.[36] However, even if prices were to surge, China has shown that it can use its heft as the region's thirstiest oil buyer to drive tougher bargains and maintain a diversity of suppliers.[37] In its quest for reliable supplies, China dramatically increased its purchases from Saudi Arabia over the past two decades. But to avoid the vulnerability associated with overdependence on Riyadh, Beijing simultaneously expanded purchases from elsewhere, like Russia.[38] By 2016, China actually started importing more oil from Russia than from Saudi Arabia.[39]

China's economic interests in the Middle East also extend beyond energy. China is a major goods exporter to Middle Eastern markets, as it is throughout the rest of the world. The region buys all manner of manufactured goods from China, from factory machinery, cars, and broadcasting (including cellular) equipment to clothing and shoes. Since 2007, the Middle East has imported more from China than from the United States.[40] Trade growth since 1993 has been nothing short of spectacular.[41] Between 1993 and 2016, China's exports to the Middle East grew twenty-five-fold, from $2.7 billion to $124 billion.[42] The region's share of global Chinese exports has doubled since 1993, and now accounts for 6 percent of China's total.[43]

In part because China relies on an uninterrupted flow of Middle Eastern energy for its domestic industry and transportation and seeks markets to sell its own products, it has been allergic to the region's unusually messy politics. Beijing has played a game of parallel diplomacy to get along with everyone. To the extent that US security operations have enabled commerce and transit throughout the region, China has taken full advantage.

In 2006, Shichor aptly observed that China's heavy economic interests had paradoxically "made Beijing politically weaker, feebler, and impotent." It is in this respect, he added, that "post-Mao China has been 'Japanized'—becoming economically strong but politically weak."[44] A decade later, his findings were more or less reprised in a 2016 RAND Corporation report, in which China was described as "an economic heavyweight . . . a diplomatic lightweight and . . . a military featherweight" in the Middle East.[45] And in May 2019 when Middle East expert Jon B. Alterman testified before Congress, he also observed that in the Middle East, China remains "very reluctant to use the military tools that Great Powers have deployed for centuries."[46]

However, there have been noteworthy exceptions to these Chinese tendencies, above all in the area of arms sales. Bruce Riedel, a longtime senior US intelligence analyst and National Security Council staffer, immediately highlighted one such example in May 2018 when he discussed the topic in his Brookings Institution office on Washington, DC's Massachusetts Avenue. "Yes, China's interests have been primarily economic, but we shouldn't overlook the security connection," he explained.[47] As "Exhibit A" of his argument, Riedel pointed to China's blockbuster sale of CSS-2 "East Wind" nuclear-capable intermediate range missiles to Saudi Arabia.

That sale came as a complete shock to US policymakers. The CIA detected the fifty missiles in 1988, a year after they had been installed. The missile deal cost Riyadh an estimated $1–1.5 billion and infuriated the Reagan administration.[48] The Saudis had approached China behind Washington's back precisely because they knew the United States would never sell nuclear-capable weapons like the CSS-2s, for these weapons introduced a potentially catastrophic degree of risk into the region. Owing to their inaccuracy, the CSS-2s were deemed suitable only for use with nuclear warheads (because they couldn't be trusted to land close enough to a target that conventional explosives would have an effect). That, in turn, made the missiles themselves targets for a preemptive attack by the Israelis similar to the 1981 strike on Iraq's Osirak nuclear reactor, since Jerusalem wouldn't want to take the chance that the missiles might be launched against them.

The CSS-2 story is revealing of a wider pattern of Chinese policy. China has repeatedly and opportunistically sold arms to Middle Eastern states, including both Saudi Arabia and Iran. In 2007, China delivered another batch of more accurate CSS-5 ballistic missiles to Riyadh, in a deal that was not publicly known until 2014.[49] In June 2019, satellite imagery of what appeared to be a new ballistic missile factory in Saudi Arabia suggested continued Chinese assistance to Riyadh.[50]

Beijing's calculation of risk in these deals was very clearly different from Washington's, and although China's arms sales have never reached the scale of American or Soviet (now Russian) deals, Beijing has been willing to deliver "game-changing" technologies to the region to line its pockets and advance its diplomatic agenda.[51] The 1988 CSS-2 sale paved the way for Riyadh to open official diplomatic relations with the People's Republic in 1990.[52]

For Iran, Russia has recently delivered the lion's share of imported weaponry.[53] But China also filled significant gaps in Tehran's missile and nuclear programs, at least until the early 2000s when the United States started to impose tougher sanctions on Chinese arms manufacturers.[54] As noted earlier in this chapter, China's arms sales to Iran date to the 1980s when Beijing enthusiastically, if indirectly, sold weapons to both belligerents in the Iran-Iraq war.[55] Along the way, Beijing opportunistically earned cash and built important technical and diplomatic ties to Tehran.

The first Chinese missiles to make a splash (quite literally) were the Silkworm anti-ship cruise missiles delivered to Iran in 1986. Although the initial Silkworms were not very effective against US military targets, they were followed in the 1990s by Chinese sales of improved anti-ship rockets. Then the China Aerospace Science and Technology Corporation transferred the relevant technologies to Iranian manufacturers so that they could make the weapons in Iran.[56] Together, these missiles and the fast attack boats equipped to launch them served as cornerstones in Iran's strategy to strike US forces in the Persian Gulf.[57]

Chinese specialists were also involved in many of Iran's other efforts to expand its defense industrial base, including in the areas of artillery, rockets, and small arms.[58] In return, Iran shared captured Soviet and French-made weapons with Chinese manufacturers eager to reverse-engineer them.[59] This pattern has persisted; in 2012, Iran appears to have shared with China an American-made "stealth" drone that crash-landed on Iranian soil.[60] Iran has thus proved itself a source of profits and valuable industrial secrets for Chinese firms.

For similar reasons, China has repeatedly involved itself in Iran's nuclear program. Chinese companies have found the relationship to be a profitable one, and Beijing, for its part, has worried less about the security consequences of Iran going nuclear than about the blowback that its sales might bring from the United States. Even after 1997, when Washington extracted a pledge from Beijing not to sell Iran "nuclear power plants, a uranium hexafluoride plant, heavy-water reactors, or a heavy water production plant," numerous reports suggest that Chinese firms continued to provide at least an important trickle, if no longer an unrestrained flood, of materials and technologies to Iran's nuclear and ballistic missile programs.[61] And according to the terms of the Joint Comprehensive Plan of Action (JCPOA), commonly known as the Iran nuclear deal, China was also intended to play a leading role in the redesign of Iran's Arak heavy water reactor, paving the way for continued nuclear cooperation.[62]

Beyond nuclear-specific trade, US officials found that a variety of Chinese firms, including the massive Zhongxing Telecommunications Equipment Corporation (ZTE), then China's largest publicly traded telecommunications manufacturer, evaded sanctions and found ways to ship sensitive high-technology items to Iran.[63] And in December 2018, the United States asked Canada to arrest and extradite Meng Wanzhou, the chief financial officer and daughter of the founder of Huawei, now China's (and the world's) largest telecommunications equipment supplier. US officials alleged that Meng had committed fraud in a scheme to circumvent US sanctions on Iran.[64]

The ZTE and Huawei cases threaten to upend what had been Beijing's balancing act: to work with Iran while also avoiding steps that would inflict deep harm to relations with Washington.[65] Peking University scholar Wu Bingbing observes that since the 1990s, China sought to "develop comprehensive relations with anti-American governments" like Iran, "and benefit from their balancing role, under the precondition of not challenging the core interests of the United States."[66]

American influence in the region is waning, however, at least in relative terms. The shock of 9/11 and the Iraq wars have fundamentally altered US relations with Middle Eastern states.[67] Both the Obama and Trump administrations have sought to shift US attention away from the region's seemingly intractable disputes.[68] Less US influence in the Middle East could leave a vacuum for Beijing to fill and fewer reasons for Beijing to hold back in its dealings with Iran.

Beijing's global ambitions also incline it to take a more active role in the Middle East. President Xi's BRI situates Iran, along with Turkey, Egypt, and Israel, as transit nodes in the grand web of infrastructure intended to link continental Eurasia from east to west.[69] In Saudi Arabia as well, Chinese companies have built, and continue to operate, many of the transportation facilities used by the millions of Muslim pilgrims traveling to Mecca for the hajj, and if Saudi leaders have their way, the kingdom will also transform itself into a global logistics hub with China's help.[70] All of this means more Chinese investment, more Chinese workers, and greater Chinese stakes in the region.[71] By the end of 2014, over 160,000 Chinese contractors were based in North Africa and the Middle East, so it is no surprise that Beijing is intent on developing a greater ability to protect its people and "overseas interests."[72]

The practical implications of this trend became stark in February 2011 when Libya collapsed into civil war. In order to help evacuate the roughly 35,000 Chinese nationals who had been working in the country, Beijing ordered its frigate *Xuzhou* to the region.[73] The mission was a first for China and demonstrated how overseas—largely commercial—activities can demand military protection, and how Beijing is increasingly inclined, and even compelled by domestic pressures, to field that protection itself rather than to leave Chinese workers at the mercy of other states or multinational humanitarian efforts.

Beijing has taken several other important steps in nearby areas. In 2008, China began contributing naval forces to multinational counterpiracy operations in the Gulf of Aden. With its warships operating farther from home, these missions offered the Chinese navy opportunities to exercise new military capabilities in the Arabian Sea. Beijing even sent nuclear-powered submarines to the region under the cover of relatively benign missions.[74] Then, in 2015, China took the unprecedented leap described in chapter 2 and announced that it would establish its first overseas military base in Djibouti, on the Horn of Africa.

China's security fears stemming from the Middle East also include the "contagion" of Chinese Muslims by the region's radical and violent ideologies. Chinese analysts believe Chinese Hui and Uighur Muslim communities are susceptible to the siren song of austere sects like the Wahhabis and radicalized Islamic groups like ISIS.[75] China's own repressive policies in Xinjiang appear counterproductive, likely to earn it the ire of a wider swath of the Muslim world, create new frictions with states in the Middle East, and turn China and its overseas interests into more frequent terrorist targets.[76]

Chinese Uighurs have indeed traveled to the Middle East to join terrorist groups, sometimes taking circuitous routes through southeast Asian smuggling networks. By 2015, as many as 1,000 Uighurs are believed to have joined ISIS, and in 2016 one Chinese expert "warned that 'many hundreds or thousands' of Uighurs . . . were involved with ISIS in Syria."[77] In 2014, the head of ISIS, Abu Bakr Al Baghdadi, specifically targeted Xinjiang and named China a top violator of Muslim rights.[78] One ISIS propaganda video from July 2015 showed a classroom of Uighur boys, one of whom threatened, "O Chinese infidels . . . we will come to you and raise this [ISIS] flag in Turkestan [Xinjiang]."[79] China has yet to deploy its own troops to Syria, the hotbed for ISIS, but one indirect indication of Beijing's security anxieties can be found in the widespread rumors that Chinese special operations are involved in the region.[80]

Although China looks set to play a greater role in the Middle East, Beijing still seems reluctant to transform the regional status quo or assume responsibility for issues beyond those it defines as relevant to its own security or economic interests. So far, Chinese diplomatic forays into the region deliver more show than substance. Beijing's first "Arab Policy Paper" released in January 2016 on the occasion of President Xi's visit to the headquarters of the League of Arab States in Cairo was a "vague, waffly document."[81] It used the trite formulation of "win-win" no fewer than eleven times.[82] Perhaps the paper's most significant contribution was to ratify a "1+2+3" characterization of China's cooperation in the region, where hydrocarbon-based energy is the top priority, infrastructure and investment come second, and nuclear, space, and alternative energy technologies are opportunities for the future.

Similarly, two relatively recent Chinese diplomatic initiatives—the first in Syria, and the second a set of proposals in 2013 and 2014 for settling the Israel-Palestine dispute—not only failed to gain traction in resolving the disputes on the ground (which hardly made them unique) but seem to have been little more than cheap gambits designed to promote China's image.[83] Throughout the conflict in Syria, Beijing has often followed Russia's lead in United Nations votes, but unlike Moscow has preferred to stick to multilateral diplomacy and to avoid ruffling too many feathers. Beijing has hosted talks, appointed a special envoy, and supported United Nations mediation with humanitarian aid, all as a means to "improve its image as a responsible stakeholder" and broaden the experience of its diplomats.[84] Similarly, in Yemen, China has bounced between policy positions, never publicly declaring itself for one side or the other, but appearing to back whichever side seemed most likely to bring the conflict to an end, for example by selling weapons to Riyadh while cautiously avoiding a backlash from Iran.[85]

Clinging to these decades-long patterns, Beijing's ideal strategy for the Middle East would be to continue advancing China's specific interests without taking on greater security responsibilities or diplomatic liabilities. The trouble is that China's new initiatives, arms sales, and investments have thrust it into the midst of a scrum where it will be very easy to end up at odds with one side or another.[86] Put a different way, China's newfound clout guarantees that the main contestants of the Middle East will routinely factor China into their own machinations, both in terms of their domestic economics and politics as well as the region's geopolitics. It is to these subjects that we now turn.

Iran's Desperate China Game

Sipping his morning coffee from a paper cup in the lobby of Washington's St. Regis Hotel, Seyed Hossein Mousavian's open collar and easy manner were fitting for a former diplomat now in comfortable residence at Princeton University's Program on Science and Global Security. We met just days after President Trump had announced the US withdrawal from the JCPOA, the international nuclear accord with Iran negotiated during the Obama administration.

Mousavian's sharp gaze and pointed comments also reflected his longtime role as the spokesman for Iran's nuclear negotiating team, someone considered a close ally to President Hassan Rouhani and an "unofficial Iranian government representative, answering queries or commenting for international news media about the nuclear program and the prospects for improved relations between Iran and the United States."[87] If anyone in the United States could offer a window into official Iranian perspectives on China, it would be Mousavian.

After the 1979 revolution, Khomeini's Iran famously maintained a strategic position of "neither East nor West," perceiving itself at odds with both sides in the Cold War. In recent years, however, Supreme Leader Ali Khamenei has argued that Iran's future lies in partnerships with the East, not the West.[88]

According to Mousavian, the Ayatollah's exhortations reflect Iran's desperation more than its popular preferences. As he sees it, "the West has practically pushed Iran to pivot East, especially toward China!"[89]

Today's hardline leaders of Iran's Islamic Republic continue to perceive themselves as they have since the 1979 revolution: locked in an existential struggle against the United States and its Middle Eastern allies like Israel and Saudi Arabia. Immediately after the revolution, the regime's foreign policies were driven by ideological fervor and revolutionary zeal, and in many ways Iran has never stopped asserting its geopolitical and sectarian influence throughout the region, unsettling neighbors with its support to political and militant proxies like Hezbollah.

Over time, however, Iran has shifted to a relatively more pragmatic approach, less bent on supporting the immediate overthrow of other Middle Eastern regimes or fomenting revolutionary movements and more focused on asserting and maintaining regional influence.[90] For instance, Tehran's constructive diplomacy in Afghanistan immediately after the United States toppled the Taliban in 2001 reflected pragmatism over ideology. And from Tehran's perspective, at least, many of Iran's policies are born of defensive motivations.[91] Iran experts Dina Esfandiary and Ariane Tabatabai explain that Iran's establishment perceives itself surrounded by a variety of security threats and aims, not surprisingly, "to deter states and non-state actors from attacking its territory, population, and interests."[92]

Washington has consistently taken a dim view of Iran's motivations. In response to Iran's revolution, regional aggression, and nuclear ambitions, the United States has played a leading role in imposing a cascading series of economic sanctions intended to limit Tehran's access to technologies, markets, and capital, including those required to exploit fully the country's oil and gas reserves. As Iran expert Suzanne Maloney chronicles in her comprehensive volume on *Iran's Political Economy since the Revolution*, Washington's first policy step in response to the 1979 seizure of the US embassy in Tehran and subsequent hostage crisis was to freeze $12 billion in Iranian assets.[93] Soon thereafter, Washington implemented a range of sanctions, including an embargo on military sales.

Since then, sanctions have featured prominently in the American policy toolkit for dealing with Iran, with varying degrees of success. One of the most effective was the international sanctions regime led by the Obama administration to curb Iran's nuclear program. It had "a dramatic impact on Iran's economy. The rial lost almost half its value over the course of 2012," and as a consequence, "for ordinary Iranians, the 2012 sanctions meant a reversion to the exigencies of the wartime economy."[94]

Decades of US-led sanctions have opened Iran's doors to other competitors, especially China, despite the fact that, as Mousavian pointed out, Iranians continue to crave Western brands, technologies, and education.[95] Mousavian anticipates that over time, and through a "phased approach," China and Iran will build on their commercial links to expand their military, cultural, and political connections. Mousavian's look ahead was compelling, even if it was probably offered more as a critique of the Trump administration's Iran policy—for unnecessarily "losing" Iran to China—than as an objective prognostication of future Sino-Iranian relations.[96]

In this context, China offers one palliative for many of Iran's economic maladies. From 2001 to 2014, Iran's overall purchases from China grew from less than $1 billion to over $24 billion. Adjusted for inflation, total trade between the two sides grew by over 1,000 percent between 2001 and 2014, and in the end accounted for 50 percent of Iran's total trade.[97] While China's share of total trade decreased after the 2015 nuclear deal went into effect, China remained Iran's top trading partner as of early 2019.[98]

Since the early 2000s, petroleum exports to China have been an essential lifeline for Iran's regime. China's (mainly oil) imports from Iran went from nearly $2.5 billion in 2001 to over $27 billion in 2014. Iran turned to China more than any other state to seek economic relief from the full effect of the US-backed sanctions regime, with China's share of Iran's total petroleum exports jumping from 26 percent in 2011 to 55 percent in 2015 (see Figure 4).[99]

Already by 2010, historian John Garver notes that "China had become the major foreign investor in Iran's energy sector, far exceeding any other country."[100] Moreover, when other firms fled from the sanctions, Chinese oil traders stepped in to deliver as much as half of Iran's imported gasoline, essential because Iran had insufficient refining capacity to meet domestic demand.[101] Even when US pressures mounted, China agreed to slow but not entirely pull away from most of its $40 billion worth of investments in Iran's energy sector.[102] One prominent energy analyst pithily summarized China's place-holding approach as, "Talk now, spend later."[103]

When the Obama administration enhanced the power of US sanctions by denying Iran and any party doing business with Iran access to American banks, China and Iran found novel ways to evade them.[104] First, they engaged in a modern form of barter, exchanging Chinese goods for Iranian oil. Iranian consumers complained of this system, dubbed "junk for oil" because their bazaars were filled with low-quality Chinese products.[105] Then again, the most realistic alternative—empty shelves—would likely have been even less popular.[106]

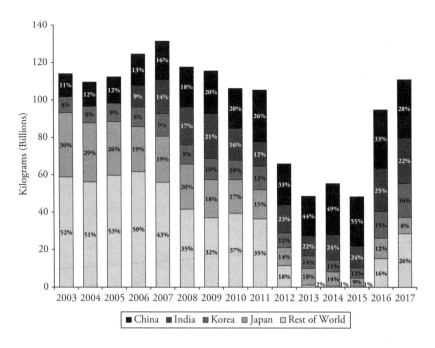

FIGURE 4 Iran Petroleum Exports
Created by the author using data from UN Comtrade Database.

Second, China engineered the Bank of Kunlun. Controlled by energy giant CNPC, the bank served as a sort of artificial firewall to protect the rest of China's banking system from US sanctions. Whereas other Chinese banks cut ties with Iranian counterparts to avoid American opprobrium, in 2012 the US Treasury Department cited the Bank of Kunlun for taking "the opposite approach by providing financial services to designated Iranian banks and facilitating the movement of millions of dollars' worth of international transactions."[107]

Kunlun was largely unaffected by US sanctions, however, and CNPC continued its use of the bank to settle tens of billions of dollars' worth of oil imports from 2012 to 2015.[108] Adam Szubin, who directed the US Treasury's Office of Foreign Assets Control (OFAC) for nine years, concluded from the episode that Kunlun was effectively immune to US sanctions unless Washington was willing to up the ante and target its huge backers in Beijing.[109]

Nor did sanctions stop a wide range of other Chinese commercial endeavors in Iran. During the 2010s, "Chinese companies . . . invested more than $5 billion in upgrading Iran's gas refinement and oil infrastructure."[110] Over that decade, China also built and rebuilt important pieces of Iran's overburdened infrastructure, like Tehran's Niayesh tunnel, one of the longest in the world, as well as the capital's new metro system.[111] All told, Chinese maneuvers around US sanctions were sufficiently effective at enabling trade and investment that at least some observers, like Iran's World Trade Center Representative, mused that "perhaps the Americans intentionally looked the other way when China threw us a lifeline."[112]

Throughout, Iranians perceived China as a second-best alternative to European technology and investment, but far better than any other option. Russia, to whom Iran has turned for much of its armaments over the past several decades, has been neither willing nor able to offer the capital, technologies, or goods required to improve Iran's energy sector, meet its manufacturing needs, or fill its shops. For Iran, Russia is an important partner, but also a jealous energy competitor (particularly with respect to natural gas) and a historical adversary dating back to the period of Russian imperial expansion.[113] China, on the other hand, is rich, energy-hungry, and comes with less historical baggage.

Yet not all Iranians are as eager as their Supreme Leader to "Look East" and welcome China's embrace. Iran's deep political cleavages are likely to be exacerbated by China's increasing involvement in ways not entirely dissimilar from what we might anticipate in Pakistan or what could emerge in a post-Nazarbayev Kazakhstan.

For now, the "winners" in Iran are clear: the regime, headed by the Supreme Leader, and complemented by the government and the Iranian Revolutionary Guard Corps (IRGC), are powerful and deeply entrenched, well positioned to take advantage of expanding ties with China. The regime exercises a stranglehold over the commanding heights of the national economy, an estimated 80 percent of which is directly or indirectly run by the state.[114] Iran's state security forces, and especially the IRGC, assumed a greater economic role in the late 1980s, when they established a range of companies in different sectors, from construction and manufacturing to agriculture and education.

During conservative president Ahmadinejad's term from 2005 to 2013, the IRGC expanded its economic role further, prompting criticism from Iran's reformists and even greater frustration within Iran's private sector.[115] The IRGC alone directly or indirectly runs as much as one-sixth of Iran's economy, amounting to roughly $10–12 billion in annual revenue in 2015.[116] Other similarly well-connected institutions, like Iran's powerful *bonyads* (religious foundations that dominate other industries), also make it nearly impossible for private companies to compete.[117]

Only radical political reforms could realistically enable healthy and sustained economic growth.[118] However, such moves are unlikely because they would also endanger the power base of Iran's powerful conservatives, and even Iran's reformist governments had only limited success in implementing change when they won political power under President Mohammad Khatami (1997–2005).[119] Iran's pragmatists and centrists, including President Hassan Rouhani, take a calibrated approach aimed at propping up the system rather than sweeping it away. Yet even Rouhani's "pro-market" schemes for economic liberalization "built around macroeconomic stability—including low inflation and a stable currency" were "dealt a direct blow" by the Trump administration's decision to reimpose sanctions in 2018.[120]

Not surprisingly, Iran's establishment figures often tout the benefits of the so-called China model: economic development without sociopolitical reform.[121] Iran's clerical regime invested in relations with China specifically "to ensure a tight grip on political power while invigorating the economy."[122] From its earliest days, the modern Sino-Iranian relationship has been mainly a government-to-government connection rather than a deeper or more organic relationship between peoples.[123] Starting in the mid-1980s, pivotal figures from within the Iranian revolution, like then-speaker of the Majlis, Ali Hashemi Rafsanjani, and then-head of the IRGC, Mustafa Muhammad-Najjar, assiduously sought closer ties with China as a means to rebuild Iran's war-torn economy.[124] Their efforts built an Iranian constituency "in government, business and industry, and to some extent in society as well—with vested interests in the advancement of the Sino-Iranian relationship."[125]

The very structure of Chinese business dealings tends to prop up Iran's dysfunctional economy. China does business through Iran's *bonyads*, IRGC enterprises, and state-run institutions like the national oil company, all reducing the pressure for Iran to reform, address corruption, or modernize its practices in ways that would invite other international partners or enable less-well-connected Iranian businesses to grow.[126] This is not to say China has had an easy time with Iran's challenging business climate.[127] To the contrary, its projects and deals have frequently been stalled or canceled because of it.

Iran's foreign policy debates do not always divide neatly along the lines of other ideological or institutional affiliations, and those distinctions are themselves complicated.[128] A pro-China sentiment is widely shared within the ruling regime, but the logic and intensity of that sentiment differs across Iran's political factions.[129] Analysts have been able to discern a fairly consistent difference between the views of Iran's conservatives on the one hand, and the views shared by pragmatists and reformists on the other.[130] To be clear, all of these factions reside within the bounds set by Iran's revolutionary state and are committed to its perpetuation.

Iran's conservatives, who tend to be most hawkish, anti-democratic, and Islamist, are most inclined to trust China and to believe that China shares a natural, "civilizational" solidarity with Iran. They perceive that relations with Beijing rest on a foundation of mutual respect. An important aspect of their trust in China is fueled by their visceral distrust of the West, and especially of the United States. That distrust is informed by ideology, but it has been reinforced by decades of tough American policies across different administrations. At present, Iran's conservatives believe that their worldview has been vindicated by the Trump administration's decision to reject the nuclear deal and restart sanctions.[131]

Rather than perceiving Chinese business practices in Iran as intentionally exploitative, Iran's conservatives counsel patience and anticipate that Chinese companies, including in the energy sector, will improve over time. For instance, they cast blame on Iran's own merchants for purchasing cheap, low-quality Chinese goods, observing that China is clearly capable of manufacturing first-rate goods for Western markets. Even in their characterization of China's repressive policies in Xinjiang, Iran's conservatives have tended to portray China as "Islam-friendly" and to lambast the "exaggerations" of the Western media.[132]

Iran's pragmatists and reformists, on the other hand, have typically been more eager to pursue economic openings with the West and more skeptical of Chinese intentions. Although they are happy to profit from Chinese investment and technology, they perceive Beijing as an unreliable, self-serving partner that has at times even played a "double game" by supporting US-led nuclear sanctions as a means to access Iran's markets without Western competition.

Whereas conservative president Ahmadinejad opened the door to major Chinese investments in the Iranian energy market, his centrist successor, Hassan Rouhani, terminated some of those agreements, citing lackluster Chinese performance. Reformist-minded Iranians have criticized Chinese companies for undercutting Iran's domestic auto manufacturers and building popular but unsafe vehicles. Some reformists have also accused conservatives of hypocritically neglecting the plight of Chinese Muslims in Xinjiang out of pure political expediency.[133]

Such debates within the Iranian political establishment reflect and echo popular views. The Iranian public was clearly unhappy with the "junk for oil" barter trade with China.[134] Iranian private companies, from textile manufacturers to flower and walnut farmers, have suffered from Chinese competition.[135] That widespread frustration has occasionally spilled into Iran's public squares, both real and virtual. After international sanctions were lifted in 2016, for instance, Iranians began a social media campaign to boycott

Chinese goods, with some citizens comparing treatment by the Chinese to that of imperial Russia in the 1828 Treaty of Turkmenchay, when the tsar carved up part of the Persian Empire.[136]

The regime's legitimacy has always been founded on populist as well as theocratic themes; along with adherence to Islamist ideology, Iran's leaders have promised a better standard of living.[137] As a consequence, when the government fails to meet the basic material demands of its people and appears increasingly dependent on a foreign power like China, it exposes itself to popular criticism.[138] Tellingly, during the "Green Revolution," the massive anti-regime protests that followed Iran's 2009 presidential elections, demonstrators were heard to chant "death to China," because they believed China had provided anti-riot equipment and "technology that enabled the regime to track dissidents' movements."[139]

These concerns had merit. In 2010, China's ZTE Corporation sold a countrywide surveillance system to Iran's largest telecommunications firm, TCI. One Iranian former telecommunications manager described it as "far more capable of monitoring citizens than I have seen in other equipment." The system would enable the government "to locate users, intercept their voice, text messaging . . . emails, chat conversations or web access."[140] ZTE described the system as a "lawful intercept solution," and according to former ZTE employees, it was indeed capable of "deep packet inspection," which enables a high level of tracking, reading, and blocking of online communication.[141]

In addition to installing Chinese-made technologies for surveillance and censorship, analyst Alex Vatanka has found that the Iranian regime emulates the Chinese state in artificially flooding cyberspace with pro-government voices and censoring dissent. In particular, "following the example of Beijing . . . the Iranian regime tasked the Islamic Revolution Guards Corps . . . and the pro-government Basij paramilitary force with producing a legion of proregime cyber-warriors under such names as the Iranian Cyber Army."[142]

Officials in Tehran have publicly declared the need for more technical coordination with China on telecommunications and internet technologies, and in 2012 Khamenei directed the creation of a "Supreme Council of Cyberspace" to censor Iranian internet content.[143] The most ambitious government initiative focused on creating a self-contained Iranian "National Information Network" (NIN) walled off from the global internet.[144]

The NIN is marketed to Iranian users as faster and cheaper, and for the state it offers the promise of near total control over content as well as easy monitoring of all users. All internet users in Iran must go through NIN to access the World Wide Web. The system appears to work; during an outbreak of anti-regime demonstrations at the end of 2017, the state completely severed the NIN's links with the global internet.[145] Perhaps not surprisingly, NIN data centers are being built by Huawei, the giant Chinese telecommunications firm that US government officials believe builds in "backdoor" access to its networks for Chinese intelligence services.[146]

Overall, China's involvement is reinforcing many of the worst, most unpopular policy tendencies of Iran's ruling regime. It is difficult to be optimistic about Iran's near-term prospects for genuine reform or revolutionary change, even though the country has experienced a spike in popular protests over recent years. Yet Iran's protesters are so far no match for a state "well-practiced in the brutal science of repression."[147] Too often, the protests are disconnected, localized, limited in scope, and founded on specific economic grievances, as Raz Zimmt of Israel's Institute for National Security Studies points out. Perhaps most important, Zimmt adds that they have yet to mobilize the urban middle class, "considered the backbone of any movements for political and social change in Iran."[148]

Under these conditions, the China factor will likely continue to play to the Iranian regime's advantage. And the more China invests in Iran, the more Beijing will itself have reason to support Iran's status quo, a pattern sure to be cheered and encouraged in Tehran's halls of power.

Saudi Arabia Also Seeks a China Fix

King Abdullah of Saudi Arabia took the maiden voyage of his reign outside the Middle East in 2006, and his first stop in Beijing was no coincidence. It marked the first time any Saudi king had visited China since 1990 when the two sides had established diplomatic relations. The Saudi Arabian ambassador to China, Saleh al-Hujeilan, remarked that the trip reflected "the great emphasis our country has attached to the relationship with China."[149]

By 2006, Saudi Arabia was beset with doubt. Above all, the durability and compatibility of the kingdom's relationship with the United States could not be taken for granted. Although that relationship had historically served as a reliable cornerstone for Riyadh, the 9/11 attacks had soured relations, not least because fifteen of the nineteen hijackers were Saudi citizens.[150] Worse, the Bush administration's ill-conceived 2003 war in Iraq had extended Iranian influence to the Saudi border, just as Riyadh had feared.

Nor was the long-range forecast any better: compared to the booming economies of Asia, US demand for Saudi oil was slackening, and there were good reasons to expect that Washington's incentives to defend the kingdom or sympathize with its concerns would wane as a consequence.[151] The combination was perilous. Moreover, because the Saudi state is based upon a "rentier" economic model—whereby its people are not taxed and expect a wide range of government services gratis, all covered by proceeds from the country's vast energy wealth—a downward trajectory in energy profits would strike the state at its very core.[152]

As a consequence, Saudi Arabia was casting about for new strategic partners even before the political shockwaves of the Arab Spring, the flood of US energy supplies brought on by the "fracking" revolution, or the Obama administration's nuclear deal with Iran, all of which reinforced Saudi anxieties in the 2010s. Mohammed Al-Sudairi, one of a tiny handful of Saudi China-watchers, explains that "King Abdullah oversaw an 'Eastward-pivot' (*itijah sharqan*) strategy that involved an active effort to court Beijing."[153] As a part of that courtship, Chinese president Hu Jintao was honored as the first foreign leader to address the Saudi Majles al-Shura, a consultative body appointed by the king. Also during that period, high-profile Saudi construction projects like the Mecca metro were awarded to Chinese state-owned companies.

In addition to their concerns about the traditional alliance with the United States, Saudi leaders faced other looming problems closer to home. Many of these were expressed less forthrightly in King Abdullah's day than they have been under his successor, King Salman, and they have clearly preoccupied the kingdom's newest crown prince, Mohammad bin Salman, or MBS. Within the kingdom, the hereditary monarchy is eager to navigate a path to tightly circumscribed political and economic reform without risking revolutionary change or ever opening the door to serious dissent.[154]

The horrific 2018 murder of Saudi columnist and dissident Jamal Khashoggi proved to the world that MBS is not pursuing a liberal agenda.[155] None of his actions is intended to divest the monarchy of its fabulous wealth or unbridled power. Nonetheless, the crown prince is pursuing modernization of a sort, as his admirers observe, and has already made some progress in "neutering the reactionary class" as part of a move to consolidate his power.[156] In addition, he has embarked on a ruthless, high-profile crackdown on some of the corruption and waste associated with the royal family and its ever-expanding coterie.

MBS's narrow expansion of Saudi rights aims to mollify a rising generation of Saudi youth and transform it into a productive workforce.[157] In an interview during his 2018 visit to the United States, MBS explained his policy moves in terms of economic pragmatism and the need to retain a capable labor force, remarking that "the environment in Saudi Arabia is pushing even Saudis outside Saudi Arabia. That is one reason we want social reforms."[158]

Today, as in 2006, Saudi Arabia tends to think of China as being at least a part—if not the only or most important part—of the solution to its core economic challenges. The first and most obvious value of China to Riyadh is as a prodigious consumer of oil, because energy sales fund Saudi Arabia's political and economic projects.[159] Unless Indian industry really catches fire, only China has the scale and purchasing power to soak up global crude supplies.

During President Hu Jintao's visit to Riyadh in February 2009, the Saudis entered a "gentleman's agreement" to guarantee oil sales and lock in long-term Chinese demand.[160] Reinforcing that commitment, Aramco has worked with ExxonMobil and Sinopec to build a major refinery and petrochemical complex in China's Fujian province specifically constructed for the type of crude pumped from Saudi fields.[161] Other big Sino-Saudi projects, like the Saudi Basic Industries Corporation (SABIC) chemical complex in Tianjin, reflect similar goals.[162]

In addition, Saudi Arabia aims to work with China to enable the kingdom's wholesale economic diversification into non-energy sectors over the next generation or longer. Diversification will be a heavy lift; as of 2017, petroleum exports accounted for roughly 87 percent of Saudi state revenues and 90 percent of export earnings.[163] In April 2016, MBS announced an ambitious blueprint for that reform effort, known as Vision 2030.[164] As an indication of his optimism and the urgency of his initiative, if not a realistic planning metric, he went so far as to declare on national television that "I think by 2020, if oil stops we can survive." He added, "we need it, we need it, but I think in 2020 we can live without oil."[165] Riyadh intends to expand Saudi non-energy industries, including manufacturing, technology, and tourism, and to build infrastructure sufficient to serve as a competitive hub for global trade and transit.[166]

Riyadh has taken steps to woo Beijing as a major partner in Vision 2030 from the start. The original eighty-four-page plan was released in Chinese among only a handful of other languages. Several months after his April launch event in Riyadh, MBS traveled to Beijing to conclude fifteen agreements under the Vision 2030 umbrella, including on "oil storage, water resources, cooperation on science and technology, and cultural cooperation."[167] The two sides also established a working-level committee linking Saudi Arabia's Council of Economic and Development Affairs and China's National Development and Reform Commission to pull China into Vision 2030 and to harmonize that Saudi plan with China's BRI.[168]

Then, in March 2017, King Salman took his thousand-member entourage on an Asia tour, highlighted by his stay in Beijing. There he signed proposals for over thirty-five projects valued at $65 billion.[169] In his official statement of support for Vision 2030, President Xi Jinping said that the "two sides should jointly build an integrated energy cooperation structure, deepen cooperation in communications, aerospace, and other fields, and discuss the setting up of a platform for financial and investment cooperation. The two sides should also continue to strengthen cooperation in culture, education, public health, science and technology, tourism, media, security, and other fields."[170]

In February 2019, facing sustained criticism in Europe and the United States for his links to the Khashoggi murder, MBS took his own tour through Asia, with stops in Pakistan, India, and China. Signaling that Saudi Arabia was keen to build partnerships beyond the United States and Europe, the crown prince received a warm welcome at each stop.[171] In Beijing, he announced a slew of agreements worth $28 billion, including a $10 billion plan for Saudi Aramco to partner with two Chinese companies to build a new refining and petrochemical complex in the Chinese city of Panjin.[172] MBS again declared his desire to integrate Vision 2030 with China's own overseas initiatives and Chinese foreign minister Wang Yi reciprocated, stating that "China and Saudi Arabia have achieved fruitful results in practical cooperation as the two countries seek greater complementarity between the Belt and Road Initiative and the Vision 2030 of Saudi Arabia."[173]

Given the central role that China now plays in global transportation infrastructure, Riyadh's prospects for realizing Vision 2030 dreams of becoming a logistics hub will depend, at least in part, on decisions made in Beijing. Chinese firms are already heavily engaged in building Saudi infrastructure. As of 2016, more than 160 Chinese companies were operating in the kingdom.[174] In 2018, Chinese firms won 13 percent of contracts across the Middle East region, including work on five major energy projects in Saudi Arabia.[175]

The Chinese are also likely to play a crucial part in a second, highly anticipated stage in the kingdom's plan for reform: the initial public offering of shares in Aramco, the national petroleum and natural gas company. Riyadh's goal for the offering is to generate roughly $100 billion, which requires a generous valuation of Aramco at $2 trillion.[176] Riyadh would use the cash to purchase other overseas assets and hedge against the uncertainty of energy prices, build and improve the national transportation infrastructure, and invest in advanced manufacturing technologies to diversify future revenue streams.[177] The public offering was originally planned for 2018, but the date had slipped more than once by late 2019, reflecting underlying concerns about its valuation, risks associated with the physical security of Saudi oil operations, lingering questions about Aramco's complicated ties to the Saudi monarchy, and the sheer complexity of the mega-deal.[178]

China could play a role in an Aramco public offering in two ways. First, although Hong Kong's political instability has made it increasingly unlikely, it is still conceivable that Aramco shares would be listed on the Hong Kong stock exchange.[179] This would make the shares attractive to a huge number of mainland Chinese investors, far more than if the sale were listed only in Saudi Arabia. Listing in Hong Kong could also shield the sale from some of the more stringent regulations and the threat of lawsuits that would be raised in London or New York.[180] All of these features make China attractive to Saudi royals, who presumably would like to sell shares to the widest market while keeping a lid on as much of Aramco's operational realities—including the vast sums paid out to princes and princesses—as possible.[181]

Second, even in the event that the IPO is listed in Tokyo, London, or only on the Saudi exchange, some significant portion of Aramco shares are likely to be sold to China's sovereign wealth fund or state-owned enterprises. Beyond that, a direct sale of Aramco shares to Chinese entities, as was rumored to be under consideration in 2017, would offer Saudi Arabia financial security if Riyadh doubts an open IPO is likely to yield sufficient cash.[182] A direct deal could include additional provisions, such as a long-term supply agreement with China, which might also prove mutually beneficial.[183] At the very least, such a deal would give Beijing an important stake in the future stability of the Saudi regime.

Some Saudi royals could worry about entering into a tighter Chinese partnership, especially one that delivers a stake of Aramco into Beijing's hands, and along with it, a greater degree of financial leverage over the kingdom. Yet, China is in many ways an ideal partner for the Saudis, who (like Iran's conservatives) have taken to touting the "China model" as a means to achieve economic and governance reforms without the messiness of political liberalization.[184] Whereas Riyadh's relations with the United States have at times been freighted with lectures about the value of liberal, democratic governance, Beijing is reliably silent on such matters.[185]

In short, the Saudi monarchy is banking on heavy Chinese financial and technical commitments to transform its economy and, in the process, to maintain the political status quo. In its courtship of China, Riyadh is a less desperate suitor than Iran, but its desire to harness Beijing to its purposes is now serious and enduring. It is founded on a sense of vulnerability and uncertainty that was only reinforced, not caused, by the West's revulsion to the Khashoggi murder. Chas Freeman, a former US ambassador to Saudi Arabia, aptly summarized the situation for the *New York Times* back in 2006, commenting that "monogamy is not enough for the Saudis anymore. They've decided to take a couple of other wives. This is a logical move by the Saudis, not one against the United States, but a step away from overdependence on America."[186]

China Enters the Middle East's Defining Competition

With its long and war-torn history, the Middle East is a wickedly complicated region that does not fit neatly into any single organizing principle. That said, understanding the hostility between Saudi Arabia and Iran helps to demystify a great deal about the region's geopolitics.

There are numerous illustrative examples. Befuddling policies, like Israel's assiduous courtship of its erstwhile foe Saudi Arabia, make sense because today's Israeli leaders perceive Iran as their most urgent threat and because, as they say, "the enemy of my enemy is my friend." Or consider Crown Prince Abdullah's adamant opposition to the George W. Bush administration's war on Iraq in 2003, a state led by the same Saddam Hussein who had gobbled up Kuwait and threatened a war on Saudi Arabia a dozen years earlier. As Saudi foreign minister Prince Saud al Faisal explained, Riyadh opposed the second Iraq war not out of any love for Saddam Hussein, but because the Saudis feared it would ultimately hand Iraq to Iran on a "golden platter."[187]

The Saudi-Iranian rivalry has numerous wellsprings, starting with the Sunni-Shia schism that dates to the death of Muhammad in 632 CE. Some of the Prophet's followers accepted the leadership of his close friend and father-in-law, Abu Bakr, while others believed the Prophet's cousin and son-in-law, Ali ibn Abi Talib, should rightfully lead. A half-century later, the split became even more irreparable when Caliph Yazid I's soldiers defeated and massacred Ali's son Husayn and seventy-two of his companions at the battle of Karbala.[188] From that point onward, the Muslim world would be divided between a Sunni majority, which accepted the legitimacy of Yazid I and his successors, and a Shia minority, which lamented the death of Husayn and still gather to mourn it every year on the Day of Ashura.

The Safavid Empire that ruled Iran from the sixteenth to early eighteenth centuries instituted Shiism as its official sectarian identity.[189] In the modern era, Iran's Shia identity remains firmly embedded in its institutions of state, especially after the 1979 revolution when Ayatollah Khomeini fused religious and temporal power in his person and became Iran's first Supreme Leader. Post-revolutionary Iran's foreign policy has routinely cultivated links with Shia minorities outside its borders, using sectarian affinities as a means to mobilize political support and advance Tehran's interests.

Most other major Muslim empires and states have identified as Sunni. In the modern period, Saudi Arabia has anointed itself the global standard bearer of Sunni Islam in one of its most austere strains. In 1925, the third Saudi kingdom captured Mecca and Medina, the two holiest pilgrimage cities of Islam, earning it an important leadership role among Muslim states.[190] The symbolic bond was reinforced by King Fahd, who in 1975 took up the mantle of "Custodian of the Two Holy Mosques" when he became crown prince. Subsequent kings Abdullah and Salman assumed the same title.[191]

The significance of this sectarian divide is neatly summarized by Vali Nasr, author of *The Shia Revival*, who writes that "the overall Sunni-Shia conflict will play a large role in defining the Middle East as a whole and shaping its relations with the outside world."[192] In addition to the Sunni-Shia split, Iran and Saudi Arabia are separated by ethnic and national differences that predate Islam.[193] The story of the Sasanian prince Firuz at the outset of this chapter offers an ancient example of animosity between Persians and Arabs.

Then again, sectarian and ethno-national difference have not always led to rivalry or violence. At various times and places they have meant rather little, and the two sides have united to pursue other common causes.[194] Prior to the 1979 revolution, for instance, Iran's Shah and his Saudi counterparts were both close allies of the United States and avoided conflict. After the revolution, their relationship has seen highs and lows.

During the early period of revolutionary fervor, Khomeini often launched into diatribes against the Saudi monarchy. He once declared, for instance, "In this age, which is the age of oppression of the Muslim world at the hands of the US and Russia and their puppets such as al-Sauds, those traitors to the great divine sanctuary must be forcefully cursed."[195] Riyadh responded with a counterrevolutionary campaign across the Muslim world, promoting and funding some of the most radical anti-Shia clerics, mosques, and militias.

Years later, however, Tehran and Riyadh found common cause in perceiving Saddam Hussein's Ba'athist regime in Iraq as their greatest strategic threat. In the late 1990s, during a period of Saudi-Iranian détente, Crown Prince Abdullah even sent a Shia ambassador to Tehran as a show of goodwill.[196]

The present uptick in hostility is also clearly motived by geopolitical events.[197] The proximate cause of the collapse in Saudi-Iranian relations dates to the 2003 US invasion of Iraq and the subsequent Arab Spring. The net consequence of these traumatic events was that powerful Arab counterweights to Iran, like Iraq and Egypt, were swept into chaos. From Riyadh's perspective, the situation went from bad to worse when the Obama administration openly pursued diplomatic negotiations with Iran to cap its nuclear program in exchange for sanctions relief. Then-king Abdullah had famously, but unsuccessfully, lobbied the United States to launch a military strike on Iran that would "cut off the head of the snake."

Deprived of its confidence in America and lacking regional counterweights to Tehran, the Saudi monarchy felt increasingly isolated.[198] Iran took full advantage of the vacuum to promote its own friends and allies in Yemen, Syria, and

Lebanon. In response, the newest generation of Saudi leaders—in the person of Crown Prince Mohammad bin Salman—has pursued an independent and aggressively anti-Iranian posture, marked for instance by decisions to launch the war in Yemen and to escalate diplomatic disputes in Lebanon and Qatar.

Riyadh is "undoubtedly obsessed with Iran," and sees the relationship in "zero-sum terms," explains Princeton professor Bernard Haykel, one of America's top experts on Saudi Arabia.[199] To gird against this perceived threat, the desert kingdom has gone on a military spending spree, disbursing $63.7 billion in 2016 alone.[200] Riyadh fervently opposed the 2015 deal that relieved international sanctions in exchange for a suspension of Iran's nuclear program, and rejoiced when President Trump withdrew from it in May 2018. Throughout the region, Saudi Arabia has financed militant proxies and governments opposed to Iran. In Yemen, Saudi forces have directly attacked the Iran-backed rebel Houthis.

For Iran, the story is somewhat more nuanced. Saudi Arabia is one of multiple enemies; Tehran does not have the luxury to obsess over just one. Iran's leaders generally place the United States and Israel at the top of the list, and have historically portrayed the Saudis as a mere American puppet. That understates, however, the core animus Iran's regime holds for the House of Saud and the extent to which its own policies have been directed at undermining Saudi interests and supplanting Saudi leadership in the region.

To accomplish these goals, Iran has pursued a strategy of "forward defense," building and backing militias in Lebanon, Syria, and Iraq to extend Iranian influence. Iran's efforts have contributed to the upending of a regional order where the United States and its friends, including Saudi Arabia, have played dominant roles for decades.[201] Iran has also seized diplomatic opportunities whenever Saudi relations soured with other states in the region, such as in Qatar or Turkey.

A revealing example of the hostility between Iran and Saudi Arabia unfolded just two weeks before the international community lifted its nuclear sanctions on Iran. On January 2, 2016, an angry mob ransacked and burned the Saudi embassy in Tehran. The incident was likely orchestrated by volunteers of Iran's Revolutionary Guards to protest the execution of a Saudi cleric named Nimr al-Nimr.[202]

The fifty-six-year-old Nimr had been a fierce critic of the Saudi regime. A gray-bearded ayatollah from the country's minority Shia sect, he delivered fiery speeches questioning the legitimacy of the Sunni-led monarchy. In one sermon delivered in 2011, he pointedly asked, "What is this country? The regime that oppresses me? The regime that steals my money, sheds my blood, and violates my honor? What does a country mean? The regime? The ruling clan? The soil? I don't know what a country means. Loyalty is only to Allah! We have declared, and we reiterate, that loyalty is to Allah, not to the Saud clan! Our loyalty is to Allah, not to this country! Our loyalty is to Allah, not to any foreign country! Our loyalty is to Allah and to those whom Allah grants authority. That's it!"[203]

The kingdom cited Nimr for treasonous incitement during Saudi Arabia's widespread protests inspired by the "Arab Spring" in 2011 and 2012 and put him to death along with forty-six other prisoners. Unlike Nimr, however, most of the rest were Sunni members of al Qaeda.[204] Riyadh and its allies in the region declared all of them to be terrorists.

Saudi Arabia responded swiftly to Iran's violation of its embassy in Tehran. Riyadh ordered its diplomats home and told Iranian diplomats to leave Saudi Arabia within forty-eight hours. Iranian authorities then enshrined the dispute by renaming the thoroughfare outside the embassy "Nimr al-Nimr Street." Nearly two and a half years later, the embassy was still shuttered when President Donald Trump withdrew the United States from the nuclear deal with Iran and reimposed sanctions.

Taken as a whole, the Nimr episode marked another dark chapter in a deteriorating relationship between Riyadh and Tehran. It also encapsulated many of the tensions that define Saudi-Iranian interactions, starting with the Sunni-Shia sectarian rift. In Syria, Yemen, Iraq, and elsewhere throughout the Middle East, Saudi-Iranian hostility has had violent repercussions. The economic and geopolitical implications of the competition are keenly felt across the globe.

The Nimr incident was distinctive for another reason as well. In an unusual bid to tamp down Middle Eastern hostilities, China sent Vice Foreign Minister Zhang Ming to Tehran and Riyadh.[205] His bland public calls for both sides to "maintain calm and exercise restraint, step up dialogue and consultations and jointly promote an amelioration of the situation" were almost certainly accompanied by more urgent appeals in private.[206] Although unannounced at that moment, Chinese president Xi Jinping was scheduled to visit Saudi Arabia and Iran later the same month, the first presidential visit to Riyadh since Hu Jintao went in 2009 and the first to Tehran since Jiang Zemin's in 2002.

Xi's trip had already been postponed from 2015 because at that time the Saudis had launched airstrikes in Yemen, and Beijing did not wish to be embroiled in that other divisive conflict. In early 2016, China was eager to keep this visit from suffering a similar derailment.[207] For the trip to proceed, Beijing needed a sufficient level of calm so as not to find itself caught in the perilous diplomatic crossfire between the Saudis and Iranians or to be perceived as favoring one side over the other. As in prior cases of Middle Eastern conflict, China once again aimed to play a calibrated, low-cost regional balancing act.

Yet Beijing's role is changing. Ten years before the Nimr execution, China probably wouldn't have thought to send an envoy at all. Ten years from now, China could well play a decisive role in any similar moment of escalating tension between Iran and Saudi Arabia. This is partly the consequence of China's own expanding economic, diplomatic, and military ties to the region. But it has more to do with the interests of the region's principal protagonists, Iran and Saudi Arabia, who are increasingly likely to perceive their relationships with China as critical means by which to satisfy not only their domestic ends, but also their geopolitical ambitions.

In short, the hostile relationship between Iran and Saudi Arabia currently frames important aspects of the region's geopolitics. In their zero-sum competition, a win by Tehran is considered a loss in Riyadh. That competition is tightly linked to the wider issue of America's role in the region, as Riyadh clearly aims to keep Washington in its corner and Iran seeks every means to resist American pressure. More than ever, both sides also view China's role as critical to their geopolitical—not just economic—agendas.

Tehran's Strategic Use of the China Card

For decades, Iran has perceived China as a vital enabler in economic, diplomatic, and military terms. Of course, Iran has other important relationships. India, for example, has been a major oil customer. Russia has been an essential source of arms and a potent partner on regional battlefields, especially in Syria. Without China, however, Tehran would not have had the wherewithal to sustain its decades-long resistance against the United States or its regional competition with the Gulf's Arab states, Saudi Arabia in particular.[208] Looking to the future, there is every reason to anticipate that Iran will place an even greater emphasis on its relationship with China as a means to pursue its geopolitical aims.

On the economic front, China has consistently provided Iran a means of surviving even some of the toughest international sanctions. This is likely to remain true. Anticipating the Trump administration's rejection of the JCPOA, China pledged $35 billion in financing and loans to support Iran's economy, including a $10 billion line of credit from the CITIC Group, a Chinese state-owned investment firm, in September 2017.[209] Not surprisingly, Esfandiary and Tabatabai concluded that "Tehran is counting on Beijing to serve as a bulwark against US-imposed isolation."[210]

Washington's about-face was warmly welcomed in Riyadh (and Jerusalem) because it meant the reimposition of tough US sanctions, including secondary sanctions on any European businesses that might try to do business in Iran. The US move left Europeans scrambling to find some means to preserve the nuclear deal and maintain commercial activities in Iran, but the uncertainty introduced by Washington immediately sent European businesses to Iran's exits.[211]

For Iranian pragmatists and reformists, this renewed dependence on China is a second-best scenario. The Rouhani government would have preferred to see the nuclear deal hold so that Iran could enjoy the benefits of commercial ties with Europe, including access to technology, capital, and trade.[212] At the very least, they believed that Iran would have been in a better negotiating position with China by having other options, especially in developing its oil and gas industry.[213]

This turn of events was consistent with the preexisting geopolitical worldview of Iran's conservatives. In Iran's domestic debate, it "proved" that they were right to see the United States and Europeans as untrustworthy, fickle partners. China, on the other hand, is "a natural strategic partner of the Islamic Republic" because it shares Iran's goal of resisting American hegemony, and only China has the economic heft to buy oil and develop Iran's energy industry in the face of American pressure.[214]

It is true that only China "has mechanisms to trade with Iran without touching the US financial system," like the bank of Kunlun, and is therefore better placed than the Europeans to seize ground in the Iranian market.[215] For precisely this reason, CNPC was poised to assume a majority stake in Iran's huge South Pars natural gas field from France's giant oil and gas company, Total, in November 2018.[216] Yet as of this writing, many Chinese companies, including CNPC, have moved cautiously so as to avoid running afoul of the United States. In October 2019, CNPC appeared to have pulled out of the South Pars project altogether, likely in response to US pressure.[217] At the same time, smaller Chinese tanker companies, including subsidiaries of CNPC and COSCO, China's (and the world's) biggest shipping operator, appear to have flouted US pressure and continued to transport Iranian oil. In September 2019, Washington slapped the subsidiaries with sanctions.[218] Iran's ability to survive the next chapter in US economic pressure will depend, in part, on its relationship with China and how Chinese companies like CNPC and COSCO deal with American pressures.

Despite evidence of Beijing's hedging, Iran's conservatives are inclined to believe that China would stand with them against the United States and its allies, and have even called for Beijing to "put pressure on Saudi Arabia in particular so that Riyadh cut its direct and indirect support to [anti-Iranian] 'terrorist groups.' "[219] Beyond that, they argued that China should work with Iran in a "serious, effective, comprehensive and honest fight against terrorism."[220] When Iranian foreign minister Javad Zarif traveled to Beijing with the speaker of the parliament, Ali Larijani, in February 2019, Zarif declared that relations with China were the "most strategic for Iran" among all other countries.[221]

Throughout its nuclear negotiations, Iran has also found it valuable to cultivate China as a diplomatic—not merely economic—partner. Facing harsh condemnation from Europe and the United States, Tehran often held out Beijing's typically bland diplomatic statements as evidence that Iran was a victim of unfair American policies, not a scofflaw of international agreements.[222] Iranians contrast China's stance with that of the United States, which they portray as unfairly using nuclear treaties to undermine Iran. In his own survey of the nuclear negotiating history, John Garver finds that throughout the process, "China delayed and diluted the sanctions ultimately confronting Iran."[223]

China's diplomatic posture could become even more useful to Tehran now that the international consensus on Iran has broken. Iran's leaders seek every opportunity to tar Washington. They benefit when China blames enflamed Middle Eastern tensions on US policies, as President Xi did ahead of a trip to Moscow in June 2019.[224]

In a further bid to reinforce diplomatic ties with China and diminish Western influence, Tehran has worked assiduously to join the SCO, the non-Western club launched by China and Russia.[225] As Iran's ambassador to Russia said in January 2016, the SCO is consistent with Iran's "fundamental principles," namely that "Iran doesn't accept the idea of a unipolar world" and "regional problems should be dealt with by countries of the corresponding region."[226]

Even though the SCO's accomplishments to date have been negligible, full membership would confer greater political legitimacy on the Islamic Republic, a quality the regime holds in short supply.[227] When Iranian president Ahmadinejad attended the SCO summit as an observer in 2005, he went so far as to propose that the group should evolve into an anti-US defense alliance, reflecting his transparent desire to use the SCO as a shield against the then-rising international pressure on Iran due to its nuclear program.[228] Although China has repeatedly claimed to endorse Iran's full SCO membership, Beijing remains nervous about finalizing that move as long as Iran still faces US sanctions.[229]

Tehran also sees great potential in putting President Xi's BRI to work for Iran's own interests, improving its economic prospects and global status.[230]

After his May 2014 meeting with Xi in Shanghai, Iranian president Hassan Rouhani publicly praised China's plans for a "revival of the Silk Road."[231] As one Iranian transportation official explained, "Our goal in the Silk Road plan is first to connect Iran's market to China's via railway for our domestic consumption and second to send Iranian and Chinese products to European markets."[232] Along the way, Iran will benefit from billions of dollars' worth of infrastructure upgrades.

In February 2016, the first-ever cargo train to run from China to Iran left Yiwu City in eastern China.[233] Passing through Kazakhstan and Turkmenistan on the course of its 6,462-mile journey, it arrived in Tehran fourteen days later. A similar trip by sea would typically take a month longer. Although the feat has been repeated several times since then, Iran's rail network will require significant upgrades to turn the trip into a routine occurrence. Beijing has already shown its willingness to jump-start that process, and in December 2017 it opened a $1.7 billion line of credit to enable the electrification of the 575-mile rail line from Tehran to Mashhad, near Iran's eastern border with Turkmenistan.[234]

Policymakers in Tehran have been thinking about their country's role in linking East Asia to Europe for decades, well before President Xi kicked off his own initiatives.[235] They know they are sitting on a corridor that links China to the Persian Gulf and Europe, which they believe should be very attractive to Beijing.[236] Railways and highways are just a start. Pipelines, especially for transporting Iran's natural gas overland, would also be major revenue generators.[237] And as two Iranian academics point out, "by controlling the strait of Hormuz, Iran is both an energy power and a maritime power," and open to a deeper Chinese partnership in ways that traditional friends of the United States, like Saudi Arabia, are not.[238]

This immediately raises the question of military ties between Iran and China. Although Russia is now Iran's top defense partner, in the 1980s China provided two-thirds of all Iranian military equipment for its war with Iraq.[239] Iran's planners might well be anticipating a similar reversal over the long run.

Iran's nuclear programs owe a great deal to China's sales and technology transfer. Without Chinese assistance, it is unlikely that Iran would now stand at the threshold of possessing nuclear weapons. Until the United States intensified its campaign to stem Chinese transfers in 1997, China was "by far Iran's most important" nuclear partner and "in effect assisted Iran in circumventing US-led international opposition to Iran's nuclear efforts."[240] From 1985 to 1997, China built essential infrastructure and shared technical know-how that helped Iranian scientists overcome engineering hurdles, including in the critical area of enriching uranium to levels required for nuclear fuel.[241]

Starting in the 1980s, Iran turned to China for a range of conventional munitions, from aircraft and tanks to small arms and spare parts. Later purchases included rocket boats, patrol boats, sea mines, anti-aircraft missile systems, and associated technologies.[242] There have been several recent indications that Iran and China have new arms deals in the works. Starting in 2014, the two sides have held a series of high-level military summits, and for the first time since the 1979 revolution, Iran hosted Chinese warships in its ports.[243] In November 2016, they signed a military cooperation agreement, and Iran's defense minister stated that "the upgrading of relations and long-term defense-military cooperation with China is one of the main priorities of the Islamic Republic of Iran's defense diplomacy."[244] As one demonstration of this upgrading, in June 2017, Chinese and Iranian warships conducted joint exercises in the Sea of Oman.[245]

It is widely rumored that China has agreed to sell 150 J-10 multirole fighter jets to Iran if and when the United Nations arms embargo is lifted.[246] Other reports suggest China could sell Iran new fast attack missile boats and cruise missiles.[247] By the original terms of the JCPOA, major conventional weapons sales would require United Nations approval until 2024, but as a permanent member of the UN Security Council, China could seek waivers sooner. Nor should it be assumed that China has strictly adhered to internationally mandated limits on arms sales to Iran. To the contrary, in January 2018 the United States sanctioned Chinese supply networks and individuals for selling sensitive technologies to Iran's ballistic missile and other military programs.[248]

Chinese-designed missiles are central to both Iran's defensive and offensive military strategies. Iran invests a relatively large share of its defense expenditures in its missile industry, a pattern that dates to its war with Iraq in the 1980s. But it was in the early 1990s that China's support really made the difference. Working with and through North Korea, the Chinese provided Iran with critical technical support and missile transfers despite the threat of US sanctions.[249]

Missiles give Iran a relatively cost-effective means to threaten retaliation against the United States and regional adversaries, like Saudi Arabia and Israel, even though all of those states field superior conventional military forces. As the director of the US Defense Intelligence Agency testified in February 2015, "Iran's overall defense strategy relies on a substantial inventory of theater ballistic missiles."[250] Without China's help, Iran's domestic missile production programs could not have developed the necessary technologies or materials as quickly or efficiently, and possibly not at all.[251]

Chinese-built missiles have also found their way, via Iran, into the hands of the Houthis in Yemen and Hezbollah in Lebanon.[252] Chinese dual-use technologies, like engines and gyroscopes, are often at the heart of Iranian-assembled weaponry, including the sorts of munitions that struck Aramco facilities in September 2019 to devastating effect.[253] US military forces have recovered seized Chinese QW-1 MANPADS in Iraq as well, though evidence linking such missiles to Iran remains circumstantial.[254] In this way, Iran harnesses Chinese military technologies to serve its regional purposes and to create special headaches for adversaries like Saudi Arabia and the United States.

These important and persistent military ties are likely to get more significant as China's own military modernization and arms trade advances. According to a report by the Stockholm International Peace Institute, which closely tracks the global arms trade, by the mid-2000s China had ingested and reverse-engineered a wide range of Russian military technologies, including combat aircraft and surface-to-air missiles, and "had rapidly transitioned into a major arms exporter." Looking ahead, the writing is on the wall: "it is more than likely that China's military technology will surpass that of Russia on all levels."[255]

Riyadh Also Courts Beijing

For Saudi Arabia, like for Iran, China's energy demand is an essential prop for the national economy. Chinese trade and investments are increasingly vital to the kingdom's bottom line. In addition, Riyadh has attempted to turn its oil sales to China into a political-economic weapon to squeeze Iran. As the world tightened sanctions on Iran prior to the negotiated nuclear settlement of 2015, Riyadh pointedly guaranteed oil supplies to meet China's growing needs. This offered Beijing a cost-free way to reduce its purchases from Iran (and satisfy US demands). In a nutshell, Saudi Arabia bought China's compliance with the sanctions regime.

Saudi tactics are revealed by a review of China's oil buying patterns. From 2006 to 2011, China's top three suppliers were Saudi Arabia, Angola, and Iran, in that order. Over the next four years, however, Saudi Arabia remained at the top of the list while Iran drifted to fourth place in 2012 and sixth place from 2013 to 2015.[256] As Yitzhak Shichor concluded from a close review of Saudi diplomatic maneuvers during the period, oil was "being used by Saudi Arabia (probably with US blessings) to engage Beijing against Iran, forcing the Chinese to do what they hate most: take sides."[257]

To be clear, there were limits to the leverage that Riyadh could extract from oil sales to Beijing. In a global buyers' market, Saudi Arabia needs Chinese demand as much as (or more than) Beijing needs Saudi supply. Riyadh was never in a position to insist that Beijing end completely its imports from Iran, and it did not. Nor did Riyadh ever threaten to cut its own sales to China. To the extent that Saudi Arabia had any leverage at all, it was with guaranteed supplies, not threatened embargoes. China's successful campaign to buy energy from a wide range of suppliers has made it less vulnerable to any single seller, even giant Saudi Arabia. During the period from 2011 to 2015, Beijing was able to substitute lost Iranian oil with purchases from Russia, Oman, Iraq, and Angola, among other sources.

Similarly, Saudi Arabia has found narrow, although still important, ways to harness its relationship with China on the military front. The CSS-2 and CSS-5 missile deals described earlier in this chapter were not the only instances in which Riyadh turned to Beijing for weapons it could not buy from the United States. The Saudis took a similar approach to the purchase of armed drones, whose sales were prohibited by the Obama administration.[258] China sold Saudi Arabia armed drones in 2014 and 2017 and agreed to construct a drone factory in the kingdom to build more.[259]

These deals are not very significant for their dollar value, which is small compared to Riyadh's transactions with American suppliers. Saudi Arabia would find it impossible to shift from American to Chinese arms in any but the most distant and hypothetical future.[260] The Saudi military is locked into US-made equipment, including its most costly, high-tech platforms, and has tens of billions of dollars' worth of arms still in the pipeline. Moreover, Saudi leaders have expressed zero interest in change. To the contrary, they are firmly invested in maintaining and building defense ties with the United States for as long as possible. For now, at least, the United States is also the only global power with a demonstrated ability to project its military forces to defend Saudi Arabia from regional threats, as it did against Saddam Hussein's Iraq in 1990 and 1991.[261]

However, Saudi arms purchases from China are significant for other reasons. Above all, they hint at the possibility that Saudi Arabia is not completely hemmed in by a relationship with the United States, in which Washington can forever limit the kingdom's access to sensitive technologies.

The head of a pro-Saudi think tank in Washington, DC, Ali Shihabi, explained that Riyadh need not be terribly concerned about relations with Washington. After all, even the Obama administration was eager to sell billions in arms to the kingdom. But then again, he said, it cannot hurt to have options, so as not to be "at the mercy of some US congressman," when future arms deals are on the table.[262]

At a maximum, Saudi arms deals with China suggest to some American security analysts the possibility that if Iran were ever to "break out" and field a nuclear weapon, Saudi Arabia could look to Beijing for help. Saudi leaders have repeatedly vowed to match Iran if it goes nuclear. MBS told CBS's *60 Minutes* co-host Norah O'Donnell in March 2018 that "Saudi Arabia does not want to acquire any nuclear bomb, but without a doubt if Iran developed a nuclear bomb, we will follow suit as soon as possible."[263]

China is treaty-bound not to share nuclear weapons and would almost certainly not wish to be recognized as abetting a nuclear arms race in the Middle East. That said, Riyadh could tempt Beijing to assist indirectly, for instance by permitting Chinese-developed warheads and delivery systems to land in Saudi Arabia by way of Pakistan. A Pakistani decision to provide access to its nuclear capabilities, perhaps in the form of "dual-key" nuclear forces stationed on Saudi soil, would not strictly require Chinese backing, but a green light from China, a permanent, veto-holding member of the UN Security Council, would help to shield Pakistan from sanctions after the fact.[264] Simon Henderson, a DC-based expert on Saudi Arabia, opined in 2006 that Riyadh "could well judge that the likely American wrath resulting from acquiring nuclear-armed missiles with the connivance of China and Pakistan is bearable."[265]

Overall, making sense of the relationship between Saudi Arabia and China requires appreciating it in comparative and historical terms.[266] When compared to the United States, China remains only a minor military partner for the kingdom, with no sign of serious change. But when stacked against prior historical periods, the past fifteen years of the Sino-Saudi relationship have seen unprecedented breakthroughs. Leaders on both sides have spent considerable time and energy building what they describe as a "strategic partnership."

Looking to the future, there is little doubt that Saudi leaders will devote an ever-greater share of their attention to relations with China. They will routinely contemplate how Beijing fits into their national ambitions, not least in terms of the conflict with Iran, even if Riyadh's influence in Beijing is limited and its connections with Washington, at least in the military arena, remain far more important.

Competing for China's Affections

Judging by Chinese policies over recent decades and by the rhetoric of its leaders, China appears committed to a Middle East strategy that avoids playing favorites among the region's main powers, incurring the wrath of the United States, or getting sucked into costly political or military commitments.[267] At the same time, leaders in Iran and Saudi Arabia will continue to court China as an increasingly active and heavily invested partner to advance their own parochial agendas, both domestic and regional. China will often oblige, and does not need to accept an exclusive relationship with either Tehran or Riyadh as it pursues energy, new markets, and geopolitical initiatives like the BRI. In the process, Beijing will at least indirectly fuel the competition between Iran and Saudi Arabia and offer reasons for the repressive leaders of both states to believe that they can put off more significant political reforms, as they have in the past.

Of the two main contestants in the Middle East, Saudi Arabia obviously prioritizes its partnership with the United States over that with China, even though ties with Washington are on fundamentally shakier ground than in the past. Riyadh will likely use its relationship with China selectively, first as an energy consumer and source of development financing and know-how, when possible as a means to squeeze Iran, and in rarer occasions as an alternative vendor of extremely sensitive military technologies.

Iran will pursue China more desperately. The ruling regime needs Beijing to save its domestic economy and to deal with external threats. Particularly after the US withdrawal from its nuclear deal, Iran has few other places to turn, especially when it comes to trade and investment. Over time, China is likely to eclipse Russia as Iran's main military partner. To achieve its ends with China, Iran holds several important attractions, starting with energy supplies and its geopolitical value as an accommodating, anti-US overland outlet to the Persian Gulf.

China's increasing involvement in Iran will likely strengthen the ruling regime's resources and tools of repression, but it is already proving unpopular. Whether China will extend a new lease on life to an ailing regime or contribute to its eventual downfall is difficult to predict. What is clear is that unlike the sorts of European (or American) commercial activities originally envisioned under the JCPOA, China's involvement in Iran comes unencumbered by pressures for Iran's legal or political change that might have held some potential to spur steady, evolutionary reform.

All told, as we have seen in the cases of South and Central Asia, the Middle East is primed for greater Chinese involvement, less reform, and more geopolitical competition. What all of this means for the United States, and how Washington should come to terms with this emerging reality, are topics for the next chapter.

CHAPTER 6 | US-China Competition in Eurasia

WHEN NINETY-TWO-YEAR-OLD MAHATHIR Mohamad announced that he would run for prime minister of Malaysia in January 2018, few observers gave him much of a chance.[1] The former prime minister had already ruled his country from 1981 to 2003, having gradually worked his way up the ranks of Malaysia's dominant political party. In 2018, however, he campaigned as an opposition candidate against his former protégé, Najib Razak. Mahathir's animating issue was corruption.

Najib practiced a brand of democratic politics laced with authoritarian tendencies, as his predecessors had before him. But Najib took it to a new extreme. He reserved for himself the portfolios of both prime minister and finance minister, and stood accused of translating his power into a vast personal fortune. Billions of dollars were diverted from Malaysia's state-owned investment fund, and a wide range of other missteps drove the state to fiscal crisis.

Even so, Najib's ruling party was so entrenched in power that when Mahathir's party won the May 9 election his own daughter breathlessly declared, "It seemed so difficult. Impossible. I didn't dare think even though I was out there and I saw the crowds."[2] Equally surprising was Mahathir's chief political partner, Anwar Ibrahim, a former deputy who, after a falling out in the late 1990s, had become Mahathir's principal political foil. Mahathir had even jailed Anwar on charges of corruption and sodomy. United primarily by their mutual desire to flush Najib from power and, as Mahathir declared, to reinstitute the "rule of law," the two made an extraordinarily unlikely pair.[3]

As a consequence, China was not alone in being caught unprepared for Malaysia's political upheaval. It was still a rude shock when Prime Minister Mahathir announced several months later that he would suspend indefinitely two huge Chinese-backed projects that had been negotiated with the Najib government: a $13.4 billion railroad deal and a $2.5 billion gas pipeline contract.[4] The blunt-spoken nonagenarian shared the news at the conclusion of a five-day trip to China in August 2018.

Although Mahathir mainly blamed Najib for treating those and similar contracts with China as piggy banks, he was critical of China as well. Speaking at the Great Hall of the People in Beijing after a meeting with Premier Li Keqiang, Mahathir observed, "We do not want a situation where there is a new version of colonialism happening because poor countries are unable to compete with rich countries." He went on to explain in an interview with the *New York Times*, "They know that when they [China] lend big sums of money to a poor country, in the end they may have to take the project for themselves."[5]

Mahathir's concern about Chinese investments in Malaysia did not end with the railroad and pipeline. Among other acquisitions, China also had a ninety-nine-year lease on a new deep-water port near Malacca to be equipped with berths adequate for cruise ships (or aircraft carriers). Separately, a mammoth Chinese condominium development called "Forest City" spans four artificial islands and was designed to house 700,000 Chinese buyers.[6]

Similar to Pakistan, Kazakhstan, or Iran, Malaysia found itself facing tough questions of how Chinese investments would play into the nation's complicated, and in this case, ethnically divided, domestic politics. In a front-page September 11, 2018, article entitled "Fears of a New 'Colonialism,'" the *Washington Post* reported that Mahathir's government was taking steps to close Forest City to non-Malaysian (mainly Chinese) buyers, effectively destroying the Chinese developer's business model.[7]

It is hard not to be struck by how quickly China's fortunes appeared to be changing in Malaysia, largely driven by an unanticipated turn of the political wheel. This was not a simple, one-sided story of Chinese strategic or economic predation. When Malaysia's leaders wanted to use China to serve their parochial interests, the door to investment was opened. After a surprising election, it looked like it might slam shut. Then, months later, Malaysia's foreign minister announced that negotiations with China to resume railway construction at a lower price point were "in the last mile," signaling that Mahathir's government was back to business with China.[8] Two weeks after that, in April 2019, Mahathir confirmed that a major Chinese-backed development project would be resurrected, with some modifications.[9]

Precisely how Kuala Lumpur will land with China is uncertain. China is too big and important a neighbor and investor for Mahathir to dismiss entirely. In any event, the episode demonstrates that Malaysia's leaders will renegotiate the terms of their relationship with China to suit their own political, national (and at times, even personal) interests.

Malaysia is not alone. Each of the last three chapters told a similar story about the importance of the motivations and intentions of states along China's western horizon. The question now is how all the pieces add up.

Making Sense of China's Western Horizon

In South Asia, Pakistan's president Musharraf originally approached China to build Gwadar to serve his own strategic agenda, not Beijing's grand designs, and subsequent Pakistani leaders have also found ways to turn Chinese resources to their own purposes. In Central Asia, Kazakhstan opened its energy industry to Chinese bailouts in the aftermath of the 2008 financial crisis, and only four years later did President Xi arrive in Nur-Sultan (Astana) to announce his "New Silk Road." And in the Middle East, the Iranian regime's nuclear tangles with the United States, not Chinese strategic plans, led Tehran's streets to be flooded with Chinese-branded automobiles, turned Iranian energy projects over to Chinese investors, and prompted the Supreme Leader to declare a preference for East over West.

These examples suggest a wider pattern: to anticipate the political consequences of China's overseas activities in any particular instance, we must appreciate the other state's preexisting domestic conditions and geopolitical relationships. Knowing what China wants, or even what China is attempting to do, is an essential starting point, but an insufficient one.

This is not to say that China is sitting still. Throughout its region—and beyond—China's influence is like a rising tide that seeps into every open crevice. Moreover, China is increasingly turning its economic ties into diplomatic, political, and even strategic advantage. Yet the specific overseas opportunities and constraints facing China are often the consequence of decisions made outside China, by other states and their leaders acting in their own interests.

To better grasp the likely implications of these developments, the previous chapters of this book assessed China's ambitions, capabilities, and history of relationships along its western horizon. Next, they explored how the internal political and economic conditions of each state would likely affect (and be affected by) its evolving relationship with China. Finally, they examined the interactive effect of China's role in the geopolitics of each sub-region.

A similar method could be applied to other cases outside Eurasia, such as in Latin America or Africa. By avoiding a narrowly functional or sectoral investigation, this approach stresses the intersection of economic, political, and military developments because actions in one policy domain will often have consequences, intended or not, for the others.

What then is China up to in continental Eurasia? In a nutshell, under President Xi, China has amplified its ambition, building on a longer history of economic and commercial activity to extend its access to resources, build its political influence, and, in certain cases, begin to improve its ability to project military power. At the extreme, Beijing's most ambitious strategists will not be fully satisfied until China achieves a dominant role, eventually displacing the influence of other major powers like the United States and Russia. Of course, some caveats are in order; this expansive Chinese vision has been only partially realized, and much of it might never come to fruition. It is not an uncontested vision in China, and it is a work-in-progress, subject to revision in its details and evolution even of its main purposes.

Moreover, even though China is increasingly assertive, it is not an aggressively expansionist power quite like Stalin's Soviet Union, or a belligerent imperialist like Kaiser Wilhelm II's pre–World War I Germany. We should not underestimate the extent to which even Xi's China remains relatively conflict-averse and conservative, reluctant to throw itself into potentially costly situations, and in numerous cases still willing to accept a silent, junior-partner role as long as China's core interests are protected. In important instances when China has expanded its overseas presence, it has acted from a sense of insecurity, for instance in 2011 when it sent a warship to war-torn Libya to help evacuate Chinese nationals.

Beijing is, however, changing how it conducts its foreign policy. Above all, China has developed a remarkable set of tools for economic statecraft. It has made itself an essential lender, investor, and trader in Pakistan, Kazakhstan, and Iran, among many other states in the region. China's centrality to the economies of these states offers various types of leverage that can be translated into political influence.[10]

Outside the economic context, Beijing has invested in new tools of diplomacy, including new institutions like the Asian Infrastructure Investment Bank, that provide China with greater opportunities for regional and global leadership. It is also in the process of reforming its own bureaucracy, for instance by creating a new foreign aid agency with improved policy planning and implementation capabilities.

Globally, China's diplomatic initiatives have raised doubts about the sustainability of American (and Western) leadership, and have the potential to drive wedges between the United States and its traditional allies and partners. This would be true even if the Trump administration were not retreating from international institutions built over decades or feuding with close allies, although those moves undeniably accelerate the process.

China's actions are not only affecting the United States and its allies. In Eurasia, they are also quietly creating new strategic options for Central Asian states once firmly in Russia's orbit, and leading influential Pakistani and Iranian leaders to perceive China as a powerful patron in the face of new tensions with India and the United States, respectively.

Militarily, Beijing is taking concrete steps that over time will enable its armed forces to act farther from China's territory. Now that China has broken the taboo of overseas facilities with its new base in Djibouti, it would not be shocking if the People's Liberation Army were to install similar bases or "dual-use facilities" in a variety of Eurasian locations. In this context, Pakistan holds particular geostrategic potential as an overland connector between western China and the Arabian Sea, although the challenging terrain along that route should not be overlooked. Next door, Iran occupies a vital position along the Persian Gulf and serves as a gateway, through Turkey, to the Mediterranean Sea. Kazakhstan, although a less likely location for Chinese military facilities, offers a huge swath of continental geography and strategically important access to plentiful energy supplies.

Although there is still little indication of a Chinese desire to position significant troop contingents outside its borders, the PLA has expanded its participation in exercises and operations that enable it to practice moving its personnel across the globe. Beijing is also developing other tools, like private security contractors and closer liaison relationships with host-nation security and intelligence services. In most cases, China is clearly eager to keep such efforts under the radar, as it has, for example, when conducting security operations along the Tajikistan-Afghanistan border.

At the same time, Chinese leadership in manufacturing and technologies will almost certainly lead China to overtake Russia as a preferred defense supplier and partner throughout much of the region. China has already made headway in increasingly vital areas, such as drones and missiles, and every time Beijing buys new, high-tech weapons from Russia the clock starts ticking on Chinese reverse-engineering efforts that eventually translate into cheaper knock-offs and increased market share. China's defense ties with Pakistan are already extensive, and Chinese-designed missiles represent a core capability in Iran's military arsenal.

It would be a mistake to see China's Eurasian expansion—in economic, political, and security realms—in an undifferentiated way. Yet even when it comes to how different regional actors perceive China and anticipate how China should factor into their own self-interested plans, some common trends emerge.

Among the region's entrenched political and economic leaders, for instance, China is an appealing, at times even essential, cash cow. Leaders in Kazakhstan, Iran, and Pakistan have all depended on Chinese bailouts in times of economic crisis. On the whole, that pattern undercuts the healthy pressure for these states to take painful but necessary reforms. China has a lot to offer Eurasia's corrupt and repressive regimes, whose leaders are allergic to the conditions on loans and assistance normally imposed by liberal Western donors and their banks.

Precisely how that Chinese support will play out is, however, a case-by-case story. The domestic political conditions in Pakistan, Kazakhstan, and Iran are strikingly different. In Pakistan, an intensifying relationship with China seems likely to worsen long-standing cleavages between the political "establishment" and those parts of society that have nearly always been excluded from power and wealth. A China-backed Pakistani state will probably become more skilled at political repression than at widespread economic development or social uplift.

In Kazakhstan, where the Nazarbayev regime has pulled off a remarkable, decades-long political balancing act, the ongoing succession drama will implicate Chinese interests, both economic and geopolitical, in ways that would have been much less significant a decade ago. Thus far, China has quietly assumed an essential role in Kazakhstan's economic future, but stayed far from the political limelight. Whether or how Beijing could be sucked into the process of political transition is unclear, but on balance, China's extensive presence is likely to exacerbate the nation's interethnic rivalries and, in particular, to prompt fears among ethnic Russians (and in Moscow itself) about Nur-Sultan's (Astana's) trajectory.

In Iran, the clerical regime finds itself ever more dependent on China, both to sustain itself against international (especially American) pressure and to repress or mollify its domestic political opposition. The experience of "oil for junk" during the last sanctions era did not endear China to the Iranian public, but the collapsing nuclear deal leaves Tehran with few options other than another desperate turn to the East. Although Iranian popular sentiment may not run as Sinophobic as in Kazakhstan, opposition groups of different stripes have already criticized the state for its close ties to Beijing, and that opposition could grow. For the time being, however, there are good reasons to anticipate that the regime has the wherewithal to successfully harness China's backing and make use of its cyber surveillance and censorship technologies to serve its own repressive ends.

Moving now to the question of China's evolving role in the sub-regional geopolitics of Eurasia, we can again draw some basic connections across disparate cases. In South Asia, Central Asia, and the Middle East, China is exacerbating or rekindling old tensions. To date, it is reasonable to assume that this has not been Beijing's intent, but rather the undesired byproduct of how states have used China to serve their own purposes.

Again, however, the specific storylines are different in each instance. In South Asia, China's tightening partnership with Pakistan emboldens Islamabad and contributes to India's fears of strategic encirclement. That encourages both sides to prepare for a future of continued hostility. China may yet find a way to use its powers of economic attraction to incentivize a more stable, even normalized, relationship between India and Pakistan, but so far most indicators point in the opposite direction.

In Central Asia, and especially in Kazakhstan, the potential for geopolitical competition between Russia and China is presently hushed up by both sides, and especially by Putin's Moscow where the obsessive need to resist Western pressure dominates nearly all other strategic calculations. Kazakhstan, for its part, is determined not to be squeezed between its powerful neighbors, and clearly seeks to benefit from its ties with both, while keeping the door open to other investors, including Europeans and Americans.

However, the current division of labor (with Russia the "gun" and China the "purse") offers an inherently unstable equilibrium. The outstanding question is whether Russia will shift to a more competitive posture—in defense of its traditionally dominant role in Central Asia—in time to counterbalance China's growing regional influence. All told, regional developments are likely to vex the Sino-Russian relationship, which in many other ways is better now than it has been throughout much of history.

In the Middle East, leaders in Saudi Arabia and Iran appreciate that because of global energy trends and the diversification of China's imports, they now need China more than China needs them. Oil sales fuel their sectarian and geopolitical competition. For the regime in Tehran, China is already the essential pillar of economic survival and, as a consequence, of political survival as well. China is likely to eclipse Russia over time as Iran's preferred arms supplier and strategic partner too. China enables Iran to resist the United States, for decades the region's most dominant external power, and to compete militarily and politically with America's traditional friends in Saudi Arabia and Israel. On balance, greater Chinese involvement will help to sustain long-standing conflicts and to further undermine already waning US influence in the Middle East.

China's commerce-first approach to Eurasia is less blatantly colonial than the imperial conquests of centuries past. Eurasian states see China's appeal among the difficult options they face; they are not being forced at gunpoint into China's orbit. Over time, however, these ties will bind. Lacking viable alternatives, states like Iran, Pakistan, or Kazakhstan are likely to develop deeper economic dependencies, their leaders and "establishments" will be indebted personally and politically to Beijing, and their militaries will rely more and more on Chinese arms. Nearly as important in this online era, their national telecommunications networks and fiber optic lines (along with sophisticated tools for domestic surveillance and political repression) will be connected to and serviced by Chinese firms like Huawei, all according to standards set in Beijing.

For these states to extricate themselves from China's influence will then be a tall order, even if the relationship becomes broadly unpopular. Just because the peoples of these nations might come to chafe under China's yoke (or, more likely, that of their own China-backed leaders) does not mean they would soon have the capacity to escape it.

Unfortunately, China's expanding influence will not necessarily bring greater stability or peace to this difficult part of the world. Beijing shows little appetite for assuming responsibility for the many existing conflicts within and among Eurasian states. China is at least as likely as Russia to act selectively as a maximizer of its own narrowly defined interests. And China's developmental model has a mixed track record.

Across states in Africa, for instance, where China tended to press a developmental aid agenda that emphasized "mutual benefit" (rather than grant aid) since at least the early 1980s, aid served as a springboard for investment, joint ventures, and new Chinese commercial projects.[11] Professor Deborah Brautigam, the author of one of the most influential studies of China's role in Africa, *The Dragon's Gift*, concludes that "in relatively well-governed, stable countries, Chinese aid and investment are likely to provide net gains. . . . In highly corrupt, unstable, authoritarian countries where governments are far less accountable, China's engagement (like that of any other country) is much less likely to produce broad gains."[12] Across continental Eurasia, one finds a great many more states from Brautigam's latter category.

The point is merely that world does not have the luxury of assuming that China would attempt to reform Eurasia in socioeconomic or political terms, or even that China will successfully pacify the region under authoritarian proxies. Continental Eurasia could simultaneously allow for much greater Chinese influence and access while remaining a hothouse for global security threats (like terrorism and the proliferation of weapons of mass destruction), political repression, and interstate conflict.

Implications for the United States

How do these developments in South Asia, Central Asia, and the Middle East affect the United States? The answers are complicated and mixed, but on the whole, it is not a good news story from an American perspective.

On the positive side, many of China's expanding economic and commercial activities in continental Eurasia pose relatively little threat to American interests in the region. In fact, the United States has often championed regional economic integration through new transportation and communications infrastructure investment. In Afghanistan, for instance, Hillary Clinton's State Department advocated a "New Silk Road" as part of an initiative to link Afghanistan with regional markets. That particular effort never panned out, lacking sufficient resources, incentives, and security, but its logic was broadly consistent with much of what Beijing is preaching as it builds new roads, railways, and ports: infrastructure boosts commerce, enhances prosperity, and promotes peace.

Similarly, the United States has favored economic reform initiatives in countries like Saudi Arabia and Pakistan, believing that such reforms can promote sustainable growth and, over time, political stability as well. Whether reform and growth are enabled by Chinese (rather than US) investment may be less important than whether they happen at all.

The United States will find other things to like about vast new Chinese investments in Eurasia, especially when they include US multinational corporations as suppliers. Honeywell has touted the BRI as a partner in its expanding Central Asian business, and General Electric has earned billions of dollars from Chinese BRI projects.[13] In addition to seizing these commercial opportunities, the United States has other means to shape portions of the regional economic integration agenda even if China plays the leading role. For instance, where roads and railways are planned and funded through multilateral organizations like the ADB (as is true for a wide range of transportation projects in Central Asia), Washington holds leverage in terms of voting power and technical expertise. That leverage offers the United States a means to encourage projects that drive economic development and connectivity without necessarily deepening dependence on China alone. Such moves should keep the door propped open to American or other non-Chinese businesses in the region. Equally, they improve the bargaining power of local authorities who might otherwise lack options other than China.

When local economies are almost exclusively dependent on China, however, the United States will see its economic interests suffer, directly or indirectly. The more continental Eurasia turns into a China-centric zone, the less level the playing field will be for US firms.[14] An example of this reality was the "Chinese Security Desk" at the Lahore airport mentioned in chapter 3, which showed the sort of favoritism that Chinese businessmen now receive in Pakistan. Of course, the kiosk is merely a sign of a wider reality: Pakistan's army has raised a separate CPEC protection force of thousands of troops to secure the sorts of investments and travel that American and other businesses have often found prohibitively costly and dangerous in recent decades. Moreover, as Chinese businesses become more entrenched in the regional economies, their familiarity with local markets, influence over standards and procedures, and dominance over vital nodes of infrastructure in high-tech, financial, and communications fields will give them an even greater advantage.[15]

The Trump administration has been more vocal than its predecessors about the various ways that Chinese overseas economic ventures have the potential to harm American interests. When then–Secretary of State Rex Tillerson spoke at the Center for Strategic and International Studies to a packed house ahead of his October 2017 trip to India, he made specific reference to the administration's concerns that Chinese investments too often displace local laborers by bringing in Chinese construction crews, and then saddle local governments with unmanageable debt.[16]

The harm to the United States in these instances tends to be indirect, and touches on political and strategic concerns as much as economic ones. If labor disputes fuel wider political grievances, instability and even violence can follow. That violence can threaten US businesses or other interests. Where crushing debt burdens force states to approach multilateral banks for relief, it is partly American funds that get tapped. And if states decide to trade equity—for instance in a project like Sri Lanka's Hambantota Port—to pay off steep Chinese loans, China can pick up assets with potential strategic value on the cheap.[17] As Indian officials have frequently observed in their critique of the BRI, ill-conceived Chinese projects can also come with environmental costs or contribute to interstate disputes over territorial claims.[18] At the very least, it is difficult to suggest that the United States comes out the winner from any of these sorts of developments.

If the implications of China's expanded economic involvement in continental Eurasia are at best mixed for the United States, the consequences of Beijing's political and diplomatic efforts are more obviously problematic. To the extent that the United States maintains an interest—pragmatic or ideological—in fostering democratic rule or defending political rights, it will rarely find a partner in Beijing. As Alexander Cooley observed in 2013, Beijing and Moscow find common cause in building and defending a "league of authoritarian gentlemen," and the consequences are "particularly grim for Eurasian countries."[19]

Eurasian leaders seeking tools and resources of repression will find China a useful partner. Not only is Beijing unwilling to criticize human rights abusers, but China is actively developing technologies and practices for surveillance, censorship, and population control that are already being exported to its neighbors.[20] As China builds a "digital silk road" of new fiber optic cables and cloud-based computing across the region, officials in states like Pakistan and Iran have in Beijing a powerful ally as they improve their tools for screening communications, tracking dissidents, or shutting down opposition parties.[21]

High-tech tools aside, the "China model" of economic development without political reform holds appeal throughout the region, where "democracy" is too often synonymous with corruption, turmoil, or inefficiency. China's own developmental miracle is impossible to miss. In some states, like Saudi Arabia, where leaders do not prioritize liberal values and their reforms are cynical moves to retain power, if a regime can win popular legitimacy without making any serious political concessions, it will try.

More broadly, new Chinese-led regional institutions like the SCO or the AIIB demonstrate Beijing's leadership and, in some cases, highlight Washington's absence. Chinese diplomatic initiatives also have some potential to drive new wedges or worsen underlying disagreements between the United States and its traditional partners and allies. In East Asia the problem is clearly more serious than in Eurasia. Chinese pressure on South Korea and the members of ASEAN, for instance, encourages those states to tread more gingerly in their ties with the United States.[22] South Asian, Central Asian, and Middle Eastern states are not currently confronted with quite the same balancing act between the United States and China. They are, however, finding more reasons to avoid unnecessary antagonism of Beijing. Not long ago, many states in Eurasia would not have given this issue serious consideration, but that is changing.

The tiny state of Georgia in the south Caucasus, for example, signed a free trade agreement with China in 2017 and in November of that same year hosted its second Belt and Road Forum.[23] This is partly an economic development play, as Tbilisi sees the potential benefits of becoming a BRI transit point. Yet Tbilisi also perceives China as a part of its diplomatic strategy to offset Russia's preponderant influence, much the same way Georgians hoped Europe and the United States could do a decade earlier.[24] Tbilisi's courtship of Beijing may not pose any direct threat to American concerns, but it does demonstrate the extent to which China offers Eurasians new alternatives for partnership and is viewed as a rising regional leader, even in countries where China feels historically and culturally alien.

China's support of regional economic integration and Beijing's own desire to promote a peaceful space along its western periphery naturally raises the hope that Chinese and American security goals in continental Eurasia will converge. In Afghanistan, for instance, US and Chinese officials have stressed their mutual desire to cooperate in resolving the Taliban insurgency. Washington and Beijing have also worked together to resolve India-Pakistan crises short of war. On paper, at least, the two also share the desire for a more peaceful Middle East and stable Central Asia, free from international terrorist groups that threaten the region and the wider world.

Yet finding common ground with China will be more easily said than done. From Washington's perspective, China is actually doing precious little to stabilize or pacify Eurasia. To the contrary, Chinese weapons—especially missiles, drones, and lesser conventional arms—help to fuel regional conflicts, while Beijing carefully sidesteps commitments that might raise costs for its businesses or diplomats. Beijing only takes serious action against terrorist groups that threaten China specifically. Nor do China and the United States always agree on how to prioritize threats when it comes to preventing the proliferation, development, or use of weapons of mass destruction and their delivery systems.[25]

China poses other security threats as well. Beijing has been opportunistic in its hunt for ways to project military power into the region by way of new bases and transportation corridors. This process is still in a nascent stage, but American strategists concerned about long-term trends fear the possible consequences of Beijing consolidating its access—if not necessarily full political control—over much of continental Eurasia. In great power competition, size matters. Access to Eurasia's resources, markets, and ports could transform China from an East Asian power to a global superpower.

Princeton professor Aaron Friedberg explains that this basic American strategic concern over the rise of a Eurasian superpower is long-standing and not China-specific. Since the early twentieth century, the United States has had an interest in preventing "the direct, physical or indirect, economic and geopolitical domination of either end of the Eurasian landmass by a hostile power or coalition. A hostile regional hegemon might be able to aggregate the resources of its neighbors and could use its preponderant position as a base from which to project power in ways threatening to the United States and its interests and allies in other regions."[26]

Historically, such "domination" meant the forcible, physical control over Eurasia's industrial and other resources, for instance by the Axis powers of World War II or the Soviet Union. China's Eurasian ambitions look different. Rather than physically seizing factories, populations, and territory and turning them to war-making potential, Chinese investments and trading relationships are buying political influence and access. The threat to American interests comes if China's influence permits Beijing to exclude American businesses from the region, if Chinese leverage forces major Eurasian states to toe an anti-American line in ways they otherwise would not, or if China begins to exploit overland routes to project significant military power westward toward Europe.

These threats may take years to develop, or they may never materialize at all. However, it is already clear that when considering economic, political, and security issues, China tends to make America's job harder throughout Eurasia, not easier. Shifting to each of the sub-regions discussed in prior chapters, similar conclusions unfold.

In South Asia, China's patronage of Pakistan has so far failed to encourage Islamabad to crack down on anti-Indian terrorists based in Pakistan. China's support for Pakistan makes it harder for Washington to coerce Islamabad on such points of disagreement. Nor have Chinese policies encouraged the normalization of bilateral relations between India and Pakistan. The risk of Indo-Pakistani war has long been a serious concern for Washington, especially after their nuclear tests in 1998. It has flared anew in recent years. An emboldened Pakistan and a deeply frustrated India are unlikely to resolve their differences anytime soon.

India's fears of China are leading New Delhi into a tighter embrace of the United States, which is a welcome development in Washington. Still, India is certain to hedge its bets and will eschew a full alliance relationship as America's junior partner, preferring to strive for an independent global role. Managing US security concerns in South Asia—including the potential that an Indo-Pakistani conflict could pull China and America into the fray—is likely to get only more complicated over time.

In Central Asia, Washington's influence and interests are both on a downward trajectory. US post–Cold War diplomacy in the region was a largely frustrating exercise, particularly when it came to promoting democratic reforms. The apex of American involvement came at earlier stages of the Afghan war when moving tens of thousands of US troops made Central Asian airbases and access routes vital. In that context, the influx of Chinese cash has only contributed to the reduction of American influence and muted already faint pressures on Central Asian autocrats for reform.

From a broader strategic perspective, Chinese moves into Central Asia highlight the strategic costs that Washington and Moscow are paying for their own disastrous relationship. US-Russia tensions have led Moscow into an ever-tighter embrace of Beijing as a means to withstand Western sanctions and diplomatic pressure. If US-Russia relations were marginally better, Moscow would likely place greater effort on constructing bulwarks to preserve its traditional geopolitical dominance in Central Asia. At present, however, Putin's Russia is not inclined to play that counterbalancing role and Xi's China has skillfully steered clear of poking the Russian bear too hard, or too blatantly, in Central Asia. Their alignment, if not precisely a "hostile coalition" of the sort referenced by Friedberg, clearly disadvantages the United States.

In the Middle East, there is little for Washington to like about Beijing's various diplomatic initiatives, and it is fair to say that China's regional involvement erodes American leverage indirectly and directly. As long as they can continue to sell to China, America's autocratic oil-producing friends like the Saudis will feel less incentive to get their political and economic houses in order. Even otherwise attractive modernizing initiatives, like Riyadh's Vision 2030, take on a different cast when bankrolled by illiberal Beijing.

More important, America's prime oil-producing adversary, Iran, sees in China a means to resist intimidation and survive sanctions. Inasmuch as Washington would prefer to see Tehran's ayatollahs deposed from power, their ability to call on Chinese support, including by making use of new tools of political repression, runs counter to US interests. New Chinese weapon sales, including missiles, complicate US military plans and threaten America's friends and allies. Over the long run, growing Chinese (and persistent Russian) influence will make the Middle East even more inhospitable to the United States.

This is not to suggest that US aims in Eurasia would be easy to achieve under any circumstance. Yet it is important to appreciate that China's involvement complicates several of America's toughest bilateral relationships, including with Russia, Iran, and Pakistan. In past decades, the United States only rarely needed to consider China's role in managing these ties. Now, not only must US policymakers factor China into their calculations, but they also need to consider how relations with Moscow, Tehran, or Islamabad (among other capitals in the region) will play back into Washington's global relationship with Beijing.

On this point, it is important to appreciate how much US interests in continental Eurasia appear to be shifting. Despite its physical distance from the region, the United States has played an exceptionally active role there for over two decades, enabled by the "unipolar moment" of the early post–Cold War and extended by the post-9/11 wars in Afghanistan and Iraq. Now, however, as Washington has reduced its military commitments to these conflicts, its attention to the region also waned, at least in relative terms.

Today, as American policymakers contemplate US interests in continental Eurasia, they tend to think less in terms of the post-9/11 or Iraq-style security threats of the past and more in terms of the return of great power competition, and especially the looming competition with China.

Evolving American Perspectives on China

In a widely circulated *Foreign Affairs* article of February 2018, former Obama administration policymakers Kurt Campbell and Ely Ratner captured Washington's new mood. They lamented the flaws now apparent in what had been long-standing, "bedrock" principles of Washington's strategy for dealing with China. Topping their list of failed US assumptions were the beliefs that "deepening commercial, diplomatic, and cultural ties would transform China's internal development and external behavior," or that "US power and hegemony could readily mold China to the United States' liking."[27]

In a remarkable roundup of expert responses to the Campbell and Ratner article, opinion ran the spectrum from "we told you so" to "we never really thought that" to "time will tell."[28] All agreed, however, that the United States is facing competition from an increasingly powerful China and that, in one way or another, Washington needs to chart a more effective path if it hopes to compete and avoid outright conflict. Where disagreement clearly lingers is over whether Beijing's policies will be driven more by a sense of security or of insecurity, the extent to which cooperative ventures are possible (and smart) in the context of a wider US-China competition, and whether a stable, mutually acceptable accommodation is even possible.

These are big disagreements, but they should not mask the broader ebbing of optimism about the rise of China that was once so pervasive in American circles. Part of the shift has been driven by China itself. Xi's China is undeniably more eager to tout its own accomplishments, and its nationalistic hyperbole "raises concerns over the extent to which Beijing will actually seek 'win-win' outcomes based (as such outcomes inevitably must be) on compromise, conciliation, and respect."[29]

Beijing's disdain for liberal, democratic values also stirs American apprehension.[30] Similar Chinese criticism is directed at international institutions that, given their origins, often tend to reflect US or Western values and interests.[31]

Alongside China's ideological challenge to the liberal order have come its more assertive military and diplomatic moves, whether in the context of maritime disputes with smaller east Asian neighbors or in the launch of major initiatives like the BRI.

So the United States is less secure about its own place in the world partly because it sees in China's rise a threat to the prevailing global pecking order. America has sat atop that order since the end of the Cold War, and in many ways, since the end of World War II.[32] As Paul Heer, a veteran US intelligence analyst with deep experience on east Asia explains, the challenge posed by China "is—first and foremost—to the long-standing US conception of its role in the international system and within East Asia in particular."[33]

To be fair, however, American anxieties also have American origins. Today's crisis of confidence would not be so acute if Americans felt their own nation to be strong, united, and firmly in step with traditional allies across the globe. That is not currently the case, and so the United States finds itself vulnerable in ways that encourage greater doubt, even pessimism, about its capacity to manage a competition with China.[34]

It would be wrong, however, to leap from these observations straight to the conclusion that the United States has already fallen into a new conflict with China, the same as its Cold War with the Soviet Union, or worse. First off, without discounting Beijing's enormous economic gains, China still trails the United States on measures of hard power and global diplomatic influence. To cite one very simple measure, in 2017 the United States spent over two-and-a-half times as much as China on its military.[35]

Second, even if the Trump administration's policies lead to a relative decoupling of US-China trade and investment, the two sides will likely remain economically interdependent in ways that the Soviet Union and United States never were.[36] Bilateral trade and investment, plus mutual exposure to international markets, give both sides trillions of reasons to avoid outright conflict.

Third, as many analysts of China's internal politics take pains to stress, we should not assume a straight-line (upward) projection of China's growth, or discount the many challenges China faces at home.[37] Even President Xi's unprecedented consolidation of power can be interpreted as an indicator that his Communist Party is grappling with dangerous contending forces and divisions within China's state and society.[38]

Fourth, when compared to the fire-breathing revolutionaries of the past, Xi's China is not launching a radical assault on the world order, but is taking a more gradual, cautious approach to its revisionism. Relative to Putin's Russia, Xi's China tends to interpret the rules to its advantage, rather than to flout them altogether.

And fifth, along similar lines, China frequently professes cooperative, risk-averse, and "win-win" intentions, even in many of its dealings with the United States, and especially in regions where old historical animosities are absent. Accordingly, for the moment we should rule out extreme characterizations of US-China ties. Better to appreciate the complexity of the relationship, acknowledging that even as the competition sharpens it is likely to permit instances of cooperation as well as conflict.

The Trump Administration's China Policy

The Trump administration quickly assumed an unabashed approach to the competition with China. For most Americans, the shift was most evident on the trade front, where the White House imposed hundreds of billions of dollars in duties, setting off reciprocal Chinese tariffs and landing the two sides in an escalating trade war. Trump's aggressive use of tariffs as a negotiating tool marked a clear break with past practice, even though previous US presidents shared similar frustrations about Chinese trade practices.

On October 4, 2018, Vice President Mike Pence sternly stepped to the podium at the conservative Hudson Institute in Washington, DC.[39] Over the next forty-five minutes, he proceeded to deliver a hard-nosed rebuke to Beijing, spotlighting instances of Chinese aggression, repression, political interference, and industrial espionage. He specifically cited China's "debt diplomacy" in states like Sri Lanka as one "of the ways that China has sought to advance its strategic interests across the world, with growing intensity and sophistication." Pence claimed that "previous administrations all but ignored China's actions. And in many cases, they abetted them."

Suggesting Trump would make a firm break with past practice, he pledged that "those days are over." The vice president then went on to outline plans for expanding the US military, sticking to a tough line on trade talks, cultivating other Asian allies and partners, and tightening scrutiny of Chinese commercial activity in the United States. He held open the possibility that the competition with China would not necessarily mean hostility, but clearly placed the onus on Beijing to "change course and return to the spirit of reform and opening that characterize the beginning of this relationship decades ago."

Pence's speech struck many observers as the clearest crystallization to date of the Trump administration's perspective on China and an unprecedented public slap against Beijing. Tone aside, however, many of the policies that Pence outlined represented iterative rather than radical departures from a trajectory established gradually over the past twenty years. Both the Obama and Bush administrations had steadily elevated China on their lists of global strategic challenges, and both devoted greater attention and resources to addressing it.[40]

As one astute State Department policymaker explained in August 2018, the Trump administration is the first to fully turn the page and embrace the view that "competition, rather than engagement" best characterizes the US relationship with China, to appreciate that "transforming China" into a more liberal society is not a realistic US goal, at least in the near term, and to begin the process of reconfiguring the entire American foreign policy apparatus to better compete with China across the globe, not merely in military terms, but in diplomatic and economic terms as well.[41]

Now China unequivocally tops the official list of US national security concerns. The 2018 summary of the *National Defense Strategy* (NDS) could not be more plain: "Inter-state strategic competition, not terrorism, is now the primary concern in US national security," and China, followed by Russia, are the main "revisionist powers" aiming to "shape a world consistent with their authoritarian model—gaining veto authority over other nations' economic, diplomatic, and security decisions."[42] China is on a path to seeking "Indo-Pacific regional hegemony in the near-term and displacement of the United States to achieve global preeminence in the future."[43]

Both the 2018 NDS and the 2017 *National Security Strategy* (NSS) identify the "Indo-Pacific" as the primary theater for America's competition with China, stretching "from the west coast of India to the western shores of the United States."[44] That geographic demarcation represents, in itself, an important shift and prioritization. For decades, US policymakers have situated China in "Asia" or the "Asia-Pacific" region. Now, by broadening the aperture to India's western coast, Washington is suggesting that China's own strategic reach has expanded and, at the same time, signaling the US intention to emphasize India's role in the competition with China. The May 2018 renaming of the Pentagon's largest area of operations, from "US Pacific Command" to "US Indo-Pacific Command," reinforced this message.[45]

To its credit, the Trump administration has never defined the competition with China in purely military terms. On July 30, 2018, at the US Chamber of Commerce, Secretary of State Mike Pompeo unveiled "America's Indo-Pacific Economic Vision" before an audience of diplomats and business leaders at the Indo-Pacific Business Forum. The secretary observed that "economic security is national security."[46] He described the Indo-Pacific's central importance to the American interest as "one of the greatest engines of the future global economy."

Pompeo then laid out what he described as an inclusive vision of a "free and open" Indo-Pacific supported by government investments in digital connectivity, energy, and infrastructure, as well as expanded financing tools to unlock billions of dollars in private investment. Pompeo specifically endorsed the Better Utilization of Investments Leading to Development (BUILD) Act. That congressional legislation authorized a new International Development Finance Corporation with the capacity to provide billions of dollars in loans for private sector US investments overseas.[47] Although Pompeo never specifically named China's BRI, his entire pitch was transparently aimed as a critique of Chinese initiatives and an invitation to Asian states to join with the United States in an effort free from "coercion or great power domination."[48]

On the diplomatic front, the Trump administration has stressed the need to maintain and forge new ties with allies and partners in the Indo-Pacific. The NDS places this goal even above fortifying the trans-Atlantic NATO alliance, citing the need to work with "key countries" in the Indo-Pacific to build "a networked security architecture capable of deterring aggression, maintaining stability, and ensuring free access to common domains."[49] The NSS highlights US plans to work with states in the region "that share respect for sovereignty, fair and reciprocal trade, and the rule of law."[50]

The Trump administration is clearly convinced that America's competition with China will be fiercest, and most conflict-prone, in the Indo-Pacific. But how is that competition likely to shape up in continental Eurasia? One long-time US official involved in China policy was willing to opine on the topic in late August 2018. Over a coffee at the venerable Swing's shop across 17th Street from the offices of the National Security Council, he explained that there was "no specific policy" on how the United States should handle its competition with China in continental Eurasia, at least when compared to the directives on the books for the Indo-Pacific.[51] In general, however, he suggested that there is "more openness to having China look west" than east.

The logic behind this openness to China's "westward look" was compelling. Above all, the United States simply does not have the same vital interests to China's west. To China's east are US treaty allies, essential trading partners, and massive commercial investments, all of which demand Washington's attention and, if necessary, defense against Chinese encroachment.

China's west is also a messy region, full of geopolitical contests, the official explained, but especially now that the United States is a net energy exporter, and not dependent on Middle Eastern or Central Asian hydrocarbons, "we don't have to be one of the contestants." Moreover, Eurasia presents a number of natural barriers to Chinese expansion, he added. Regional powers like Russia, India, Turkey, and Iran will all have self-interested reasons to resist Beijing's encroachment on their traditional spheres of influence. Cultural differences and China's own heavy-handedness mean that "familiarity will breed contempt" over time.

These are all logical reasons for the United States to formulate a different strategy for China's western reaches than it has in the east. In addition, to the extent that the United States has other pressing—if perhaps less vital—interests in continental Eurasia, Washington may still find instances when working cooperatively with Beijing pays off for both sides. The threats posed by terrorism, organized crime, and civil wars should offer at least some grounds for common cause. Even during the Cold War, Washington and Moscow were at times able to bridge their many differences in pursuit of mutual aims like nuclear nonproliferation. The barriers to cooperation with Beijing would seem less than they were with Moscow, although they will rise if US-China relations take a nosedive elsewhere.

By the same token, it would be shortsighted to overlook the reality that what China does in continental Eurasia is likely, over time, to have momentous consequences for the broader US-China competition. Influential Chinese strategists perceive the region as a zone of strategic potential, the vast "heartland" territory from which Beijing can realize its superpower-sized aspirations.[52] Via Central Asia and the Middle East, China can secure an overland route to practically inexhaustible energy supplies. Via Pakistan and Iran, China can gain access to the waters of the Arabian Sea and Persian Gulf. Rail and road networks will enable China to more easily project military power to Europe's doorstep. Of course, none of this will happen overnight, and some of it may never happen at all. Yet the prospect is hardly inconsequential to American interests.

Moreover, as recounted earlier, China's influence tends to maintain or exacerbate the principal geopolitical competitions of South Asia, Central Asia, and the Middle East, at least from the American point of view. On balance, China's influence favors authoritarian states, weakens democratic systems, and threatens political reform.

When taken as a whole, Trump administration officials are right to believe that the region along China's western horizon should not be America's first priority. It is equally true, however, that Washington cannot afford to discount, much less ignore, what happens there. As the United States formulates a specific policy for dealing with China in continental Eurasia, it should therefore be differentiated but not divorced from the global strategic competition.

Strategic Options for the United States

With that in mind, what realistic strategic alternatives does the United States have? One systematic way to approach the question is by considering American strategies for dealing with China in continental Eurasia along a spectrum, from least competitive to most competitive. Of course, this would comprise only a piece of any real US strategy for South Asia, Central Asia, or the Middle East, where the United States has other goals, commitments, and interests. Still, it is a reasonable place to begin.

At one end of that spectrum, an extreme option for the United States would be "strategic withdrawal" or "benign neglect." In brief, rather than competing for regional influence, Washington would more or less concede to Beijing a continental Eurasian sphere of influence. The logic of this strategy begins with the realistic recognition that in many parts of continental Eurasia, US interests are relatively narrow and Washington's influence is limited. Kazakhstan provides a good example of that reality, where even major energy investments by American firms like Chevron provide relatively limited political influence in Nur-Sultan.

In addition to the inherent limits of American influence, much of the region faces severe developmental challenges—both political and economic—and is populated with warring, fragile states. So why not just leave it to Beijing to sort out? Stepping into a series of quagmires and meeting the natural resistance of other rivalrous states could be precisely the cure for China's global ambition. For the United States, channeling China's ambitions westward rather than eastward could distract Beijing from the Indo-Pacific zone of America's most vital interest.

One potential problem with this strategy is that Beijing shows about as much proclivity as Russia for seriously shouldering most of these Eurasian burdens, which is to say, very little at all. To the contrary, it is possible to envision China cautiously sidestepping Eurasia's quagmires while advancing a narrower agenda of military power projection, market capture, and resource extraction. Other downsides to China's expanded regional presence—from Beijing's support to repressive regimes to the reduction of commercial opportunities for American businesses—were enumerated earlier in this chapter as well.

That said, it is important to appreciate what this first strategic option suggests about the limits of US interests and aspirations in South Asia, Central Asia, and the Middle East. At present, America has a more "negative" than "positive" agenda there. Washington is, on balance, more concerned about mitigating real or potential threats than it is hopeful about reaping rewards. The contrast with the Indo-Pacific, where the United States already has important allies and friends, is instructive.

A different, perhaps more positive, way of framing this first option would be as part of a "strongpoint defense" strategy, in which the United States would compete with China by building and maintaining America's closest relationships in Asia while taking care not to spread itself thin across inhospitable, distant, or less essential territories. This asymmetrical approach would lead the United States to play to its strengths and avoid a costly game of one-upmanship with China. In the Cold War context, the principal advocate of "strongpoint defense," George Kennan, urged the United States to focus "on areas that were both defensive and vital, without worrying too much about the rest."[53] Of course, the United States did not stick to Kennan's preferred approach; it instead pursued a far more costly and expansive competition with the Soviet Union. In the twenty-first century, the limits of American power and resources are likely to favor a measured, Kennan-esque approach to competition with China.

A second option, "peaceful accommodation," is suggested by the work of scholars like Lyle Goldstein at the US Naval War College.[54] For Goldstein, it is incumbent upon the United States to work constructively with China, to realize the potential benefits of China's growing power rather than aiming to contain or balance it.[55] The core goal, from Goldstein's perspective, is to help Washington and Beijing avoid a repetition of the devastating great power conflicts of the past. Kori Schake and Anja Manuel, two former US policymakers also looking for ways to escape the historical pattern of rivalry between great powers and rising competitors, also argue for "prioritizing goodwill" with China.[56] They note that this won't "preclude disagreements of competition," but will require efforts at "resolving conflicts in private and prioritizing problem-solving in public."[57]

If accommodation with China is possible anywhere, continental Eurasia might not be a bad place to try. US-China competition is less heated there, and the two sides share some important goals. Indeed, some US policy initiatives in the region already fall into this category, such as the Obama administration's efforts to harmonize American and Chinese policy in Afghanistan. By working with Beijing to educate Afghan diplomats and improve Afghan agricultural practices, Washington hoped not merely that it could leverage Chinese resources to support mutually beneficial goals, but also that the process would establish patterns of cooperation with China that could be expanded and possibly also replicated in other settings.[58]

Cooperation won't happen on its own, however. It will require hard work and likely some concessions by both sides. The US and Chinese government agencies active overseas were not built for transparency or cooperation of this sort. Merely harmonizing assistance programming requires an unusual degree of transparency and coordination. In other more sensitive matters, such as diplomatic negotiations over Afghanistan or Iran, the complications obviously multiply.

Overcoming suspicion is always a challenge as well. After delivering a February 2016 lecture in Islamabad about the potential for US-China cooperation on aid programming in Pakistan, I experienced some of that suspicion firsthand. A visiting Chinese PLA officer pressed her finger into my chest and harangued me with, "We know what you are doing! You are working to contain China! We will never share information about our assistance programs in Pakistan because you would just use it to sabotage us."[59]

Not all Chinese experts feel similarly, but it is essential to appreciate that neither side is currently very well placed to undertake a comprehensive approach to accommodation with the other. Realistically, especially when US-China relations are so fraught on other issues, this strategy would have to be implemented piecemeal and selectively, possibly starting where the overlap in American and Chinese interests and the benefits to collaboration are most obvious.

One variant of "peaceful accommodation" would be the "constructive participation" recommended by Gal Luft in a 2017 report on China's BRI for the Atlantic Council think tank. Luft argued that the United States should publicly embrace the many regional connectivity and energy projects Beijing has planned in continental Eurasia, but should only "support cherry-picked projects that correspond with its geopolitical rationale and ideological worldview, while resisting those elements of the initiative that undermine its strategic interests."[60] At its most ambitious, Luft's vision for constructive participation could also serve as a platform for deeper and broader cooperation with China. Framed narrowly, however, it could also serve as a more tactical policy option.

In continental Eurasia the policy rationale would be less linked to transforming US-China relations globally, and more about securing specific, tangible gains for American interests. As Luft observes, Chinese initiatives like BRI are happening whether the United States is involved or not, so rather than sidelining itself as it did when Beijing built the Asian Infrastructure Investment Bank, Washington should seek opportunities as they arise and avoid looking like the skunk at every Chinese party.

Luft's point is likely to appeal to certain American business leaders (especially in the energy and construction sectors), who would prefer that Washington help them profit from the bonanza of Chinese BRI investments. It could also hold appeal where US policymakers can achieve tangible wins from partnering with Chinese counterparts, such as intelligence sharing on specific terrorist organizations or criminal networks.

A third strategic option takes the United States to a more competitive posture with China. A strategy of "critical publicity" would emphasize Washington's use of public diplomacy as a tool to expose harmful Chinese activities, highlight US values, and mobilize popular opinion in ways that play to America's advantage. Along these lines, historian Hal Brands, who has written extensively on US grand strategy, argues that the United States would be smart to "highlight the authoritarian, brutal aspects of Chinese rule," as a smart means to deal "with an authoritarian challenger that is not shying away from ideological competition."[61] Where the "China model" of economic growth without political reform is popular, Washington could tirelessly point out its shortcomings.

In the Indo-Pacific, the United States is already implementing a strategy of public criticism. When Trump administration officials describe their strategy for a "Free and Open" Indo-Pacific, they highlight the US preference for human rights and a liberal order, and contrast that vision with an authoritarian Chinese model.[62] When testifying before the Senate Armed Services committee as a nominee to head US Pacific (now Indo-Pacific) Command in April 2018, Admiral Philip Davidson pointedly observed that "China wants to shape a world aligned with its own authoritarian model," inconsistent with US respect for the principles of "international law, freedom of navigation and overflight, and the free flow of commerce and ideas."[63]

Where China's economic and political policies tend to undermine democrats and strengthen repressive regimes, Aaron Friedberg observes that "as always, sunlight is the best disinfectant."[64] Collecting and disseminating credible information is most appropriately handled by independent news media and researchers, but the United States could do more to bolster and make use of their efforts.[65] America could invest more heavily in US broadcasting and information operations, perhaps through a reinvention of the Cold War–era US Information Agency.[66] Along these lines, the State Department already has a "Global Engagement Center" with a congressional mandate to confront anti-American propaganda efforts, especially online. If placed under consistent, senior leadership and armed with sufficient personnel and resources, an office of this sort could effectively train its attention on China.[67]

A "critical publicity" strategy could also lead the United States to develop and share technologies that would better enable foreign journalists to operate in repressive political environments and assist foreign audiences to circumvent firewalls and other barriers to posting and accessing uncensored content on the internet.[68] US officials could also develop training, education, and information-sharing programs to improve the technical quality of overseas reporting on Chinese contracts, loans, and other business deals. Local investigations and public disclosures of Chinese business and political practices are likely to be more compelling to local audiences than any statements released by Washington itself.

According to the US State Department, Congress has appropriated more than $145 million since 2008 for "activities that advance Internet freedom."[69] The United States is also a member of the Freedom Online Coalition, established in 2011 "to support Internet freedom and protect fundamental human rights— free expression, association, assembly, and privacy online—worldwide."[70] These efforts constitute a start, but given China's huge investments in broadcasting as well as censorship technologies, the United States could do considerably more, unilaterally or through multilateral institutions.

A fourth strategic option of "selective competition" would require the United States to outdo at least some of China's new economic and diplomatic initiatives in continental Eurasia.[71] Narrowly conceived, this could mean providing viable alternatives for infrastructure financing to states concerned about falling into Chinese debt traps or otherwise vulnerable to Chinese economic coercion.

As Robert Blackwill, a former US ambassador to India and senior national security official in the George W. Bush administration, explains, this approach would almost certainly require the United States to work with other allies, like Japan, "to identify geoeconomic vulnerabilities and to design resiliency and diversification efforts to address those vulnerabilities."[72] Given the scale of Chinese financing, however, Washington and its partners would need to act in a targeted and coordinated fashion, both to prioritize instances in which economic vulnerabilities are most likely to expose states to political and strategic influence and, equally, to avoid incentivizing states to take on Chinese loans recklessly, confident in bailouts from the United States.

The Trump administration's endorsement of the BUILD Act, which would create a beefed-up development credit agency, appears to follow this logic. So did the October 2017 announcement by the US Overseas Private Investment Corporation that it would team up with its Japanese counterparts to "offer high-quality United States–Japan infrastructure investment alternatives in the Indo-Pacific region."[73] A similar US agreement was also signed with the Europeans. The Heritage Foundation's Jeff Smith documents other efforts by the Japanese to use generous overseas development assistance funds as a way to outbid China, for instance in building Bangladesh's first deep-water port.[74]

Conceived in a broader way, "selective competition" would lead the United States to pursue a variety of additional diplomatic initiatives to blunt or dilute China's influence in continental Eurasia. In the Indo-Pacific, Washington's main strategic innovation over the past three administrations has arguably been its courtship of New Delhi as a regional counterweight to Beijing. Minor multilateral outgrowths of that effort include the Quad dialogue (with India,

Japan, and Australia) and trilateral ministerial-level meetings (with India and Japan).[75]

Applying a similar approach in continental Eurasia, Washington could put considerably more effort into bilateral and multilateral ties with select states in Central Asia and the Middle East. The primary US aim would be to offer states along China's western horizon realistic alternatives to Chinese-sponsored initiatives and multilateral institutions. Like with India, Washington would not aim to compel a quick "with us or against us" decision, but to demonstrate that the United States can be an effective partner in supporting their core aspirations of territorial sovereignty and autonomy. Of course, Washington will not find other "Indias" in Eurasia. As the world's largest democracy and the only state with a population of China's magnitude, India is unique. But that fact need not negate the potential for improving US ties with other states in the region, even at the margins.

The United States has much to offer, including access to advanced technology and intelligence, arms deals, educational opportunities, or direct financial assistance. Sometimes even relatively small US initiatives can have a disproportionate impact. US air pollution technologies offer one example of how the United States has important scientific and technical resources that resonate widely in other societies, including China itself.

In 2008, American officials installed an air pollution monitor on the rooftop of the US embassy in Beijing. In 2011, Beijing tried to force the embassy to stop publicizing data on the city's disastrous air quality, but when Washington refused to budge and China's own bloggers used US data to criticize municipal authorities for inadequate action against the smog, the tide turned for good. Soon China adopted new air quality standards based on the US model.[76] In India, a similar US embassy air monitoring program helped satisfy public thirst for reliable data as well as for American air filtration technologies. The US embassy followed up with additional outreach, including scientific workshops on how to tackle air pollution.[77] In both China and India, American air pollution initiatives paid scientific, environmental, social, and even political dividends well beyond the small scale of official US investments.

Outreach by the United States could go wide or deep. If wide, Washington would pursue an inclusive and expansive set of activities, making American partnership more appealing and accessible to the widest range of states in Eurasia. That approach would permit the United States to seize opportunities where they arise, for instance in smaller states of Central Asia, the Caucasus, and the Middle East where Chinese policies become unpopular or new local leaders, for their own reasons, decide to recalibrate relations with Beijing.

Alternatively, Washington could focus on improving ties with a few select partners in continental Eurasia, such as Kazakhstan, that are more clearly central to China's regional expansion initiatives but remain relatively open to forging closer ties with the United States, if only to hedge against Chinese influence.

Washington's decisions about where to compete with China would depend, in part, on whether a specific location (territory, state, region) appears likely to hold significant strategic value to Beijing. By that measure, even states like Kazakhstan, where inherent US interests are relatively minor, could become more consequential because they offer China benefits in terms of regional connectivity, influence, and access to vital resources. On the other hand, some states—especially those plagued by violent political turmoil—may actually create more headaches for China than benefits. In such cases, Washington could do well to steer clear.

"Selective competition" could also include a defensive strategy, meaning that Washington could give greater weight to its competition with China in dealings with states like Iran, Russia, and Pakistan, where US ties are frayed or fraying. A defensive "selective competition" would not require Washington to pursue closer ties with these states, much less to set aside its concerns about Iran's nuclear program, Russia's aggression against Ukraine, or Pakistan's support to the Afghan Taliban and anti-Indian terrorists. Instead, Washington would begin by considering how these states could find alternatives to near-exclusive economic dependence upon China that will, over time, likely translate into political and military dependence as well.

For instance, as the Trump administration has reimposed sanctions on Iran, US policymakers could factor the competition with China into how they treat European and Indian businesses and investors seeking to work in Iran. In some cases, it could be smarter to constrain but not threaten wholesale these non-Chinese channels of access and, indirectly, of influence in Iran.

Turning to the Russian case, Washington could aim to drive a wedge between Moscow and Beijing, for instance by publicly calling attention to the many ways in which China is displacing Russia from military and diplomatic leadership in Eurasia, or by stressing the political implications of Russia's growing economic dependence on China. The success of this effort would depend less on "creating" friction between Moscow and Beijing where none exists, but on shining a light on sensitive issues that Xi and Putin would otherwise try to sweep under the carpet.

In the case of Pakistan, US officials could emphasize the issue of territorial sovereignty, where Pakistanis are already sensitive to Chinese encroachments, as a means to encourage some distance between Islamabad and Beijing. Once again, the goal would not necessarily be to tighten links between Islamabad and Washington, but only to point out natural areas of Pakistani political discomfort in ways that could make Islamabad more circumspect about its vulnerability to China.

Finally, there is the US strategic option of "militarized competition." Each of the previous options emphasizes diplomatic and economic tools more than military ones. This reflects the current reality that Chinese policies in continental Eurasia have been less militarized, and are in that respect quite unlike the disputes and arms races of the Indo-Pacific (especially the South and East China Seas).

Yet it is possible to anticipate that in time China's military footprint across continental Eurasia will expand in more open and dramatic ways. China's new base at Djibouti is only a start. If China were to develop dual-use ports or bases along Pakistan's Arabian Sea coast, or set up a permanent presence in Iran along the Strait of Hormuz, Washington would have to consider its own military responses. The threat to American interests need not be direct to warrant a response; China's military presence could just limit the ease with which the United States moves its own forces to and through the region in the event of a war or other contingency.

At the very least, US officials would need to determine whether new Chinese military initiatives demand attention in the first place, if they can be peacefully accommodated, if they are likely to prompt countermoves by other states (like India, Saudi Arabia, or Russia), and whether they alter the relative priority that the United States should place on military operations in continental Eurasia as compared to the world's other regions. Beyond that, US officials could develop new partnerships and alliances with regional powers, both as a means to secure American military access and to share the military burden. Finally, the US military and intelligence community could invest in technologies, platforms, and personnel that would allow them to respond effectively to Chinese forces in this new regional theater. Such investments could be costly, however, and would first require a wider strategic and political debate over American priorities.

An American Strategy

These strategic options, from "benign neglect" to "militarized competition," fall along a spectrum, but they also comprise a menu from which US policymakers will need to pick and choose over time, recalibrating according to their shifting preferences and in response to Chinese actions. As the broader shape of the US-China competition is not set in stone, neither can Washington settle on a single, narrow path.

In practical terms, some of these policy options are likely to be mutually exclusive. For instance, just as the Trump administration's trade war with China cast a dark shadow over US-China relations in many other sectors, it would be challenging to promote "peaceful accommodation" initiatives in instances where Washington is simultaneously waging a campaign of "critical publicity." Prioritizing aims and appreciating how one policy may foreclose another is therefore essential.

US policymakers will also need to revise their policies in the face of shifting realities on the ground in continental Eurasia. As the cases in this book demonstrate, the character of China's evolving role in South Asia, Central Asia, and the Middle East is contingent on local decisions, interests, relationships, and conflicts.

Even if America's primary global strategic concern is China, an effective policy response requires filtering the competition through the sieve of local realities. Rather than developing a global, one-size-fits-all strategy, Washington needs to develop differentiated state-by-state and sub-regional policies. The more attuned US policymakers are to local developments, the better equipped they will be to anticipate where and how Beijing is likely to make strategic inroads overseas.

The alternative would be a mindlessly competitive US strategy, in which every Chinese initiative requires an American response. An example of this tendency was on display in the Malaysia story that opened this chapter. As the new Mahathir government was struggling with how to deal with China, the *Washington Post*'s editorial board chastised the Trump administration for launching "a new Indo-Pacific development program with a paltry $115 million in funding," and went on to suggest that "a real alternative for countries like Malaysia will require far more than that."[78] The *Post*'s logic was clear: China is delivering major infrastructure investments in the region. The United States is in a global competition with China. To win the competition, Washington should outspend China.

The logic proposed by this book is quite different. The United States would be better advised not to ape Chinese initiatives, whether by matching dollars for yuan in infrastructure investments or otherwise. Instead, in continental Eurasia the United States should select carefully its theaters of competition, remain open to the possibility of at least tactical cooperation with Beijing, pursue lower-cost initiatives likely to win local partners and drive wedges among adversaries, and invest in the capacity to compete militarily over the long haul if necessary.

To succeed, American policy and intelligence analysts need to devote at least as much attention to figuring out how "Eurasians" perceive and deal with China as they do to tracking Chinese initiatives in the region. At present, this is not the case, judging by the large and rapidly growing body of research on Beijing's regional and global initiatives, compared to the paucity of work on how other Eurasian states factor China into their own economic, political, and strategic calculations. The BRI, in particular, draws a disproportionate share of attention, and is too often framed uncritically and narrowly in terms of regional connectivity and infrastructure projects, without adequate attention to historical, political, or strategic context.

US policymakers need to take local political-economic conditions and strategic competitions more seriously, and should at least attempt to understand them as the states of the region do. Sometimes this should lead the United States to support Chinese-backed investment schemes because they are intelligently linked to local, national, and regional development plans. Washington would be smart to help Eurasian states develop their own technical capabilities to judge the value of Chinese investments, negotiate the most beneficial deals, and anticipate the long-term consequences of loans and other more complicated financial arrangements.[79] Washington has already undertaken similar steps in southeast Asia. In 2018, an expert team from the US Agency for International Development provided technical advice to Myanmar as it renegotiated terms for a multibillion-dollar Chinese-funded deep-water port and industrial zone.[80]

Americans need to be realistic about the central role China now plays in the global economy. Energy producers like Saudi Arabia and Kazakhstan cannot help seeing China as an essential consumer, and Washington should not expect otherwise. Nor should Washington expect Eurasians to "buy American" unless American goods and services are competitive in ways Eurasians value relative to Chinese alternatives. Washington should not even assume that Eurasian states fear China's influence or feel vulnerable to Chinese interference any more than they already fear or resent other external powers such as Russia (or in some cases, even the United States itself).

The Trump administration's global effort to steer states away from buying Huawei wireless equipment illustrates the policy challenge facing Washington. Even close American partners like the United Kingdom (not to mention a number of US telecommunications providers) have found that Huawei products offer an attractive value for money.[81] At present, neither American nor European firms can outdo Huawei's 5G networks. Moreover, many Eurasian states assume Western equipment providers could just as well be penetrated by American spy agencies, have no greater reason to fear that China would monitor or sabotage their networks, and prefer not to choose sides in a commercial competition between Western and Chinese companies. If Washington is serious about keeping China from dominating the Eurasian telecommunications market, it will need to offer something better than a blunt "with us or against us" message.[82]

At times, appreciating the "local rules" of Eurasia may mean that the United States should stand aside and watch corrupt regimes saddle themselves with Chinese debt, spurring a popular backlash. Or it may mean ignoring Chinese investments altogether and focusing on what Eurasian leaders and their people value more, such as educational opportunities, clean drinking water, arms sales, or budgetary support. Fortunately, the United States still has many cards to play in all of these areas. American universities, in particular, remain the envy of the world, attractive to students and professors eager to engage in cutting-edge research and to be immersed in the free flow of ideas. The contrast even with the very best universities located in illiberal societies, including in China, is stark. As a source of global power and influence, America's universities should not be underestimated (or under-resourced) by US policymakers.

At times, Washington will have pressing interests in Eurasia that should not be subordinated to its global competition with China. For example, US security concerns in South Asia, from terrorism to the war in Afghanistan, are significant in and of themselves. Averting a nuclear war between India and Pakistan can (and should) assume an urgency and importance ahead of the long-term strategic competition with China. Where Washington and Beijing can work together on such issues, both could find advantage.

By better understanding the specific interests and motivations of Eurasian leaders, US policymakers can view states not merely as "pro" or "anti" China, but as more or less inclined to see value in Chinese solutions to their domestic and strategic challenges. The distinction is crucial because it clarifies the fact that where the United States (or other powers) bring better options to the table, states are inclined to turn to them instead. China's appeal to other states tends to flow not from ideological conviction or solidarity, but from Beijing's deep pockets and claims to "non-interference." This is a powerful combination, but not an invincible one.

It is also a good reminder that no state in the region is primarily concerned with the US-China competition, but all will be seeking ways to advance their own purposes by it. That, in turn, suggests the United States should avoid being suckered into expensive relationships with states simply because their leaders threaten to seek closer Chinese ties. In continental Eurasia, especially, Washington often enjoys the luxury to call such bluffs. When considering where to compete with China, US policymakers should prioritize issues of inherent national interest over competition for the sake of competition.

All of this is not to discount the strategic significance of Beijing's growing presence and influence in continental Eurasia. China enjoys a critical advantage in proximity. The United States will need to seize fleeting openings for influence, sometimes at the margins. In Kazakhstan, for instance, pressure from both Moscow and Beijing has encouraged leaders in Nur-Sultan (Astana) to seek ways to "loosen their geopolitical constraints," and this, as scholars from the Carnegie Endowment for International Peace have astutely recognized, creates "opportunities for carefully calibrated engagement" by the United States, to include trade and investment as well as support for certain reforms in the economic and security sectors.[83]

Elsewhere, like in Pakistan, Iran, and Russia, the United States would be smart to appreciate that widespread, if latent, suspicion of China (some, unfortunately, born of pure racism) will likely prop the door open to narrow American overtures. Over the long run, it will not serve the US interest to so punish these lesser adversaries that they have nowhere to turn for help but Beijing. That said, balancing the value of accommodation against clear and present US frustrations with Moscow, Tehran, and Islamabad will not be easy.

China also enjoys advantages in dealing with repressive and autocratic regimes. Where leaders and other elites are purely concerned with their own gains rather than some conception of the national interest, they are more easily "captured" through outright or indirect bribery.[84] Beijing plays that game effectively and ruthlessly. China's cultivation of ties with the Pakistani establishment, for instance, has built a powerful cheering squad that drowns out or stifles popular criticism of China. In many states, China has won over ruling parties and influential business leaders who stand to gain from the relationship even as the wider population remains skeptical or even actively Sinophobic. Beijing is also, like Moscow, increasingly skilled at controlling old-fashioned airwaves and new media, so it will invariably turn these tools to the project of cultivating public opinion.[85] These tools can be deployed in liberal democracies as well as illiberal states.

As a rule, the United States would only taint itself by attempting to match China's insidious support to illiberal regimes and corrupt elites. At the opposite extreme, when US diplomats and leaders publicly criticize the repressive policies of other states, they run the risk of alienating strongmen in ways that prove costly to other American aims and even, if they are not careful, of undermining the legitimacy of local opposition groups. Unfortunately, many of Washington's past practices for indirectly supporting liberal activists within illiberal societies, such as supporting foundations that deliver grants and training to nongovernmental organizations and research institutions, are finding it increasingly difficult to operate overseas. Across the globe, authoritarian and authoritarian-leaning states have imposed new laws and regulations that limit the effectiveness of these groups or even ban them outright.

America's policy tools are therefore limited, but Washington should redouble its efforts to make technical tools for information access more universal and less easily censored.[86] The US government needs to work with partners in the private sector to build and disseminate new workarounds in the game of cat and mouse with state censors increasingly backed by Chinese tactics and technologies. By arming local journalists and opposition groups with unfettered access to information and audiences, corrupt games of "elite capture" are more likely to be unmasked.

Conclusion

For millennia, China has been linked to other parts of Eurasia via overland and maritime flows of people, goods, and ideas. Now, however, Beijing is developing an unprecedented, thoroughly modern presence across the continent, spearheaded by economic relationships but not limited to them. China was once a minor, even peripheral factor in US policy calculations in South Asia, Central Asia, and the Middle East. Now and into the future Beijing will play an increasingly significant role.

Yet China's new initiatives and ambitions are playing out against the backdrop of Eurasian realities, some long-standing and others changeable. Eurasian leaders are self-interested, their societies are motivated by strong domestic preferences and riven by political cleavages, and their states are engaged, sometimes obsessively, in competitive regional relationships. Beijing cannot run roughshod over these realities or avoid them entirely. To the contrary, China's own interests will be shaped and implicated in regional dynamics in new, complicated ways.

For US policymakers, a clear grasp of local histories, interests, and relationships will be essential to advance America's specific diplomatic, economic, and security interests in Eurasia, whether in common cause with Beijing or when working at cross purposes. Likewise, that fine-grained appreciation for the Eurasian theater will prove invaluable in the global geopolitical competition with China that now looms in America's future.

NOTES

Preface

1. This account is confirmed by a retired senior Pakistani diplomat, who said the "Chinese agreed to finance and build the port 'as a favor' to Pakistan, not out of recognition of the port's commercial or strategic value," according to Arif Rafiq in "The China-Pakistan Economic Corridor: Barriers and Impact," United States Institute of Peace, 25 October 2017, https://www.usip.org/publications/2017/10/china-pakistan-economic-corridor, p. 6. Also during his trip to Beijing, Musharraf was quoted as saying that "cooperation and friendship between the two countries should be cemented in the new century." From "Musharraf Gets China's 'Unconditional Support,' " *The Hindu*, 19 January 2000, https://www.thehindu.com/2000/01/19/stories/01190006.htm.

2. Michael Dorgan, "China Rolls Out Red Carpet for Pakistani Leader," *San Jose Mercury News*, 19 January 2000.

3. Author conversation, Alexandria, Virginia, 13 April 2017.

4. Musharraf confirmed that the Chinese were not expecting his request and that it was entirely his idea. He related that he had researched the potential for Gwadar as a deep sea port and had also looked into the challenges of building pipelines and railways overland from China to Pakistan before raising these ideas to an initially skeptical, but never dismissive, Chinese leadership. (Author conversation, Alexandria, Virginia, 13 April 2017.)

5. David R. Sands, "China Suspected in Port Deal—Beijing Naval Vessels Expected to Dock at Pakistani Site," *Washington Times*, 31 May 2001.

6. "Gwadar Project Launched," *Dawn*, 22 March 2002.

7. Andrew Small, *The China-Pakistan Axis* (Oxford: Oxford University Press, 2015), pp. 100–105.

8. The original "string of pearls" report was Juli A. MacDonald, Amy Donahue, and Bethany Danyluk, "Energy Futures in Asia: Final Report," Booz Allen Hamilton, 2004.

9. Robert D. Kaplan, *Monsoon: The Indian Ocean and the Future of American Power* (New York: Random House, 2010), p. 69.

Chapter 1

1. In fact, as noted in chapter 3, the emissary from the Han court sought military allies to assist in fierce wars along China's expanding imperial borders.

2. Nadège Rolland, "China's New Silk Road," National Bureau of Asian Research Commentary, 12 February 2015, https://www.nbr.org/publication/chinas-new-silk-road/.

3. "Vision and Actions on Jointly Building Silk Road Economic Belt and 21st-Century Maritime Silk Road," Report Issued by the National Development and Reform Commission, Ministry of Foreign Affairs, and Ministry of Commerce of the People's Republic of China, March 2015, http://en.ndrc.gov.cn/newsrelease/201503/t20150330_669367.html.

4. "Towards a Community of Common Destiny," *China Daily*, 30 March 2015, http://europe.chinadaily.com.cn/opinion/2015-03/30/content_19946478.htm.

5. Wade Shepard, *Ghost Cities of China: The Story of Cities without People in the World's Most Populated Country* (London: Zed Books, 2015).

6. Walter Russell Mead describes China's export of surplus economic capacity as a "Lenin trap" and foreshadows how China's overcapacity can lead to "imperialism with Chinese characteristics." See "Imperialism Will Be Dangerous for China," *Wall Street Journal*, 17 September 2018, https://www.wsj.com/articles/imperialism-will-be-dangerous-for-china-1537225875.

7. He Yafei, "Chinese Overcapacity Crisis Can Spur Growth through Overseas Expansion," *South China Morning Post*, 7 January 2014, https://www.scmp.com/comment/insight-opinion/article/1399681/chinas-overcapacity-crisis-can-spur-growth-through-overseas. Chinese officials report serious overcapacity issues in areas like steel and glass, with manufacturers operating at only 70–75 percent of capacity. See "China Needs to Address Industrial Overcapacity: Top Economic Planner," *Xinhua*, 6 March 2013, http://news.xinhuanet.com/english/business/2013-03/06/c_132213294.htm.

8. The concept of a "Chinese Marshall Plan" as a "roundabout subsidy" to Chinese industry is explained by Jiayi Zhou, Karl Hallding, and Guoyi Han in "The Trouble with China's 'One Belt One Road' Strategy," *The Diplomat*, 26 June 2015, http://thediplomat.com/2015/06/the-trouble-with-the-chinese-marshall-plan-strategy/.

9. For more on the concept of "performance legitimacy," see Yuchao Zhu, "Performance Legitimacy and China's Political Adaptation Strategy," *Journal of Chinese Political Science,* vol. 16 (2011): pp. 123–140.

10. Joseph Hope, "Returning Uighur Fighters and China's National Security Dilemma," *China Brief,* vol. 18, no. 13, 25 July 2018, https://jamestown.org/program/returning-uighur-fighters-and-chinas-national-security-dilemma/. For details on the ambiguity surrounding the specific number of Uighur fighters in Syria, see Ben Blanchard, "China Envoy Says No Accurate Figure on Uighurs Fighting in Syria," *Reuters,* 20 August 2018, https://www.reuters.com/article/us-mideast-crisis-syria-china/china-envoy-says-no-accurate-figure-on-uighurs-fighting-in-syria-idUSKCN1L508G.

11. Bizenjo's briefing is quoted in "China-Pakistan Economic Corridor: Opportunities and Risks," *Asia Report No. 297*, International Crisis Group, 29 June 2018, p. 17. See also "China to Get 91pc Gwadar Income, Minister Tells Senate," *Dawn,* 25 November 2017, https://www.dawn.com/news/1372695.

12. "China-Pakistan Economic Corridor: Opportunities and Risks," pp. 19–20.

13. For routine updates on Gwadar and CPEC, see CPECWire, a website managed by analyst Arif Rafiq, at http://www.cpecwire.com. On the general problem of how heavy-handed security operations in Gwadar can contribute to insurgency, see "China-Pakistan Economic Corridor: Opportunities and Risks," pp. 20–22.

14. Victoria Gatenby, "Gunmen Attack Chinese Consulate in Karachi," *Al Jazeera English*, 23 November 2018, https://www.youtube.com/watch?v=UpunbhxYr6Q.

15. Saeed Shah and Eva Dou, "Militants Attack Chinese Consulate in Pakistan," *Wall Street Journal,* 23 November 2018, https://www.wsj.com/articles/militants-attack-chinese-consulate-in-pakistan-1542957610.

16. Murat Sofuoglu, "Who Are the BLA and Why Did They Attack a Chinese Consulate in Pakistan?" *TRT World*, 23 November 2018, https://www.trtworld.com/magazine/who-are-the-bla-and-why-did-they-attack-a-chinese-consulate-in-pakistan-21909.

17. Saleem Shahid, "Three Chinese Engineers among Five Injured in Dalbandin Suicide Attack," *Dawn,* 12 August 2018, https://www.dawn.com/news/1426550.

18. "Baloch versus Beijing: How Chinese Investment in Pakistan Has Energised a Violent Separatist Movement," *Agence France-Presse*, 15 May 2019, https://www.scmp.com/news/asia/south-asia/article/3010258/baloch-versus-beijing-how-chinese-investment-pakistan-has.

19. In international politics, "relative gain is more important than absolute gain!" observes Kenneth N. Waltz in his seminal *Man, the State, and War* (New York: Columbia University Press, 1959), p. 198.

20. "Vision and Actions on Jointly Building Silk Road Economic Belt and 21st-Century Maritime Silk Road."

21. Sewall Chan, "Former Hong Kong Official Pleads Not Guilty in Africa Bribery Case," *New York Times*, 8 January 2018, https://www.nytimes.com/2018/01/08/world/asia/hong-kong-patrick-ho-bribery-chad-senegal.html.

22. William Jones, "New Paradigm of the Belt and Road Presented at Washington Seminar," *Executive Intelligence Review*, 9 December 2016, http://www.larouchepub.com/other/2016/4350obor_paradigm_dc.html.

23. Francis Fukuyama, "The End of History?" *The National Interest*, no. 16 (Summer 1989): pp. 3–18.

Chapter 2

1. Ahmad Shah Ghanizada, "China Appoints Sun Yuxi Special Envoy for Afghanistan," *Khaama Press*, 19 July 2014, https://www.khaama.com/china-appoints-sun-yuxi-special-envoy-for-afghanistan-8334/.

2. Ambassador Sun was not the first Chinese diplomat to play an active role on this portfolio, but he was the first to be named as special envoy to Afghanistan. Ambassador Luo Zhaohui, who served in Islamabad from 2006 to 2010, covered the region as director general for Asian Affairs in China's foreign ministry from 2011 to 2014 and dealt extensively with American diplomats on Af-Pak issues during that period. This point was made by James Schwemlein in our phone conversation on 23 July 2018.

3. Author email conversation with Dan Feldman, 26 June 2018.

4. These initiatives included the training of Afghan diplomats and agricultural assistance programs. Author email conversation with Dan Feldman, 26 June 2018; author phone conversation with Dan Feldman, 23 July 2018.

5. Author meeting with Sun Yuxi, Washington, DC, 14 August 2014.

6. Author email conversation with Joseph DeTrani, 7 July 2018.

7. "The Turbulent Time Period When the Ambassador's Wife Was in Afghanistan," Ministry of Foreign Affairs of the People's Republic of China, 27 August 2004, http://www.fmprc.gov.cn/web/ywfc_673029/t154600.shtml. Translation courtesy of Woqing Wang.

8. Kai Qi, "Sun Yuxi: Defining Diplomat with Loyalty, Eruditeness, Intelligence, and Agility," China Talk, 19 July 2013, http://www.china.com.cn/fangtan/2013-07/19/content_29473462.htm. Translation courtesy of Woqing Wang.

9. Author phone conversation with James Schwemlein, 23 July 2018.

10. Author phone conversation with Dan Feldman, 23 July 2018.

11. Author phone conversation with James Schwemlein and Dan Feldman, 23 July 2018.

12. The initial story of Taliban talks in China was reported by Nathan Hodge, Habib Khan Totakhil, and Josh Chin, "China Creates New Avenue for Afghan Peace Talks," *Wall Street Journal*, 6 January 2015, https://www.wsj.com/

articles/china-creates-new-avenue-for-afghan-peace-talks-1420564492. May talks were reported by Edward Wong and Mujib Mashal, "Taliban and Afghan Peace Officials Have Secret Talks in China," *New York Times*, 25 May 2015, https://www.nytimes.com/2015/05/26/world/asia/taliban-and-afghan-peace-officials-have-secret-talks-in-china.html.

13. For a helpful review of China's 2014–2016 "peacebroker" role in Afghanistan, see Raffaello Pantucci, "China's Big Hedge," Durham Global Strategy Institute, 29 May 2016, https://raffaellopantucci.com/2016/05/29/chinas-big-hedge/. For reporting on the so-called Quadrilateral Coordination Group meetings, see Franz-Stefan Gady, "Afghanistan to Start Peace Talks with Taliban by the End of February," *The Diplomat*, 8 February 2016, https://thediplomat.com/2016/02/afghanistan-to-start-peace-talks-with-taliban-by-the-end-of-february/.

14. Peter Frankopan, *The Silk Roads: A New History of the World* (London: Bloomsbury, 2015), p. xiv.

15. Frankopan, *The Silk Roads*, p. xiv. For more on Balasaghun, see p. 92. The point is reinforced by the work of Central Asia scholar S. Frederick Starr, who concludes that "during the four or five centuries around AD 1000 it was Central Asia, the one world region that touched all these other centers [in India, China, the Middle East, and Europe], that surged to the fore." See S. Frederick Starr, *Lost Enlightenment: Central Asia's Golden Age from the Arab Conquest to Tamerlane* (Princeton: Princeton University Press, 2013), p. 4.

16. See RAND analyst Andrew Scobell, "China's Search for Security in the Greater Middle East," in *The Red Star & the Crescent*, edited by James Reardon-Anderson (London: C. Hurst & Co. Ltd, 2018), p. 23. Scobell cites the work of a professor of international relations at Beijing University: An Weihua, "Sa Zhong Dong xi ['Greater Middle East' Analysis]," *Guoji zhengzhi yanjiu* [*Studies of International Politics*], no. 92 (2004): pp. 81–88.

17. For more on Ming geostrategy, and especially the dynasty's shift from a maritime to continental focus, see Jakub Grygiel, *Great Powers and Geopolitical Change* (Baltimore: Johns Hopkins University Press, 2006), pp. 123–163.

18. Making a similar point, Nadège Rolland writes, "For most of China's long history, its identity has primarily been that of a continental power.′Given the constraints and opportunities that China faces on both its land and sea frontiers, BRI's continental dimension will likely once again emerge as particularly important. On the other hand, China's maritime and naval expansion is relatively recent and has received disproportionate attention in the West, both because of its novelty and because it has brought China into direct contact with the United States and its Asian allies." See Nadège Rolland, *China's Eurasian Century? Political and Strategic Implications of the Belt and Road Initiative* (Seattle: The National Bureau of Asian Research, 2017), p. 4.

19. Raffaello Pantucci, "Looking West: China and Central Asia," *Testimony before the US-China Economic and Security Review Commission*, 18 March 2015, https://www.uscc.gov/sites/default/files/USCC%20Testimony_Pantucci_China%20in%20Central%20Asia_March%202015.pdf.

20. For more on the Cold War and post–Cold War history of Xinjiang and the region's ties to Central Asia, see Michael Clarke, "Xinjiang and China's Relations with Central Asia, 1991–2001: Across the 'Domestic-Foreign Frontier'?" *Asian Ethnicity*, vol. 4, no. 2 (June 2003): pp. 207–224.

21. James D. Frankel, "Chinese-Islamic Connections: An Historical and Contemporary Overview," *Journal of Muslim Minority Affairs*, vol. 36, no. 4 (2016): p. 576.

22. Lilian Craig Harris, "Xinjiang, Central Asia, and the Implications for China's Policy in the Islamic World," *The China Quarterly*, no. 133 (March 1993): p. 112.

23. Harris, "Xinjiang, Central Asia, and the Implications for China's Policy in the Islamic World," p. 114.

24. Simon Denyer, "Terrorist Attack on Market in China's Restive Xinjiang Region Kills More Than 30," *Washington Post*, 22 May 2014, https://www.washingtonpost.com/world/terrorist-attack-on-market-in-chinas-restive-xinjiang-region-kills-more-than-30/2014/05/22/06fab2dc-93d4-4cda-ae78-caa913819e15_story.html.

25. Adrian Zenz, "Reeducation Returns to China," *Foreign Affairs*, 20 June 2018, https://www.foreignaffairs.com/articles/china/2018-06-20/reeducation-returns-china. See also Adrian Zenz, "'Thoroughly Reforming Them towards a Healthy Heart Attitude': China's Political Re-education Campaign in Xinjiang," *Central Asian Survey*, DOI: 10.1080/02634937.2018.1507997. For a review of reporting and research on China's ongoing crackdown in Xinjiang, see James Millward, "'Reeducating' Xinjiang's Muslims," *New York Review of Books*, 7 February 2019, https://www.nybooks.com/articles/2019/02/07/reeducating-xinjiangs-muslims/.

26. Josh Chin and Clément Bürge, "Twelve Days in Xinjiang: How China's Surveillance State Overwhelms Daily Life," *Wall Street Journal*, 19 December 2017, https://www.wsj.com/articles/twelve-days-in-xinjiang-how-chinas-surveillance-state-overwhelms-daily-life-1513700355.

27. David S. G. Goodman traces aspects of this "colonization" effort back to the 1980s. See "The Campaign to 'Open Up the West': National, Provincial-Level, and Local Perspectives," *China Quarterly*, no. 178 (June 2004): p. 331.

28. Raffaello Pantucci, "Looking West: China and Central Asia."

29. Specifically, China works bilaterally with Central Asian states as well as through the SCO's "Regional Anti-Terrorist Structure," or RATS, which maintains a website at http://ecrats.org/en/.

30. "Vision and Actions on Jointly Building Silk Road Economic Belt and 21st-Century Maritime Silk Road.".

31. Rolland writes that "Beijing envisions that a new, Chinese-led international order will . . . arise in Eurasia. BRI is thus the main instrument of the grand strategy that will help China regain its 'great power-ness' returning it to the dominant position from which it was unjustly removed and from which it has been absent for far too long." See Rolland, *China's Eurasian Century?*, p. 128. Rolland is careful to observe that there are contending Chinese views on the BRI, and it is clearly a debate over just how "strategic" the entire initiative actually is. See, for instance, Lee Jones and Jinghan Zeng, "Understanding China's 'Belt and Road Initiative': Beyond 'Grand Strategy' to a State Transformation Analysis," *Third World Quarterly* (2019), DOI: 10.1080/01436597.2018.1559046.

32. Rolland, *China's Eurasian Century?*, p. 128.

33. Rolland succinctly observes that "As China gains political influence over its neighborhood, it will be able to push back against US dominance and reclaim its own regional strategic space." See Rolland, *China's Eurasian Century?*, p. 120.

34. Peking University professor Wang Jisi argued this point in an often-cited 2012 article "Marching Westwards: The Rebalancing of China's Geostrategy," *International and Strategic Studies*, no. 73 (2012), pp. 1–11. But as Rolland points out, similar themes were articulated more than a decade earlier by one of China's most prominent military minds who was also a member of President Xi's inner circle, General Liu Yazhou. In a 2007 article, General Liu championed the idea that Beijing should construct a "Europe-Asia land bridge to form a greater Euro-Asian symbiotic economic belt and use the countless economic links and common interests with countries to the west in order to dismantle the US encirclement of China." See Rolland, *China's Eurasian Century?*, pp. 117–118.

35. Even the concept of the Silk Road as a true long-distance trading route is likely incorrect. It is better understood as "a stretch of shifting, unmarked paths across massive expanses of deserts and mountains" along which a relatively small quantity of cargo was transported but which nevertheless "did actually transform cultures both east and west." See Valerie Hansen, *The Silk Road: A New History* (Oxford: Oxford University Press, 2012), p. 5.

36. Kent E. Calder, *The New Continentalism: Energy and Twenty-First-Century Eurasian Geopolitics* (New Haven: Yale University Press, 2012).

37. "Energy is to the New Silk Road what silk was to its ancestors," finds Calder. See Calder, *The New Continentalism*, p. 1. Brookings scholar Geoffrey Kemp reached a similar conclusion in his 2010 book *The East Moves West*, writing that "the momentum that is pulling these two regions together is driven primarily by economic factors, especially Asia's need for the Middle East's fossil fuels." See Geoffrey Kemp, *The East Moves West: India, China, and Asia's Growing Presence in the Middle East* (Washington, DC: Brookings, 2010), p. 229.

38. For a thorough review of each of these initiatives, see Rolland, *China's Eurasian Century?*, pp. 7–42. See also Evan A. Feigenbaum, "China Didn't Invent Asian Connectivity," *Macropolo*, 26 June 2017, https://macropolo.org/china-didnt-invent-asian-connectivity/.

39. GDP data (both nominal and purchasing power parity) for China and the United States can be found in the *World Economic Outlook Database*, International Monetary Fund, April 2019, https://www.imf.org/external/pubs/ft/weo/2019/01/weodata/index.aspx.

40. Former CIA China analyst Christopher K. Johnson believes that BRI is "best understood as a response to frequent complaints about the failures of past administrations—former President Jiang Zemin and Premier Zhu Rongji with the Great Western Development Campaign in the 1990s and their respective successors, Hu Jintao and Wen Jiabao, with their efforts to turn around the northeast in the 2000s—to successfully develop these areas." See Christopher K. Johnson, "President Xi Jinping's 'Belt and Road' Initiative: A Practical Assessment of the Chinese Communist Party's Roadmap for China's Global Resurgence," CSIS, March 2016, p. 20. Rolland traces the BRI's lineage to prior Chinese policies too, but shifts the focus slightly, writing that "from an economic perspective, BRI can be seen as the third phase of China's reform and opening-up policy, a rationalization and an outward expansion of various earlier efforts." See Rolland, *China's Eurasian Century?*, p. 108; see also p. 96 on similar points.

41. Elizabeth Economy records this history and also observes that although China has made significant overseas investments, it is "rarely the lead investor in any region of the world." See Elizabeth C. Economy, *The Third Revolution: Xi Jinping and the New Chinese State* (Oxford: Oxford University Press, 2018), pp. 208–209. For other examples of how analysts see the BRI as an evolution of China's "Going Out" or "Going Global" strategy, see Rolland, *China's Eurasian Century?*, p. 101; Johnson, "President Xi Jinping's 'Belt and Road' Initiative," pp. v, 6.

42. Regarding Figure 1 data, "Chinese outward FDI" includes FDI from China, Hong Kong SAR, and Macao SAR as defined by United Nations Conference on Trade and Development (UNCTAD). Data retrieved from "Foreign Direct Investment: Inward and Outward Flows and Stock, Annual 1970–2017," United Nations Conference on Trade and Development, accessed 19 June 2019, http://unctadstat.unctad.org/wds/TableViewer/tableView.aspx?ReportId=96740. Upon visiting the homepage, filter the data by year ("1999–2017"), flow ("outward"), measure ("US Dollars at current prices in millions"), and economy ("China," "Hong Kong SAR," and "Macao SAR" underneath the Individual economies section).

43. For Chinese FDI surpassing USA FDI, see "China Go Abroad," EY, August 2017, https://www.ey.com/Publication/vwLUAssets/EY-china-overseas-investment-report-issue-6-en/$FILE/EY-china-overseas-investment-report-issue-6-en.pdf.

44. Data for Figure 2 are from "China Global Investment Tracker," American Enterprise Institute, accessed 19 June 2019, https://www.aei.org/china-global-investment-tracker/?ncid=txtlnkusaolp00000618. Click "Download The Full Data Set," and then filter by "Country," or by "Region," to isolate the relevant data in the "Dataset 1 + 2" tab. Central Asia includes Kazakhstan, Kyrgyzstan, Tajikistan, Turkmenistan, and Uzbekistan. South Asia includes Afghanistan, Bangladesh, India, Maldives, Nepal, Pakistan, and Sri Lanka. All other regions defined by American Enterprise Institute and the Heritage Foundation. Data include "construction contracts" and "investments" as defined by American Enterprise Institute and the Heritage Foundation.

45. For Asia, see "China Rises to 16 Asian Countries' Biggest Trading Partners," *People's Daily Online*, 12 January 2018, http://en.people.cn/n3/2018/0112/c90000-9314972.html. For Europe, see "China," European Commission, accessed 12 July 2018, http://ec.europa.eu/trade/policy/countries-and-regions/countries/china/.

46. In Latin America, for example, China's quest for commodities and energy led to surging trade from 1990 to 2005, when imports from the region to China grew eighteenfold, from $1.5 billion to $27 billion. At the same time, Latin American hunger for cheap Chinese goods drove imports at a similar torrid pace, from $1.3 billion in 1990 to $23.3 billion in 2005. See Francisco E. González, "Latin America in the Economic Equation—Winners and Losers: What Can Losers Do?," in *China's Expansion into the Western Hemisphere: Implications for Latin America and the United States*, edited by Riordan Roett and Guadalupe Paz (Washington, DC: Brookings, 2008), p. 149.

47. "Chinese Travellers of All Sorts Have Become Ubiquitous," *The Economist*, 17 May 2018, https://www.economist.com/special-report/2018/05/17/chinese-travellers-of-all-sorts-have-become-ubiquitous. For size of countries, see "The World Factbook," Central Intelligence Agency, accessed 11 July 2018, https://www.cia.gov/library/publications/the-world-factbook/rankorder/2119rank.html.

48. "For China's Elite, Studying Abroad Is De Rigueur," *The Economist*, 17 May 2018, https://www.economist.com/special-report/2018/05/17/for-chinas-elite-studying-abroad-is-de-rigueur.

49. Rolland, *China's Eurasian Century?*, pp. 41, 99; Johnson, "President Xi Jinping's 'Belt and Road' Initiative," p. v.

50. Rolland, *China's Eurasian Century?*, p. 97.

51. Aaron L. Friedberg, *A Contest for Supremacy: China, America, and the Struggle for Mastery in Asia* (New York: W. W. Norton, 2011), p. 218.

52. Friedberg, *A Contest for Supremacy*, pp. 215–244.

53. All spending figures come from China Power Team, "What Does China Really Spend on Its Military?," *China Power*, 28 December 2015, updated 13 June 2019, https://chinapower.csis.org/military-spending/.

54. For data on UN Peacekeeping Missions, see "Troop and Police Contributors," United Nations Peacekeeping, accessed 18 July 2018, https://peacekeeping. un.org/en/troop-and-police-contributors.

55. On the history of China's changing military strategies, see M. Taylor Fravel, "Shifts in Warfare and Party Unity: Explaining China's Changes in Military Strategy," *International Security*, vol. 42, no. 3 (Winter 2017/ 2018): pp. 37–83.

56. For a concise overview of these developments, see Economy, *The Third Revolution*, pp. 200–207. For up-to-date tracking of China's "island-building" activities, see the CSIS Asia Maritime Transparency Initiative website at "China Island Tracker," https://amti.csis.org/island-tracker/china/.

57. "China began considering creating an ADIZ after a midair collision between its F-8 fighter jet and a US EP-3 reconnaissance aircraft over the South China Sea in April 2001, according to senior officials of government-affiliated research institutes." See "China Overturned Draft Air Defense Zone, Expanded It toward Japan," *Asahi Shimbun*, 12 January 2014, https:// web.archive.org/web/20140216065721/http://ajw.asahi.com/article/asia/china/ AJ201401120021.

58. MacDonald, Donahue, and Danyluk, "Energy Futures in Asia: Final Report."

59. For reporting and analysis of the Libya operation, see Gabe Collins and Andrew S. Erickson, "Implications of China's Military Evacuation of Citizens from Libya," *The China Brief*, vol. 11, issue 4, 11 March 2011, https:// jamestown.org/program/implications-of-chinas-military-evacuation-of-citizens-from-libya/.

60. Tania Branigan, "Chinese State TV Unveils Global Expansion Plan," *Guardian*, 8 December 2011, https://www.theguardian.com/world/2011/dec/ 08/china-state-television-global-expansion. For $6.6 billion figure, see Gordon G. Chang, "Beijing's Propaganda Goes Global," *Forbes*, 6 May 2009, https:// www.forbes.com/2009/05/05/global-times-beijing-cctv-peoples-daily-opinions-columnists-xinhua/.

61. For information on the rebrand and location of CGTN, see "About Us," CGTN.com, accessed 31 July 2018, https://www.cgtn.com/home/info/about_ us.do.

62. For excellent pieces on how President Xi's foreign policy builds on, and differs from, that of his predecessors, see Evan Osnos, "Make China Great Again," *New Yorker*, 8 January 2018, https://www.newyorker.com/magazine/2018/ 01/08/making-china-great-again; and Jeffrey A. Bader, "How Xi Jinping Sees The Word . . . and Why," *Brookings Institution*, February 2016, https:// www.brookings.edu/wp-content/uploads/2016/07/xi_jinping_worldview_ bader-1.pdf. For analysis that stresses the important continuities from Hu Jintao to Xi Jinping, see Rush Doshi, "Hu's to Blame for China's Foreign Assertiveness?," *Brookings Institution*, 22 January 2019, https://www.brookings. edu/articles/hus-to-blame-for-chinas-foreign-assertiveness/.

63. On Xi's consolidation of power, see for instance, Economy, *The Third Revolution*, pp. 22–25. One specific example of Xi's consolidating policy trends is his more extensive use of "leading small groups." See Christopher K. Johnson, Scott Kennedy, and Mingda Qiu, "Xi's Signature Governance Innovation: The Rise of Leading Small Groups," *CSIS Commentary*, 17 October 2017, https://www.csis.org/analysis/xis-signature-governance-innovation-rise-leading-small-groups.

64. Related and interesting debates have swirled over whether Xi's consolidation efforts are a sign of strength or weakness, and over how his efforts will ultimately pan out for the Communist Party's hold on power. For a window into such discussions, see David Shambaugh, "The Coming Chinese Crackup," *Wall Street Journal*, 6 March 2015, https://www.wsj.com/articles/the-coming-chinese-crack-up-1425659198.

65. For a very useful introduction to the Jiang Shigong essay, see David Ownby and Timothy Creek, "Jiang Shigong on 'Philosophy and History: Interpreting the "Xi Jinping Era" through Xi's Report to the Nineteenth National Congress of the CCP,'" *The China Story*, 11 May 2018, https://www.thechinastory.org/cot/jiang-shigong-on-philosophy-and-history-interpreting-the-xi-jinping-era-through-xis-report-to-the-nineteenth-national-congress-of-the-ccp/.

66. Ownby and Creek, "Jiang Shigong.".

67. Ownby and Creek, "Jiang Shigong.".

68. Jiang appreciates that the three eras are "not those understood by academic historians but must be analyzed from a political angle. Using historical divisions to express political thought is a basic method employed by traditional Chinese philosophy." Indeed, this is an effort to use history in the "construction of legitimacy in the Chinese political order." See Ownby and Creek, "Jiang Shigong."

69. On Deng Xiaoping's prioritization of economic growth, see Rolland, *China's Eurasian Century?*, p. 122.

70. Yan observed that "the Chinese government did not provide any official clarification" about the differences between KLP and SFA, but suggested that the two strategies were intended to advance different Chinese goals. Simply put, he argued that whereas KLP was mainly about "making money," SFA is more about "making friends." See Yan Xuetong, "From Keeping a Low Profile to Striving for Achievement," *Chinese Journal of International Politics*, vol. 7, no. 2 (2014): pp. 154, 165, 166, https://academic.oup.com/cjip/article/7/2/153/438673.

71. The meeting brought together "all six of Xi's Politburo Standing Committee (PBSC) colleagues, the rest of the full Politburo, China's leading foreign policy practitioners, and hundreds of other officials from China's provincial-level administrations, the military, SOEs, and the state bureaucracy." See Johnson, "President Xi Jinping's 'Belt and Road' Initiative," p. 15.

72. Michael D. Swaine observed that China had "entered into a 'new era' marked by greater self-confidence, expanded goals, and an unambiguous desire to occupy a position of global leadership alongside the United States and other major powers." See Michael D. Swaine, "Chinese Views of Foreign Policy in the 19th Party Congress," *China Leadership Monitor*, Winter 2018, Issue 55, 23 January 2018, https://www.hoover.org/research/chinese-views-foreign-policy-19th-party-congress. Similarly, China-watcher Bonnie Glaser concluded that "the main takeaway for the international community is that Xi Jinping is extremely confident in China's growing national power and sees international trends working in China's favor. Against the background of China's expanding global interests, these assessments suggest that the international community may face an even more assertive China in the years to come." See Bonnie Glaser, "Xi Jinping's 19th Party Congress Speech Heralds Greater Assertiveness in Chinese Foreign Policy," *CSIS Commentary*, 26 October 2017, https://www.csis.org/analysis/xi-jinpings-19th-party-congress-speech-heralds-greater-assertiveness-chinese-foreign-policy.

73. As will be made clear in chapter 6, the Trump administration has been even more forthright in its characterization of the US-China relationship as one of competition between great powers.

74. Yan Xuetong, "From Keeping a Low Profile," p. 160.

75. Yan Xuetong, "From Keeping a Low Profile," p. 182.

76. Yan Xuetong, "From Keeping a Low Profile," p. 184.

77. On this history of the non-interference principle in Chinese policy after 1949, see Chen Zheng, "China Debates the Non-Interference Principle," *Chinese Journal of International Politics*, vol. 9, no. 3 (September 2016): p. 351, https://academic.oup.com/cjip/article/9/3/349/2352052.

78. This point about Mao's revolutionary agenda in the context of non-interference was made by Professor Wang Yizhou in "New Direction for China's Diplomacy," *Beijing Review*, no. 10, 5 March 2012, http://www.bjreview.com/Cover_Stories_Series_2014/2012-03/05/content_628359.htm.

79. "Rulers have almost universally sought international legal sovereignty. . . . In contrast, domestic autonomy has frequently been transgressed. Westphalian norms have been decoupled from behavior. While the principle of nonintervention has been widely accepted, it has often been challenged by alternatives such as human rights." On this and related points, see Stephen D. Krasner, *Sovereignty: Organized Hypocrisy* (Princeton: Princeton University Press, 1999), pp. 223–224.

80. Mathieu Duchâtel, Olivier Brauner, and Zhou Hang, "Protecting China's Overseas Interests: The Slow Shift away from Non-Interference," *SIPRI Policy Paper* 41, June 2014, p. vi.

81. Duchâtel, Brauner, and Zhou Hang, "Protecting China's Overseas Interests," p. vi. In a subsequent 2016 article, Chinese scholar Chen Zheng concluded that a "loose pragmatic consensus" favoring "moderately adjusting" China's

stance had emerged, although the debate has not been settled. See Chen Zheng, "China Debates the Non-Interference Principle," p. 349, also 359. See also p. 366 for a "map" of where different prominent Chinese academics stand on this debate.

82. Chen Zheng, "China Debates the Non-Interference Principle," p. 352.

83. "Creative involvement" is associated with Wang Yizhou, while "constructive involvement" is the term employed by Professor Zhao Huasheng of Fudan University. See Duchâtel, Brauner, and Zhou Hang, "Protecting China's Overseas Interests," pp. 18–19. Wang Yizhou, a professor of international relations at Peking University, argues such ideas do not violate non-interference but offer "enrichment." Nor, he says, is "creative involvement" an endorsement of the "interventionism" of Western powers. It requires a "new and active attitude," but also "obeying the United Nations charter, being invited or accepted by local people or a majority of political parties in the state concerned, and conforming to the wishes of most of its neighboring counties." Wang adds that it "stresses diplomatic mediation and economic assistance instead of a military-first approach or armed suppression." Wang points to China's diplomatic mediation efforts in Sudan, participation in Korean six-party talks, counterpiracy missions off the Somali coast, and assistance programs in Africa as examples of this approach. See Wang Yizhou, "New Direction for China's Diplomacy."

84. "Hambantota Harbour Dream Come True," Sri Lanka Ports Authority, http://portcom.slpa.lk/news_events_220.asp.

85. Sirisena's quote is from December 2014, and referenced in Neil DeVotta, "China's Influence in Sri Lanka: Negotiating Development, Authoritarianism, and Regional Transformation," in *Rising China's Influence in Developing Asia*, edited by Evelyn Goh (Oxford: Oxford University Press, 2016), p. 130. DeVotta skillfully explains that Sri Lanka (similar to the cases explored in this book) has not always been a mere hapless victim in its relations with China. To the contrary, "it is the ruling elite in Colombo that has been trying to mobilize Chinese investment, presence, and interest to promote its own domestic political, commercial, and regional strategic agendas." See Goh, "Introduction," p. 19. Even the Hambantota port was a Sri Lankan initiative pitched to Indian and American governments before Beijing eventually stepped in. See DeVotta, "China's Influence," pp. 143–144.

86. Chen Zheng, "China Debates the Non-Interference Principle," p. 370.

87. Go Yamada, "Is China's Belt and Road Working? A Progress Report from Eight Countries," *Nikkei Asian Review*, 28 March 2018, https://asia.nikkei.com/Spotlight/Cover-Story/Is-China-s-Belt-and-Road-working-A-progress-report-from-eight-countries.

88. "The evidence that Beijing is engaged in a coordinated campaign to enmesh borrowers in debt—and then strong-arm debtors or snatch away prized strategic assets—is thin . . . of 40 cases across 24 countries, only the Sri

Lankan case involved a confirmed asset seizure." See Nathaniel Taplin, "One Belt, One Road, and a Lot of Debt," *Wall Street Journal*, 2 May 2019, https://www.wsj.com/articles/one-belt-one-road-and-a-lot-of-debt-11556789446.

89. Robert A. Manning and Bharath Gopalaswamy, "Is Abdulla Yameen Handing Over the Maldives to China?," *Foreign Policy*, 21 March 2018, https://foreignpolicy.com/2018/03/21/is-abdulla-yameen-handing-over-the-maldives-to-china/.

90. Mohamed Nasheed, "A Villain in Paradise," *Indian Express*, 7 February 2018, https://indianexpress.com/article/opinion/columns/a-villain-in-paradise-maldives-president-abdulla-yameen-5053962/.

91. Mohamed Nasheed, "A Villain in Paradise."

92. On the "absolute nonsense" comment, see Sanaina Kumar and Angela Stanzel, "The Maldives Crisis and the China-India Chess Match," *The Diplomat*, 15 March 2018, https://thediplomat.com/2018/03/the-maldives-crisis-and-the-china-india-chess-match/. On the official Chinese statement of non-interference and the use of the economic development minister as envoy to China, see "China Says It Doesn't Want Maldives to Be Another 'Flashpoint' in Ties with India, Warns against External Interference," *Firstpost*, 9 February 2018, https://www.firstpost.com/world/china-hopes-its-ties-with-india-wont-be-impacted-by-maldives-crisis-warns-against-external-interference-in-island-nation-4343537.html.

93. Zaheena Rasheed, "Ibrahim Mohamed Solih Sworn In as New Maldives President," *Al Jazeera*, 17 November 2018, https://www.aljazeera.com/news/2018/11/ibrahim-mohamed-solih-sworn-maldives-president-181117111139762.html.

94. Historically, New Delhi has had fewer qualms about political interference in its smaller neighbors, but found it difficult to compete with China's deep pockets, at least directly. Then again, the fact that domestic political developments in both Sri Lanka and the Maldives turned in India's favor suggests that China's deep pockets are not, in themselves, sufficient guarantees of political influence. Robert Manning and Bharath Gopalaswamy, analysts at the Atlantic Council think tank, found in the Maldives episode an instructive case of China "throwing cash around to create dependent client states." See Manning and Gopalaswamy, "Is Abdulla Yameen Handing Over the Maldives to China?".

95. "Don't mistake Xi's recalibration for retreat," writes Frederick Kempe in "China's Global Power Play," *Atlantic Council*, 28 April 2019, https://www.atlanticcouncil.org/blogs/new-atlanticist/china-s-global-power-play.

96. On the August 2018 meeting, see Nadège Rolland, "Reports of Belt and Road's Death Are Greatly Exaggerated," *Foreign Affairs*, 29 January 2019, https://www.foreignaffairs.com/articles/china/2019-01-29/reports-belt-and-roads-death-are-greatly-exaggerated. On the April 2019 meeting, see Laura Zhou, "China's Belt and Road Forum Ends with More Support

and US$64 Billion in New Deals, But Is It Job Done for Beijing?" *South China Morning Post*, 27 April 2019, https://www.scmp.com/news/china/diplomacy/article/3007967/chinas-belt-and-road-forum-ends-more-support-and-us64-billion. For Xi's quote, see Xi Jinping, "Working Together to Deliver a Brighter Future for Belt and Road Cooperation," Opening Ceremony of the Second Belt and Road Forum for International Cooperation, 26 April 2019, http://govt.chinadaily.com.cn/a/201904/26/WS5cc5663c498e079e6801f3c0.html.

97. Rolland correctly finds that "it is not just a series of engineering and construction plans linked together to complete a fragmented Eurasian transportation network but a thoroughly considered and ambitious vision for China as the rising regional leader, in which Xi has invested great personal capital, and which is backed up by considerable financial and human resources." Rolland, *China's Eurasian Century?*, p. 43.

98. Again, the most thorough overview of the BRI is found in Rolland, *China's Eurasian Century?*, pp. 43–92. Also extremely helpful for tracking BRI developments is the "Reconnecting Asia" project at the Center for Strategic and International Studies, which includes analysis and an interactive database of new infrastructure projects in Asia at https://reconnectingasia.csis.org/.

99. Jonathan E. Hillman, "How Big Is China's Belt and Road?" *CSIS Commentary*, 3 April 2018, https://www.csis.org/analysis/how-big-chinas-belt-and-road. Joy-Perez and Scissors offer good reasons to anticipate that the total will be closer to the low-end estimate. They argue that "the BRI will not hit $1 trillion in value until well into the 2020s." See "The Chinese State Funds Belt and Road but Does Not Have Trillions to Spare," American Enterprise Institute, March 2018, http://www.aei.org/publication/the-chinese-state-funds-belt-and-road-but-does-not-have-trillions-to-spare/.

100. Michael D. Swaine, "Chinese Views and Commentary on the 'One Belt, One Road,'" *China Leadership Monitor*, Summer 2015, issue 47, 14 July 2015, https://www.hoover.org/research/chinese-views-foreign-policy-19th-party-congress.

101. "Meeting Asia's Infrastructure Needs," Asian Development Bank, February 2017, https://www.adb.org/publications/asia-infrastructure-needs.

102. "Vision and Actions on Jointly Building Silk Road."

103. "Beijing has also backed the initiative with a considerable financial commitment, earmarking $40 billion for the Silk Road Economic Belt, $25 billion for the Maritime Silk Road, $50 billion for the AIIB, and $40 billion for the SRF." See Michael Clarke, "The Belt and Road Initiative: China's New Grand Strategy?" *Asia Policy*, no. 24 (July 2017): p. 71.

104. Rolland, *China's Eurasian Century?*, p. 58.

105. The China Development Bank announced in May 2015 that it would invest over $890 billion, and Export-Import Bank of China would do similarly. See Rolland, *China's Eurasian Century?*, p. 58.

106. For an overview of the AIIB, see Martin A. Weiss, "Asian Infrastructure Investment Bank (AIIB)," Congressional Research Service, 3 February 2017, https://fas.org/sgp/crs/row/R44754.pdf.

107. "AIIB Approves Membership of Algeria, Ghana, Libya, Morocco, Serbia, Togo," Asian Infrastructure Investment Bank, 19 December 2018, https://www.aiib.org/en/news-events/news/2018/20181219_001.html.

108. On this point, see Eswar Prasad, "How China Aims to Limit the West's Global Influence," *New York Times*, 1 September 2017, https://www.nytimes.com/2017/09/01/opinion/china-west-democracy.html.

109. Jane Perlez, "China Creates a World Bank of Its Own, and the US Balks," *New York Times*, 4 December 2015, https://www.nytimes.com/2015/12/05/business/international/china-creates-an-asian-bank-as-the-us-stands-aloof.html.

110. Natalie Lichtenstein, *A Comparative Guide to the Asian Infrastructure Investment Bank* (Oxford: Oxford University Press, 2018), p. 12.

111. Lichtenstein, *A Comparative Guide*, p. 13.

112. On the Trump administration's last-minute decision to send National Security Council senior director for Asia Matthew Pottinger to the BRI Forum in May 2017, see Jane Perlez and Yufan Huang, "Behind China's $1 Trillion Plan to Shake Up the Economic Order," *New York Times*, 13 May 2017, https://www.nytimes.com/2017/05/13/business/china-railway-one-belt-one-road-1-trillion-plan.html. The United States did not send a high-level representative to the second BRI Forum in April 2019, but that meeting was less well attended overall. See "Second Belt and Road Forum Top-Level Attendees," *The Diplomat*, 27 April 2019, https://thediplomat.com/2019/04/second-belt-and-road-forum-top-level-attendees/.

113. This last point was made to me and Nadège Rolland by a Chinese expert in Beijing, December 2016. She recalls the same comment in Rolland, *China's Eurasian Century?*, pp. 157–158.

114. On this uncertainty of repayment and the use of concessional loans in Pakistan, see Jeremy Page and Saeed Shah, "China's Global Building Spree Runs into Trouble in Pakistan," *Wall Street Journal*, 22 July 2018, https://www.wsj.com/articles/chinas-global-building-spree-runs-into-trouble-in-pakistan-1532280460.

115. For details on the type of assistance China provides, see Axel Dreher, Andreas Fuchs, Bradley Parks, Austin M. Strange, and Michael J. Tierney, "Aid, China, and Growth: Evidence from a New Global Development Finance Dataset," Working Paper 46, AIDDATA, October 2017, p. 2, http://docs.aiddata.org/ad4/pdfs/WPS46_Aid_China_and_Growth.pdf. For data on China's aid from 2003 to 2016, see "Data: Chinese Foreign Aid," China Africa Research Initiative, accessed 1 August 2018, http://www.sais-cari.org/data-chinese-foreign-aid-to-africa.

116. Lily Quo makes use of the AIDDATA Working Paper 46 in her article, helpfully highlighting the figures about grant versus non-grant aid. See Lily Quo, "China's 'Rogue Aid' to Africa Isn't as Much or as Controversial as We Thought," *Quartz Africa*, 19 October 2017, https://qz.com/1104209/chinas-rogue-aid-to-africa-isnt-as-much-or-as-controversial-as-we-thought/.

117. Quo, "China's 'Rogue Aid' to Africa."

118. As Alex Thier, a former leader in the US Agency for International Development during the Obama administration, put it, "Chinese aid is spread through the mercantilist Ministry of Commerce, the Foreign Ministry, the quasi-state banks, and other domestically-oriented entities like the Ministry of Public Health, the Army, and the Earthquake Agency." See Alex Thier, "China's New Development Agency: Five Expert Views," ODI, https://www.odi.org/comment/10624-china-s-new-development-agency-five-expert-views.

119. As analyst Wang Huiyao pointed out, ideas for addressing the "Balkanized" nature of institutional responsibilities had been "floating around in Beijing circles for years." See Wang Huiyao, "China's Immigration and Aid Agencies a Sign of Global Aspirations," *Financial Times*, 28 March 2018, https://www.ft.com/content/6701c95c-3278-11e8-ac48-10c6fdc22f03.

120. Kristin Huang, "China Must Act More Wisely in Giving Out Foreign Aid, Says Xi Jinping," *South China Morning Post*, 9 February 2017, https://www.scmp.com/news/article/2069414/chinas-president-xi-wants-wiser-approach-foreign-aid-donation.

121. "China Unveils Cabinet Restructuring Plan," *China Daily*, 14 March 2018, http://www.chinadaily.com.cn/a/201803/14/WS5aa7ffd3a3106e7dcc141675.html. See also Denghua Zhang, "China's New Aid Agency," *The Lowy Interpreter*, 19 March 2018, https://www.lowyinstitute.org/the-interpreter/china-s-new-aid-agency.

122. "China Says New Agency Will Improve Foreign Aid Coordination," *Reuters*, 12 March 2018, https://www.reuters.com/article/us-china-parliament-aid/china-says-new-agency-will-improve-foreign-aid-coordination-idUSKCN1GP02J.

123. "China Unveils Int'l Development Cooperation Agency," *Xinhua*, 18 April 2018, http://www.xinhuanet.com/english/2018-04/18/c_137120544.htm.

124. See, for instance, Denghua Zhang, "Diplomacy Will Have More Weight in China's Foreign Aid Program," Devpolicyblog, 2 May 2018, http://www.devpolicy.org/diplomacy-more-weight-chinas-foreign-aid-program-20180502/.

125. For samples of this sort of analysis, see Wang Binbin, "After China's Ministerial Shake-Up, What's Next for South-South Climate Cooperation," Chinadialogue, 19 June 2018, https://www.chinadialogue.net/article/show/single/en/10685-Opinion-After-China-s-ministerial-shake-up-what-s-next-for-South-South-climate-cooperation-; and Marina Rudyak, "Will China's New Aid Agency Be Effective?" *The Lowy Interpreter*, 20 April 2018, https://www.lowyinstitute.org/the-interpreter/will-china-new-aid-agency-be-effective.

126. Lisa Cornish, "China's New Aid Agency: What We Know," *Devex*, 20 April 2018, https://www.devex.com/news/china-s-new-aid-agency-what-we-know-92553.

127. According to Denghua Zhang, "The government has said the objective of this new agency is to promote aid coordination, and one of their main tasks will be aid planning rather than aid implementation. So Mr. Wang is an ideal person to direct this work." See Cornish, "China's New Aid Agency."

128. On CIDCA's assuming responsibility for concessionary loans, see " 'China-Aid' to Fund CPEC Projects from Now On," China-Pakistan Economic Corridor, http://www.cpecinfo.com/news/china-aid-to-fund-cpec-projects-from-now-on/NTM0Ng==. On pulling personnel and other capabilities from the Ministry of Commerce, Peking University researcher Wang Binbin writes, "CIDCA will also benefit from established overseas aid systems moved over from the Ministry of Commerce (including material aid, complete project delivery, technical cooperation and training)." See Wang Binbin, "After China's Ministerial Shake-Up, What's Next for South-South Climate Cooperation," Chinadialogue, 19 June 2018, https://www.chinadialogue.net/article/show/single/en/10685-Opinion-After-China-s-ministerial-shake-up-what-s-next-for-South-South-climate-cooperation-. On Chinese ambassadors seeking more reporting relevant to the new aid agency, see Graeme Smith's comments in Jenny Lei Ravelo and Lisa Cornish, "5 Questions on China's Planned Foreign Aid Agency," *Devex*, 16 March 2018, https://www.devex.com/news/5-questions-on-china-s-planned-foreign-aid-agency-92349.

129. Author email conversation with Janet Eom, who cited interviews with Beijing-based experts and policymakers, 11 July 2018.

130. For a concise analysis about how China's different tools of statecraft might stack up, see Evan A. Feigenbaum, "Is Coercion the New Normal in China's Economic Statecraft?" *Macro Polo*, 25 July 2017, https://macropolo.org/coercion-new-normal-chinas-economic-statecraft/. Aaron Friedberg has carefully charted the historical progression of China's economic statecraft, from a mainly defensive crouch to the increasingly active use of trade and investment for political influence and even the restructuring of the global economic system. See Aaron L. Friedberg, "Globalization and Chinese Grand Strategy," *Survival*, vol. 60, no. 1, pp. 7–40, https://doi.org/10.1080/00396338.2018.1427362. Citing similar Chinese activities, Jeff Smith perceives that Beijing is wielding "instruments of economic power in more overtly coercive, punitive, and intrusive ways." See Smith, "China's Belt and Road Initiative," p. 16, http://report.heritage.org/bg3331.

131. Feigenbaum neatly sets out the Chinese approach to Korea over THAAD in "Is Coercion the New Normal in China's Economic Statecraft?".

132. Echo Huang, "China Inflicted a World of Pain on South Korea in 2017," *Quartz*, 21 December 2017, https://qz.com/1149663/china-south-korea-relations-in-2017-thaad-backlash-and-the-effect-on-tourism/.

133. Keith Bradsher, "Amid Tension, China Blocks Vital Exports to Japan," *New York Times*, 22 September 2010, https://www.nytimes.com/2010/09/23/business/global/23rare.html.

134. Ellen Nakashima, "US Pushes Hard for a Ban on Huawei in Europe, but the Firm's 5G Prices Are Nearly Irresistible," *Washington Post*, 29 May 2019, https://www.washingtonpost.com/world/national-security/for-huawei-the-5g-play-is-in-europe--and-the-us-is-pushing-hard-for-a-ban-there/2019/05/28/582a8ff6-78d4-11e9-b7ae-390de4259661_story.html.

135. Norman Pearlstine, David Pierson, Robyn Dixon, David S. Cloud, Alice Su, and Max Hao Lu, "The Man Behind Huawei," *Los Angeles Times*, 10 April 2019, https://www.latimes.com/projects/la-fi-tn-huawei-5g-trade-war/.

136. The Trump administration's order authorizing these commercial bans is found at The White House, "Executive Order on Securing the Information and Communications Technology and Services Supply Chain," 15 May 2019, https://www.whitehouse.gov/presidential-actions/executive-order-securing-information-communications-technology-services-supply-chain/.

137. For example, as early as 2004, President Hu Jintao ordered China's military to gear up for "new historic missions," which was interpreted to mean improving its capacity to protect Chinese interests both at home and abroad. See Michael S. Chase and Kristen Gunness, "The PLA's Multiple Military Tasks: Prioritizing Combat Operations and Developing MOOTW Capabilities," *China Brief*, 21 January 2010, https://jamestown.org/program/the-plas-multiple-military-tasks-prioritizing-combat-operations-and-developing-mootw-capabilities/.

138. These figures were drawn from a speech by Foreign Minister Wang Yi in 2016, and found in Timothy R. Heath, *China's Pursuit of Overseas Security* (Santa Monica, CA: RAND Corporation, 2018), p. 1, https://www.rand.org/pubs/research_reports/RR2271.html.

139. For more detail on this reform process that was officially announced in November 2015, see Fravel, "Shifts in Warfare and Party Unity," p. 81.

140. Author conversation with Senior Colonel and PLA Academy of Military Science Senior Fellow Ding Hao, Beijing, 7 December 2017.

141. For more on these reforms, including political motivations and operational implications, see Phillip C. Saunders and Joel Wuthnow, "China's Goldwater-Nichols? Assessing PLA Organizational Reforms," INSS Strategic Forum, April 2016, http://www.dtic.mil/dtic/tr/fulltext/u2/1006824.pdf. These authors and other experts identify China's 2015 defense white paper as a source for official Chinese views on the evolution of modern warfare and external security challenges and the need to develop new military capabilities

to address them. See "China's Military Strategy," The State Council Information Office of the People's Republic of China, May 2015, http://www.china.org.cn/china/2015-05/26/content_35661433.htm.

142. Author conversation with PLA Colonel Wang Guifang, Beijing, 7 December 2017.

143. For more on this debate, see Duchâtel, Braüner, and Zhou Hang, "Protecting China's Overseas Interests," p. vi.

144. As a 2013 Chinese Defense White Paper explained: "With the gradual integration of China's economy into the world economic system, overseas interests have become an integral component of China's national interests." The significance of the 2013 Defense White Paper was highlighted in Duchâtel, Braüner, and Zhou Hang, "Protecting China's Overseas Interests," p. 3. The White Paper is found at Information Office of the State Council, "The Diversified Employment of China's Armed Forces," April 2013, http://english.gov.cn/archive/white_paper/2014/08/23/content_281474982986506.htm.

145. Fravel, "Shifts in Warfare and Party Unity," p. 81.

146. "China is putting power projection components into place—carrier air, land attack cruise missiles on multi-mission destroyers, and amphibious forces—that, when assembled as a task force, are very credible. . . . When combined with modern destroyers as escorts and an aircraft carrier to provide air defense, China will have a distant-seas power projection capability for the first time since Admiral Zheng He's last voyage (1431–33)." See Michael McDevitt, "China's Far Seas Navy: The Implications of the 'Open Seas Protection' Mission," CNA, Revised April 2016, p. 11, https://www.cna.org/cna_files/pdf/China-Far-Seas-Navy.pdf.

147. Andrew S. Erickson and Austin Strange, *Six Years at Sea . . . and Counting: Gulf of Aden Anti-Piracy and China's Maritime Commons Presence* (Washington, DC: Jamestown Foundation, 2015).

148. Erica Downs, Jeffrey Becker, and Patrick deGategno, "China's Military Support Facility in Djibouti: The Economic and Security Dimensions of China's First Overseas Base," CNA, July 2017, pp. vi, 29–31, https://www.cna.org/CNA_files/PDF/DIM-2017-U-015308-Final2.pdf.

149. Downs, Becker, and deGategno, "China's Military Support Facility in Djibouti," pp. 25–28.

150. The base at Djibouti represented nothing short of "a fundamental shift in China's foreign and security policy." See Downs, Becker, and deGategno, "China's Military Support Facility in Djibouti," p. iii.

151. Official Chinese statements are cited in Downs, Becker, and deGategno, "China's Military Support Facility in Djibouti," p. 1.

152. Downs, Becker, and deGategno, "China's Military Support Facility in Djibouti," p. 1.

153. US Marine General Thomas Waldhauser testified before the House Armed Services Committee that "there are some indications of (China) looking for additional facilities, specifically on the eastern coast (of Africa) . . . so Djibouti happens to be the first—there will be more." See Bertil Lintner, "Djibouti: The Casablanca of a New Cold War," *Asia Times*, 28 November 2018, http://www.atimes.com/article/djibouti-the-casablanca-of-a-new-cold-war/. On the potential for a new Chinese base in Cambodia, see Jeremy Page, Gordon Lubold, and Rob Taylor, "Deal for Naval Outpost in Cambodia Furthers China's Quest for Military Network," *Wall Street Journal*, 22 July 2019, https://www.wsj.com/articles/secret-deal-for-chinese-naval-outpost-in-cambodia-raises-u-s-fears-of-beijings-ambitions-11563732482.

154. For several examples of these Chinese analysts, see Joel Wuthnow, "Chinese Perspectives on the Belt and Road Initiative: Strategic Rationales, Risks, and Implications," *China Strategic Perspectives*, no. 12 (October 2017): pp. 22–23, http://inss.ndu.edu/Portals/68/Documents/stratperspective/china/ChinaPerspectives-12.pdf.

155. Minnie Chan, "As Overseas Ambitions Expand, China Plans 400 Per Cent Increase to Marine Corps Numbers, Sources Say," *South China Morning Post*, 13 March 2017, https://www.scmp.com/news/china/diplomacy-defence/article/2078245/overseas-ambitions-expand-china-plans-400pc-increase. David Brewster catalogues these PLA shifts and rightly concludes that there will "be a risk of mission creep." See "The Forces Needed to Protect the Belt and Road," *The Lowy Interpreter*, 28 November 2018, https://www.lowyinstitute.org/the-interpreter/forces-needed-protect-belt-and-road.

156. Heath, *China's Pursuit of Overseas Security*, p. 26.

157. Article 69 of the law allows government officials to exchange counter-terrorism intelligence with foreign countries and conduct "enforcement cooperation." Article 71 allows China security forces to "assign people to leave the country on counter-terrorism missions," upon reaching agreement with relevant countries. Translation courtesy of US-China Business Council and ChinaLawTranslate.com. See "Unofficial Translation of the Counter-Terrorism Law of the People's Republic of China," The US-China Business Council, https://www.uschina.org/china-hub/unofficial-translation-counter-terrorism-law-peoples-republic-china.

158. "Chinese Police in Closer Law Enforcement Cooperation with Foreign Peers," *Xinhua*, 24 September 2017, http://www.xinhuanet.com/english/2017-09/24/c_136634614.htm. This figure was an increase from 2012, when thirty-eight officers were stationed in twenty-three countries. For 2012 figures, see Duchâtel, Braüner, and Zhou Hang, "Protecting China's Overseas Interests," p. 54.

159. Duchâtel, Brauner, and Zhou Hang, "Protecting China's Overseas Interests," p. 3.

160. Author conversation with officials from the China Association of Friendship, Beijing, 8 December 2017.

161. Thanks to Joshua T. White for his helpful recollections from that meeting.

162. Alessandro Arduino, *China's Private Army: Protecting the New Silk Road* (Singapore: Palgrave Pivot, 2018), p. 163.

163. Arduino, *China's Private Army*, p. 37.

164. Arduino, *China's Private Army*, p. 43.

165. Helena Legarda and Meia Nouwens, "Guardians of the Belt and Road," Mercator Institute for China Studies, 16 August 2018, https://www.merics.org/en/china-monitor/guardians-of-belt-and-road.

166. Duchâtel, Braüner, and Zhou Hang, "Protecting China's Overseas Interests," p. 55; also on the same point, see Arduino, *China's Private Army*, p. 35; Helena Legarda and Meia Nouwens, "Guardians of the Belt and Road."

167. On the slightly murky issue of China's private security contractors carrying arms, see Charles Clover, "Chinese Private Security Companies Go Global," *Financial Times*, 26 February 2017, https://www.ft.com/content/2a1ce1c8-fa7c-11e6-9516-2d969e0d3b65.

168. Meia Nouwens, "China's Use of Private Companies and Other Actors to Secure the Belt and Road across South Asia," *Asia Policy*, vol. 14, no. 2 (April 2019): p. 19.

169. Emily Feng and Charles Clover, "Drone Swarms vs Conventional Arms: China's Military Debate," *Financial Times*, 24 August 2017, https://www.ft.com/content/302fc14a-66ef-11e7-8526-7b38dcaef614; Office of the Secretary of Defense, "Annual Report to Congress: Military and Security Developments Involving the People's Republic of China," https://www.defense.gov/Portals/1/Documents/pubs/2014_DoD_China_Report.pdf; Elizabeth Shim, "China Deploying Drones for 'Surveillance and Strikes,'" *United Press International*, 29 December 2017, https://www.upi.com/China-deploying-drones-for-surveillance-and-strikes/5811514558053/; Laura Zhou, "Chinese Navy Deploys Drones in South China Sea Missile Drills," *South China Morning Post*, 15 June 2018, https://www.scmp.com/news/china/diplomacy-defence/article/2150957/chinese-navy-deploys-drones-south-china-sea-missile; "China Deploys Radars, Drones on Indo-Tibet Border to Curb Infiltration," *Press Trust of India*, 13 July 2018, https://www.tribuneindia.com/news/world/china-deploys-radars-drones-on-indo-tibet-border-to-curb-infiltration/155310.html.

170. On Trump administration amendments to US drone export policies, see Michael C. Horowitz and Joshua A. Schwartz, "A New US Policy Makes It (Somewhat) Easier to Export Drones," *Washington Post*, 20 April 2018, https://www.washingtonpost.com/news/monkey-cage/wp/2018/04/20/a-new-u-s-policy-makes-it-somewhat-easier-to-export-drones/.

171. "Is China at the Forefront of Drone Technology?" ChinaPower Project, Center for Strategic and International Studies, https://chinapower.csis.org/china-drones-unmanned-technology/.

172. "Is China at the Forefront of Drone Technology?"

173. "Is China at the Forefront of Drone Technology?"

174. China's efforts to secure its overseas interests will likely be "characterized by an overlapping mixture of People's Liberation Army troops, paramilitary forces, civilian contractors, and local security forces provided by nations hosting major Chinese assets," according to Heath, *China's Pursuit of Overseas Security*, p. x.

175. "Speech by Foreign Minister Wang Yi at the Opening of Symposium on International Developments and China's Diplomacy in 2017," 10 December 2017, http://www.fmprc.gov.cn/mfa_eng/wjbxw/t1518130.shtml. Wang Yi had made similar comments at the 19th Party Congress in October 2017, calling the BRI "the largest international cooperation platform in the world and the most popular international public product." See Swaine, "Chinese Views of Foreign Policy in the 19th Party Congress."

176. "Speech by Foreign Minister Wang Yi at the Opening of Symposium on International Developments and China's Diplomacy in 2017."

177. As Sinologist David Shambaugh wrote in his 2013 book, China "enjoys the trappings of being a major world power: being a permanent member of the UN Security Council, a member of the G-20, a participant in all major international summits, etc. On the other hand, with the possible exception of its central role in the Six Party Talks process on North Korea, Chinese officials remain remarkably reactive and passive in these venues. China does not lead." He adds with respect to multilateral settings, "China repeatedly takes a low-key, backseat approach in its diplomacy." But, "On the other hand, China's bilateral diplomacy is extremely active." See David L. Shambaugh, *China Goes Global: The Partial Power* (Oxford: Oxford University Press, 2013), pp. 45–46.

178. In July 2018, for example, he used a BRICS summit—a group founded in 2009 that now counts Brazil, Russia, India, and South Africa as members—to urge support for "an open world economy." He also declared the need "to be resolute in rejecting unilateralism and protectionism." See "Full Text of Chinese President's Speech at BRICS Business Forum in South Africa," *Xinhua*, 26 July 2018, http://www.xinhuanet.com/english/2018-07/26/c_137348197.htm.

179. "China's President Is the Country's Most-Traveled Leader Since Communism—And Maybe the Strongest," *Los Angeles Times*, 25 December 2015, http://www.latimes.com/world/asia/la-fg-china-president-travel-20151225-story.html.

180. Another example of China stepping out of the shadows on the global stage and expressing "the need for new leadership at the United Nations and in

international affairs, and on China's ability and willingness to take on a greater role in both" is described by Jim Hoagland, recounting the story of Chinese defense minister Wei Fenghe's interaction with UN Security Council members in November 2018. See Jim Hoagland, "The Wrong Way to Answer China's Global Aims," *Washington Post*, 8 January 2019.

181. In 2015, Shambaugh found that although China's publicity blitz took off in 2007, "it has intensified under President Xi Jinping." David Shambaugh, "China's Soft Power Push," *Foreign Affairs*, July/August 2015, https://www. foreignaffairs.com/articles/china/2015-06-16/china-s-soft-power-push.

182. Hilton Yip, "China's $6 Billion Propaganda Blitz Is a Snooze," *Foreign Policy*, 23 April 2018, https://foreignpolicy.com/2018/04/23/the-voice-of-china-will-be-a-squeak/.

183. Lily Quo, "China State Media Merger to Create Propaganda Giant," *Guardian*, 21 March 2018, https://www.theguardian.com/world/2018/mar/21/ china-state-media-merger-to-create-propaganda-giant.

184. Elias Groll, "Chinese Media Targeted in Foreign Agent Crackdown," *Foreign Policy*, 6 February 2019, https://foreignpolicy.com/2019/02/06/chinese-media-targeted-in-foreign-agent-crackdown/.

185. "Chinese Ambassador to Pakistan Zhao Lijian in Twitter Spat with Cyril Almeida Says Fed Up of Criticism of CPEC," *Financial Express*, 21 December 2016, https://www.financialexpress.com/world-news/chinese-ambassador-to-pakistan-zhao-lijian-in-twitter-spat-with-cyril-almeida-says-fed-up-of-criticism-of-cpec/481115/.

186. For more on the park, see Kyle Haddad-Fonda, "China's Massive, Garish Theme Park for the Muslim World," *Foreign Policy*, 11 May 2016, http:// foreignpolicy.com/2016/05/11/chinas-massive-garish-new-theme-park-for-the-muslim-world-hui-minority-yinchuan/.

187. Haddad-Fonda, "China's Massive, Garish Theme Park.".

188. "Ningxia has supplanted Xinjiang as Beijing's approved destination for Muslim visitors, part of a conscious strategy to shift focus from the Uighur to the Hui." See Haddad-Fonda, "China's Massive, Garish Theme Park."

189. Janis Mackey Frayer, "China's Islamic-Themed 'Hui Culture Park' Is No Tourism Mecca," *NBC News*, 10 July 2016, https://www.nbcnews.com/news/ china/china-s-islamic-themed-hui-culture-park-no-tourism-mecca-n588036.

190. "Chart of the Day: The Growth of China's Confucius Institutes," *Caixin*, 30 November 2018, https://www.caixinglobal.com/2018-11-30/chart-of-the-day-the-growth-of-chinas-confucius-institutes-101354066.html.

191. Bethany Allen-Ebrahimian, "This Beijing-Linked Billionaire Is Funding Policy Research at Washington's Most Influential Institutions," *Foreign Policy*, 28 November 2017, https://foreignpolicy.com/2017/11/28/this-beijing-linked-billionaire-is-funding-policy-research-at-washingtons-most-influential-institutions-china-dc/.

192. John Fitzgerald, "Academic Freedom and the Contemporary University: Lessons from China," *The Journal of the Australian Academy of the Humanities*, vol. 8 (2017): p. 14, who cites Chang Ping, "Chinese Students Studying Abroad a New Focus of CCP's 'United Front Work,'" *China Change*, 9 June 2015, https://chinachange.org/2015/06/09/chinese-students-studying-abroad-a-new-focus-of-ccps-united-front-work/.

193. Josh Rogin, "University Rejects Chinese Communist Party-Linked Influence Efforts on Campus," *Washington Post*, 14 January 2018, https://www.washingtonpost.com/opinions/global-opinions/university-rejects-chinese-communist-party-linked-influence-efforts-on-campus/2018/01/14/c454b54e-f7de-11e7-beb6-c8d48830c54d_story.html.

194. For reporting on Chinese interference in Australia, see "Power and Influence" *ABC News*, 5 June 2017, http://www.abc.net.au/4corners/power-and-influence-promo/8579844.

195. Malcolm Turnbull, "Speech Introducing the National Security Legislation Amendment (Espionage and Foreign Interference) Bill 2017," 7 December 2017, https://www.malcolmturnbull.com.au/media/speech-introducing-the-national-security-legislation-amendment-espionage-an.

196. Economy, *The Third Revolution*, p. 82.

197. For examples of direct and indirect pressure, see Paul Mozur, "China Tries to Extract Pledge of Compliance from US Tech Firms," *New York Times*, 16 September 2015, https://www.nytimes.com/2015/09/17/technology/china-tries-to-extract-pledge-of-compliance-from-us-tech-firms.html; Paul Mozur and Jane Perlez, "China Quietly Targets US Tech Companies in Security Reviews," *New York Times,* 16 May 2016, https://www.nytimes.com/2016/05/17/technology/china-quietly-targets-us-tech-companies-in-security-reviews.html; "China's New Cyber-Security Law Is Worryingly Vague," *The Economist*, 1 June 2017, https://www.economist.com/news/business/21722873-its-rules-are-broad-ambiguous-and-bothersome-international-firms-chinas-new-cyber-security; Katie Benner and Sui-Lee Wee, "Apple Removes New York Times Apps from Its Store in China," *New York Times*, 4 January 2017, https://www.nytimes.com/2017/01/04/business/media/new-york-times-apps-apple-china.html. For offensive cyber-attacks, see "China's Great Cannon," Mapping Global Media Policy, 4 April 2015, http://www.globalmediapolicy.net/node/13276; Adam Segal, "What's the Future of Chinese Hacking," *Motherboard*, 30 July 2016, https://motherboard.vice.com/en_us/article/ezpa5w/future-of-chinese-hacking.

198. Gary King, Jennifer Pan, and Margaret E. Roberts, "How Censorship in China Allows Government Criticism but Silences Collective Expression," *American Political Science Review*, vol. 107, no. 2 (May 2013): pp. 1–18, http://j.mp/2nxNUhk.

199. For more information, see Thomas Lum, Patricia Moloney Figliola, and Matthew C. Weed, "China, Internet Freedom, and US Policy," Congressional Research Service, 13 July 2012, https://fas.org/sgp/crs/row/R42601.pdf.

200. Adrian Shahbaz, "Freedom on the Net 2018: The Rise of Digital Authoritarianism," Freedom House, October 2018, https://freedomhouse.org/sites/default/files/FOTN_2018_Final%20Booklet_11_1_2018.pdf.

201. Andrew J. Nathan, "China's Challenge," in *Authoritarianism Goes Global*, edited by Larry Diamond, Marc F. Plattner, and Christopher Walker (Baltimore: Johns Hopkins University Press, 2016), p. 31.

202. For an instructive debate over how and why the US policy debate over China has evolved in this way, see "Did America Get China Wrong? The Engagement Debate," *Foreign Affairs*, July/August 2018, https://www.foreignaffairs.com/articles/china/2018-06-14/did-america-get-china-wrong; and Kurt M. Campbell and Ely Ratner, "The China Reckoning: How Beijing Defied American Expectations," *Foreign Affairs*, vol 97, no. 2 (March/April 2018), https://www.foreignaffairs.com/articles/united-states/2018-02-13/china-reckoning.

203. Aaron L. Friedberg, "Competing with China," *Survival*, vol. 60, no. 3 (2018): p. 7.

204. President Xi's signature BRI is most properly appreciated as "a grand strategy that advances China's goal of establishing itself as the preponderant power in Eurasia and a global power second to none." Rolland, *China's Eurasian Century?*, p. xi.

205. Although Chinese commentators rarely question the overarching wisdom of President Xi's signature foreign policy initiative, some have raised doubts about its implementation prospects. Others are not fully convinced Beijing has the wherewithal to overcome its lack of operational experience in a complicated Eurasian environment, fear that the financial and security risks in Eurasia are higher than anticipated, or sense that Beijing is too impatient and is moving too quickly. See Rolland, *China's Eurasian Century?*, pp. 152–157.

206. For an insightful first take on the various hurdles described in this paragraph in the context of the BRI, see Rolland, *China's Eurasian Century?*, pp. 159–173.

Chapter 3

1. Bin Yang, "The Rise and Fall of Cowrie Shells: The Asian Story," *Journal of World History*, vol. 22, no. 1 (2011): pp. 1–25.

2. Xi Jinping, "Promote Friendship between Our People and Work Together to Build a Bright Future," Ministry of Foreign Affairs of the People's Republic of China, 7 September 2013, https://www.fmprc.gov.cn/mfa_eng/wjdt_665385/zyjh_665391/t1078088.shtml. For critical commentary, see Tansen Sen, "Silk Road Diplomacy – Twists, Turns and Distorted History," YaleGlobal Online, 23 September 2014, https://yaleglobal.yale.edu/content/silk-road-diplomacy-twists-turns-and-distorted -history.

3. Tansen Sen, *India, China, and the World: A Connected History* (London: Rowman & Littlefield, 2017), p. 38.

4. Tansen Sen, *India, China, and the World*, p. 39.

5. For a discussion of Faxian's travels, including a map, see Tansen Sen, *India, China, and the World*, pp. 125–127.

6. Tansen Sen, *India, China, and the World*, p. 41.

7. Tansen Sen, *India, China, and the World*, pp. 81–106.

8. Tansen Sen, *India, China, and the World*, pp. 44–45.

9. Tansen Sen, *India, China, and the World*, p. 200; Geoff Wade, "The Zheng He Voyages: A Reassessment," *Journal of the Malaysian Branch of the Royal Asiatic Society*, vol. 78, no. 1 (2005): p. 51, https://www.jstor.org/stable/41493537.

10. Tansen Sen, "The Impact of Zheng He's Expeditions on Indian Ocean Interactions," *Bulletin of the School of Oriental and African Studies*, vol. 79, no. 3 (October 2016): p. 617.

11. Wade, "The Zheng He Voyages," pp. 37–58.

12. Zachary Reddick, "The Zheng He Voyages Reconsidered: A Means of Imperial Power Projection," *Quarterly Journal of Chinese Studies*, vol. 3, no. 1 (Autumn 2014): pp. 57–58.

13. Wade, "The Zheng He Voyages," p. 45.

14. Wade, "The Zheng He Voyages," pp. 47–51. For more detail on Zheng He's 1411 battle in Sri Lanka, see Tansen Sen, *India, China, and the World*, pp. 210–215.

15. Tansen Sen, "The Impact of Zheng He's Expeditions on Indian Ocean Interactions," pp. 609–636; Wade, "The Zheng He Voyages."

16. For a colorful and detailed history of the Zheng He period as well as the subsequent Ming Dynasty decision to end its maritime expeditions, see Louise Levathes, *When China Ruled the Seas: The Treasure Fleet of the Dragon Throne, 1405–1433* (Oxford: Oxford University Press, 1994), especially pp. 155–181.

17. Tansen Sen, *India, China, and the World*, p. 278.

18. Tensen Sen devotes considerable attention to the context and consequence of Pan-Asianism throughout chapter 4 of *India, China, and the World*, pp. 293–378.

19. On Pakistan's Cold War alliance with the United States, see Dennis Kux, *The United States and Pakistan 1947–2000: Disenchanted Allies* (Washington, DC: Woodrow Wilson Center, 2001).

20. On this period, see John W. Garver, *Protracted Contest: Sino-Indian Rivalry in the Twentieth Century* (Seattle: University of Washington Press, 2001), pp. 190–191.

21. Tansen Sen, *India, China, and the World*, pp. 379, 409–411.

22. Garver, *Protracted Contest*, pp. 3, 11–16.

23. See map of "Overlap of Perceived Indian and Chinese Historic Spheres of Influence," Garver, *Protracted Contest*, p. 15.

24. On the contemporary historical evolution of the China-Pakistan relationship, see Small, *The China-Pakistan Axis*.

25. Dennis Kux was the political counselor and the author of the best history of US-Pakistan diplomatic relations. See Kux, *The United States and Pakistan 1947–2000*, pp. 182–184, 188–192.

26. On China's strategic interests in South Asia, see Daniel S. Markey and James West, "Behind China's Gambit in Pakistan," Council on Foreign Relations Expert Brief, 12 May 2016, https://www.cfr.org/expert-brief/behind-chinas-gambit-pakistan.

27. See Ruan Zongze, "Belt and Road Initiative: A New Frontier for Win-Win Cooperation," China Institute of International Studies, 21 July 2017, http://www.ciis.org.cn/english/2017-07/21/content_39050638.htm.

28. "Ascending the Saga of National Progress," Ministry of Planning, Development and Reform, Government of Pakistan, 2015, p. 7.

29. "Long Term Plan for China-Pakistan Economic Corridor (2017–2030)," Ministry of Planning, Development and Reform, Government of Pakistan, 2017, http://cpec.gov.pk/long-term-plan-cpec.

30. "Long Term Plan for China-Pakistan Economic Corridor (2017–2030)," p. 9.

31. "Long Term Plan for China-Pakistan Economic Corridor (2017–2030)," p. 2.

32. "Briefing on China-Pakistan Economic Corridor," Chinese Embassy in Pakistan, 26 October 2018, http://www.cpecinfo.com/news/briefing-on-cpec-at-chinese-embassy-news-briefing-meeting-(2018-10-26)/NjExOQ==. For more on the next steps envisioned for CPEC in agriculture, industry, and development assistance, see Arif Rafiq, "CPEC's New Pivot," *CPECWire*, 3 March 2019, https://cpecwire.com/analysis/china-pakistan-economic-corridor-cpec-new-pivot-changes/.

33. Much has been written about India's global ambitions. Excellent American assessments include Ashley J. Tellis, India as a Leading Power (Washington, DC: Carnegie Endowment for International Peace, 2016), https://carnegieendowment.org/2016/04/04/india-as-leading-power-pub-63185; Alyssa Ayres, *Our Time Has Come: How India Is Making Its Place in the World* (Oxford: Oxford University Press, 2018); and Teresita C. Schaffer and Howard B. Schaffer, *India at the Global High Table: The Quest for Regional Primacy and Strategic Autonomy* (Washington, DC: Brookings Institution Press, 2016).

34. For a short summary of these territorial disputes, see Ayres, *Our Time Has Come*, pp. 126–128.

35. Ankit Panda, "The Political Geography of the India-China Crisis at Doklam," *The Diplomat*, 13 July 2017, https://thediplomat.com/2017/07/the-political-geography-of-the-india-china-crisis-at-doklam/; Ankit Panda, "What's Driving the India-China Standoff at Doklam?," *The Diplomat*, 18 July 2017, https://thediplomat.com/2017/07/whats-driving-the-india-china-standoff-at-doklam/.

36. For more on what brought the crisis to an end, see Abhijnan Rej, "India's Clever Use of the BRICS Card in Doklam Standoff," *Livemint*, 15 September

2017, http://www.livemint.com/Opinion/c4ws2jwOqP7ALa7Y0RbC1M/Indias-clever-use-of-the-BRICS-card-in-Doklam-standoff-reso.html.

37. As Oriana Skylar Mastro puts it, "this action-reaction cycle of China pushing the boundaries literally and figuratively, and the Indian imperative to respond to establish deterrence, is bound to lead to another standoff. The only question is when the next time will be that China pushes too far and triggers an Indian military response." See Oriana Skylar Mastro's contribution in "One Year after They Almost Went to War, Can China and India Get Along?" A ChinaFile Conversation, 14 June 2018, http://www.chinafile.com/conversation/one-year-after-they-almost-went-war-can-china-and-india-get-along.

38. On specific defensive infrastructure investments near Doklam, including nearby deployments of advanced fighters, as well as new Chinese sentry posts, helipads, and trenches, see Joel Wuthnow's contribution in "One Year after They Almost Went to War, Can China and India Get Along?" A ChinaFile Conversation, 14 June 2018, http://www.chinafile.com/conversation/one-year-after-they-almost-went-war-can-china-and-india-get-along.

39. Analyst Frank O'Donnell estimates that by 2021, India should "be able to draw on an estimated 221,000 forces . . . close to the border." For its part, China's "superior military logistical network" should enable Beijing to field similar numbers of troops to the border region within a month. See Frank O'Donnell, "Stabilizing Sino-Indian Security Relations: Managing Strategic Rivalry after Doklam," Carnegie-Tsinghua Center for Global Policy, Carnegie Endowment for International Peace, 2018, pp. 6, 13–14.

40. India expert Ashley Tellis notes that India's rise to great power status will take time. See Tellis, "India as a Leading Power," p. 5.

41. Professor Mohan Malik of the Asia-Pacific Center for Security in Honolulu observes that "China has been concerned about India moving too close to the United States and Japan. . . . Should India challenge or aspire to emerge as China's equal or peer competitor—and do so with help from Japan and the United States—then the entire gamut of contentious bilateral issues are open for review and recasting." See Mohan Malik, "China and India: The Roots of Hostility," *The Diplomat*, 12 September 2017, https://thediplomat.com/2017/09/china-and-india-the-roots-of-hostility/.

42. Author conversations with Chinese academics and think tank analysts as part of a SAIS-PKU Dialogue, Beijing, 5–9 December 2017.

43. For more on the prospects of the Quad, see Ankit Panda, "US, Japan, India, and Australia Hold Senior Official-Level Quadrilateral Meeting in Singapore," *The Diplomat*, 8 June 2018, https://thediplomat.com/2018/06/us-japan-india-and-australia-hold-senior-official-level-quadrilateral-meeting-in-singapore/.

44. Tanvi Madan, "Dancing with the Dragon? Deciphering India's 'China Reset,'" *War on the Rocks*, 26 April 2018, https://warontherocks.com/2018/04/dancing-with-the-dragon-deciphering-indias-china-reset/.

45. Brahma Chellaney, "India-China Summit Highlights Modi's Hope vs Xi's Strategy," *Nikkei Asian Review*, 1 May 2018, https://asia.nikkei.com/Opinion/India-China-summit-highlights-Modi-s-hope-vs-Xi-s-strategy2.

46. The best treatment of the political controversies surrounding these decisions is found in Rafiq, "The China-Pakistan Economic Corridor," pp. 31–35.

47. Peer Muhammad, "CPEC: Rs20b for Western, Rs110b for Eastern Route, NHA Admits," *Express Tribune*, 20 October 2015, http://www.tribune.com.pk/story/975849/cpec-rs20b-for-western-rs110b-for-eastern-route-nha-admits/.

48. Khawar Ghumman, "Parties Give Go-Ahead to China-Pak Corridor," *Dawn,* 29 May 2015, https://www.dawn.com/news/1184885; "Decisions Taken in the All Parties Conference Held under the Chairmanship of the Prime Minister on 15th January 2016 Islamabad," 15 January 2016, https://pmo.gov.pk/press_release_detailes.php?pr_id=1306.

49. "Energy Projects Worth $25b to Be Completed under CPEC: Ahsan Iqbal," *Express Tribune*, 10 January 2016, https://tribune.com.pk/story/1025092/energy-projects-worth-25b-to-be-completed-under-cpec-ahsan-iqbal/. "Energy Projects Worth $25b to Be Completed Under CPEC."

50. Adnan Aamir, "Rural Pakistan Voices Dissatisfaction over Belt & Road," *Nikkei Asian Review*, 31 December 2018, https://asia.nikkei.com/Spotlight/Belt-and-Road/Rural-Pakistan-voices-dissatisfaction-over-Belt-Road.

51. "China-Pakistan Economic Corridor: Opportunities and Risks," p. 16.

52. "Agriculture Statistics," Pakistan Bureau of Statistics, http://www.pbs.gov.pk/content/agriculture-statistics.

53. Half of Pakistan's rural households are "landless or near-landless," according to Cynthia Caron, "Pakistan Property Rights and Resource Governance Profile," *USAID Country Profile*, April 2018, p. 1. On the political significance of landholdings in Pakistan, large and small, see Anatol Lieven, *Pakistan: A Hard Country* (New York: Public Affairs, 2011), pp. 219–220. On Pakistan's incomplete land reforms, see Stephen Philip Cohen, *The Idea of Pakistan* (Washington, DC: Brookings Institution Press, 2004), p. 258; Ian Talbot, *Pakistan: A Modern History* (New York: Palgrave Macmillan, 2005), pp. 164–166.

54. "Long Term Plan for China-Pakistan Economic Corridor (2017–2030)," p. 18.

55. Vaqar Ahmed, "Making China-Pakistan Agri Cooperation Politically Safe," *Arab News*, 28 December 2018, http://www.arabnews.pk/node/1426546.

56. Ahmed, "Making China-Pakistan Agri Cooperation Politically Safe."

57. Interview with Pakistani landowner, Washington, DC, 7 July 2017.

58. See "China-Pakistan Economic Corridor: Opportunities and Risks," pp. 23–24.

59. Andrew Small, "Buyer's Remorse: Pakistan's Elections and the Precarious Future of the China-Pakistan Economic Corridor," *War on the Rocks*, 27 July 2018, https://warontherocks.com/2018/07/buyers-remorse-pakistans-elections-and-the-precarious-future-of-the-china-pakistan-economic-corridor/.

60. "Dispute over CPEC Is with Nawaz-Led Govt, Not with China: Imran," *Dawn*, 25 December 2016, https://www.dawn.com/news/1304419.

61. Jamil Anderlini, Henny Sender, and Farhan Bokhari, "Pakistan Rethinks Its Role in Xi's Belt and Road Plan," *Financial Times*, 9 September 2018, https://www.ft.com/content/d4a3e7f8-b282-11e8-99ca-68cf89602132.

62. "No Rollback of CPEC, Pakistan Assures China," *Express Tribune*, 10 September 2018, https://tribune.com.pk/story/1799826/1-pakistan-china-react-angrily-financial-times-report-cpec/; "Wary of Debt Trap, Govt Rethinks Silk Road Projects," *Dawn*, 1 October 2018, https://www.dawn.com/news/1436109/wary-of-debt-trap-govt-rethinks-silk-road-projects.

63. "General Qamar Javed Bajwa, Chief of Army Staff (COAS) Called on Chinese President Xi Jinping on Special Invitation," Inter-Services Public Relations, 19 September 2018, https://www.ispr.gov.pk/press-release-detail.php?id=4940.

64. An example of the appeals China made to the incoming Imran Khan government can be found in this op-ed by China's ambassador to Pakistan: Yao Jing, "A Community of Shared Future with Pakistan," *China Daily*, 28 August 2018, http://global.chinadaily.com.cn/a/201808/28/WS5b8487b1a310add14f3880c5.html.

65. On Imran Khan's early efforts to refocus CPEC, see Syed Irfan Raza, "CPEC Focus Must Be on Job Creation, Agriculture: Imran," *Dawn*, 9 October 2018, https://www.dawn.com/news/1437770.

66. "Briefing on China-Pakistan Economic Corridor."

67. Saibal Dasgupta, "Pakistani PM Visits China as Fiscal Crisis Looms," *Voice of America*, 2 November 2018, https://www.voanews.com/a/pakistan-imran-khan-china-xi-jinping/4639850.html.

68. "IMF Survey: Pakistan Gets $6.6 Billion Loan from IMF," *International Monetary Fund*, accessed 4 September 2013, https://www.imf.org/en/News/Articles/2015/09/28/04/53/socar090413a.

69. Ismail Dilawar, "China's Silk Road Push in Pakistan Edges Out US Investments," *Bloomberg*, 12 April 2017, https://www.bloomberg.com/news/articles/2017-04-12/china-s-silk-road-push-in-pakistan-edges-out-u-s-investments.

70. Data reported and defined by the State Bank of Pakistan. To access data, see "Net Inflow of Foreign Private Investment—Country-wise (New Format)," State Bank of Pakistan, http://www.sbp.org.pk/ecodata/NIFP_Arch/index.asp.

71. Faseeh Mangi, "China's Billions Luring Once Shy Foreign Investors to Pakistan," *Bloomberg*, 6 November 2016, https://www.bloomberg.com/news/articles/2016-11-07/china-s-billions-luring-once-shy-foreign-investors-to-pakistan. According to the State Bank of Pakistan—which published different 2016 figures—foreign investment also grew in 2017 and 2018. See "Summary of Foreign Investment in Pakistan," State Bank of Pakistan, accessed 20 June 2019, http://www.sbp.org.pk/ecodata/NetinflowSummary.pdf.

72. Author conversation with Sibtain Fazal Haleem, Lahore, Pakistan, 29 February 2016.

73. For details on the project, see "China Export-Import Bank Commits Loan of 165.226 Billion Rupees to Pakistan for Lahore Orange Line Metro Train Project," Aid Data, accessed 21 August 2017, http://china.aiddata.org/projects/37280?iframe=y; Khalid Hasnain, "$1.6bn Chinese Soft Loan for Elevated Metro Train," *Dawn*, 4 March 2014, https://www.dawn.com/news/1090941; "Chinese Bank to Give Rs162 bn for Lahore Metro Train," *The News International*, 22 December 2015, https://www.thenews.com.pk/print/83509-Chinese-bank-to-give-Rs162-bn-for-Lahore-metro-train; Kevin Smith, "China Signs Funding Agreement for Lahore Metro," *International Railway Journal*, 23 December 2015, http://www.railjournal.com/index.php/asia/funding-agreed-for-lahore-metro-line.html.

74. "'Massive Kickbacks' Behind Launching Loss-Making Projects, Claims Imran," *Geo News*, 7 March 2018, https://www.geo.tv/latest/185219-massive-kickbacks-behind-launching-loss-making-projects-claims-imran. See also Page and Shah, "China's Global Building Spree Runs into Trouble in Pakistan.".

75. Small, *The China-Pakistan Axis*, p. 112.

76. On Zardari's twenty-nine visits to China, see Tom Hussain, "In Pakistan, Chinese Money Grapples with a Karachi-Lahore Divide," *South China Morning Post*, 16 September 2018, https://www.scmp.com/week-asia/geopolitics/article/2163956/pakistan-chinese-money-grapples-karachi-lahore-divide.

77. The "Panama Papers," a trove of legal documents leaked in 2016, indicated that Sharif's three children owned previously undisclosed properties in London. At the time the properties were purchased, Sharif's children were minors, indicating that Sharif had initiated the transactions. In 2017, Pakistan's supreme court unanimously disqualified Sharif from parliament for failing to report the assets in 2013 election documents and for false declarations. In 2018, the supreme court effectively banned Sharif from political office. See Bill Chappell, "Pakistan's High Court Ousts Prime Minister Sharif in Panama Papers Fallout," *NPR*, 28 July 2017, http://www.npr.org/sections/thetwo-way/2017/07/28/539954118/pakistans-high-court-ousts-prime-minister-sharif-in-panama-papers-fallout; Sune Engel Rasmussen, "Pakistani Court Removes PM Nawaz Sharif from Office in Panama Papers Case," *Guardian*, 28 July 2017, https://www.theguardian.com/world/2017/jul/28/pakistani-court-disqualifies-pm-nawaz-sharif-from-office. For more on the 2018 ruling, see Kamran Haider and Ismail Dilawar, "Pakistan Court Orders Lifetime Political Ban Against Sharif," *Bloomberg*, 13 April 2018, https://www.bloomberg.com/news/articles/2018-04-13/pakistan-court-orders-lifetime-political-ban-against-sharif.

78. For an earlier detailed look at corruption in Pakistan, see Raymond W. Baker, *Capitalism's Achilles Heel* (New Jersey: John Wiley & Sons, 2005), pp. 76–87.

79. I have heard several versions of a similar speech by Ahsan Iqbal, each time observing how Pakistan under the PML-N moved from "world's most dangerous state" to a stable, secure, and vibrant emerging economy. One such speech was delivered at the Leaders in Islamabad Business Summit, in Islamabad, Pakistan, 15 March 2018.

80. Shahid Javed Burki, "China's Road Can Be Pakistan's Route to Rescue," *Business Times*, 9 August 2018, https://www.businesstimes.com.sg/opinion/chinas-road-can-be-pakistans-route-to-rescue.

81. "PTV Apologises for 'Typo' during PM's China Speech," *Express Tribune*, 5 November 2018, https://tribune.com.pk/story/1840556/1-ptv-apologises-typo-pms-china-speech/.

82. Jaffrelot notes how "The convergence of civil and military authorities within an establishment comprising 2,000 families offers a key to the interpretation of the country's stability paradox: whether political parties or the army are in power, it is the interests of one and the same class that are protected—as shown by the persistently low tax burden, the absence of land reform and the continuously high level of military expenditure." Christophe Jaffrelot, *The Pakistan Paradox: Instability and Resilience* (New York: Oxford University Press, 2015), pp. 634–635, and throughout pp. 197–371.

83. On the Karachi-Lahore business divide, see Hussain, "In Pakistan, Chinese Money Grapples with a Karachi-Lahore Divide."

84. "Pakistan's economy clearly needs reform to better serve its people, and many officials say CPEC will help in this regard." See "China-Pakistan Economic Corridor: Opportunities and Risks," p. i. Dr. Ishrat Husain, one of Pakistan's most prominent economists, outlines "policy reforms and institutional arrangements that should enable Pakistan to derive maximum benefits for the economy, for a large segment of the population, and minimize risks" from CPEC. See Ishrat Husain, "CPEC and Pakistan's Economy: A Way Forward," Working Paper #020, Centre of Excellence China-Pakistan Economic Corridor, 5 March 2018, p. 13.

85. CPEC "would change the image of Pakistan into an investor-friendly country," write Anam Kuraishi and Mustafa Hyder, in "The Reality of China-Pakistan Economic Corridor (CPEC): Facts vs. Fiction," Pakistan-China Institute, September 2017, p. 35. On the latter point, economist Shahid Javed Burki writes, "China will provide Pakistan finance, management practices and technologies it does not have at this time but needs for sustained and inclusive development." See "The State of the Economy: China Pakistan Economic Corridor Review and Analysis, 10th Annual Report 2017," The Shahid Javed Burki Institute at NetSol, p. 17 (see also related recommendations for Pakistani economic reforms, pp. 144–146), www.sjbipp.org/publications/AR/reports/AR-10-17.pdf.

86. Early intimations of these concerns, especially over whether Pakistan's private sector would be fully informed and engaged in CPEC, can be found in "China Pakistan Economic Corridor: A Primer," *PRIME Analytical Reports, Unlocking Business Potential for Growth, Policy Research Institute of Market Economy*, vol. 1, no. 2 (15 September 2015).

87. Arif Rafiq, "Pakistan's Imran Khan Heads to China," *The National Interest*, 4 November 2018, https://nationalinterest.org/feature/pakistan's-imran-khan-heads-china-major-implications-belt-and-road-initiative-34897.

88. Saeed Shah and Jeremy Page, "China Readies $46 Billion for Pakistan Trade Route," *Wall Street Journal*, 16 April 2015, https://www.wsj.com/articles/china-to-unveil-billions-of-dollars-in-pakistan-investment-1429214705.

89. Daniel S. Markey, *No Exit from Pakistan: America's Tortured Relationship with Islamabad* (New York: Cambridge University Press, 2013), p. 36.

90. Nadia Naviwala, "Pakistan's $100B Deal with China: What Does It Amount To?" *Devex,* 24 August 2017, https://www.devex.com/news/pakistan-s-100b-deal-with-china-what-does-it-amount-to-90872.

91. For outstanding credit, see Syed Sajid Ali and Sadia Badar, "Dynamics of Circular Debt in Pakistan and Its Resolution," *The Lahore Journal of Economics*, vol. 15 (September 2010): p. 62. For conversions into USD, see "Historic Lookup," X-Rates, accessed 22 August 2017, http://www.x-rates.com/historical/?from=USD&amount=1&date=2009-12-31.

92. For a helpful explanation of circular debt in Pakistan, see Ali and Badar, "Dynamics of Circular Debt in Pakistan and Its Resolution," 61–74.

93. "The Causes and Impacts of Power Sector Circular Debt in Pakistan," Planning Commission of Pakistan, March 2013, http://climateinfo.pk/frontend/web/attachments/data-type/USAID%20(2013)%20The%20Causes%20and%20Impacts%20of%20Power%20Sector%20Circular%20Debt.pdf; Institute of Public Policy, "The State of the Economy: From Survival to Revival," The Shaid Javed Burki Institute of Public Policy at NetSol, June 2013, http://www.sjbipp.org/publications/AR/reports/AR-06-13.pdf.

94. "More Outages Feared as Circular Debt Rises," *Express Tribune*, 31 May 2018, https://tribune.com.pk/story/1723069/2-outages-feared-circular-debt-rises/. For conversion to USD, see "Currency Calculator," X-Rates, accessed 22 June 2018, https://www.xe.com/currencyconverter/convert/?Amount=573&From=INR&To=USD. For GDP, see "Pakistan" The World Bank, https://data.worldbank.org/country/pakistan. GDP as of 2016, the latest year for which data are available.

95. Without fixing circular debt, new power plants could even do more harm than good because they would likely operate at a net loss. See Naviwala, "Pakistan's $100B Deal with China."

96. Author interview, Pakistan, 2 March 2016.

97. "China-Pakistan Economic Corridor: Opportunities and Risks," p. 7.

98. Drazen Jorgic and Brenda Goh, "Braving Security Fears, Chinese Seek 'Silk Road' Riches in Pakistan," *Reuters*, 27 August 2017, https://www.reuters.com/article/us-china-silkroad-pakistan-insight-idUSKCN1B801X.

99. Raza Khan, "15,000 Troops of Special Security Division to Protect CPEC Projects, Chinese nationals," *Dawn*, 12 August 2016, https://www.dawn.com/news/1277182.

100. Drazen Jorgic and Jibran Ahmad, "Pakistan Scrambles to Protect China's 'Silk Road' Pioneers," *Reuters*, 11 June 2017, https://www.reuters.com/article/us-pakistan-china-islamic-state/pakistan-scrambles-to-protect-chinas-silk-road-pioneers-idUSKBN1920KL.

101. "CPEC Security: China to Train Pakistan Civil Armed Forces on Modern Lines: Ambassador," *Times of Islamabad*, 16 September 2017, https://timesofislamabad.com/16-Sep-2017/cpec-security-china-to-train-pakistan-civil-armed-forces-on-modern-lines-ambassador.

102. "China-Pakistan Economic Corridor: Opportunities and Risks," p. 7.

103. On Pakistan's various new "sovereign obligations" to China—from energy projects to roads and ports—see Rafiq, "The China-Pakistan Economic Corridor: Barriers and Impact," pp. 44–47.

104. "Chinese Prisoners Working on CPEC Projects: MNA," *Dawn*, 27 February 2018, https://www.dawn.com/news/1392023; "Rumors Claiming Prisoners Being Used as Labours in CPEC Projects Are False, Says China," *Pakistan Today*, 23 December 2016, https://www.pakistantoday.com.pk/2016/12/23/rumours-claiming-prisoners-being-used-as-labours-in-cpec-projects-are-false-says-china/.

105. Sajjad Akbar Shah, "Chinese Workers Thrash Policemen in Khanewal," *Dawn*, 5 April 2018, https://www.dawn.com/news/1399531.

106. In December 2017, Khurram Hussain, a senior journalist investigating CPEC, said, "we still know very little about CPEC. The material that would tell us more is still vigorously concealed." See "China-Pakistan Economic Corridor: Opportunities and Risks," p. 10. Moreover, the lack of transparency in Pakistan's deals with China became a special bone of contention with the International Monetary Fund when Imran Khan's government approached the multilateral lender for a bailout in late 2018. See Xie Yu, "IMF Warns Pakistan of Risks of Working with China," *South China Morning Post*, 9 October 2018, https://www.scmp.com/news/asia/south-asia/article/2167574/pakistan-poised-seek-bailout-imf-stabilise-economy-chinese-debt.

107. John Hurley, Scott Morris, and Gailyn Portelance, "Examining the Debt Implications of the Belt and Road Initiative from a Policy Perspective," Policy Paper 121, Center for Global Development, March 2018, https://www.cgdev.org/sites/default/files/examining-debt-implications-belt-and-road-initiative-policy-perspective.pdf.

108. Rafiq, "The China-Pakistan Economic Corridor: Barriers and Impact," pp. 46–47; "China-Pakistan Economic Corridor: Opportunities and Risks," pp. 10–11.

109. Shahbaz Rana, "Pakistan to Pay China $40b on $26.5b CPEC Investments in 20 years," *Express Tribune*, 26 December 2018, https://tribune.com.pk/story/1874661/2-pakistan-pay-china-40-billion-20-years/.

110. Aqil Shah, "Pakistan: Voting Under Military Tutelage," *Journal of Democracy*, vol. 30, no. 1 (January 2019): p. 141.

111. For a short overview of China-Pakistan security ties, see Markey, *No Exit from Pakistan*, pp. 188–192; and for a more comprehensive look, see Small, *The China-Pakistan Axis*.

112. Farhan Bokhari, "Game-Changer: Pakistan Army Takes Lead Role in CPEC Initiative," *Janes Defence Weekly*, 31 August 2016.

113. See "Importer/Exporter TIV Tables," Stockholm International Peace Research Institute, accessed 29 May 2019, http://armstrade.sipri.org/armstrade/page/values.php.

114. On the barriers to US drone sales, see Levi Maxey, "Will China Start Selling the 'AK-47' of Drones?" *The Cipher Brief*, 15 October 2017, https://www.thecipherbrief.com/article/tech/will-china-start-selling-ak-47-drones.

115. The Missile Technology Control Regime signatories agree to start from a "strong presumption of denial" when considering whether to sell large drones capable of carrying significant payloads. Russia and most Western countries are signatories. See "Frequently Asked Questions," Missile Technology Control Regime, accessed 31 August 2017, http://mtcr.info/frequently-asked-questions-faqs/.

116. Maria Abi-Habib, "China's 'Belt and Road' Plan in Pakistan Takes a Military Turn," *New York Times*, 19 December 2018, https://www.nytimes.com/2018/12/19/world/asia/pakistan-china-belt-road-military.html.

117. For CH-3 sales, see "Trade Registers," Stockholm International Peace Research Institute, accessed 23 August 2017, http://armstrade.sipri.org/armstrade/page/trade_register.php. The drones were scheduled for delivery from 2013 to 2016.

118. Adam Rawnsley, "Meet China's Killer Drones," *Foreign Policy*, 14 January 2016, http://foreignpolicy.com/2016/01/14/meet-chinas-killer-drones/.

119. For details on the CH-3, see Clay Dillow, "China: A Rising Drone Weapons Dealer to the World," *CNBC*, 5 March 2016, https://www.cnbc.com/2016/03/03/china-a-rising-drone-weapons-dealer-to-the-world.html. For more on Pakistan's drone program, see Farhan Bokhari and James Hardy, "Update: Pakistan Successfully Fires Missile from Indigenous UAV," *Jane's Defence Weekly*, 18 March 2015; Farhan Bokhari, "Pakistan Claims First Ever Night-Time Attack Using Indigenously Built UAV," *Jane's Defence Weekly*, 26 October 2015.

120. "'Largest Deal': China to Sell 48 High-End Military Drones to Pakistan," *The News (Pakistan)*, 9 October 2018, https://www.thenews.com.pk/latest/378678-largest-deal-china-to-sell-48-high-end-military-drones-to-pakistan.

121. Ayesha Siddiqua observes that the military has permeated three key sectors: agriculture, manufacturing, and services. See Ayesha Siddiqua, *Military Inc.* (Pluto Press: London, 2007), pp. 112–128.

122. Siddiqua, *Military Inc.*, p. 236.

123. Frontier Works Organization Pakistan, "Investment Projects," Rawalpindi, Pakistan, 2018. See also https://www.fwo.com.pk.

124. Author conversation with FCO CEO General Muhammed Afzal, Washington, DC, January 19, 2018. Also, "Baloch militants have killed scores of Pakistani workers employed on CPEC projects, including three labourers in Turbat district working for the military-run Frontier Works Organization on the Gwadar-Quetta highway in May 2017, and ten construction workers in Gwadar earlier the same month, also working on CPEC projects." See "China-Pakistan Economic Corridor: Opportunities and Risks," pp. 21–22.

125. As Aqil Shah writes, "The impact of decades of US policies toward Pakistan has been corrosive for democratization and civilian supremacy . . . the United States has typically set aside concerns about human rights and democracy in favor of short-term strategic goals in Pakistan and has shielded successive allied military governments from the diplomatic, financial, and political costs associated with overthrowing constitutional governments." See Aqil Shah, *The Army and Democracy: Military Politics in Pakistan* (Cambridge: Harvard University Press, 2014), p. 281.

126. S. Akbar Zaidi, "A Dictator by Any Name," *Dawn*, 1 December 2017, https://www.dawn.com/news/1372376.

127. For more on the US policy challenge of democracy promotion in Pakistan during the Musharraf era, see Markey, *No Exit from Pakistan*, pp. 82–83, 129–134.

128. Abi-Habib, "China's 'Belt and Road' Plan in Pakistan Takes a Military Turn."

129. Zafar Bhutta, "Otic Fibre Cable Connecting Pakistan, China to Be Inaugurated Today," *Express Tribune*, 13 July 2018, https://tribune.com.pk/story/1756458/2-optic-fibre-cable-connecting-pakistan-china-inaugurated-today/.

130. Qurat ul ain Siddiqui and Jahanzaib Haque, "Exclusive: The CPEC Plan for Pakistan's Digital Future," *Dawn*, 3 October 2017, https://www.dawn.com/news/1361176.

131. "Watchdog: Pakistan's Military Courts 'Disaster' for Human Rights," *Voice of America*, 16 January 2019, https://www.voanews.com/south-central-asia/watchdog-pakistans-military-courts-disaster-human-rights.

132. Pakistan originally intended to shut down the courts in 2017, but extended them into 2019. See Asad Hashim, "Pakistan to Renew Military Courts for 'Terror' Suspects," *Al Jazeera*, 22 March 2017, http://www.aljazeera.com/news/2017/03/pakistan-renews-military-courts-terror-suspects-170321143432673.html.

133. "Govt Set to Extend Military Courts for Two Years," *Express Tribune*, 30 December 2018, https://tribune.com.pk/story/1877453/1-govt-set-extend-military-courts-two-years/. See also "Army Chief Confirms Death Sentences of 11 'Hardcore Terrorists': ISPR," *Dawn*, 23 November 2018, https://www.dawn.com/news/1447212/army-chief-confirms-death-sentences-of-11-hardcore-terrorists-ispr.

134. "Govt Set to Extend Military Courts for Two Years."

135. Kiran Stacey and Farhan Bokhari, "Pakistan Orders Expulsion of 29 International NGOs," *Financial Times*, 13 December 2017, https://www.ft.com/content/15d38124-de54-11e7-a8a4-0a1e63a52f9c.

136. Ben Farmer, "Aid to 11 Million at Risk as Pakistani Intelligence Gives 18 Charities and NGOs Their Marching Orders," *Telegraph*, 18 October 2018, https://www.telegraph.co.uk/news/2018/10/18/aid-11-million-risk-pakistani-intelligence-gives-18-charities/.

137. "Government Kicks Out 18 INGOs After Rejecting Final Appeal," *Dawn*, 6 December 2018, https://www.dawn.com/news/1449827.

138. "Foreigners Must Have NOC to Enter Gwadar: BoI," *Dawn,* 18 February 2016, https://www.dawn.com/news/1240315.

139. On Saeed's role in the MML, see Yelena Biberman and Niloufer Siddiqui, "Pakistani Militants Have Created Their Own Political Party. Can It Actually Win Votes?" Monkey Cage Blog, *Washington Post*, 8 May 2018, https://www.washingtonpost.com/news/monkey-cage/wp/2018/05/07/pakistani-militants-are-joining-elections-now-what/?utm_term=.60139522fd60. For more on Saeed's history and ties with the Pakistani military, see Markey, *No Exit from Pakistan*, pp. 99–103. On LeT more generally, see Stephen Tankel, *Storming the World Stage* (New York: Columbia/Hurst Press, 2011).

140. "China-Pakistan Economic Corridor: Opportunities and Risks," p. i.

141. "Who Was Behind the Consulate Attack," *The News*, 23 November 2018, https://www.thenews.com.pk/latest/397270-who-was-behind-the-chinese-consulate-attack.

142. Saeed Shah and Eva Dou, "Militants Attack Chinese Consulate in Pakistan," *Wall Street Journal*, 23 November 2018, https://www.wsj.com/articles/militants-attack-chinese-consulate-in-pakistan-1542957610.

143. Usman Shahid, "Balochistan: The Troubled Heart of the CPEC," *The Diplomat*, 23 August 2016, http://thediplomat.com/2016/08/balochistan-the-troubled-heart-of-the-cpec/.

144. "Transcript of RAW Agent Kulbhushan's Confessional Statement," *Dawn*, accessed 22 September 2017, https://www.dawn.com/news/1248786.

145. Author conversation with Pakistani embassy official, Washington, DC, 23 March 2017.

146. Kay Johnson, "Pakistan Army Chief Accuses India of Undermining China Investment Corridor," *Reuters*, 12 April 2016, http://www.reuters.com/article/us-pakistan-india-port-idUSKCN0X92JQ.

147. The best accounting of the Jadhav case so far comes in Praveen Swami, "India's Secret War," *Frontline* (India), 31 January 2018, https://frontline.thehindu.com/the-nation/indias-secret-war/article10055129.ece.

148. Meeting with former senior Indian diplomat, 25 March 2017, Washington, DC.

149. On the tragic and frustrating history of Indo-Pakistani conflict, see Stephen P. Cohen, *Shooting for a Century* (Washington, DC: Brookings, 2013).

150. For a short review of recent developments in the Indo-Pakistani nuclear race, see Max Fischer, "India, Long at Odds with Pakistan, May Be Rethinking Nuclear First Strikes," *New York Times*, 31 March 2017, https://www.nytimes.com/2017/03/31/world/asia/india-long-at-odds-with-pakistan-may-be-rethinking-nuclear-first-strikes.html.

151. "Surgical Strike II Special Media Briefing by Ranbir Singh, Official Spokesperson, 29 Sep," YouTube, accessed 23 September 2017, https://www.youtube.com/watch?v=4eQKiioW9NI.

152. For an example of one such account, see Surendra Singh, "Surgical Strike a Copybook Execution of Precise Planning," *Times of India*, 9 February 2017, http://timesofindia.indiatimes.com/india/surgical-strike-a-copybook-execution-of-precise-planning/articleshow/57049047.cms.

153. Manu Balachandran, "Balochistan and Kashmir: Modi Has Reminded Pakistan That It Lives in a Glass House," *Quartz India*, 16 August 2016, https://qz.com/758424/narendra-modis-mention-of-balochistan-will-change-india-pakistan-relations-forever/.

154. "Ajit Doval Warns Pakistan 'You Do One More Mumbai, You Lose Balochistan,'" *YouTube*, accessed 22 September 2017, https://www.youtube.com/watch?v=N7ESR5RU3X4&feature=youtu.be.

155. "Chinese Scholars 'Deeply Disturbed' by PM Modi's Reference to Balochistan," *Times of India*, 28 August 2016, http://timesofindia.indiatimes.com/india/Chinese-scholars-deeply-disturbed-by-PM-Modis-reference-to-Balochistan/articleshow/53900481.cms.

156. "Chinese Scholars 'Deeply Disturbed' by PM Modi's Reference to Balochistan."

157. On conflicting Indian and Pakistani accounts of the skirmish, see Lara Seligman, "Did India Shoot Down a Pakistani Jet? US Count Says No," *Foreign Policy*, 4 April 2019, https://foreignpolicy.com/2019/04/04/did-india-shoot-down-a-pakistani-jet-u-s-count-says-no/.

158. Patrick Wintour, "Who Will Pull India and Pakistan back from the Edge This Time?" *Guardian*, 27 February 2019, https://www.theguardian.com/world/2019/feb/27/who-will-pull-india-and-pakistan-back-from-the-edge-this-time.

159. Figures calculated by adding India's and Pakistan's respective imports from and exports to China. For India-China bilateral trade data, see "India Trade Summary 2017," World Integration Trade Solution, accessed 19 June 2019, https://wits.worldbank.org/CountryProfile/en/Country/IND/Year/2017/SummaryText/. For Pakistan-China bilateral trade data, see "Pakistan Trade Summary 2017," World Integrated Trade Solution, accessed 19 June 2019, https://wits.worldbank.org/CountryProfile/en/Country/PAK/Year/LTST/Summarytext.

160. Over 60 percent of Chinese FDI was for automobiles, as of 2015. For China's FDI ranking into India, see "Quarterly Fact Sheet," Department for Promotion of Industry and Internal Trade, accessed 19 June 2019, https://dipp.gov.in/sites/default/files/FDI_Factsheet_27May2019.pdf.

161. For 2014–2016, see Sarah Watson, "Beyond a Himalayan Standoff: India Is Still Navigating the New Normal on Chinese Investment," *The Diplomat*, 8 August 2017, http://thediplomat.com/2017/08/beyond-a-himalayan-standoff-india-is-still-navigating-the-new-normal-on-chinese-investment/. For 2016–2017, see Suparna Dutt D'Cunha, "How China Is Positioning Itself among India's Top 10 Investors Despite Bilateral Differences," *Forbes*, 1 May 2018, https://www.forbes.com/sites/suparnadutt/2018/05/01/how-china-is-positioning-itself-among-the-top-10-investors-in-india-despite-bilateral-differences/#31fd8cee1dac.

162. Peggy Sito, "India and Russia Tipped to Be the Big Winners from China's Massive 'Belt and Road' Investment," *South China Morning Post*, 13 May 2017, http://www.scmp.com/business/article/2094224/india-and-russia-tipped-be-big-winners-chinas-massive-belt-and-road.

163. "China's Xi Jinping Signs Landmark Deals on India Visit," *BBC News*, 18 September 2014, http://www.bbc.com/news/world-asia-india-29249268.

164. "The fDi Report 2017," fDi Intelligence, accessed September 14, 2017, http://bcckenya.org/assets/documents/The-fDi-Report-2017.pdf.

165. For more on the Pakistani Taliban, see Mona Kanwal Sheikh, *Guardians of God: Inside the Religious Mind of the Pakistani Taliban* (Oxford: Oxford University Press, 2016).

166. For a comprehensive overview of Pakistan's National Action Plan and National Counter Terrorism Authority, see Shuja Nawaz, "Countering Militancy and Terrorism in Pakistan," United States Institute of Peace, October 2016, pp. 1–16; Zeeshan Salahuddin, "20 Points to Pakistan?" *Foreign Policy*, 29 June 2015, http://foreignpolicy.com/2015/06/29/20-points-to-pakistan/.

167. National Consortium for the Study of Terrorism and Responses to Terrorism, "Annex of Statistical Information," Homeland Security Science and Technology Center of Excellence, July 2016, https://www.state.gov/documents/organization/257738.pdf; National Consortium for the Study of Terrorism and Responses to Terrorism, "Annex of Statistical Information," Homeland Security Science and Technology Center of Excellence, July 2017, https://www.state.gov/documents/organization/272485.pdf.

168. Shannon Tiezzi, "After Peshawar School Attack, China Pledges Deeper Anti-Terror Co-op with Pakistan," *The Diplomat*, 18 December 2014, http://thediplomat.com/2014/12/after-peshawar-school-attack-china-pledges-deeper-anti-terror-co-op-with-pakistan/.

169. "Chinese Foreign Minister Appreciates Progress on Zarb-e-Azb," *Express Tribune*, 9 December 2015, https://tribune.com.pk/story/1006910/chinese-foriegn-minister-appreciates-progress-on-zarb-e-azb/.

170. For details on exercises, see "Chinese and Pakistani Special Forces Hold Joint Anti-Terrorism Drills," *Defence Blog*, 7 November 2016, http://defence-blog.com/news/chinese-and-pakistani-special-forces-hold-joint-anti-terrorism-drills.html; "Pakistan, China to Continue Working against Terror," *Dawn*, 16 September 2015, https://www.dawn.com/news/1207284; Ankit Panda, "China, Pakistan Conclude Bilateral Counterterrorism Exercises," *The Diplomat*, 8 January 2019, https://thediplomat.com/2019/01/china-pakistan-conclude-bilateral-counterterrorism-exercises/.

171. "Afghanistan, China, Pakistan, Tajikistan Issue Joint Statement on Anti-Terrorism," China Military Online, 4 August 2016, http://eng.mod.gov.cn/TopNews/2016-08/04/content_4707491.htm.

172. There have been a wide range of reports commissioned that show the economic benefits that would accrue from Indo-Pakistani peace and make the case for building peace through improved trade and commercial ties. A small sampling includes Mahmud Ali Durrani, *India and Pakistan: The Cost of Conflict and the Benefits of Peace* (Karachi: Oxford University Press, 2001); Shuja Nawaz and Mohan Guruswamy, *India and Pakistan: The Opportunity Costs of Conflict* (Washington, DC: Atlantic Council of the United States, 2014); Ilmas Futehally and Seemu Bhatt, *Cost of Conflict between India and Pakistan* (Mumbai: Strategic Foresight Group, 2004).

173. This balanced approach manifested in neutral rhetoric (omitting pro-Pakistani language about the need for multilateral negotiations) and a softer defense posture (no longer implying that China would absolutely come to Pakistan's aid if conflict erupted). See Garver, *Protracted Conflict*, pp. 227–234.

174. For a detailed account of Chinese military aid to Pakistan, see Garver, *Protracted Conflict*, pp. 234–248 and 324–331.

175. For 2001–2002, see Polly Nayak and Michael Krepon, "US Crisis Management in South Asia's Twin Peaks Crisis," Stimson Center, September 2014, https://www.stimson.org/sites/default/files/file-attachments/Twin_Peaks_Crisis.pdf. For 2008, see Polly Nayak and Michael Krepon, "The Unfinished Crisis: US Crisis Management after the 2008 Mumbai Attacks," Stimson Center, February 2012, https://www.stimson.org/sites/default/files/file-attachments/Mumbai-Final_1_1.pdf.

176. Nayak and Krepon, "The Unfinished Crisis."

177. The AIIB projects in Pakistan were the National Motorway M-4 (approved June 2016) and the Tarbela 5 Hydropower Extension Project (approved

September 2016). See "Approved Projects," Asian Infrastructure Bank, accessed 14 September 2016, https://www.aiib.org/en/projects/approved/.

178. " 'If it wasn't for the BRICS meeting happening so soon,' " said Zhang Guihong, an India expert at Shanghai's Fudan University, " 'the stand-off would have lasted much longer.' " Quoted in Malik, "China and India." See also Rej, "India's Clever Use of the BRICS Card in Doklam Standoff."

179. For recent interviews on the common Pakistani perspective that China is a useful shield against international pressure, see "China-Pakistan Economic Corridor: Opportunities and Risks," p. 4.

180. Small, *The China-Pakistan Axis*, pp. 19–25.

181. For more on this period, see Steve Coll, *Ghost Wars: The Secret History of the CIA, Afghanistan, and Bin Laden, from the Soviet Invasion to September 10, 2001* (New York: Penguin, 2004); Kux, *The United States and Pakistan, 1947–2000*; George Crile, *Charlie Wilson's War* (New York: Grove Press, 2003).

182. Mukund Padmanabhan, "China's Hold Stopped Designation of LeT, Jaish Leaders," *The Hindu*, 7 June 2011, http://www.thehindu.com/opinion/op-ed/chinas-hold-stopped-designation-of-let-jaish-leaders/article2082626.ece.

183. Author interview, 16 May 2012, Islamabad, Pakistan.

184. "BRICS Leaders Xiamen Declaration," BRICS 2017 China, 4 September 2017, http://www.brics.utoronto.ca/docs/170904-xiamen.pdf.

185. Sutirtho Patranobis, "Mention of Pak, Afghan Terror Groups in BRICS Declaration a Mistake by China," *Hindustan Times*, 6 September 2017, http://www.hindustantimes.com/world-news/brics-declaration-adding-terror-groups-based-in-pak-afghan-is-a-costly-mistake-by-china-say-experts/story-ZujyLPpfKXlu3qaA99bzJN.html.

186. For similar arguments on Pakistani responses to Chinese pressure, see "China-Pakistan Economic Corridor: Opportunities and Risks," p. 7.

187. Some analysts have suggested that China was willing to vote against Pakistan to enable its candidate to be elected Financial Action Task Force (FATF) vice president, a likely precursor step to winning the presidency. See "India Congratulates China on Being Elected FATF Vice President," *India Today*, 25 February 2018, https://www.indiatoday.in/india/story/india-congratulates-china-on-being-elected-fatf-vice-president-1177331-2018-02-25.

188. Jarrett Blanc and James Schwemlein, "Financial Crimes and Punishment," *Foreign Policy*, 30 October 2018, https://foreignpolicy.com/2018/10/30/financial-crimes-and-punishment/.

189. Almeida's column landed him in hot water with the army. See Mohammed Hanif, "Censorship under Military Dictators Was Bad. It May Be Worse in a Democracy," *New York Times*, 17 October 2018, https://www.nytimes.com/2018/10/17/opinion/pakistan-almeida-censorship-dawn.html.

190. Cyril Almeida, "For Nawaz, It's Not Over till It's Over," *Dawn*, 12 May 2018, https://www.dawn.com/news/1407192.

191. Asad Hashim, "Pakistan's Cyril Almeida named IPI's World Press Freedom Hero," *Al Jazeera*, 24 April 2019, https://www.aljazeera.com/news/2019/04/pakistan-cyril-almeida-named-ipi-world-press-freedom-hero-190424094705064.html.

192. Maria Abi-Habib and Michael Schwirtz, "China Blocks UN Vote to Blacklist Pakistani Militant Leader," *New York Times*, 13 March 2019, https://www.nytimes.com/2019/03/13/world/asia/china-pakistan-masood-azhar.html.

193. Sarah Zheng, "Why China Dropped Its Opposition to UN Blacklisting of Pakistan-Based Terror Chief Masood Azhar," *South China Morning Post*, 2 May 2019, https://www.scmp.com/news/china/diplomacy/article/3008614/why-china-dropped-its-opposition-un-blacklisting-pakistan.

194. Andrew Small, "Why China is Playing a Tougher Game on the NSG This Time Around," *Herald*, 23 June 2016, https://herald.dawn.com/news/1153439.

195. Stephen Philip Cohen, *The Idea of Pakistan* (Washington, DC: Brookings Institution Press, 2004), pp. 25–77.

196. Some of these dates reflect a consensus, but not exact knowledge, of Pakistan's nuclear timeline. See Garver, *Protracted Conflict*, pp. 313–331. For missile assistance, see Small, *The China-Pakistan Axis*, pp. 39–42.

197. As Feroz Khan has documented, the Chinese "built the turnkey missile factory at Fatehjung, which not only allowed production of the M-series missiles but also provided Pakistan . . . [with] an infrastructure as well as a training facility to bring a new generation of missile scientists into the art of solid propellant production." See Feroz Hassan Khan, *Eating Grass: The Making of the Pakistani Bomb* (Stanford, CA: Stanford Security Series, 2012), pp. 242.

198. Jeff M. Smith, *Cold Peace: China-India Rivalry in the Twenty-First Century* (Plymouth: Lexington Books, 2014), pp. 133 and 202–203.

199. In November 2018, Pakistan had an estimated 140–150 nuclear warheads, while India had 130–140. See Hans M. Kristensen and Robert S. Norris, "Status of World Nuclear Forces," Federation of American Scientists, https://fas.org/issues/nuclear-weapons/status-world-nuclear-forces/.

200. Ashley J. Tellis, C. Christine Fair and Jamison Jo Medby, *Limited Conflicts under the Nuclear Umbrella: Indian and Pakistani Lessons from the Kargil Crisis* (Santa Monica, CA: RAND Corporation, 2001); S. Paul Kapur, *Dangerous Deterrent: Nuclear Weapons Proliferation and Conflict in South Asia*, 1st Ed. *Studies in Asian Security* (Stanford, CA: Stanford University Press, 2007).

201. In a helpful overview of Pakistan's nuclear doctrine and arsenal, this Pakistani strategy is described as "full spectrum deterrence." See Toby Dalton and Michael Krepon, "A Normal Nuclear Pakistan," Stimson Center and Carnegie Endowment for International Peace, 2015, http://carnegieendowment.org/files/NormalNuclearPakistan.pdf.

202. Christopher Clary and Ankit Panda, "Safer at Sea? Pakistan's Sea-Based Deterrent and Nuclear Weapons Security," *Washington Quarterly*, vol. 40, no.

3 (Fall 2017): pp. 149–168, https://doi.org/10.1080/0163660X.2017.1370344. See also Diana Wueger, "Through a Periscope Darkly: The Nuclear Undersea Competition in Southern Asia Is Just Beginning," *War on the Rocks*, 18 October 2017, https://warontherocks.com/2017/10/through-a-periscope-darkly-the-nuclear-undersea-competition-in-southern-asia-is-just-beginning/.

203. For more on the potential for Sino-Indian military confrontation, see Daniel S. Markey, "Armed Confrontation Between India and China," Council on Foreign Relations, November 2015, https://www.cfr.org/sites/default/files/pdf/2015/11/CPA_ContingencyPlanningMemo_27.pdf.

204. Harsh V. Pant and Ritika Passi, "India's Response to China's Belt and Road Initiative: A Policy in Motion," *Asia Policy*, no. 24 (July 2017): p. 88.

205. Quoted in Pant and Passi, "India's Response to China's Belt and Road Initiative," p. 89.

206. Smith, "China's Belt and Road Initiative, p. 8.

207. David Brewster, "Between Giants: The Sino-Indian Cold War in the Indian Ocean," *Notes de L'ifri, Asie Visions*, no. 103, Institut Francais des Relations Internationales, December 2018, pp. 8, 10–14, https://www.ifri.org/sites/default/files/atoms/files/brewster_sino_indian_cold_war_2018.pdf.

208. Brewster, "Between Giants," p. 8.

209. Brewster, "Between Giants," p. 11.

210. China has claimed that these ports are for commercial or benign purposes, only to later develop capabilities that India views as militarily threatening. For a good example of this dynamic playing out at the People's Liberation Army base in Djibouti, see Abhijit Singh, "China's Military Base in Djibouti: Strategic Implications for India," *War on the Rocks* and Stimson Center, 21 August 2017, https://warontherocks.com/2017/08/chinas-military-base-in-djibouti-strategic-implications-for-india/. For an example of the gap between China's statements and India's interpretation of them, see Jeremy Page, "Beijing Agrees to Operate a Key Port, Pakistan Says," *Wall Street Journal*, 23 May 2011, https://www.wsj.com/articles/SB10001424052702303654804576339323765033308.

211. Brewster focuses on Indian concerns about China's involvement in the Maldives. See Brewster, "Between Giants," pp. 15–25.

212. For more extensive discussions of Sino-Indian competition, see C. Raja Mohan, *Samudra Manthan: Sino-Indian Rivalry in the Indo-Pacific* (Washington, DC: Carnegie Endowment for International Peace, 2012); also David Brewster, ed., *India and China at Sea: Competition for Naval Dominance in the Indian Ocean* (Oxford: Oxford University Press, 2018).

213. "China's Strength Draws US and India Together," *Jane's Intelligence Review*, 5 May 2015.

214. The most dramatic of these Chinese missteps was likely in Myanmar, over the issue of the Myitsone Dam project. See Mike Ives, "A Chinese-Backed Dam Project Leaves Myanmar in a Bind," *New York Times*, 31 March 2017, https://

www.nytimes.com/2017/03/31/world/asia/myanmar-china-myitsone-dam-project.html.

215. On this point, see C. Raja Mohan, "Mind the Power Gap," *Indian Express*, 2 August 2017, http://indianexpress.com/article/opinion/columns/india-china-standoff-mind-the-power-gap-4777926/.

216. Abhijit Singh, "India's Naval Interests in the Pacific," in *India and China at Sea: Competition for Naval Dominance in the Indian Ocean*, edited by David Brewster (Oxford: Oxford University Press, 2018), p. 177.

217. Singh, "India's Naval Interests in the Pacific," in *India and China at Sea*, pp. 178–179.

218. Kamal Dev Bhattarai, "The China-India-Nepal Triangle," *The Diplomat*, 25 April 2018, https://thediplomat.com/2018/04/the-china-india-nepal-triangle/.

219. When Washington's ties to Islamabad frayed toward the end of the Obama administration, some Indians held out hope that Pakistan would finally find itself diplomatically isolated and more susceptible to Indian pressure. The Indian foreign office actively worked to promote that isolation. Yet China's friendship with Pakistan effectively blunted that initiative. See Jayanth Jacob, Saubhadra Chatterji, and Imtiaz Ahmad, "Uri Attack: India to Isolate Pakistan Globally; Death Toll Rises to 18," *Hindustan Times*, 19 September 2016, http://www.hindustantimes.com/india-news/uri-attack-india-will-gather-evidence-isolate-pakistan-globally/story-5qqHbNoiRHXQsK2ok6M7wJ.html.

Chapter 4

1. For an extended profile of Nur-Sultan (Astana) with stunning photos, see Oliver Wainwright, "Secret Stans 'Norman Said the President Wants a Pyramid': How Starchitects Built Astana," *Guardian*, 17 October 2017, https://www.theguardian.com/cities/2017/oct/17/norman-foster-president-pyramid-architects-built-astana.

2. Peter B. Golden, *Central Asia in World History* (Oxford: Oxford Univerity Press, 2011), pp. 1–3.

3. Starr, *Lost Enlightenment*, p. 67.

4. On the financial (and moral) costs of silk in Rome, see Frankopan, *The Silk Roads*, pp. 17–18. On the use of silk as currency, see Hansen, *The Silk Road*, p. 96, plate 5A.

5. Hansen, *The Silk Road*, p. 5.

6. Hansen, *The Silk Road*, p. 13.

7. On Chinese demand for Central Asian horses, see Andre Gunder Frank, "The Centrality of Central Asia," *Studies in History*, vol. 8, no. 1 (1992): pp. 54–55, 71, DOI:10.1177/025764309200800103; also Peter C. Perdue, *China Marches West: The Qing Conquest of Central Eurasia* (Cambridge, MA: The Belknap Press of Harvard University Press, 2005), pp. 33–36.

8. James A. Millward and Peter C. Perdue, "Political and Cultural History of the Xinjiang Region through the Late Nineteenth Century," in *Xinjiang: China's Muslim Borderland*, edited by S. Frederick Starr (London: Routledge, 2004), p. 39.

9. Millward and Perdue, "Political and Cultural History of the Xinjiang Region," in *Xinjiang: China's Muslim Borderland*, p. 42.

10. Although their works were penned in Arabic, Starr points out that "A Central Asian who wrote in Arabic a millennium ago was no more an Arab than a Japanese who writes a book in English is an Englishman." Starr, *Lost Enlightenment*, p. 16.

11. Starr finds multiple causes for Central Asia's decline, but finally concludes that the "closing of the Muslim mind in Central Asia" was most attributable to the Sunni-Shiite divide. See Starr, *Lost Enlightenment*, pp. 522–539.

12. Joseph F. Fletcher, "China and Central Asia, 1368–1884," in *The Chinese World Order*, edited by John King Fairbank (Cambridge, MA: Harvard University Press, 1968), p. 207.

13. Fletcher recounts the lengths that the Ming Yongle emperor was willing to go to secure Central Asian horses. See Fletcher, "China and Central Asia, 1368–1884," in *The Chinese World Order*, pp. 207–216.

14. Golden, *Central Asia in World History*, pp. 95–100.

15. Igor Torbakov, "Managing Imperial Peripheries," in *The New Great Game*, edited by Thomas Fingar (Stanford, CA: Stanford University Press, 2016), p. 241.

16. Peter Hopkirk, *The Great Game: The Struggle for Empire in Central Asia* (New York: Kodansha International, 1992), pp. 11–15.

17. Golden, *Central Asia in World History*, p. 108.

18. Golden, *Central Asia in World History*, p. 109.

19. Perdue, *China Marches West*, p. 113.

20. Perdue, *China Marches West*, pp. 50, 120.

21. Golden, *Central Asia in World History*, p. 118. On the origins of the Zunghar state, see Perdue, *China Marches West*, pp. 101–109.

22. Perdue, *China Marches West*, p. 1.

23. Perdue, *China Marches West*, p. 10.

24. Peter C. Perdue discusses the "unboundedness of Central Eurasia" in Perdue, *China Marches West*, pp. 19–23, and the specific challenge of shifting borders between China and Russia on p. 43.

25. Fletcher, "China and Central Asia, 1368–1884," in *The Chinese World Order*, pp. 223–224. On this tumultuous period, see also Harris, "Xinjiang, Central Asia, and the Implications for China's Policy in the Islamic World," p. 114.

26. For example, "class warfare was for the Muslim East the struggle of an oppressed Muslim people against the European imperialist-colonialist forces." See Golden, *Central Asia in World History*, p. 132.

27. Golden, *Central Asia in World History*, p. 134.

28. As Swanström writes, "ties between the minority population in Xinjiang and the Central Asian states are strong and there has traditionally not been a clear border between the people in Central Asia and Xinjiang, aside from the theoretical border given on maps." See Niklas Swanström, "China and Central Asia: A New Great Game or Traditional Vassal Relations?," *Journal of Contemporary China*, vol. 14, no. 45 (2005): p. 571, doi: 10.1080/10670560500205001.

29. For an example of one such delay, see Vasili Rukhadze, "Completion of Baku-Tbilisi-Kars Railway Project Postponed Again," *Eurasia Daily Monitor*, 2 March 2016, https://jamestown.org/program/completion-of-baku-tbilisi-kars-railway-project-postponed-again/.

30. Wade Shepard was a helpful travel guide for my trip to Khorgos, and has so far written about three trips to Khorgos from 2015 to 2017, from which he has gained a perspective on the evolution of the place from empty sand dunes to fast-growing city. See Wade Shepard, "Why Kazakhstan Is Building a 'New Dubai' on the Chinese Border," *Forbes*, 28 February 2016, https://www.forbes.com/sites/wadeshepard/2016/02/28/will-a-place-called-khorgos-become-the-next-dubai/2/#6a744795132b; Wade Shepard, "The Western Europe–Western China Expressway to Connect the Yellow Sea with the Baltic," *Forbes*, 10 July 2016, https://www.forbes.com/sites/wadeshepard/2016/07/10/the-western-europe-western-china-expressway-to-connect-the-yellow-sea-with-the-baltic/#39a558126c95; Wade Shepard, "Khorgos: The New Silk Road's Central Station Comes to Life," *Forbes*, 20 February 2017, https://www.forbes.com/sites/wadeshepard/2017/02/20/khorgos-the-new-silk-roads-central-station-comes-to-life/#dc17b08c22ee.

31. Shepard, "Khorgos."

32. Andrew Higgins, "China's Ambitious New 'Port': Landlocked Kazakhstan," *New York Times*, 1 January 2018, https://www.nytimes.com/2018/01/01/world/asia/china-kazakhstan-silk-road.html.

33. Higgins, "China's Ambitious New 'Port.'"

34. Small traders are permitted only 110 lbs. of duty-free merchandise and one visit per month, severely limiting the economic impact of the trade zone. This weight restriction was the result of Russian pressure, reflecting its own concerns about China's market access. See Andrew Higgins, "A Visa-Free Zone Welcomes Your Wallet. But Maybe Not Your Beard," *New York Times*, 8 January 2018, https://www.nytimes.com/2018/01/08/world/asia/kazakhstan-china-border.html.

35. Kemal Kirisci and Philippe Le Corre, "The New Geopolitics of Central Asia: China Vies for Influence in Russia's Backyard," Order from Chaos, Brookings Institution, 2 January 2018, https://www.brookings.edu/blog/order-from-chaos/2018/01/02/the-new-geopolitics-of-central-asia-china-vies-for-influence-in-russias-backyard/.

36. A number of Western journalists have made the trek to Khorgos to survey the scene and connect the dots between infrastructure development and politics. One particularly worthwhile read is by Ben Mauk (with beautiful photos and video clips from Andrea Frazzetta) in "Can China Turn the Middle of Nowhere into the Center of the World Economy?," *New York Times Magazine*, 30 January 2019, https://www.nytimes.com/interactive/2019/01/29/magazine/china-globalization-kazakhstan.html.

37. On Chinese voting shares in the ADB, see "ADB Annual Report 2017," Asian Development Bank, 31 December 2017, https://www.adb.org/sites/default/files/page/30786/ar2017-oi-appendix1.pdf. China's involvement in the CAREC process that created "Corridor 1b" can be traced to the 2006 "Comprehensive Action Plan," which Chinese experts helped to formulate. Key Chinese policy speeches from 2006 include H. E. Mr. Zeng Peiyan, "Building a Harmonious Region by Strengthening Partnership and Improving Cooperation Mechanism," 20 October 2006, http://182.50.129.37/uploads/events/2006/5th-MC/Speech-PRC-Vice-Premier.pdf; Li Yong, "Keynote Speech at the 5th Ministerial Conference on Central Asia Regional Economic Cooperation," 20 October 2006, http://182.50.129.37/uploads/events/2006/5th-MC/PRC-Opening-Statement-on-CAP.pdf. China retains a strong influence in CAREC infrastructure projects by retaining a leadership role in Operations Group 1, which oversees ADB investments in Central Asia, and by actively participating in Transport Sector Coordinating Committee meetings. Alexander Cooley notes China's clever leveraging of ADB resources to serve its own infrastructure agenda in Central Asia. See Alexander Cooley, *Great Games, Local Rules* (Oxford: Oxford University Press, 2012), p. 88, and cites Jonathan Holslag, who concludes that "China has thus become the main driver of regional and sub-regional initiatives on transport, but it has cleverly left the *ownership* to others." See Jonathan Holslag, "China's Road to Influence," *Asian Survey* vol. 50, no. 4 (July/August 2010): pp. 641–662, http://hdcswpsa2016.wikispaces.com/file/view/china's+road+to+influence.pdf, p. 653.

38. For instance, between 2013 and 2017, China's Ex-Im Bank provided $697.9 million to build parts of Kyrgyzstan's North-South Road Project, which hooks into CAREC's Corridor 1 and Corridor 3. These corridors are the principal CAREC arteries connecting China with Central Asia, Russia, and Europe. For details on China's funding, see "Development Coordination," Asian Development Bank, accessed 8 March 2018, https://www.adb.org/sites/default/files/linked-documents/48401-007-dc.pdf. For details on how the North-South Road Project connects into CAREC corridors, see "ADB, Kyrgyz Republic Sign Agreement for North-South Alternate Road Corridor Rehabilitation," Asian Development Bank, 1 December 2016, https://www.adb.org/news/adb-kyrgyz-republic-sign-agreement-north-south-alternate-road-corridor-rehabilitation. For a list of Chinese-backed projects, see "Projects List," CAREC, accessed 12 June 2018, https://test0302.carecprogram.

org/?page_id=1726&paged=1&funding_agency[]=china-development-bank-prc&funding_agency[]=china-export-import-bank&funding_agency[]=peoples-republic-of-china&funding_agency[]=ministry-of-communications-peoples-republic-of-china&funding_agency[]=peoples-republic-of-china-prc-regional-cooperation-and-poverty-reduction-fund.

39. For "resources," see "China EXIM Bank Loans Tajikistan 49 Million USD for Second Phase of the Dushanbe-Kulyab-Khorog-Kulma Road Upgrade (linked to ID #40063)," AIDDATE, accessed 9 March 2018, http://china.aiddata.org/projects/40440; "Activity of Chinese Companies," Grata International, http://www.gratanet.com/uploads/user_11/files/client_note_Yessimkhanov.pdf. For "technical expertise," see "Uzbekistan," Huawei, accessed 9 March 2018, http://www.huawei.com/en/about-huawei/sustainability/win-win-development/social-contribution/seeds-for-the-future/uzbekistan.

40. Jack Farchy and James Kynge, "Map: Connecting Central Asia," *Financial Times*, 9 May 2016, https://www.ft.com/content/ee5cf40a-15e5-11e6-9d98-00386a18e39d.

41. "BTK Route Aims to Be Integral to China's Belt and Road Initiative," *Xinhua*, 1 November 2017, http://www.xinhuanet.com/english/2017-11/01/c_136718382.htm.

42. According to Yerkhat Iakaliev, it costs $70/container to ship by sea versus $800/container to ship by land. Author conversation with Yerkhat Iakaliev, 27 April 2017, Nur-Sultan (Astana), Kazakhstan. Western media sources have also reported on the discrepancy between shipping costs, though giving the cost differential as 100 percent. For example, see Julie Maniken and Violet Law, "China's Bold Gambit to Cement Trade with Europe—Along the Ancient Silk Road," *Los Angeles Times*, 1 May 2016, http://www.latimes.com/world/asia/la-fg-china-silk-road-20160501-story.html.

43. Henrik Rodemann and Simon Templar, "The Enablers and Inhibitors of Intermodal Rail Freight between Asia and Europe," *Journal of Rail Transport Planning and Management*, vol. 4, no. 3 (2014): pp. 74–75, https://doi.org/10.1016/j.jrtpm.2014.10.001.

44. "Country Analysis Brief: Kazakhstan," US Energy Information Administration, 10 May 2017, http://www.ieee.es/en/Galerias/fichero/OtrasPublicaciones/Internacional/2017/EIA_Country_Aanlysis_Kazakhstan_10may2017.pdf. For a list of pipeline construction projects, see Yelena Kalyuzhnova and Julian Lee, "China and Kazakhstan's Oil and Gas Partnership at the Start of the Twenty-First Century," *Emerging Markets Finance & Trade*, vol. 50, no. 5 (September/October 2014): pp. 206–221, http://www.tandfonline.com/doi/pdf/10.2753/REE1540-496X500515.

45. Kashagan is Kazakhstan's most important offshore oil field. Its proven reserves of 13 billion barrels is equivalent to the entire proven reserves of Brazil. For more on Kashagan, see "Kazakhstan Consortium Achieves First

Oil Production from Kashagan Field," North Caspian Operation Company, 19 September 2013, https://www.eia.gov/todayinenergy/detail.php?id=13011. For China's entry, see Raffaello Pantucci and Sarah Lain, "China's Eurasian Pivot," RUSI, 31 May 2017, p. 32, https://rusi.org/publication/whitehall-papers/chinas-eurasian-pivot-silk-road-economic-belt.

46. See Zhang Junmian, "China, Kazakhstan Deepen Energy Cooperation," Belt and Road Portal, 21 July 2017, https://eng.yidaiyilu.gov.cn/home/rolling/20467.htm. Estimates tend to vary in the 25 to 33 percent range. For example, see Erica Downs, "Looking West: China and Central Asia," *Testimony before the US-China Economic and Security Review Commission,* 18 March 2015, https://www.uscc.gov/sites/default/files/Downs%20Testimony_031815.pdf; Kalyuzhnova and Lee, "China and Kazakhstan's Oil and Gas Partnership," pp. 206–221.

47. "China to Put $2.16b on Gas Pipeline," *Xinhua,* 29 December 2007, http://www.chinadaily.com.cn/china/2007-12/29/content_6357734.htm.

48. Downs, "Looking West, China and Central Asia."

49. "38.7 bln Cubic Meters of Gas Piped to China from Central Asia," *Xinhua,* 5 January 2018, http://www.xinhuanet.com/english/2018-01/05/c_136874692.htm.

50. "China's CNPC Imports First Gas from Kazakhstan ahead of Winter," *Reuters,* 22 October 2017, https://www.reuters.com/article/china-gas-imports/chinas-cnpc-imports-first-gas-from-kazakhstan-ahead-of-winter-idUSL4N1MY186. The Central Asia–China Gas Pipeline also draws from Uzbekistan, and another stretch from Tajikistan is in the works. See "Tajik Energy Minister Confirms Work Resumed on Central Asia–China Gas Pipeline," *IntelliNews,* 2 February 2018, http://www.intellinews.com/tajik-energy-minister-confirms-work-resumed-on-central-asia-china-gas-pipeline-136162/.

51. "Kazakhstan to Double Natural Gas Exports to China to 10 Bcm/Year in 2019," *S&P Global,* 15 October 2018, https://www.spglobal.com/platts/en/market-insights/latest-news/natural-gas/101518-kazakhstan-to-double-natural-gas-exports-to-china-to-10-bcmyear-in-2019.

52. "Central Asia–China Gas Pipeline to Hit Maximum Capacity—PetroChina," *Reuters,* 12 November 2018, https://af.reuters.com/article/commoditiesNews/idAFL4N1XN3DF.

53. "China's government and companies' interest in the oil and gas sector in Kazakhstan has clearly been driven by the fact that the two countries share a long land border, allowing China to reduce its dependence on seaborne crude oil, which it sees as vulnerable both to piracy, particularly in the Malacca Strait and off the coast of East Africa, and to any future military blockade by the US Navy." Kalyuzhnova and Lee, "China and Kazakhstan's Oil and Gas Partnership, pp. 216.

54. Downs, "Looking West, China and Central Asia," p. 3.

55. Edward C. Chow and Leigh E. Hendrix, "Central Asia's Pipelines: Field of Dreams and Reality," *National Bureau of Asian Research Special Report #23*, September 2010, pp. 29–42.

56. "Uranium and Nuclear Power in Kazakhstan," World Nuclear Organization, February 2018, http://www.world-nuclear.org/information-library/country-profiles/countries-g-n/kazakhstan.aspx.

57. "Kazakhstan to Produce Nuclear Fuel for China," *Reuters*, 26 May 2017, https://www.reuters.com/article/us-kazakhstan-china-nuclearpower/kazakhstan-to-produce-nuclear-fuel-for-china-idUSKBN18M1KP. For an updated projection on when shipments will occur, see "Uranium and Nuclear Power in Kazakhstan," World Nuclear Association, April 2019, http://www.world-nuclear.org/information-library/country-profiles/countries-g-n/kazakhstan.aspx.

58. Kazakhstan primarily exports non-enriched uranium that requires further processing before countries can use it for fuel. See "Kazakhstan to Produce Nuclear Fuel for China," *Reuters*, 26 May 2017, https://www.reuters.com/article/us-kazakhstan-china-nuclearpower/kazakhstan-to-produce-nuclear-fuel-for-china-idUSKBN18M1KP.

59. Anastasia, "Nazarbayev Back from China with 51 Joint Projects," *The Eurasian Press Agency*, 6 September 2016, http://eurasiatx.com/nazarbayev-back-from-china-with-51-join-projects/; "Kazakhstan, China to Create 50 Joint Enterprises," *Kazinform*, 21 September 2016, http://www.inform.kz/en/kazakhstan-china-to-create-50-joint-enterprises_a2951403.

60. Emily Feng and Henry Foy, "China-Kazakhstan Border Woes Dent Silk Road Ambitions," *Financial Times*, 20 December 2017, https://www.ft.com/content/1606d70a-9c31-11e7-8cd4-932067fbf946.

61. Assel G. Bitabaraova, "Unpacking Sino-Central Asian Engagement along the New Silk Road: A Case Study of Kazakhstan," *Journal of Contemporary East Asia Studies*, vol. 7, no. 2 (January 2019), https://www.tandfonline.com/doi/full/10.1080/24761028.2018.1553226.

62. Data for Kazakhstan's imports can be retrieved at UN Comtrade Database by selecting reporter (Kazakhstan), partner (China), imports, and "TOTAL-Total of all HS commodities." See "UN Comtrade Database," United Nations, accessed 22 June 2018, https://comtrade.un.org/data/.

63. Data for China–Central Asia can be retrieved at UN Comtrade Database by selecting reporter (China), partner (Kazakhstan, Kyrgyzstan, Tajikistan, Turkmenistan, and Uzbekistan), "All" trade, and "TOTAL-Total of all HS commodities." See "UN Comtrade Database," United Nations, accessed 22 June 2018, https://comtrade.un.org/data/.

64. For 2017, see "European Union, Trade in Goods with Central Asia 5," European Commission, 16 April 2018, http://trade.ec.europa.eu/doclib/docs/2013/november/tradoc_151896.pdf. For 2018, see "European Union, Trade in Goods

with Central Asia 5," European Commission, 6 March 2019, https://webgate.
ec.europa.eu/isdb_results/factsheets/region/details_central-asia-5_en.pdf.

65. More on Chinese loans to Central Asia will follow later in this chapter. Carla
P. Freeman, "New Strategies for an Old Rivalry? China-Russia Relations in
Central Asia after the Energy Boom," *The Pacific Review* (2017): pp. 1–20,
https://doi.org/10.1080/09512748.2017.1398775, pp. 10–11.

66. For the $5 billion loans, see "China Lends Crisis-Hit Kazakhstan $10bln,"
Reuters, 16 April 2009, https://uk.reuters.com/article/china-kazakhstan-
loans/china-lends-crisis-hit-kazakhstan-10-bln-idUKLG94896920090416;
Rick Carew and Guy Chazan, "China Makes Big New Bet on Kazakhstan's
Oil," *Wall Street Journal*, 1 October 2009, https://www.wsj.com/articles/
SB125428493302451733. For Kazakhmys loan, see Jeffrey Sparshott,
"Kazakhyms Sells Stake in Power Station," *Wall Street Journal*, 13 October
2009, https://www.wsj.com/articles/SB10001424052748704107204574470613642627876; "Kazakhmys Announces Development of the Major Copper Project
at Bozshakol," Kazakhmys, 25 August 2011, http://kase.kz/files/emitters/GB_
KZMS/gb_kzms_reliz_250811_e.pdf.

67. Data for 2007 and 2010 found at "Gross Inflow of Direct Investment in
Kazakhstan from Foreign Direct Investors: Breakdown by Countries,"
National Bank of Kazakhstan, accessed 12 February 2018, http://www.
nationalbank.kz/?docid=469&switch=english.

68. On this point, see Stephen Blank, "The Impact of China's Economic and
Security Interests in Continental Asia on the United States," 20 May
2009, https://www.uscc.gov/sites/default/files/5.20.09%20Blank.pdf; Erica
Downs, "Inside China, Inc.: China Development Bank's Cross-Border
Energy Deals," Brookings Institution, March 2011, https://www.brookings.
edu/wp-content/uploads/2016/06/0321_china_energy_downs.pdf; Cesar
B. Martinez Alvarez, "China-Kazakhstan Energy Relations between 1997
and 2012," *Journal of International Affairs*, 1 January 2016, https://jia.sipa.
columbia.edu/china-kazakhstan-energy-relations-1997-2012; Alexander
Cooley, "The Emerging Political Economy of OBOR," Center for Strategic
and International Studies, October 2016, p. 9 https://www.csis.org/analysis/
emerging-political-economy-obor.

69. Daniel C. O'Neill, "Risky Business: The Political Economy of Chinese
Investment in Kazakhstan," *Journal of Eurasian Studies*, vol. 5, no. 2 (2014): pp.
145–156, https://doi.org/10.1016/j.euras.2014.05.007, p. 148.

70. "China's generous loans are contributing to a serious debt spiral in Central
Asia." See Marlene Laruelle, ed., *China's Belt and Road Initiative and Its Impact
in Central Asia* (Washington, DC: George Washington University Central
Asia Program, 2018), p. xi.

71. Alexander Cooley, "The Emerging Political Economy of OBOR," p. 4.

72. John Hurley, Scott Morris, and Gailyn Portelance, "Examining the Debt
Implications of the Belt and Road Initiative from a Policy Perspective," CGD

Policy Paper 121, March 2018, p. 20, https://www.cgdev.org/publication/
examining-debt-implications-belt-and-road-initiative-a-policy-perspective.

73. Paolo Sorbello, "Turkmenistan's Ongoing Gas Quandary," *The Diplomat*, 25
    April 2017, https://thediplomat.com/2017/04/turkmenistans-ongoing-gas-
    quandary/.

74. For an extensive review of Turkmenistan, see Annette Bohr,
    Turkmenistan: Power, Politics, and Petro-Authoritarianism (London: Chatham
    House, 2016); note specific concerns about possible overdependence on
    China, p. 78.

75. Catherine Putz, "Russia Is Buying Turkmen Gas Again. Why?" *The Diplomat*,
    25 April 2019, https://thediplomat.com/2019/04/russia-is-buying-turkmen-
    gas-again-why/.

76. According to Xinjiang's director and Party chief of the Department of
    Commerce. See "Boom to Place Xinjiang as Central Asia's Economic Hub,"
    Global Times, 7 April 2016, http://www.globaltimes.cn/content/992232.shtml.

77. On this point, see Raffaello Pantucci, "Looking West: China and
    Central Asia."

78. For more on this topic, see Michael Clarke, "Looking West: China and Central
    Asia," *Testimony before the US-China Economic and Security Review Commission*,
    18 March 2015, https://www.uscc.gov/sites/default/files/Clarke%20Testimony_
    3.18.15.pdf.

79. Joseph Hope, "Returning Uighur Fighters and China's National Security
    Dilemma," *China Brief*, vol. 18, issue 13 (25 July 2018), https://jamestown.org/
    program/returning-uighur-fighters-and-chinas-national-security-dilemma/.
    For other estimates, see Mathieu Duchâtel, "China's Foreign Fighters
    Problem," *War on the Rocks*, 25 January 2019, https://warontherocks.com/2019/
    01/chinas-foreign-fighters-problem/.

80. Clarke, "Looking West: China and Central Asia."

81. Niklas Swanström and Par Nyren, "China's March West: Pitfalls and
    Challenges in Greater Central Asia," Institute for Security and Development
    Policy, 10 January 2017, http://isdp.eu/publication/chinas-pitfalls-challenges-
    gca/.

82. Clarke, "Looking West: China and Central Asia."

83. For examples of statements and agreements, see "China, Kazakhstan Eye
    Stronger Cross-Border, Security Cooperation," *Xinhua*, 8 June 2017, http://
    www.xinhuanet.com/english/2017-06/08/c_136350731.htm; "China,
    Kazakhstan Pledge More Security Cooperation," *Xinhua*, 4 December 2014,
    http://english.gov.cn/state_council/state_councilors/2014/12/04/content_
    281475019330899.htm; "Sino-Kazakhstan Joint Declaration on Further
    Deepening Comprehensive Strategic Partnership," China International Water
    Law Programme, accessed 8 March 2018, https://www.internationalwaterlaw.
    org/documents/regionaldocs/China-Kazakhstan_declaration_7_Sept_2013-
    CIWL_unofficial_translation.pdf.

84. M. Tayor Fravel recounts this China-Kazakhstan history in M. Taylor Fravel, *Strong Borders, Secure Nation* (Princeton: Princeton University Press, 2008), pp. 160–163. On Central Asian concerns about renegotiating borders with China, see Sebastien Peyrouse, "Discussing China: Sinophilia and Sinophobia in Central Asia," *Journal of Eurasian Studies*, vol. 7, no. 1 (2016): pp. 14–23, https://www.sciencedirect.com/science/article/pii/S1879366515000251. Peyrouse notes that although most of the border issues have been resolved, significant cross-border river management issues are not ("Discussing China," p. 15). See also Sebastien Peyrouse, "China and Central Asia," in *The New Great Game*, edited by Thomas Fingar (Stanford, CA: Stanford University Press, 2016).

85. Author conversation with Nargis Kassenova, 28 April 2017, Almaty, Kazakhstan.

86. Author conversation with Adil Kaukenov, 28 April 2017, Almaty, Kazakhstan.

87. Kaukenov was likely referring to a Chinese promise to offer 30,000 scholarships in SCO countries over the next ten years. See Martha Brill Olcott, "China's Unmatched Influence in Central Asia," Carnegie Endowment for International Peace, 18 September 2013, http://carnegieendowment. org/2013/09/18/china-s-unmatched-influence-in-central-asia-pub-53035. According to the China Scholarship Council, in 2016 the number of Kazakhs studying in China has increased to 12,000, a 500 percent jump in ten years. See Jake Farchy, "Kazakh Language Schools Shift from English to Chinese," *Financial Times*, 9 May 2016, https://www.ft.com/content/ 6ce4a6ac-0c85-11e6-9456-444ab5211a2f.

88. China's use of scholarships as a propaganda vehicle in a wide range of BRI countries is described in "Why China Is Lavishing Money on Foreign Students," *The Economist*, 24 January 2019, https://www.economist.com/china/ 2019/01/26/why-china-is-lavishing-money-on-foreign-students.

89. Author conversation with Daniyar Kosnazarov, 27 April 2017, Nur-Sultan (Astana), Kazakhstan.

90. Cooley, *Great Games, Local Rules*.

91. As Cooley argues, Central Asia's predatory elites are well positioned to reap benefits from Chinese efforts, with patterns of graft and "rent-seeking" as likely to become further entrenched as to be reformed. Cooley, "The Emerging Political Economy of OBOR," pp. 10–14. He concludes that "recent experiences in Central Asia suggest that while OBOR has the potential to fund valuable new transit infrastructure, it also risks stirring domestic political competition, fueling networks of graft and rent-seeking, and not fulfilling its transformative potential."

92. On Kazakhstan as an authoritarian developmental state, see Sean Roberts, "The Perils of the Autocratic Developmental State," *Georgetown Journal of Asian Affairs* (Winter 2016), https://asianstudies.georgetown.edu/sites/

asianstudies/files/files/upload/gjaa._2.2_roberts.pdf. For a brief summary of human rights concerns, see *Amnesty International Report 2017/18: The State of the World's Human Rights* (London: Amnesty International, 2018), pp. 220–222.

93. Elya Altynsarina, "New Kazakh President Sworn In, Praises Predecessor, Pledges Continuity," *Astana Times*, 20 March 2019, https://astanatimes.com/2019/03/new-kazakh-president-sworn-in-praises-predecessor-pledges-continuity/.

94. Dmitri Trenin, *Twitter* post, 19 March 2019.

95. Nastassia Astrasheuskaya and Henry Foy, "Tokayev Wins Vote to Become Kazakhstan's Second President," *Financial Times*, 10 June 2019, https://www.ft.com/content/47bf45bc-8b4e-11e9-a24d-b42f641eca37.

96. "Protests against Kazakhstan's 'Stage-Managed' Election Test Tokayev's Legitimacy," *World Politics Review*, 19 June 2019, https://www.worldpoliticsreview.com/trend-lines/27961/protests-against-kazakhstan-s-stage-managed-election-test-tokayev-s-legitimacy.

97. Joanna Lillis, *Dark Shadows: Inside the Secret World of Kazakhstan* (London: I. B. Tauris, 2019), p. 16.

98. Raushan Nurshayeva and Dimitry Solovyov, "Kazakh Leader Apologizes for 97.7 Percent Re-Election Victory," *Reuters*, 27 April 2015, https://www.reuters.com/article/us-kazakhstan-election-results/kazakh-leader-apologizes-for-97-7-percent-re-election-victory-idUSKBN0NI09220150427.

99. Michael Mesquita, "Kazakhstan's Presidential Transition and the Evolution of Elite Networks," *Demokratizatsiya*, vol. 24, no. 3 (Summer 2016): pp. 371–397, p. 377.

100. See Barbara Junisbai, "A Tale of Two Kazakhstans: Sources of Political Cleavage and Conflict in the Post-Soviet Period," *Europe-Asia Studies*, vol. 62, no. 2 (February 2010): pp. 235–269, https://www.tandfonline.com/doi/abs/10.1080/09668130903506813; see p. 256 on the president's power to appoint, remove and rotate akims, or regional governors. As she notes, these regional officials are even rotated to the senate and ambassadorships so they never build up strong constituencies in any one place (p. 258).

101. Mesquita, "Kazakhstan's Presidential Transition," pp. 371–397.

102. See Junisbai, "A Tale of Two Kazakhstans," p. 263.

103. As Alexander Cooley finds, for instance, "a number of Eurasian countries view OBOR as a politically critical initiative to guard against becoming dependent on Moscow." Cooley, "The Emerging Political Economy of OBOR," p. 9.

104. Author conversation with Daniyar Kosnazarov, 29 April 2017, Almaty, Kazakhstan.

105. Sebastien Peyrouse, "Discussing China," p. 14. On the evolution of China's role in Central Asia, see also Zhao Huasheng, "Central Asia in Chinese Strategic Thinking," in *The New Great Game*, edited by Thomas Fingar (Stanford, CA: Stanford University Press, 2016), p. 171–189.

106. Peyrouse, "Discussing China," p. 14.

107. See Marlene Laruelle and Sebastien Peyrouse, *The "Chinese Question" in Central Asia. Domestic Order, Social Changes, and the Chinese Factor* (London, New York: Hurst and Columbia University Press, 2012), especially pp. 72–81.

108. Cooley, "The Emerging Political Economy of OBOR," p. 7.

109. Peyrouse, "Discussing China," p. 22.

110. Author conversation with Karla Jamankulova, 27 April 2017, Nur-Sultan (Astana), Kazakhstan.

111. Dena Sholk, "Kazakhstan's Land Reforms," *The Diplomat*, 15 June 2016, https://thediplomat.com/2016/06/kazakhstans-land-reforms/.

112. On Sauytbay, see Nathan Vanderklippe, "'Everyone Was Silent, Endlessly Mute': Former Chinese Re-Education Instructor Speaks Out," *Globe and Mail*, 2 August 2018, https://www.theglobeandmail.com/world/article-everyone-was-silent-endlessly-mute-former-chinese-re-education/; Mauk, "Can China Turn the Middle of Nowhere into the Center of the World Economy?"; James Millward, "'Reeducating' Xinjiang's Muslims," *New York Review of Books*, 7 February 2019, https://www.nybooks.com/articles/2019/02/07/reeducating-xinjiangs-muslims/.

113. Catherine Putz correctly identified many of these issues in her essay written before the Sauytbay story broke. See "Carefully, Kazakhstan Confronts China about Kazakhs in Xinjiang Re-Education Camps," *The Diplomat*, 14 June 2018, https://thediplomat.com/2018/06/carefully-kazakhstan-confronts-china-about-kazakhs-in-xinjiang-re-education-camps/. Reid Sandish updated the analysis in "She Fled China's Camps—but She's Still Not Free," *Foreign Policy*, 6 February 2019, https://foreignpolicy.com/2019/02/06/she-fled-chinas-camps-but-shes-still-not-free/.

114. Dake Kang, "China Allowing 2,000 Ethnic Kazakhs to Leave Xinjiang Region," *Associated Press*, 9 January 2019, https://www.apnews.com/6c0a9dcdd7bd4a0b85a0bc96ef3dd6f2.

115. "Kazakhstan Arrests a Man Who Exposed China's Gulag," *The Economist*, 14 March 2019; Reid Standish, "Astana Tries to Silence China Critics," *Foreign Policy*, 11 March 2019, https://foreignpolicy.com/2019/03/11/uighur-china-kazakhstan-astana/.

116. "China Issues Warning to Tourists amid Confusion Over Visas to Kazakhstan," *South China Morning Post*, 17 June 2017, http://www.scmp.com/news/china/diplomacy-defence/article/2098785/china-issues-warning-tourists-amid-confusion-over-visas.

117. Jack Farchy, "China Seeking to Revive the Silk Road," *Financial Times*, 9 May 2016, https://www.ft.com/content/e99ff7a8-0bd8-11e6-9456-444ab5211a2f.

118. For Russia and European, see "Kazakhstan Planning to Introduce a 72-hour Visa-Free Regime for Indian Citizens—A. Mukhamediuly," The Prime Minister of Kazakhstan, 25 January 2018, https://primeminister.kz/en/news/all/15958. For Americans, see "30-day Visa Free to Kazakhstan," US Embassy and Consulate in Kazakhstan, accessed 13 June 2018, https://kz.usembassy.gov/30-day-visa-free-kazakhstan/.

119. Pantucci, "Looking West: China and Central Asia." For China's presence in Aktobe, see Raffaello Pantucci and Alexandros Petersen, "Chinatown, Kazakhstan?" China in Central Asia, 20 September 2012, http://chinaincentralasia.com/2012/09/20/chinatown-kazakhstan/.

120. For Chinese energy companies' employment tendencies, see "As China Invests, Many Kazakhs Say: Not Too Fast," *National Public Radio*, 7 June 2011, https://www.npr.org/templates/transcript/transcript.php?storyId=136822829. For information on temporary camps, see Tom Miller, *China's Asian Dream* (London: Zed Books, 2017).

121. Luca Anceschi and Bruce Pannier, "Is This Kazakhstan's New Transitional Government?" *Radio Free Europe Radio Liberty*, 23 September 2016, https://www.rferl.org/a/is-this-kazakhstans-new-transitional-government/28008984.html; Bruce Pannier, "Nazarbaev's Decision to Leave Office Just Might Be His Greatest Legacy," *Radio Free Europe Radio Liberty*, 19 March 2019, https://www.rferl.org/a/nazarbaev-s-decision-to-leave-office-just-might-be-his-biggest-legacy/29830474.html.

122. Parliament granted Nazarbayev a seat on key decision-making bodies after leaving office and immunity to him and his family. See Mesquita, "Kazakhstan's Presidential Transition," p. 376. As of February 2019, there were indications Nazarbayev might seek an early re-election to power. See "Kazakh Leader Seeks Legal Advice on End of Term, Hinting at Snap Election," *Channel News Asia*, 4 February 2019, https://www.channelnewsasia.com/news/world/kazakh-leader-seeks-legal-advice-on-end-of-term--hinting-at-snap-election-11202952.

123. Nargis Kassenova, "Passing Central Asia Power Batons: What Can We Expect?" PONARS Eurasia, http://www.ponarseurasia.org/article/passing-central-asian-power-batons-kassenova-schatz-mcglinchey-part-2. For more on the history of Central Asia's patronage politics, see Eric McGlinchey, *Chaos, Violence, Dynasty: Politics and Islam in Central Asia* (Pittsburgh: University of Pittsburgh Press, 2011), pp. 8–9; Cooley, *Great Games, Local Rules*, pp. 16–18.

124. Quote from Henry Hale, "25 Years after the USSR: What's Gone Wrong?" *Journal of Democracy*, vol. 27, no. 3 (July 2016). Also see Henry Hale, *Patronal Politics* (Washington, DC: George Washington University, 2014).

125. For more on Kazakhstan's hordes and their relationship to politics, see Martha Olcott, *Kazakhstan: Unfulfilled Promise?* (Washington, DC: Carnegie Endowment For Peace, 2012), pp. 183–189.

126. Cooley, *Great Games, Local Rules*, p. 18.

127. Eric McGlinchey, *Chaos, Violence, Dynasty: Politics and Islam in Central Asia* (Pittsburgh: University of Pittsburgh Press, 2011), p. xi.

128. Edward Schatz, "Passing Central Asia Power Batons: What Can We Expect?," PONARS Eurasia, http://www.ponarseurasia.org/article/passing-central-asian-power-batons-kassenova-schatz-mcglinchey-part-2. A short list of possible successors to Nazarbayev, all of whom would essentially favor continuity over

change, can be found in Mesquita, "Kazakhstan's Presidential Transition," p. 380. Each would likely reshuffle the composition of the ruling coalition only at the margins so as to avoid a powerful backlash.

129. Nargis Kassenova, "Passing Central Asia Power Batons: What Can We Expect?," PONARS Eurasia, http://www.ponarseurasia.org/article/passing-central-asian-power-batons-kassenova-schatz-mcglinchey-part-2.

130. See Scott Radnitz, "Post Succession Scenarios in Central Asia," PONARS Eurasia, August 2015, http://www.ponarseurasia.org/memo/post-succession-scenarios-central-asia, for an extended analysis that explores this possibility.

131. Barbara Junisbai's study in the mid-2000s mapped out the membership of the first and second tier of these groups, with the former more tightly aligned with the president than the latter. See Junisbai, "A Tale of Two Kazakhstans."

132. See Junisbai, "A Tale of Two Kazakhstans," p. 247.

133. See Junisbai, "A Tale of Two Kazakhstans," p. 264.

134. Roberts, "The Perils of the Autocratic Developmental State," p.78.

135. Author conversation with expert analyst, 26 April 2017, Nur-Sultan (Astana), Kazakhstan.

136. Author conversation with expert analyst, 26 April 2017, Nur-Sultan (Astana), Kazakhstan.

137. Author conversation with Sultan Akimbekov, 28 April 2017, Almaty, Kazakhstan.

138. Peyrouse, "Discussing China," p. 16. Fravel also observes the link between Chinese pressure and Kazakhstan's action against Uighur groups in 1999. See Fravel, *Strong Borders, Secure Nation*, p. 162. And Laruelle and Peyrouse state that Chinese secret services may have even entered Kazakhstani territory to track down Uighur dissidents (Marlene Laruelle and Sebastien Peyrouse, "China as a Neighbor: Central Asian Perspectives and Strategies," Central Asia-Caucuses Institute, 2009, https://www.silkroadstudies.org/resources/pdf/Monographs/2009_BOOK_Laruelle-Peyrouse_China-Central-Asia.pdf, p. 73).

139. Peyrouse, "Discussing China," p. 18.

140. Paul Stronski, "Kazakhstan's Autocratic President Resigns. What Happens Next?" *Quick Take*, Carnegie Endowment for International Peace, 20 March 2019, https://carnegieendowment.org/2019/03/20/kazakhstan-s-autocratic-president-resigns.-what-happens-next-pub-78646.

141. Peyrouse identifies Alexander Mashkevich and Vladimir Kim, both of whom are major metal exporters to China and frequently named as top Kazakhstani oligarchs. See Peyrouse, "Discussing China," p. 18. Farkhad Sharip also identifies Nazarbayev's son-in-law, Timur Kulibayev, as a figure who, along with Massimov, enjoys extremely close ties with China. See Farkhad Sharip, "Chinese Pawns on the Kazakh Political Chessboard: Massimov versus Kulibayev?," *Eurasia Daily Monitor*, 16 May 2011, https://jamestown.org/program/chinese-pawns-on-the-kazakh-political-chessboard-masimov-versus-kulibayev/. Another useful speculative piece on post-Nazarbayev leadership options is Natalie Hall,

"Who Will Run Post-Nazarbayev Kazakhstan?," *The Diplomat*, 30 October 2018, https://thediplomat.com/2018/10/who-will-run-post-nazarbayev-kazakhstan/.

142. Author conversation, 24 April 2017, Moscow, Russia.

143. Martha Brill Olcott, the author of a modern history of Kazakhstan, explains that "the Kazakh national revival made local Russians uncomfortable from the start" of Kazakhstan's period of independence from the Soviet Union in 1991. Olcott, *Kazakhstan: Unfulfilled Promise?*, p. 72.

144. "Kazakhstan to Change from Cyrillic to Latin Alphabet," *DW*, 27 October 2017, http://www.dw.com/en/kazakhstan-to-change-from-cyrillic-to-latin-alphabet/a-41147396.

145. Figures from Olcott, *Kazakhstan: Unfulfilled Promise?*, p. 293; Casey Michel, "Why Are Russians Leaving Kazakhstan," *The Diplomat*, 23 February 2016, https://thediplomat.com/2016/02/why-are-russians-leaving-kazakhstan/.

146. For a map of Russian ethnic populations in Kazakhstan, see Dmitry Gorenburg, "Russian Military Intervention in Kazakhstan," American Enterprise Institute, January 2018, https://www.aei.org/wp-content/uploads/2018/01/Russian-Military-Intervention-in-Kazakhstan.pdf.

147. Paul Stronski, "Kazakhstan at Twenty-Five: Stable but Tense," Carnegie Endowment for Peace, 4 February 2016, http://carnegieendowment.org/2016/02/04/kazakhstan-at-twenty-five-stable-but-tense-pub-62642.

148. Sean Roberts, "The Perils of the Autocratic Developmental State," *Georgetown Journal of Asian Affairs* (Winter 2016), https://asianstudies.georgetown.edu/sites/asianstudies/files/files/upload/gjaa._2.2_roberts.pdf, p. 79. As Central Asia expert Paul Stronski writes, "Kazakhstan would be a place where the Kremlin could easily replicate the Ukraine scenario if it chose to." See Stronski, "Kazakhstan at Twenty-Five."

149. Author conversation with US official, 1 February 2018, Washington, DC. See "United States and Kazakhstan: An Enhanced Strategic Partnership for the 21st Century," The White House, 16 January 2018, https://www.whitehouse.gov/briefings-statements/united-states-kazakhstan-enhanced-strategic-partnership-21st-century/.

150. Author conversation, 24 April 2017, Moscow, Russia. Other Russian experts expressed similar sentiments, stating that "Russia is not going to pull a Crimea in northern Kazakhstan." (Author conversation with Andrei Kazantsev, 24 April 2017, Moscow, Russia.)

151. For a discussion of different Kazakhstani views on the Ukraine scenario, see Lillis, *Dark Shadows*, pp. 115–126.

152. For more on how Russians have understood their close ties with northern Kazakhstan or "Southern Siberia," see Casey Michel, "South of Southern Siberia," *Intersection*, 4 February 2016, http://intersectionproject.eu/article/russia-world/south-southern-siberia; Casey Michel, "Kazakhstan-Russia Relations: With Liberals like These . . . ," *The Diplomat*, 11 June 2015, https://thediplomat.com/2015/06/kazakhstan-russia-relations-with-liberals-like-these/.

As Michel writes, "it's upon Nazarbayev's departure that questions come. When a time of transition can turn to a time of turbulence. When a shuffle can slip into a vacuum, and within that vacuum, little green men can find their footing." See Casey Michel, "Putin's Chilling Kazakhstan Comments," *The Diplomat*, 3 September 2014, https://thediplomat.com/2014/09/putins-chilling-kazakhstan-comments/.

153. Dmitry Gorenburg, "Russian Military Intervention in Kazakhstan," American Enterprise Institute, January 2018, https://www.aei.org/wp-content/uploads/2018/01/Russian-Military-Intervention-in-Kazakhstan.pdf.

154. For an overview of Russian interests in Central Asia, see Dmitri Trenin, "Russia and Central Asia," in *Central Asia: Views from Washington, Moscow, and Beijing* (New York: M. E. Sharpe, 2007).

155. "Putin aims to create a new Russian empire, pushing Central Asian states to declare themselves with or against Russia under significant pressure from Moscow." Author conversation with Rasul Jumaly, 28 April 2017, Almaty, Kazakhstan. Syroyezhkin, a former Soviet KGB agent, was arrested in 2019 for passing classified documents to Chinese agents. The case "exposes Kazakhstan's growing unease over China's clout." See Thomas Grove, "A Spy Case Exposes China's Power Play in Central Asia," *Wall Street Journal*, 10 July 2019, https://www.wsj.com/articles/a-spy-case-exposes-chinas-power-play-in-central-asia-11562756782.

156. Cooley, *Great Games, Local Rules*, p. 57.

157. Author conversation with Konstantin Syroyezhkin, 29 April 2017, Almaty, Kazakhstan.

158. Bobo Lo, *Axis of Convenience* (London: Royal Institute of International Affairs, 2008), p. 113.

159. Roger McDermott, "Kazakhstan-Russia," Danish Institute for International Studies, 9 January 2013, p. 48, https://www.diis.dk/en/research/kazakhstan-russia. See also Sebastien Peyrouse, "Russia–Central Asia: Advances and Shortcomings of the Military Partnership," *Strategic Studies Institute*, 2011, https://ssi.armywarcollege.edu/pdffiles/PUB1063.pdf.

160. McDermott, "Kazakhstan-Russia," p. 48.

161. Russia used to hold 11 million hectares, but pressure from Kazakhstan has forced Russia to cede 2 million hectares in recent years; see McDermott, "Kazakhstan-Russia," p. 49. For recent Russian concessions, see Farkhad Sharip, "Public Protests against Russian Military Presence Mounting in Kazakhstan," *Eurasia Daily Monitor*, 9 November 2017, https://jamestown.org/program/public-protests-russian-military-presence-mounting-kazakhstan/ and "Russia Returns Leased Lands to Kazkahstan," *Kazpravda*, 17 April 2015, https://www.kazpravda.kz/en/news/politics/russia-returns-leased-lands-to-kazakhstan/.

162. McDermott, "Kazakhstan-Russia." While Russia has the lease until 2050, Baiknour's relative importance to Russia may decrease. See Catherine Putz,

"Kazakh-Russian Space Cooperation Muddles Forward," *The Diplomat*, 15 July 2016, https://thediplomat.com/2016/07/kazakh-russian-space-cooperation-muddles-forward/; John C. K. Daly, "Beset by Cash Flow Problems, Russia and Kazakhstan Consider Leasing Baikonur Cosmodrome to Other Countries," *Eurasia Daily Monitor*, 14 July 2016, https://jamestown.org/program/beset-by-cash-flow-problems-russia-and-kazakhstan-consider-leasing-baikonur-cosmodrome-to-other-countries/.

163. Guy Plopsky, "Russia's Big Plans for Air Defense in Central Asia," *The Diplomat*, 7 April 2017, https://thediplomat.com/2017/04/russias-big-plans-for-air-defense-in-eurasia/.

164. As of 2016, Kazakhstan spent 0.08 percent of its GDP on defense. See "Military Expenditure (% of GDP)," World Bank, accessed 9 March 2018, https://data.worldbank.org/indicator/MS.MIL.XPND.GD.ZS?locations=KZ.

165. As a member of the CSTO, Kazakhstan can purchase weapons from Russia at the discounted price available to Russia's domestic defense companies. See John Keaney, "CSTO: A Military Pact to Defend Russian Influence," American Security Project, 1 February 2017, https://www.americansecurityproject.org/csto-a-military-pact-to-defend-russian-influence/.

166. Data downloaded at "IMPORTER/EXPORTER TIV TABLES," Stockholm International Peace Research Institute, accessed 19 June 2019, http://armstrade.sipri.org/armstrade/page/values.php; For examples of Kazakhstan's military deals with Russia, see Reuben F Johnson, "Kazakhstan Signs MiG-31 Upgrade Contract with Russia," *Jane's Defence Weekly*, 4 September 2007; Trefor Moss, "Kazakhstan Set to Receive Russian S-300 Systems," *Jane's Missiles & Rockets*, 2 March 2009.

167. "Russia, Kazakhstan Sign Contract for Supply of 12 Su-30SM Jets," *TASS*, 12 September 2017, http://tass.com/defense/965105/.

168. Carla Freeman observes that Russia "launched a new soft power campaign in the region, seeking to improve the regional penetration of Russian-language media (for example, *Rossotrudnichestvo, Russkii Mir, Russia Today, Russia Beyond the Headlines*, and *Voice of Russia*) and fostering new cultural links to Russia via funding for university programs as well as pro-Russian civil society organizations." See Freeman, "New Strategies for an Old Rivalry?," p. 12.

169. Alma Sultangaliyeva, "Kazakhstan and Its Neighbors: Opportunities and Limitations," Institute of World Economics and Politics, September 2016, pp. 35, http://iwep.kz/files/attachments/article/2016-09-23/kazakhstan_and_its_neighbors_opportunities_and_limitations.pdf.

170. For a thorough retelling of Kazakhstan's modern history, see Olcott, *Kazakhstan: Unfulfilled Promise?*

171. A 2007 estimate placed the number at 73 percent and a 2016 estimate placed the figure at 75 percent, though estimates vary. See Sebastien Peyrouse, "The Russian Minority in Central Asia," Woodrow Wilson International Center for Scholars, 2008, https://www.wilsoncenter.org/sites/default/files/OP297_

russian_minority_central_asia_peyrouse_2008.pdf . Paul Goble, "Ethnic Russians Leaving Central Asia and with Them, Putin's Hopes for Influence," *Eurasia Daily Monitor*, 2 February 2016, https://jamestown.org/program/ethnic-russians-leaving-central-asia-and-with-them-putins-hopes-for-influence/.

172. Data for Kazakhstan's trade can be retrieved at UN Comtrade Database by selecting reporter (Kazakhstan), partner ("All"), Trade Flows ("Import," then "Export"), and "TOTAL-Total of all HS commodities." See "UN Comtrade Database," United Nations, accessed 20 June 2019, https://comtrade.un.org/data/.

173. Frol Leandoer, "Kazakh-Russian Trade Turnover to Grow up to 40 Percent This Year, Says Russian Trade Representative," *Astana Times*, 11 September 2017, https://astanatimes.com/2017/09/kazakh-russian-trade-turnover-to-grow-up-to-40-percent-this-year-says-russian-trade-representative/.

174. Author conversation with Alexander Gabuev, 24 April 2017, Moscow, Russia. Carla Freeman also finds that China-Russia relations were strong during the years of the energy boom, roughly 2000–2008. See Freeman, "New Strategics for an Old Rivalry?," pp. 7–10.

175. On the interplay between Russia and China over Central Asian energy, see Lo, *Axis of Convenience*, pp. 102–103.

176. "Annual Report of 'KazTransGas' JSC 2017," KazTransGas, http://www.kaztransgas.kz/images/01_reports/ktg_annual_report_2017-eng.pdf. On China's entry, see Joanna Lillis, "Kazakhstan: China's Deep Pockets Make Beijing a Potent Energy Player in Central Asia," *Eurasianet*, 20 April 2009, https://eurasianet.org/kazakhstan-chinas-deep-pockets-make-beijing-a-potent-energy-player-in-central-asia; "Chinese Bank to Allot $1.8bn for Gas Pipe Construction in Kazakhstan," *Azernews*, 13 December 2012, https://www.azernews.az/oil_and_gas/47478.html.

177. "Moscow sees Eurasia as a power base that will allow it to remain a major power. Moscow believes that the future world order will consist of macro-blocs, and that in order to have leverage over world affairs, countries will need to be affiliated to one, or better still to dominate one. That vision was evident in an article that President Vladimir Putin wrote about the EEU in 2012." Mathieu Duchâtel, François Godement, Kadri Liik, Jeremy Shapiro, Louisa Slavkova, Angela Stanzel, and Vessela Tcherneva, "Eurasian Integration: Caught between Russia and China," European Council on Foreign Relations, 7 June 2016, http://www.ecfr.eu/article/essay_eurasian.

178. Author conversation with Rasul Jumaly, 28 April 2017, Almaty, Kazakhstan.

179. Author conversation with Rakhim Oshakbayev, 27 April 2017, Nur-Sultan (Astana), Kazakhstan. This history of the EAEU is also recounted by Paul Stronski, "Kazakhstan at Twenty-Five." As Alexander Cooley observes, "the EEU is a Russian-led, regional bloc designed to give preferential treatment to an internal market within its post-Soviet members and affiliates." See Cooley, "The Emerging Political Economy of OBOR," p. 9.

180. Sultangaliyeva, "Kazakhstan and Its Neighbors," p. 40. On the origins and evolution of the EAEU, see Evgeny Vinokurov, "Eurasian Economic Union: Current State and Preliminary Results," *Russian Journal of Economics*, vol. 3, no. 1 (2017): pp. 54–70. See also Ivan Safranchuk, "Russia in a Reconnecting Eurasia," Center for Strategic and International Studies, September 2016, https://csis-prod.s3.amazonaws.com/s3fs-public/publication/160907_Safranchuk_RussiaReconnectingEurasia_Web.pdf; Ivan Safranchuk, "Russian Policy in Central Asia: Strategic Context," L'Observatoire Franco-Russe, November 2014, http://obsfr.ru/fileadmin/Policy_paper/PP8_EN_Safrantchouk.pdf.

181. Russia's external tariff became the common external tariff for EAEU countries, meaning that Kazakhstan had to raise its tax levels when it joined the organization. For EAEU details, see David Tarr, "The Eurasian Economic Union among Russia, Belarus, Kazakhstan, Armenia, and the Kyrgyz Republic: Can It Succeed Where Its Predecessor Failed?," Vanderbilt University, 29 September 2015, https://as.vanderbilt.edu/gped/documents/DavidTarrEurasianCustomsUnion--prospectsSept282015.pdf.

182. Niklas Swanström, "The Security Dimension of the China-Central Asia Relationship: China's Military Engagement with Central Asian Countries," Institute for Security & Development Policy, 18 March 2015, https://www.uscc.gov/sites/default/files/Swanström%20Testimony_3.18.15.pdf, p. 5.

183. Swanström, "The Security Dimension of the China-Central Asia Relationship," p. 5.

184. Alexander Cooley points this out in "Cooperation Gets Shanghaied: China, Russia, and the SCO," *Foreign Affairs*, 14 December 2009, https://www.foreignaffairs.com/articles/china/2009-12-14/cooperation-gets-shanghaied. Alexander Lukin explains that "Russian agencies responsible for economic cooperation" hold that "the SCO should not be engaged in active implementation of multilateral projects." See Alexander Lukin, *China and Russia: The New Rapprochement* (Cambridge: Polity Press, 2018), p. 123.

185. "SCO Leaders Begin Conference in Astana," Agencia EFE, 8 June 2017, https://www.efe.com/efe/english/portada/sco-leaders-begin-conference-in-astana/50000260-3291612.

186. Li Xin, "Chinese Perspective on the Creation of a Eurasian Economic Space," Valdai Discussion Club, November 2016, http://valdaiclub.com/files/12585/, p. 6. See also Nadège Rolland, "A China-Russia Condominium over Eurasia," *Survival*, vol. 61, no. 1, (2019): p. 9, https://doi.org/10.1080/00396338.2019.1568043.

187. For example, see "China and Russia Sign the Joint Declaration of Feasible Study on Eurasian Economic Partnership Agreement," Ministry of Commerce, 6 July 2017, http://english.mofcom.gov.cn/article/newsrelease/significantnews/201707/20170702605903.shtml. As Alexander Cooley notes, "China has already agreed to formally deal with EEU representatives, thus giving the Russian-led organization the international standing and legitimacy that Moscow craves." Cooley, "The Emerging Political Economy of OBOR," p. 9.

188. On Russia's efforts to "accept and use Chinese power," and specifically to involve itself in China's BRI rather than to oppose it, see Sebastien Peyrouse, "The Evolution of Russia's Views on the Belt and Road Initiative," *Asia Policy*, no. 24 (2017): pp. 96–102.

189. Author conversation, 28 April 2017, Almaty, Kazakhstan.

190. A good recent review of China-Russia relations is found in Michael S. Chase, Evan S. Medeiros, J. Stapleton Roy, Eugene B. Rumer, Robert Sutter, and Richard Weitz, *Russia-China Relations: Assessing Common Ground and Strategic Fault Lines*, National Bureau of Asian Research, July 2017. Other pieces that have contributed to this debate include Stephen Kotkin, "The Unbalanced Triangle," *Foreign Affairs*, September/October 2009, https://www.foreignaffairs.com/reviews/review-essay/unbalanced-triangle; Gilbert Rozman, *The Sino-Russian Challenge to World Order* (Stanford, CA: Stanford University Press, 2014); Raffaello Pantucci, "China and Russia's Soft Competition in Central Asia," *China in Central Asia*, 14 October 2015, http://chinaincentralasia.com/2015/10/14/china-and-russias-soft-competition-in-central-asia/.

191. There are outliers to this consensus. See, for instance, Alexander Khramchikhin and Andrei Piontkovsky, "If Anyone Is Going to Attack Russia, It Will Be China—and When China Does So, It Will Win, Khramchikhin Says," Johnson's Russia List, 6 November 2014, http://russialist.org/if-anyone-is-going-to-attack-russia-it-will-be-china-and-when-china-does-so-it-will-win-khramchikhin-says/; Andrei Piontkovsky, "Life after Decline," Jamestown Foundation, 6 July 2016, https://jamestown.org/program/%D0%B0ndrei-piontkovsky-life-after-decline/.

192. Alexander Lukin notes that some prominent Chinese (Yan Xuetong, Zhang Wenmu, Dai Xü) have urged closer alliance-like ties with Russia. See Lukin, *China and Russia*, pp. 61–62.

193. For a very brief historical review of China-Russia relations, see Yu Bin, "Between Past and Future: Implications of Sino-Russian Relations for the United States," *Asia Policy*, vol. 13, no. 1 (January 2018): pp. 12–18.

194. "Xi Tells Russian Media He Cherishes Deep Friendship with Putin," *Global Times*, 5 June 2019, http://www.globaltimes.cn/content/1153186.shtml.

195. Although Lukin's recounting of this history is decidedly biased, it offers a useful window into Moscow's characterization of post–Cold War developments. See Lukin, *China and Russia*, pp. 2–33. For a helpful (and concise) American point of view on the post–Cold War history of US-Russian relations, see Eugene Rumer, Richard Sokolsky, Paul Stronski, and Andrew S. Weiss, *Illusions vs. Reality: Twenty-Five Years of US Policy toward Russia, Ukraine, and Eurasia* (Washington, CA: Carnegie Endowment for International Peace, 2017), pp. 7–11. Many other books have attempted to make sense of the challenge to American leadership in the post–Cold War era, including Richard Haass, *A World in Disarray: American Foreign Policy and the Crisis of the Old Order* (New York: Penguin, 2018).

196. Lo, *Axis of Convenience.*

197. Lo, *Axis of Convenience*, p. 3.

198. Lo, *Axis of Convenience*, pp. 193–194.

199. Indeed, Lukin's book reads as if it were partially motivated as a rejoinder to Lo. Lukin strenuously objects to the notion that Sino-Russian relations are tenuous or destined for divergence, suggesting that such interpretations are more likely driven by ideological biases rather than "maximum objectivity." See Lukin, *China and Russia*, pp. ix, xiii, xvi.

200. Lukin, *China and Russia*, pp. xi, 3, 6–8.

201. Lukin, *China and Russia*, pp. 2–8.

202. Eugene B. Rumer makes the important observation that "Russian foreign policy is controlled exclusively by a close-knit circle of the country's elite, whose chief preoccupation is preserving the domestic stability and security of the ruling regime. A productive relationship with the West would require from Russia significant domestic changes that make the West an incompatible partner for the Kremlin. Beijing, by contrast, does not confront Moscow with such demands." See Chase, Medeiros, Roy, Rumer, Sutter, and Weitz, *Russia-China Relations*, p. 15. Elizabeth Wishnick makes the broader observation that "Russia and China oppose what the United States stands for . . . their unity reflects a convergence on issues they view as existentially important for regime survival." See Elizabeth Wishnick, "The New China-Russia-US Triangle," National Bureau of Asian Research, 15 December 2015, https://www.nbr.org/wp-content/uploads/pdfs/publications/121615_Wishnick_ChinaRussiaUS.pdf.

203. Aspects of this development in Chinese policy are explored in chapter 2. See also Larry Diamond, Marc F. Plattner, and Christopher Walker, eds., *Authoritarianism Goes Global: The Challenge to Democracy* (Baltimore: Johns Hopkins University Press, 2016).

204. For details of the 2013 deal, see Courtney Weaver and Neil Buckley, "Russia and China Agree $270bn Oil Deal," *Financial Times*, 21 June 2013, https://www.ft.com/content/ebc10e76-da55-11e2-a237-00144feab7de. For oil supplier rankings, see Edward Chow and Andrew Staley, "Russia's National Oil Champion Goes Global," Center for Strategic and International Studies, February 2018, https://www.csis.org/analysis/russias-national-oil-champion-goes-global.

205. "Gazprom Completed Bulk of Activities at Power of Siberia Pipeline," *TASS*, 21 December 2018, http://tass.com/economy/1037463.

206. Calculation based on forecasted demand of 317 bcm in 2020. See Chen Aizhu, "China's Soaring Natural Gas Output Unable to Meet Demand Set Loose in Pollution Fight," *Reuters*, 4 February 2018, https://www.reuters.com/article/us-china-pollution-gas-production/chinas-soaring-natural-gas-output-unable-to-meet-demand-set-loose-in-pollution-fight-idUSKBN1FP006.

207. Paul Stronski and Nicole Ng, "Cooperation and Competition: Russia and China in Central Asia, the Russian Far East, and the Arctic," Carnegie

Endowment for International Peace, February 2018, pp. 20–21, https://carnegieendowment.org/2018/02/28/cooperation-and-competition-russia-and-china-in-central-asia-russian-far-east-and-arctic-pub-75673.

208. On Russia's legitimate concerns about reverse engineering, see Igor Danchenko, Erica Downs, and Fiona Hill, "One Step Forward, Two Steps Back?" Brookings Institution, August 2010, p. 3, https://www.brookings.edu/wp-content/uploads/2016/06/08_china_russia_energy_downs_hill.pdf.

209. Author conversation with Alexander Gabuev, 24 April 2017, Moscow, Russia. On the estimated $3 billion S-400 sale, see Franz-Stefan Gady, "Russia Starts Delivery of S-400 Defense Systems to China," *The Diplomat*, 22 January 2018, https://thediplomat.com/2018/01/russia-starts-delivery-of-s-400-missile-defense-systems-to-china/. On the estimated $2 billion SU-35 sale and China's apparent intention to reverse engineer the aircraft's engine, see Franz-Stefan Gady, "China Takes Delivery of 10 Russian Su-35 Fighter Jets," *The Diplomat*, 4 January 2018, https://thediplomat.com/2018/01/china-takes-delivery-of-10-russian-su-35-fighter-jets/.

210. Richard Weitz, "Sino-Russian Security Ties," in *Russia-China Relations: Assessing Common Ground and Strategic Fault Lines*, National Bureau of Asian Research, July 2017, p. 29; "Importer/Exporter TIV Tables," Stockholm International Peace Research Institute, accessed 21 June 2019, http://armstrade.sipri.org/armstrade/page/values.php.

211. Lyle J. Goldstein, "Watch Out: China and Russia Are Working Together at Sea," *The National Interest*, 13 April 2016, http://nationalinterest.org/blog/the-buzz/watch-out-china-russia-are-working-together-sea-15767; Lukin, *China and Russia*, pp. 157–158.

212. "Russian Defense Minister Suggests Signing Russian-Chinese Military Cooperation Roadmap," *TASS*, 7 June 2017, http://tass.com/defense/950215.

213. Peter Zwack, "Russia and China's Growing Military Interaction; Surprised?" *The National Interest*, 9 September 2018, https://nationalinterest.org/feature/russia-and-china's-growing-military-interaction-surprised-30822; Zi Yang, "Vostok 2018: Russia and China's Diverging Common Interests," *The Diplomat*, 17 September 2018, https://thediplomat.com/2018/09/vostok-2018-russia-and-chinas-diverging-common-interests/.

214. Eugene B. Rumer, "Russia's China Policy: This Bear Hug Is Real," in *Russia-China Relations: Assessing Common Ground and Strategic Fault Lines*, National Bureau of Asian Research, July 2017, p. 24.

215. Similar points can be found in Lukin, *China and Russia*, pp. 165–169.

216. Author conversation with Asset Ordabayev, 27 April 2017, Nur-Sultan (Astana), Kazakhstan.

217. This is precisely the point made in Cooley, *Great Games, Local Rules*, p. 9.

218. Reuel R. Hanks, "'Multi-Vector Politics' and Kazakhstan's Emerging Role as a Geo-Strategic Player in Central Asia," *Journal of Balkan and Near Eastern Studies*, vol. 11, no. 3 (2009): p. 261, DOI: 10.1080/19448950903152110.

219. Hanks, "'Multi-Vector politics,'" p. 267.

220. Author conversation, 26 October 2017, Moscow, Russia.

221. Lukin appears to take at face value an obviously misleading 2009 claim by China's former ambassador to Russia, Li Fenglin, that "China has no intention of becoming a leader at either the regional or global levels. China understands Russia's desire to preserve its traditional influence in Central Asia." To advance similar arguments, he also repeatedly cites Beijing's official advocacy of "equal partnership with Russia." See Lukin, *China and Russia*, pp. 57, 62.

222. Lukin asserts that "it is premature to speak of China's overall superiority or of any broad asymmetry [of power with Russia]," and goes on to suggest that China could stumble in its growth, writing, "Of course, the simplest approach is to extrapolate from current trends, but such predictions are often flawed." See Lukin, *China and Russia*, p. x.

223. Russia's GDP was $1.65 trillion and China's $14.17 trillion. See "GDP, Current Prices," International Monetary Fund, accessed 30 January 2019, https://www.imf.org/external/datamapper/NGDPD@WEO/OEMDC/ADVEC/WEOWORLD/.

224. As early as 2008, Russia started to import more from China than from any other state, and by 2017, 21 percent of all Russian imports arrived from China. Data for Russia's imports can be retrieved at UN Comtrade Database by selecting reporter (Russian Federation), partner ("All"), imports, and "TOTAL-Total of all HS commodities." See "UN Comtrade Database," United Nations, accessed 22 June 2018, https://comtrade.un.org/data/. Data for Russia's exports can be retrieved at UN Comtrade Database by selecting reporter (Russian Federation), partner ("All"), exports, and "TOTAL-Total of all HS commodities." See "UN Comtrade Database," United Nations, accessed 22 June 2018, https://comtrade.un.org/data/.

225. Data for China's exports can be retrieved at UN Comtrade Database by selecting reporter (China), partner ("All"), exports, and "TOTAL-Total of all HS commodities." See "UN Comtrade Database," United Nations, accessed 20 June 2019, https://comtrade.un.org/data/. 2017 is the latest year for which data are available for China exports.

226. Lukin, *China and Russia*, p. xi.

227. Eliot Cohen observes that the early history of the United States and Canada was defined by war, and also finds that rumors of conflict persisted through much of the nineteenth century. See Eliot A. Cohen, *Conquered into Liberty: Two Centuries of Battles along the Great Warpath That Made the American Way of War* (New York: Free Press, 2011).

228. On the Russian Far East, see Lo, *Axis of Convenience*, chapter 4. For more dire views, see Michael Khodarkovsky, "So Much Land, Too Few Russians," *New York Times*, 16 September 2016, https://www.nytimes.com/2016/09/17/opinion/so-much-land-too-few-russians.html; and work by Andrei Piontkovsky, such as Piontkovsky, "Life after Decline."

229. Stronski and Ng, "Cooperation and Competition," p. 21.
230. Marcin Kaczmarski, "The Bear Watches the Dragon: The Russian Debate on China," Marka Karpia Centre for Eastern Studies, 2013, p. 21, https://www.osw.waw.pl/sites/default/files/pw_31_en_net.pdf.
231. Stronski and Ng, "Cooperation and Competition," p. 25.
232. Author conversation, 24 April 2017, Moscow, Russia.
233. "The Expanding Kabul-Beijing Military Ties," Center for Strategic and Regional Studies, 6 March 2016, http://csrskabul.com/en/blog/the-expanding-kabul-beijing-military-ties/; "China Pledges over $70 Million to Support the Afghan Military," *Khaama Press*, 1 March 2016, http://www.khaama.com/china-pledges-over-70-million-to-support-the-afghan-military-0216.
234. Jessica Donati and Ehsanullah Amiri, "China Offers Afghanistan Army Expanded Military Aid," *Wall Street Journal*, 9 March 2016, https://www.wsj.com/articles/china-offers-afghanistan-army-expanded-military-aid-1457517153; "Afghanistan Urges China to Support the Afghan Air Force," *Khaama Press*, 29 February 2016, http://www.khaama.com/afghanistan-urges-china-to-support-the-afghan-air-force-0211; "China Approves $73 Million to Assist Afghan Military," *Middle East Press*, 1 March 2016, http://middleeastpress.com/english/china-approves-73-million-to-assist-afghan-military/.
235. Joshua Kucera, "China Proposes New Central Asian Military Alliance," *Eurasianet*, 21 March 2016, http://www.eurasianet.org/node/77896.
236. As Niklas Swanström notes, "nowhere else has China engaged in the same number of military exercises or had the same depth of regional cooperation in security issues." See Swanström, "The Security Dimension of the China-Central Asia Relationship." The SCO Peace Mission exercises have taken place routinely since 2003. In 2006 and 2015 China and Kazakhstan also undertook joint tactical anti-terror exercises. See Bruce Pannier, "China/Kazakhstan: Forces Hold First-Ever Joint Terrorism Exercises," *RadioFreeEurope*, 24 August 2006, https://www.rferl.org/a/1070801.html; "Kazakh, Chinese Militaries Hold Anti-Terrorism Drills in Kazakhstan (PHOTOS)," *Kazinform*, 5 November 2015, http://www.inform.kz/en/kazakh-chinese-militaries-hold-anti-terrorism-drills-in-kazakhstan-photos_a2836291; Martin Breitmaier, "China's Rise and Central Asia's Security," European Institute for Security Studies, June 2016.
237. The quote is from Andrey Serenko of the Russian think tank Center for the Study of Contemporary Afghanistan, in an *Izvestiya* interview, cited in Kucera, "China Proposes New Central Asian Military Alliance."
238. The quote is from Central Asia analyst Alexander Knyazev's article in *Nezavisimaya Gazeta*, cited in Joshua Kucera, "China Proposes New Central Asian Military Alliance."
239. Joshua Kucera, "Don't Worry, Russia: China's Not Starting A 'Central Asian NATO,'" *Eurasianet*, 5 April 2016, http://www.eurasianet.org/node/78136.

240. The analyst was Xiao Bin, a research fellow at the Institute of Russian, Eastern European, and Central Asian Studies, Chinese Academy of Social Sciences, cited in Joshua Kucera, "Don't Worry, Russia."

241. Kucera, "China Proposes New Central Asian Military Alliance."

242. Umed Partov, "Beijing Encroaching on Moscow's Military Dominance in Tajikistan," *Eurasia Daily Monitor*, 17 November 2016, https://jamestown.org/program/beijing-encroaching-moscows-military-dominance-tajikistan/.

243. Joshua Kucera, "Report: China Building Military Base on Afghan-Tajik Border," *Eurasianet*, 7 January 2018, https://eurasianet.org/s/report-china-building-military-base-on-afghan-tajik-border; Joshua Kucera, "Report: China Denies Plans to Build Military Base on Afghan-Tajik Border," *Eurasianet*, 7 February 2018, https://eurasianet.org/s/china-denies-plans-to-build-military-base-on-afghan-tajik-border; Kemel Toktomushev, "China's Military Base in Afghanistan," *The Diplomat*, 18 January 2018, https://thediplomat.com/2018/01/chinas-military-base-in-afghanistan/.

244. "Rivals for Authority in Tajikistan's Gorno-Badakhshan," *International Crisis Group Briefing*, no. 87, 14 March 2018, https://www.crisisgroup.org/europe-central-asia/central-asia/tajikistan/b87-rivals-authority-tajikistans-gorno-badakhshan. See also Gerry Shih, "In Central Asia's Forbidding Highlands, A Quiet Newcomer: Chinese Troops," *Washington Post*, 18 February 2019, https://www.washingtonpost.com/world/asia_pacific/in-central-asias-forbidding-highlands-a-quiet-newcomer-chinese-troops/2019/02/18/78d4a8d0-1e62-11e9-a759-2b8541bbbe20_story.html.

245. "China in Talks over Military Base in Remote Afghanistan," *Express Tribune*, 2 February 2018, https://tribune.com.pk/story/1624513/3-china-talks-military-base-remote-afghanistan/.

246. Craig Nelson and Thomas Grove, "Russia, China Vie for Influence in Central Asia as US Plans Afghan Exit," *Wall Street Journal*, 18 June 2019, https://www.wsj.com/articles/russia-china-vie-for-influence-in-central-asia-as-u-s-plans-afghan-exit-11560850203.

247. Joshua Kucera, "Has China Made Its First Big Military Sale in Central Asia?" *Eurasianet*, 6 February 2015, https://eurasianet.org/s/has-china-made-its-first-big-military-sale-in-central-asia.

248. For air defense system, see Joshua Kucera, "Turkmenistan Shows Off New Chinese Rockets," *Eurasianet*, 2 April 2016, https://eurasianet.org/s/turkmenistan-shows-off-new-chinese-rockets.

249. "Trade Registers," Stockholm International Peace Research Institute Arms Transfer Database, accessed 20 June 2019, http://armstrade.sipri.org/armstrade/page/trade_register.php; Gabriel Dominguez and Neil Gibson, "Kazakhstan Parades Newly Acquired UAVs," *Jane's Defence Weekly*, 20 May 2017; Richard D Fisher Jr., "Kazakhstan Purchases Two Chinese Wing-Loong UAVs," *Jane's Defence Weekly*, 7 June 2016.

250. Charles Forrester, "Kazakhstan Looks to Start UAV Assembly in 2017," *Jane's Defence Weekly*, 20 September 2016; "Memorandum on Technology Transfer on Production of Large-Caliber Ammunition Signed at 'Kadex-2016,'" Government of the Republic of Kazakhstan, 3 June 2016, http://www.government.kz/en/novosti/1001265-memorandum-on-technology-transfer-on-production-of-large-caliber-ammunition-signed-at-kadex-2016.html.

251. David Harrison, "Kazakhstan's Defence Cooperation with China," China in Central Asia, 26 February 2015, http://chinaincentralasia.com/2015/02/26/kazakhstans-defence-cooperation-with-china/.

252. On China's encroachment on Russian security "turf" in Central Asia, especially with respect to arms sales, see Yau Tsz Yan, "What Drives Chinese Arms Sales in Central Asia?" *The Diplomat*, 11 September 2019, https://thediplomat.com/2019/09/what-drives-chinese-arms-sales-in-central-asia/. According to one Moscow-based analyst in 2017, Russian officials have quietly shared their frustration with their Chinese counterparts who explained that all of their moves so far have been driven strictly by security concerns in Xinjiang. Author conversation, 24 April 2017, Moscow, Russia.

253. Ivan Nechepurenko, "Suicide Bomber Attacks Chinese Embassy in Kyrgyzstan," *New York Times*, 30 August 2016, https://www.nytimes.com/2016/08/31/world/asia/bishkek-china-embassy-kyrgyzstan.html.

254. Olga Dzyubenko, "Kyrgyzstan Says Uighur Militant Groups behind Attack on China's Embassy," *Reuters*, 6 September 2016, https://www.reuters.com/article/us-kyrgyzstan-blast-china/kyrgyzstan-says-uighur-militant-groups-behind-attack-on-chinas-embassy-idUSKCN11C1DK.

255. For his part, Cooley argues that "Beijing is likely to calculate that more direct interference in the security and political affairs of its neighbors is warranted." See Cooley, "The Emerging Political Economy of OBOR," p. 10.

256. Former military attaché Ben Lowsen considers the contingency of China sending PAP units to Central Asia in Ben Lowsen, "Like a Good Neighbor: Chinese Intervention through the Shanghai Cooperation Organization," in *The People's Liberation Army and Contingency Planning in China*, edited by Andrew Scobell, Arthur S. Ding, Phillip C. Saunders, and Scott Herold (Washington, DC: National Defense University Press, 2015), p. 260, http://ndupress.ndu.edu/Portals/68/Documents/Books/PLA-contingency/PLA-Contingency-Planning-China.pdf.

257. Richard Weitz, "China's Military Goals, Policy, Doctrine, and Capabilities in Central Asia," in *Central Asia after 2014*, edited by Stephen Blank (Carlisle, PA: US Army War College, November 2013), p. 92.

258. On the "Differences in Chinese and Russian Views of Multipolarity, Global Governance, and the International Order," see Stronski and Ng, "Cooperation and Competition," p. 8.

259. Lo, *Axis of Convenience*, p. 87.

260 | NOTES FOR PAGES 114–115

260. Danchenko, Downs, and Hill, "One Step Forward, Two Steps Back?," pp. 2–3. On Russia as "vassal state," see Kaczmarski, "The Bear Watches the Dragon."

261. Angela Stent, *Putin's World: Russia against the West and with the Rest* (New York: Twelve, 2019), p. 2.

262. After surveying some of China's more bellicose actions and rhetoric over the recent past, Lukin writes, "at the same time, Chinese leaders continue to adopt a moderate tone in their official statements." Later, after noting more aggressive Chinese moves to build a naval base and use economic sanctions, he approvingly cites a speech by Xi Jinping to conclude that "China is generally not interested in confrontation with anyone." Lukin, *China and Russia*, pp. 21, 27.

263. Joshua Kurlantzik, "China's Charm Offensive in Southeast Asia," *Current History* (September 2006): pp. 270–276, http://carnegieendowment.org/files/kurlantzick_southeastasia_china.pdf.

264. All of this, as southeast Asia analyst Joshua Kurlantzik summarized, was a reflection of the fact that "China has spent much of the past two years provoking its neighbors—and the United States as well." See Joshua Kurlantzik, "The Belligerents," *New Republic*, 27 January 2011, https://newrepublic.com/article/82211/china-foreign-policy.

265. For the Carnegie Endowment's Dmetri Trenin, the Sino-Russian relationship shows no sign of deterioration. He writes, "Many in the West have been waiting for decades for a Sino-Russian clash in Central Asia. Their wait will never end." See "Russia, China Are Key and Close Partners," *China Daily*, 5 June 2019, http://www.chinadaily.com.cn/a/201906/05/WS5cf6f85da3105191427010c6.html.

266. Igor Torbakov makes a similar observation: "it is also useful to keep in mind that Central Asia is only one element—and not necessarily the most important one—of Moscow and Beijing's strategic universes." See Torbakov, "Managing Imperial Peripheries," in *The New Great Game*, p. 251.

267. Rolland's review of Sino-Russian relations also stresses the potential for Eurasian condominium in the medium term, but also observes that "As time goes on, problems might emerge in the Sino-Russian relationship. Russia may eventually realise that China poses a profound threat to its interests and ambitions and decide to get serious about competition. But it took the United States nearly a quarter of a century to come to a similar conclusion. Over the medium-term, a Sino-Russian condominium over Eurasia will probably continue to take shape." See Rolland, "A China-Russia Condominium over Eurasia," p. 19.

268. Central Asia expert Paul Stronski makes a similar point about the potential for Kazakhstan's instability: "Moving into the future, Kazakhstan may simultaneously face geopolitical insecurity outside its borders, economic trouble due to prolonged low oil prices, and political uncertainty at home." See Stronski, "Kazakhstan at Twenty-Five."

269. For more on this point, see Laruelle, ed., *China's Belt and Road Initiative and Its Impact in Central Asia*, p. xi.

Chapter 5

1. Beijing has identified both Tehran and Riyadh as "Comprehensive Strategic Partners." See "China, Iran Lift Bilateral Ties to Comprehensive Strategic Partnership," *China Daily*, 23 January 2016, http://www.chinadaily.com.cn/world/2016xivisitmiddleeast/2016-01/23/content_23215522.htm; also "Saudi Arabia, China Upgrade Relations to Comprehensive Strategic Partnership," *Saudi Gazette*, 21 January 2016, http://saudigazette.com.sa/article/147023.

2. Xenophon, *Cyropaedia*, vol. I: *Books 1–4*, trans. Walter Miller (Cambridge, MA: Harvard University Press, 1914), pp. 7, 9.

3. Historian John Garver explains this point in greater detail in his book on contemporary China-Iran relations that remains a definitive source. John W. Garver, *China & Iran: Ancient Partners in a Post-Imperial World* (Seattle: University of Washington Press, 2006), pp. 13–17. For a recent example of this rhetoric about ancient civilizational ties, see "Iran-China Bilateral Relations Growing," *Mehr News Agency*, 15 April 2018, https://en.mehrnews.com/news/133379/Iran-China-bilateral-relations-growing.

4. William Watson, "Iran and China," in *The Cambridge History of Iran*, edited by E. Yarshater (Cambridge: Cambridge University Press, 1983), p. 537.

5. Josef Wiesehöfer, "The Late Sasanian Near East," in *The New Cambridge History of Islam*, edited by C. Robinson (Cambridge: Cambridge University Press, 2010), p. 143.

6. Matthew P. Canepa, "Distant Displays of Power: Understanding Cross-Cultural Interaction among the Elites of Rome, Sasanian Iran, and Sui-Tang China," *Ars Orientalis*, vol. 38 (2010): p. 123.

7. Chase F. Robinson, "The Rise of Islam, 600–705," in *The New Cambridge History of Islam*, edited by C. Robinson (Cambridge: Cambridge University Press, 2010): pp. 173–225.

8. When the Arabs conquered the Sasanian Empire, "Persia was swallowed whole . . . Yet it did survive, in some sense, in Islamic garb." See David Morgan, "Sasanian Iran and the Early Arab Conquests," *Journal of the Economic and Social History of the Orient*, vol. 54, no. 4 (2011): pp. 528–536. On the booty and other resources from the conquest of Persia, see also Robinson, "The Rise of Islam, 600–705," in *The New Cambridge History of Islam*, pp. 199–202.

9. Canepa, "Distant Displays of Power," pp. 124, 138; also on this period, see Watson, "Iran and China," in *The Cambridge History of Iran*, pp. 537–558.

10. Chiu Ling-Yeong, "Persians, Arabs, and Other Nationals in T'ang China: Their Status, Activities, and Contributions," *Journal of the Hong Kong Branch of the Royal Asiatic Society*, vol. 13 (1973): pp. 58–72.

11. James D. Frankel, "Chinese-Islamic Connections: An Historical and Contemporary Overview," *Journal of Muslim Minority Affairs*, vol. 36, no. 4 (2016): p. 573.

12. Garver, *China & Iran*, p. 23.

13. Watson, "Iran and China," in *The Cambridge History of Iran*, p. 547; also Canepa, "Distant Displays of Power," p. 146, note 17.

14. Canepa, "Distant Displays of Power," p. 130. See also Matteo Compareti, "The Last Sasanians in China," *Encylopaedia Iranica*, (2009), http://www.iranicaonline.org/articles/china-xv-the-last-sasanians-in-china.

15. Levathes, *When China Ruled the Seas*, pp. 140–151; Barbara Bennett Peterson, "The Ming Voyages of Cheng Ho (Zheng He), 1371–1433," *The Great Circle*, vol. 16, no. 1 (1994): pp. 45–46.

16. Ralph Kauz and Roderich Ptak, "Hormuz in Yuan and Ming Sources," *Bulletin de l'Ecole Francaise d'Extreme-Orient*, vol. 88 (2001): p. 56; Levathes, *When China Ruled the Seas*, p. 172.

17. For updates on China's relations with a wider range of Middle Eastern states, see Jonathan Fulton, "China's Changing Role in the Middle East," The Atlantic Council, June 2019, https://www.atlanticcouncil.org/images/publications/Chinas_Changing_Role_in_the_Middle_East.pdf; Jon B. Alterman, "Chinese and Russian Influence in the Middle East," Statement before the US House Foreign Affairs Subcommittee on the Middle East, North Africa, and International Terrorism, 9 May 2019.

18. For a summary of early relations between communist China and revolutionary Iran, see Baris Adibelli, "Sino-Iranian Relations since the Cold War," in *The Emerging Middle East–East Asia Nexus*, edited by Anoushiravan Ehteshami and Yukiko Miyagi (New York: Routledge, 2015), pp. 110–114.

19. For a brief history of early relations between communist China and Saudi Arabia, see Jonathan Fulton, *China's Relations with the Gulf Monarchies* (London: Routledge, 2019), pp. 80–94.

20. "This alliance between the Wahhabi and the Al Saud family has endured, surviving defeat and collapse, for more than two and a half centuries. Individuals from the two families have often intermarried over the years. In today's Saudi Arabia, many senior government officials are appointed from among this family." See Ali al Shihabi, *The Saudi Kingdom* (Princeton: Markus Wiener Publications, 2016), pp. 169–174.

21. Fulton, *China's Relations with the Gulf Monarchies*, p. 81.

22. Fulton, *China's Relations with the Gulf Monarchies*, p. 85.

23. Author conversation with Yitzhak Shichor, Jerusalem, Israel, 26 June 2017.

24. Yitzhak Shichor, *The Middle East in China's Foreign Policy, 1949–1977* (Cambridge: Cambridge University Press, 1979), p. 192.

25. Shichor, *The Middle East in China's Foreign Policy*, pp. 6–7. These limitations, and especially the Cold War framing of Middle Eastern geopolitics, are also noted by other historians of the period. According to John Calabrese, in the

Middle East "the presence and activities of the superpowers have supplied not only incentives and opportunities for China to act, but have also imposed constraints and costs on China's acting." The Calabrese quote comes from an insightful literature review by Matteo Legrenzi and Fred H. Lawson, "China's Gulf Policy: Existing Theories, New Perspectives," *Middle East Policy*, vol. 8, no. 2 (Summer 2015): p. 59. See also John Calabrese, *China's Changing Relations with the Middle East* (London: Pinter Publishers, 1991). Another classic history by Hashim S. H. Behbehani, *China's Foreign Policy in the Arab World, 1955–75: Three Case Studies* (London: KPI Limited, 1981) also stresses the Cold War framing of Chinese policies in the Middle East, focusing attention particularly on how Beijing perceived the region through the lens of its own attempts to project global leadership through the 1955 Bandung Conference (pp. 2–6), then its opposition to "Soviet revisionism" and "US imperialism" in the 1960s (pp. 6–9), and in the early 1970s, its efforts to promote "Third World" solidarity (pp. 9–17).

26. As John Garver and Jon Alterman observe at the outset of their comprehensive 2008 report for the Center for Strategic and International Studies, "a thirst for energy guides much of China's policy in the Middle East, with other commercial, military, and diplomatic interests playing a subsidiary role." Jon B. Alterman and John W. Garver, *The Vital Triangle: China, the United States and the Middle East* (Washington, DC: Center for Strategic and International Studies, 2008), p. 3.

27. Erica S. Downs, *China's Quest for Energy Security* (Santa Monica, CA: RAND Corporation, 2006), p. 12.

28. Downs, *China's Quest for Energy Security.*

29. Suzanne Maloney, *Iran's Political Economy since the Revolution* (Cambridge: Cambridge University Press, 2015), p. 32.

30. On the early ties between President Franklin Delano Roosevelt and Ibn Saud, see Bruce Riedel, *Kings and Presidents: Saudi Arabia and the United States since FDR* (Washington, DC: Brookings Institution, 2008), pp. 6–12.

31. Data for China's oil imports by reporter (China) and partner (available Middle East countries) can be retrieved from UN Comtrade Database's main webpage. Selecting commodity code 2709, "Petroleum oils and oils obtained from bituminous minerals; crude," for HS (as reported) commodity codes, "imports," for trade flows, years 2000 through 2017, "China" as reporter, and specific countries as partners. Final figures include China's import data from the following, if available: Bahrain, Cyprus, Egypt, Iran, Iraq, Israel, Jordan, Kuwait, Lebanon, Oman, Qatar, Saudi Arabia, Syria, Turkey, United Arab Emirates, and Yemen. China does not report imports from every country each year. See "UN Comtrade Database," United Nations, accessed 20 June 2019, https://comtrade.un.org/data/.

32. Data for China's oil imports by reporter (China) and partner (available Middle East countries and World) can be retrieved at UN Comtrade Database by

selecting commodity code 2709, "Petroleum oils and oils obtained from bituminous minerals; crude." Figures include China's import data from the following, if available: Bahrain, Cyprus, Egypt, Iran, Iraq, Israel, Jordan, Kuwait, Lebanon, Libya, Oman, Qatar, Saudi Arabia, Syria, Turkey, United Arab Emirates, and Yemen. China does not report exports to every country each year. See "UN Comtrade Database," United Nations, accessed 15 June 2018, https://comtrade.un.org/data/.

33. Michael Lelyveld, "China's Oil Import Dependence Climbs as Output Falls," *Radio Free Asia*, 4 December 2017, https://www.rfa.org/english/commentaries/ energy_watch/chinas-oil-import-dependence-climbs-as-output-falls-12042017102429.html.

34. Shashank Mohan, "What Does the Drop in Oil Prices Mean for the Chinese Economy?," Aspen Institute, 24 July 2015, https://www.aspeninstitute.it/ aspenia-online/article/what-does-drop-oil-prices-mean-chinese-economy.

35. Samantha Gross, "Lower for Longer: The Implications of Low Oil and Gas Prices for China and India," Brookings Institution, 19 October 2017, https:// www.brookings.edu/wp-content/uploads/2017/10/fp_20171019_lower_longer_ china_india.pdf.

36. Anjli Raval and Neil Hume, "Oil Industry Loses Fear Factor but Finds Little to Cheer," *Financial Times*, 29 September 2017, https://www.ft.com/ content/f54146e2-a502-11e7-9e4f-7f5e6a7c98a2 ; Linda Capuano, "Annual Energy Outlook 2018," US Energy Information Administration, 6 February 2018, https://www.eia.gov/pressroom/presentations/Capuano_02052018.pdf.

37. Andrea Ghiselli, "China and the Middle East: Growing Influence and Divergent Perceptions," Middle East Institute, 17 April 2018, http://www. mei.edu/content/map/china-and-middle-east-growing-influence-and-divergent-goals. China may begin pressuring Saudi Arabia to accept oil payments in renminbi, similar to China's setup with Iran, Russia, and Angola. See Sam Meredith, "China Will 'Compel' Saudi Arabia to Trade Oil in Yuan—and That's Going to Affect the US Dollar," *CNBC*, 11 October 2017, https://www. cnbc.com/2017/10/11/china-will-compel-saudi-arabia-to-trade-oil-in-yuan--and-thats-going-to-affect-the-us-dollar.html.

38. China's crude imports from Saudi Arabia in 2013 were ten times their totals in 2000. See Yitzhak Shichor, "Sweet and Sour: Sino-Saudi Crude Collaboration and US-Crippled Hegemony," in *Sino-US Energy Triangles: Resource Diplomacy Under Hegemony*, edited by David Zweig and Yufan Hao (London: Routledge, 2016), p. 79.

39. Chen Aizhu and Meng Meng, "Russia Beats Saudi Arabia as China's Top Crude Oil Supplier in 2016," *Reuters*, 23 January 2017, https://www.reuters. com/article/us-china-economy-trade-crude/russia-beats-saudi-arabia-as-chinas-top-crude-oil-supplier-in-2016-idUSKBN1570VJ.

40. Trade includes all goods (not services), and China's exports include those from Hong Kong. Data are exports to Middle East as reported by China, Hong

Kong, and America. Data can be retrieved at UN Comtrade Database by selecting "TOTAL—Total of all HS commodities," by reporter (China, Hong Kong, America) and partner (available Middle East countries). Middle East includes the following countries: Bahrain, Cyprus, Egypt, Iran, Iraq, Israel, Jordan, Kuwait, Lebanon, Oman, Qatar, Saudi Arabia, Syria, Turkey, United Arab Emirates, and Yemen. Note that America and China do not report exports to every country each year. See "UN Comtrade Database," United Nations, accessed 15 June 2018, https://comtrade.un.org/data/.

41. For helpful breakdowns of all Chinese imports to Saudi Arabia, see the Observatory of Economic Complexity's visualization of UN Comtrade data at "What Does China Export to Saudi Arabia? (2017)" accessed 20 May 2019, https://atlas.media.mit.edu/en/visualize/tree_map/hs92/export/chn/sau/show/ 2017/; and for Iran, see https://atlas.media.mit.edu/en/visualize/tree_map/hs92/ export/chn/irn/show/2017/.

42. Exports includes all goods (not services). Data are exports to Middle East as reported by China. Data can be retrieved at UN Comtrade Database by selecting "TOTAL—Total of all HS commodities," by reporter (China) and partner (available Middle East countries) for 1993 and 2016. Middle East includes the following countries: Bahrain, Cyprus, Egypt, Iran, Iraq, Israel, Jordan, Kuwait, Lebanon, Oman, Qatar, Saudi Arabia, Syria, Turkey, United Arab Emirates, and Yemen. Note that China does not report exports to every country each year. See "UN Comtrade Database," United Nations, accessed 15 June 2018. Inflation figures calculated at "US Inflation Calculator," US Inflation Calculator, accessed 17 May 2018, http://www.usinflationcalculator. com.

43. Exports includes all goods (not services). Data are exports to Middle East as reported by China, and exports to "World" as reported by China. Data can be retrieved at UN Comtrade Database by selecting "TOTAL—Total of all HS commodities," by reporter (China) and partner (available Middle East countries and World) for 2016. Middle East includes the following countries: Bahrain, Cyprus, Egypt, Iran, Iraq, Israel, Jordan, Kuwait, Lebanon, Oman, Qatar, Saudi Arabia, Syria, Turkey, United Arab Emirates, and Yemen. Note that China does not report exports to every country each year. See "UN Comtrade Database," United Nations, accessed 15 June 2018.

44. Yitzhak Shichor, "Competence and Incompetence: The Political Economy of China's Relations with the Middle East," *Asian Perspective*, vol. 30, no. 4 (2006): p. 65.

45. Andrew Scobell and Alireza Nader, *China in the Middle East: The Wary Dragon* (Santa Monica, CA: RAND Corporation, 2016), p. 2. Scobell and Nader helpfully go on to note that China's sense of insecurity in the Middle East had propelled Beijing to adopt a "wary dragon" strategy. This means "avoiding taking sides in Middle East conflicts and controversies" and limiting even the "public articulation of a Middle East policy."

46. Jon B. Alterman, "Chinese and Russian Influence in the Middle East," Statement before the US House Foreign Affairs Subcommittee on the Middle East, North Africa, and International Terrorism, 9 May 2019.

47. Author interview with Bruce Riedel, Washington, DC, 8 May 2018.

48. See also Riedel, *Kings and Presidents*, pp. 93–94. For more on the backstory of the missile sale, Riedel cites the memoir of the then-head of Saudi air defenses General Prince Khalid bin Sultan (Khalid bin Sultan with Patrick Seale, *Desert Warrior* [New York: HarperCollins, 1995], pp. 138–42). For an earlier, nearly contemporary, overview of the negotiations and sale—including the estimated price—see Yitzhak Shichor, *East Wind over Arabia: Origins and Implications of the Sino-Saudi Missile Deal* (Berkeley: Institute of East Asian Studies, University of California at Berkeley, 1989), especially pp. 26–31. See also David B. Ottaway, *The King's Messenger: Prince Bandar Bin Sultan and America's Tangled Relationship with Saudi Arabia* (New York: Walker and Company, 2008), p. 67. For the size of the deal, see "Trade Registers," Stockholm International Peace Research Institute, accessed 1 May 2018, http://armstrade.sipri.org/armstrade/page/trade_register.php.

49. On the CSS-5 (or DF-21) sale, see Ethan Meick, "China's Reported Ballistic Missile Sale to Saudi Arabia," US-China Economic and Security Review Commission, 16 June 2014, https://www.uscc.gov/sites/default/files/Research/Staff%20Report_China%27s%20Reported%20Ballistic%20Missile%20Sale%20to%20Saudi%20Arabia_0.pdf.

50. Phil Mattingly, Zachary Cohen, and Jeremy Herb, "Exclusive: US Intel Shows Saudi Arabia Escalated Its Missile Program with Help from China," *CNN*, 5 June 2019, https://www.cnn.com/2019/06/05/politics/us-intelligence-saudi-arabia-ballistic-missile-china/index.html.

51. To put Chinese sales to Saudi Arabia in comparative context, between 2010 and 2014, Saudi Arabia imported four times more arms than it had in the preceding five-year period. Despite this exploding demand, which by 2014 put Saudi Arabia at the top of the global list of arms importers, Riyadh completed only one deal with China and roughly fifty arms deals or deliveries with the United States. See "The United States Leads Upward Trend in Arms Exports, Asian and Gulf States Arms Imports Up, Says SIPRI," Stockholm International Peace Research Institute, 16 March 2015, https://www.sipri.org/media/press-release/2015/united-states-leads-upward-trend-arms-exports-asian-and-gulf-states-arms-imports-says-sipri. For a list of US–Saudi Arabia and China–Saudi Arabia deals, see "Trade Registers," Stockholm International Peace Research Institute, accessed 1 May 2018, http://armstrade.sipri.org/armstrade/page/trade_register.php. For Saudi Arabia becoming the top arms importer in 2014, see "Saudi Arabia Becomes World's Biggest Arms Importer," *Agence France-Presse*, 9 March 2015, https://www.theguardian.com/world/2015/mar/09/saudi-arabia-becomes-worlds-biggest-arms-importer.

52. Scobell and Nader, *China in the Middle East*, pp. 24–26.

53. Russia-Iran arms transfers since 2000 are valued at more than twice the level of China-Iran arms transfers since 2000. As of 2017, Russia remains "Iran's main supplier of conventional weaponry and a significant supplier of missile-related technology." See Kenneth Katzman, "Iran's Foreign and Defense Policies," Congressional Research Service, 7 November 2017, http://www.refworld.org/pdfid/5a168ebb4.pdf. For a breakdown of Russian and Chinese weapons exports into Iran, see "Importer/Exporter TIV Tables," Stockholm International Peace Research Institute, accessed 18 June 2018, http://armstrade.sipri.org/armstrade/page/values.php. For detail on how arms "value" is calculated, see "Sources and Methods," Stockholm International Peace Research Institute, accessed 18 June 2018, https://www.sipri.org/databases/armstransfers/sources-and-methods/.

54. Joel Wuthnow, "China-Iran Military Relations at a Crossroads," *China Brief*, vol. 15, issue 3 (February 2015), https://jamestown.org/program/china-iran-military-relations-at-a-crossroads/; Christian LeMiere, "Tighter Bonds—China Strengthens Ties with Iran," *Jane's Intelligence Review*, 11 November 2009.

55. Garver, *China & Iran*, pp. 168–170.

56. Garver, *China & Iran*, pp. 182–183.

57. Scott Harold and Alireza Nader, "China and Iran: Economic, Political, and Military Relations," RAND, 2012, p. 7.

58. Garver, *China & Iran*, p. 173.

59. Garver, *China & Iran*, pp. 173–178.

60. David Cenciotti, "Chinese Delegation Currently in Iran to Copy the US Stealthy RQ-170 Drone Captured in 2011," *The Aviationist*, 16 August 2012, https://theaviationist.com/2012/08/16/chinese-delegation-rq170/; David Axe, "It Won't Be Easy for Iran to Dissect, Copy US Drone," *Wired*, 12 December 2011, https://www.wired.com/2011/12/cia-drone-secrets/.

61. For details on China's pledge, see Garver, *China & Iran*, pp. 153–154. For examples of Chinese assistance, see "China's Alliance with Iran: Building for Long-Term Influence," *Jane's Intelligence Review*, 9 May 2006; Glenn R. Simpson and Jay Solomon, "Fresh Clues of Iranian Nuclear Intrigue," *Wall Street Journal*, 16 January 2009, https://www.wsj.com/articles/SB123206759616688285; LeMiere, "Tighter Bonds"; "US Sanctions Iran Officials, Chinese Network over Missile Program," *Reuters*, 18 May 2017, https://www.cnbc.com/2017/05/18/us-sanctions-iran-officials-chinese-network-over-missile-program.html.

62. Dina Esfandiary and Ariane Tabatabai, *Triple Axis: Iran's Relations with Russia and China* (London: I. B. Tauris, 2019), p. 174. At this writing, China appears to have suspended Arak cooperation. See "Iran Nuclear Chief Criticizes China for Not Helping with Reactor," *Radio Farda*, 31 January 2019, https://en.radiofarda.com/a/iran-nuclear-chief-criticizes-china-for-not-helping-arak-reactor/29743934.html.

63. ZTE, in particular, "engaged in a scheme to ship more than 20 million US-origin items to Iran. ZTE used multiple avenues to evade US sanctions and export control regulations, including establishing shell companies, falsifying customs documents, and then actively misleading investigators when details of the conspiracy came to light." See Jerrica Goodson and Valerie Lincy, "Lesson Learned or Business as Usual?," Iran Watch Report, Wisconsin Project on Nuclear Arms Control, 4 April 2017, https://www.iranwatch. org/sites/default/files/zte_report_complete_1.pdf, p. 1. See also reports and briefs from the Wisconsin Project on Nuclear Arms Control, https://www. wisconsinproject.org.

64. Kate Conger, "Huawei Executive Took Part in Sanctions Fraud, Prosecutors Say," *New York Times*, 7 December 2018, https://www.nytimes.com/2018/12/ 07/technology/huawei-meng-wanzhou-fraud.html.

65. As RAND analysts Scobell and Nader pointed out in 2016, Iran has been among a small handful of "states that are both firmly outside the global US network of allies and partners and possess sufficient power and determination to challenge US policies." Scobell and Nader, *China in the Middle East*, p. 12.

66. Wu Bingbing, "Strategy and Politics in the Gulf as Seen from China," in *China and the Persian Gulf: Implications for the United States*, edited by Bryce Wakefield and Susan L. Levenstein (Washington, DC: Woodrow Wilson International Center for Scholars, 2011), p. 19.

67. As Jon B. Alterman writes, "20 years ago, every government in the Middle East was either friendly to the United States government or seeking to become more so. While the United States was not exactly triumphant, it was unquestionably dominant." He adds, "As we consider conditions now, we should recall that, 20 years ago, China was completely peripheral to the region." See Jon B. Alterman, "Chinese and Russian Influence in the Middle East," Statement before the US House Foreign Affairs Subcommittee on the Middle East, North Africa, and International Terrorism, 9 May 2019.

68. Two close observers of US foreign policy, Richard Fontaine and Michael Singh, explain that China now finds itself in a world where "first the Obama and now the Trump administration have evinced a desire to focus foreign policy attention on Asia rather than the Middle East's intractable conflicts." See "Middle Kingdom Meets Middle East," *The American Interest*, 3 April 2017, https://www.the-american-interest.com/2017/04/03/middle-kingdom-meets-middle-east/.

69. On Iran's role in BRI, see Alex Vatanka, "China Courts Iran: Why One Belt, One Road Will Run through Tehran," *Foreign Affairs*, 1 November 2017, https://www.foreignaffairs.com/articles/china/2017-11-01/china-courts-iran. On the Israeli portion of this regional network, see Yoram Evron, "Can China Participate in Middle East Stabilization Efforts by Supporting Regional Connectivity?," East West Center, 6 December 2016, https://

www.eastwestcenter.org/system/tdf/private/apb363.pdf?file=1&type=node
&id=35906.

70. Deborah Lehr, "The Middle East Is the Hub for China's Modern Silk Road,"
Middle East Institute, 15 August 2017, http://www.mei.edu/content/map/
middle-east-hub-china-s-modern-silk-road.

71. A similar point is made in John Calabrese, "Fate of the Dragon in the
Year of the Red Fire Monkey: China and the Middle East 2016," Middle
East Institute, 3 February 2016, http://www.mei.edu/content/map/
fate-dragon-year-monkey-china-and-middle-east-2016.

72. Andrea Ghiselli, "Growing Overlap Between Counter-Terrorism and Overseas
Interest Protection Acts as New Driver of Chinese Strategy," *China Brief*, vol.
16, issue 9 (June 2016), https://jamestown.org/program/growing-overlap-
between-counter-terrorism-and-overseas-interest-protection-acts-as-new-
driver-of-chinese-strategy/.

73. Fontaine and Singh, "Middle Kingdom Meets Middle East."

74. "China's Nuclear Sub Mission in Gulf of Aden 'Could Cause Unease among
Neighbours,'" *South China Morning Post*, 28 April 2015, http://www.scmp.com/
news/china/diplomacy-defence/article/1777792/chinese-nuclear-submarine-
completes-anti-piracy-mission. For more on China's counterpiracy missions
in the context of its naval development, see Andrew S. Erickson and Austin
M. Strange, *Six Years at Sea and Counting: Gulf of Aden Anti-Piracy and China's
Maritime Commons Presence* (Washington, DC: Jamestown Foundation, 2015).

75. Mohammed Turki Al-Sudairi, "Hajjis, Refugees, Salafi Preachers, and a
Myriad of Others: An Examination of Islamic Connectivities in the Sino-
Saudi Relationship," in *The Red Star & the Crescent*, edited by James Reardon-
Anderson (London: C. Hurst & Co., 2018), p. 238.

76. China's crackdown against Uighurs has the potential to cause friction with
Iran's ayatollahs, who have previously criticized China's actions in Xinjiang
and Iran's tepid response. See Robert F. Worth, "Clerics Fault a Mute Iran as
Muslims Die in China," *New York Times*, 13 July 2009, https://www.nytimes.
com/2009/07/14/world/middleeast/14iran.html.

77. James M. Dorsey, "China's Uyghurs: A Potential Time Bomb," in *The Red Star
& the Crescent*, edited by James Reardon-Anderson (London: C. Hurst & Co.
Ltd, 2018), p. 251; Scobell and Nader, *China in the Middle East*, p. 14. Quote
is from Mordechai Chaziza, "Syria's Civil War: Stage for Greater Chinese
Involvement in the Middle East?," *Middle East Review of International Affairs*,
vol. 20, no. 2 (Summer 2016): p. 3.

78. Dorsey, "China's Uyghurs," in *The Red Star & the Crescent*, p. 248.

79. Dorsey, "China's Uyghurs," in *The Red Star & the Crescent*, p. 251.

80. There have been reports of Chinese special forces in Syria, but these remain
unconfirmed. For example, see Dr. Jacques Neriah, "Chinese Troops Arrive
in Syria to Fight Uygher Rebels," Jerusalem Center for Public Affairs, 20
December 2017, http://jcpa.org/chinese-troops-arrive-syria-fight-uyghur-rebels/.

Also Andrew Small, "The Implications of China's Changing Counter-Terrorism Calculus for Its Middle East Policy," China and the Middle East: Contemporary Perspectives Conference, Tel Aviv University, 6 June 2018.

81. "Well-Wishing," *The Economist*, 23 January 2016, https://www.economist.com/china/2016/01/23/well-wishing. See also Ministry of Foreign Affairs of the People's Republic of China, "Xi Jinping Delivers Important Speech at Headquarters of the League of Arab States," 22 January 2016, https://www.fmprc.gov.cn/mfa_eng/topics_665678/xjpdstajyljxgsfw/t1334587.shtml.

82. "Full Text of China's Arab Policy Paper," *Xinhua*, 13 January 2016, http://english.gov.cn/archive/publications/2016/01/13/content_281475271412746.htm.

83. "Beijing's early 2010s proposals for Middle Eastern crises were mostly a tool to promote its political role, image, and influence in the region—at the expense of the United States and its world order principles—while limiting its responsibilities and investment and not entering deeply into regional politics." See Yoram Evron, "China's Diplomatic Initiatives in the Middle East: The Quest for a Great-Power Role in the Region," *International Relations*, vol. 31, no. 2 (2017): p. 127.

84. Chaziza, "Syria's Civil War," p. 3.

85. Samuel Ramani, "China's Role in the Yemen Crisis," *The Diplomat*, 11 August 2017, https://thediplomat.com/2017/08/chinas-role-in-the-yemen-crisis/.

86. An author at *The Economist* put his finger on the point when he wrote that "in the long run, China may find it hard to avoid taking sides," and its "new rules of Middle Eastern diplomacy could end up resembling familiar Western meddling." See "Well-Wishing."

87. Thomas Erdbrink, "Diplomat Back in Iran after Exile in the US," *New York Times*, 31 December 2013, https://www.nytimes.com/2014/01/01/world/middleeast/ally-of-irans-president-living-in-us-returns-home.html.

88. "Eastern Promise: Ayatollah Shifts towards China and Russia, as Iran's Patience with West Wears Thin," *Agence France-Presse*, 26 February 2018, http://www.scmp.com/news/world/middle-east/article/2134694/eastern-promise-ayatollah-shifts-towards-china-and-russia; "'Look East!,' Says Khamenei, Disappointed with Europe's Efforts to Save JCPOA," *Radio Farda*, 18 October 2018, https://en.radiofarda.com/a/look-east-says-khamenei-disappointed-with-europe-s-efforts-to-save-jcpoa/29550531.html.

89. Author conversation with Seyed Hossein Mousavian, Washington, DC, 11 May 2018.

90. Esfandiary and Tabatabai, *Triple Axis*, pp. 42, 51.

91. Esfandiary and Tabatabai, *Triple Axis*, p. 124.

92. Esfandiary and Tabatabai, *Triple Axis*, p. 125.

93. Maloney, *Iran's Political Economy*, pp. 429–431.

94. Maloney, *Iran's Political Economy*, p. 471.

95. Of course, Mousavian is not the only one to have made a similar observation. As China–Middle East scholar John Calabrese wrote in 2006, "the United States has been the pivotal third party in Sino-Iranian relations, serving as both an enabling and a complicating factor. The US arms embargo and economic sanctions against Iran have indirectly benefited China. Pressure by Washington on its Western allies—and the possibility that they might one day accede to it—has reinforced Tehran's inclination to 'Look East' for both commercial and strategic partners. The prohibition on US companies from doing business in Iran has created space, particularly in the energy sector, which Chinese enterprises along with other foreign firms . . . have competed with one another to fill." See John Calabrese, "China and Iran: Partners Perfectly Mismatched," Jamestown Foundation, August 2006, pp. 4–5, https://jamestown.org/wp-content/uploads/2006/08/Jamestown-ChinaIranMismatch.pdf.

96. Mousavian makes complementary points in Seyed Hossein Mousavian, "The Strategic Disaster of Leaving the Iran Deal," *Foreign Affairs*, 10 May 2018, https://www.foreignaffairs.com/articles/iran/2018-05-10/strategic-disaster-leaving-iran-deal.

97. Data as reported by China. Data for China's imports and exports with Iran can be retrieved at UN Comtrade Database by selecting reporter (China), partner (Iran), trade flows of "import," and "export" and "TOTAL—Total of all HS commodities" for any series of years. Total China-Iran trade calculated by adding imports and exports together, as complete historical data is unavailable at UN Comtrade. See "UN Comtrade Database," United Nations, accessed 17 May 2018, https://comtrade.un.org/data/. For the percent of Iran's total trade, see the Observatory of Economic Complexity's visualization of UN Comtrade data at "Iran," Observatory of Economic Complexity, accessed 21 June 2018, https://atlas.media.mit.edu/en/profile/country/irn/.

98. In 2017, the last year for which UN Comtrade data is available, China accounted for 49 percent of Iran's export market and provided 37 percent of Iran's imports. For complete historical data on Iran's trade, see the Observatory of Economic Complexity's visualization of UN Comtrade data at "Iran," Observatory of Economic Complexity, accessed 21 June 2018, https://atlas.media.mit.edu/en/profile/country/irn/. For 2019, see "China-US Trade War Can Create Opportunities for Iran," *Mehr News Agency*, 7 January 2019, https://en.mehrnews.com/news/141285/China-US-trade-war-can-create-opportunities-for-Iran.

99. Due to inconsistencies in Iran's reporting data for exports to individual countries, the data shown here are China's, Japan's, Korea's, and India's reported imports of Iranian oil, along with all other countries' reported imports from Iran. Data can be retrieved from the UN Comtrade Database's main website by selecting reporter ("China," "Japan," "Korea," "India," or

"All"), partner ("Iran"), trade flows ("import"), and "2709—Petroleum oils and oils obtained from bituminous minerals; crude," as the HS commodity code, for a range of years. See "UN Comtrade Database," United Nations, accessed 20 June 2019, https://comtrade.un.org/data/.

100. John W. Garver, "Is China Playing a Dual Game in Iran?" *Washington Quarterly*, vol. 34, no. 1 (Winter 2010): p. 76.

101. Erica Downs, "China-Gulf Energy Relations," in *China and the Persian Gulf,* edited by Bryce Wakefield and Susan Levenstein (Washington, DC: Woodrow Wilson International Center for Scholars, 2011), p. 69.

102. Barbara Slavin, "Iran Turns to China, Barter to Survive Sanctions," Atlantic Council, 10 November 2011, p. 3, http://www.atlanticcouncil.org/publications/ issue-briefs/iran-turns-to-china-barter-to-survive-sanctions-1; Scobell and Nader, *China in the Middle East*, pp. 62–63.

103. Downs, "China-Gulf Energy Relations," in *China and the Persian Gulf*, p. 72.

104. On US secondary sanctions, see Richard Goldberg, "Europe's Sanctions-Blocking Threats Are Empty," *Foreign Policy*, 20 February 2018, http:// foreignpolicy.com/2018/02/20/europes-iran-deal-threats-are-empty-trump-iran-eu/.

105. Indira A. R. Lakshmanan and Pratish Narayanan, "India and China Skirt Iran Sanctions with 'Junk for Oil,'" *Bloomberg News*, 30 March 2012.

106. Thomas Erdbrink, "Iran Staggers as Sanctions Hit Economy," *New York Times*, 30 September 2013, https://www.nytimes.com/2013/10/01/world/middleeast/ iran-staggers-as-sanctions-hit-economy.html.

107. "Treasury Sanctions Kunlun Bank in China and Elaf Bank in Iraq for Business with Designated Iranian Banks," US Department of the Treasury, 31 July 2012, https://www.treasury.gov/press-center/press-releases/Pages/tg1661. aspx.

108. Peter Harrell, "The Path to Renewed Oil Sanctions on Iran," *Foreign Affairs*, 8 August 2018, https://www.foreignaffairs.com/articles/iran/2018-08-08/ path-renewed-oil-sanctions-iran.

109. Author conversation with Adam Szubin, Washington, DC, 11 May 2018.

110. Mercy A. Kuo, "US-Iran Tensions: Impact on China-Iran Ties," *The Diplomat*, 3 June 2019, https://thediplomat.com/2019/06/us-iran-tensions-impact-on-china-iran-ties/.

111. Owen Matthews, "China: Iran's New Best Friend," *Newsweek*, 1 February 2016, http://www.newsweek.com/2016/02/12/china-irans-hassan-rouhani-xi-jinping-421614.html.

112. Thomas Erdbrink, "China Deepens Its Footprint in Iran after Lifting of Sanctions," *New York Times*, 24 January 2016, https://www.nytimes.com/2016/ 01/25/world/middleeast/china-deepens-its-footprint-in-iran-after-lifting-of-sanctions.html.

113. For more on Iran-Russia relations, including mutual suspicions and the limits to their strategic cooperation, see Mohsen Milani, "Iran and Russia's

Uncomfortable Alliance," *Foreign Affairs*, 31 August 2016, https://www.foreignaffairs.com/articles/iran/2016-08-31/iran-and-russias-uncomfortable-alliance; also see Esfandiary and Tabatabai, *Triple Axis*, pp. 163–166.

114. Adam Nossiter, "Rouhani Goes Shopping in Europe as Iran Enjoys New Economic Freedoms," *New York Times*, 28 January 2016, https://www.nytimes.com/2016/01/29/world/europe/iran-hassan-rouhani-france.html.

115. Maloney, *Iran's Political Economy*, pp. 342–345. Maloney goes on to observe similar frustrations related to the creation of the Construction Basij (pp. 345–347).

116. Parisa Hafezi and Louis Charbonneau, "Iranian Nuclear Deal Set to Make Hardline Revolutionary Guards Richer," *Reuters*, 6 July 2015, https://www.reuters.com/article/us-iran-nuclear-economy-insight-idUSKCN0PG1XV20150706.

117. Maloney, *Iran's Political Economy*, pp. 244–245. Ray Takeyh, *Hidden Iran* (New York: Henry Holt, 2006), p. 38.

118. As Ray Takeyh writes, "the fundamentals of economic reform, including decentralization, free competition, and the rule of law cannot be instituted without endangering the conservatives' lucrative power base." See Takeyh, *Hidden Iran*, pp. 38–39.

119. Takeyh, *Hidden Iran*, pp. 51–52.

120. Djavad Salehi-Isfahani, "Iran's Economic Reforms in Retreat," Brookings Institution, 4 December 2018, https://www.brookings.edu/blog/future-development/2018/12/04/irans-economic-reforms-in-retreat/.

121. On Iranian "pragmatists" and their use of the China model, see among others Takeyh, *Hidden Iran*, p. 40.

122. This important point is made by Calabrese in "China and Iran," p. 6.

123. For example, China has opened only one Confucius Institute in Iran (2009), limiting the opportunities for Iranian citizens to learn more about China. See "Iran's First Confucius Institute Opens in Tehran," *Xinhua*, 13 January 2009, http://www.china.org.cn/international/2009-01/13/content_17098977.htm.

124. Calabrese, "China and Iran," p. 5.

125. Calabrese, "China and Iran," p. 6.

126. On China's murky business ties with these facets of the Iranian economy, see Calabrese, "China and Iran," p. 12. As Bazoobandi writes, "the Chinese 'state capitalism' seems to have great synergy with Iran's increasingly IRGC-dominant system." See Sara Bazoobandi, "Sanctions and Isolation, the Driving Force of Sino-Iranian Relations," *East Asia*, vol. 32 (2015): p. 269.

127. In 2019, the World Bank ranked Iran 128 out of 190 states in its "Ease of Doing Business" survey. See World Bank, "Rankings & Ease of Doing Business Score," http://www.doingbusiness.org/en/rankings.

128. Farideh Farhi and Saideh Lotfian, "Iran's Post-Revolution Foreign Policy Puzzle," in *Worldviews of Aspiring Powers: Domestic Foreign Policy Debates in China, India, Iran, Japan, and Russia* (Oxford: Oxford University Press, 2012), pp. 114–140. Payam Mohseni charts factional dynamics along two

axes: economic policy (statist versus laissez-faire) and ideological legitimacy (theocratic versus republican). See Payam Mohseni, "Economic Privatization, Factional Politics, and Regime Transformation," in *Power and Change in Iran: Politics of Contention and Conciliation*, edited by Daniel Brumberg and Farideh Farhi (Bloomington: Indiana University Press, 2016), 36–79.

129. Raz Zimmt, "Long for the West, Settling for the East: The Iranian Perspective," China and the Middle East: Contemporary Perspectives Conference, Tel Aviv University, 6 June 2018. Also, as Alex Vatanka of the Middle East Institute observes, "hardliners, particularly those found in the ranks of the Islamic Revolutionary Guard Corps (IRGC), continue to argue for closer ties to China. Even the moderate faction in President Hassan Rouhani's government views China as an essential player that can complement Iran's overall attempts to break its former international isolation" (Vatanka, "China Courts Iran").

130. Anoushiravan Ehteshami, Niv Horesh, and Ruike Xu, "Chinese-Iranian Mutual Strategic Perceptions," *The China Journal*, no. 79, 9 August 2017. On Iran's political factions, see also Takeyh, *Hidden Iran*, pp. 31–57.

131. By many accounts, Washington's "maximum pressure" campaign has played to the political and economic advantage of the most repressive and hawkish factions in the Iranian state, including the IRGC. " 'The Guards are consolidating power because the national security environment in Iran justifies why they should take control of media, of intelligence, and the like,' says Vali Nasr, dean of the Paul H. Nitze School of Advanced International Studies at Johns Hopkins University. 'In an ironic way, Trump is achieving regime change in Iran, but not the one he wanted.' " See Glen Carey and Ladane Nasseri, "Trump's Iran Policy Is Not Changing the Regime's Actions," *Bloomberg Businessweek*, 23 April 2019, https://www.bloomberg.com/news/articles/2019-04-22/trump-s-iran-policy-is-not-changing-the-regime-s-behavior.

132. On these and related points about Iran's conservatives, see Ehteshami, Horesh, and Xu, "Chinese-Iranian Mutual Strategic Perceptions," pp. 2, 4, 7–9, 19–20.

133. On these and related points about Iran's reformists, see Ehteshami, Horesh, and Xu, "Chinese-Iranian Mutual Strategic Perceptions," pp. 4, 8, 9.

134. Author conversation with Raz Zimmt, Tel Aviv, Israel, 27 June 2017.

135. Maloney, *Iran's Political Economy*, p. 359; Bazoobandi, "Sanctions and Isolation, the Driving Force of Sino-Iranian Relations"; Marybeth Davis, James Lecky, Torrey Froscher, David Chen, Abel Kerevel, and Stephen Schlaikjer, "China-Iran: A Limited Partnership," CENTRA Technology, Inc., October 2012, pp. 52–53.

136. For boycotts and Treaty of Turkmenchay, see Zimmt, "Long for the West, Settling for the East."

137. "By creating expectations of economic windfalls, greater egalitarianism, and an improvement in the plight of *mostazafan* [poor], Iranian leaders effectively

undercut the theocratic basis of their authority and bolstered a competing rationale based on delivery of a better life." Maloney, *Iran's Political Economy*, pp. 503–504.

138. For a recent roundup on the possibility that Iran's economic crisis will translate into political change, see Keith Johnson, "Iran's Economy Is Crumbling, but Collapse Is a Long Way Off," *Foreign Policy*, 13 February 2019, https://foreignpolicy.com/2019/02/13/irans-economy-is-crumbling-but-collapse-is-a-long-way-off-jcpoa-waivers-sanctions/.

139. Herald and Nader, "China and Iran: Economic, Political, and Military Relations," pp. 13–14.

140. Steve Stecklow, "Special Report: Chinese Firm Helps Iran Spy on Citizens," *Reuters*, 22 March 2012, https://www.reuters.com/article/us-iran-telecoms/special-report-chinese-firm-helps-iran-spy-on-citizens-idUSBRE82L0B820120322.

141. Stecklow, "Special Report: Chinese Firm Helps Iran Spy on Citizens."

142. Alex Vatanka, "Iran Abroad," in *Authoritarianism Goes Global*, p. 73.

143. Vatanka, "Iran Abroad," in *Authoritarianism Goes Global*, p. 73. For examples of Iran-China cyber cooperation, see "Iran, China to Expand ICT Cooperation," *Financial Tribune*, 15 June 2015, https://financialtribune.com/articles/sci-tech/18983/iran-china-to-expand-ict-cooperation.

144. Initially, the NIN was to be an entirely separate Iranian internet, as noted in Christopher Rhoads and Farnaz Fassihi, "Iran Vows to Unplug Internet," *Wall Street Journal*, 28 May 2011, https://www.wsj.com/articles/SB10001424052748704889404576277391449002016.

145. *Guards at the Gate: The Expanding State Control over the Internet in Iran* (New York: Center for Human Rights in Iran, 2018), p. 34, https://www.iranhumanrights.org/wp-content/uploads/EN-Guards-at-the-gate-High-quality.pdf; Simin Kargar, "Iran's National Information Network: Faster Speeds, but at What Cost?" *Internet Monitor*, 21 February 2018, https://thenetmonitor.org/bulletins/irans-national-information-network-faster-speeds-but-at-what-cost.

146. *Guards at the Gate*, p. 41. On Huawei, see Zachary Karabell, "The Huawei Case Signals the New US-China Cold War over Tech," *Wired*, 11 March 2019, https://www.wired.com/story/huawei-case-signals-new-us-china-cold-war-tech/.

147. Karim Sadjadpour, "The Battle for Iran," *The Atlantic*, 31 December 2017, http://carnegieendowment.org/2017/12/31/battle-for-iran-pub-75132.

148. Raz Zimmt, "A Year of Protests in Iran: Situation Assessment," *INSS Insight*, No. 1118, 19 December 2018, https://www.inss.org.il/publication/year-protests-iran-situation-assessment/.

149. "Beijing and Riyadh Sign Oil and Gas Deal," *International Herald Tribune*, 24 January 2006.

150. For a contemporaneous analysis that stressed similar points, see Richard L. Russell, "Oil-for-Missiles," *Wall Street Journal*, 25 January 2006.

151. "The specter of this declining reliance raises questions—at least in the mid-term—about the future of the now-60 year old US security umbrella in the Gulf. After all, energy has historically underpinned the special security partnership between the US and Saudi Arabia." Mohammed Turki Al-Sudairi, "Sino-Saudi Relations: An Economic History," Gulf Research Center, August 2012, p. 6.

152. Fulton, *China's Relations with the Gulf Monarchies*, pp. 50–52.

153. "Featured Young China Watcher—Mohammed Al-Sudairi: Research Fellow and Head of Asian Studies, King Faisal Center for Research and Islamic Studies," *Young China Watchers*, 10 March 2018, http://www.youngchinawatchers.com/featured-young-china-watcher-mohammed-al-sudairi-research-fellow-and-head-of-asian-studies-king-faisal-center-for-research-and-islamic-studies/.

154. As retired US foreign service officer Jerry Feierstein observes, "Saudi Arabia under King Salman and the crown prince will remain an authoritarian state, with little scope offered for popular participation, let alone peaceful political dissent." Jerry Feierstein, "Saudi Arabia: Liberalization, Not Democratization," *Foreign Service Journal*, May 2018, http://www.afsa.org/saudi-arabia-liberalization-not-democratization.

155. On the Khashoggi murder as part of a wider crackdown on dissent, including women's rights, see Mark Mazzetti and Ben Hubbard, "It Wasn't Just Khashoggi: A Saudi Prince's Brutal Drive to Crush Dissent," *New York Times*, 17 March 2019, https://www.nytimes.com/2019/03/17/world/middleeast/khashoggi-crown-prince-saudi.html.

156. Quote from author conversation with Ali Shihabi, Washington, DC, 30 April 2018. See also Thomas L. Friedman's controversial column on his meeting with MBS, Thomas L. Friedman, "Saudi Arabia's Arab Spring, at Last," *New York Times*, 23 November 2017, https://www.nytimes.com/2017/11/23/opinion/saudi-prince-mbs-arab-spring.html.

157. For assessments of MBS, his reform agenda, and prospects, see Dexter Filkins, "A Saudi Prince's Quest to Remake the Middle East," *New Yorker*, 9 April 2018, https://www.newyorker.com/magazine/2018/04/09/a-saudi-princes-quest-to-remake-the-middle-east; F. Gregory Gause III, "Fresh Prince: The Schemes and Dreams of Saudi Arabia's Next King," *Foreign Affairs*, May/June 2018, https://www.foreignaffairs.com/articles/middle-east/2018-03-19/fresh-prince.

158. Margherita Stancati, "Saudi Prince Calls for Stepped-Up Pressure on Iran," *Wall Street Journal*, 29 March 2018, https://www.wsj.com/articles/saudi-prince-calls-for-stepped-up-pressure-on-iran-1522365518. See also "Crown Prince Mohammed bin Salman Talks to TIME about the Middle East, Saudi Arabia's Plans and President Trump," *Time*, 5 April 2018, http://time.com/5228006/mohammed-bin-salman-interview-transcript-full/.

159. Mohammed Turki Al-Sudairi charts the history of the Sino-Saudi economic ties at length, and concludes that "energy is now at the heart of the relationship." See Al-Sudairi, "Sino-Saudi Relations," p. 3.

160. Downs, "China-Gulf Energy Relations," in *China and the Persian Gulf: Implications for the United States*, p. 62.

161. Al-Sudairi, "Sino-Saudi Relations," p. 9.

162. See Jean-François Seznec, "China and the Gulf in 2010: A Political Economic Survey" in *China and the Persian Gulf: Implications for the United States*, p. 57; also see Shichor, "Sweet and Sour," in *Sino-US Energy Triangles*, p. 77.

163. Page last updated on March 6, 2019, though economic information only contains data as late as 2017. "Saudi Arabia," The World Factbook, Central Intelligence Agency, accessed 14 March 2019, https://www.cia.gov/library/publications/the-world-factbook/geos/sa.html.

164. Simeon Kerr and Anjli Raval, "Sweeping Saudi Plan Threatens to Shift Foundations of Kingdom," *Financial Times*, 25 April 2016, https://www.ft.com/content/80cedc7c-0b05-11e6-9456-444ab5211a2f.

165. Megan Darby, "Saudi Prince: From 2020, We Can Survive without Oil," *Climate Home News*, 25 April 2016, https://www.climatechangenews.com/2016/04/25/saudi-prince-from-2020-we-can-survive-without-oil/.

166. Mohammed bin Salman, "Our Vision: Saudi Arabia, the Heart of the Arab and Islamic Worlds, the Investment Powerhouse, and the Hub Connecting Three Continents," https://vision2030.gov.sa/en/foreword.

167. "Saudi Arabia Signs Initial Deals with China on Prince's Visit," *Reuters*, 30 August 2016, https://www.reuters.com/article/us-saudi-china-agreements/saudi-arabia-signs-initial-deals-with-china-on-princes-visit-idUSKCN1151HT. See also Wang Mouzhou, "What the Saudi Shake Up Means for China," *The Diplomat*, 9 November 2017, https://thediplomat.com/2017/11/what-the-saudi-shake-up-means-for-china/ for a discussion of the "natural synergies" of developing solar power in sun-soaked Saudi Arabia with Chinese solar panels.

168. "Featured Young China Watcher."

169. Margherita Stancati and Brian Spegele, "Saudis Seek US, Asian Investment to Diversify Economy" *Wall Street Journal*, 16 March 2017, https://www.wsj.com/articles/saudis-seek-u-s-asian-investment-to-diversify-economy-1489695797.

170. "China's Xi Expresses Support for Saudi Arabia's 'Vision 2030' Plan," *Xinhua*, 16 March 2017.

171. Ben Hubbard and Javier C. Hernandez, "Amid Trouble with the West, Saudi Arabia Looks East," *New York Times*, 20 February 2019, https://www.nytimes.com/2019/02/20/world/middleeast/saudi-arabia-pakistan-india-china.html.

172. "Saudis Signal Allure of China with $10 Billion Refinery Deal," *Bloomberg News*, 22 February 2019, https://www.bloomberg.com/news/articles/2019-02-22/saudi-aramco-to-build-10-billion-chinese-refinery-with-partners.

173. "Saudi Crown Prince Visit Builds on Partnership of Trust: Chinese FM," *Arab News,* 22 February 2019, http://www.arabnews.com/node/1456556/saudi-arabia.

174. "Interview: Beijing, Riyadh Share Great Potential for Cooperation: Chinese Envoy," *Xinhua*, 17 January 2016.

175. For the 2018 figure, see Karen E. Young, "The Gulf's Eastward Turn: The Logic of Gulf-China Economic Ties," American Enterprise Institute, February 2018, https://www.aei.org/wp-content/uploads/2019/02/The-Gulfs-Eastward-Turn.pdf. For map of energy projects in Saudi Arabia, see Robin Mills, Sarmad Ishfaq, Roa Ibrahim, and Aaron Reese, "China's Road to the Gulf: Opportunities for the GCC in the Belt and Road Initiative," emerge85, October 2017, https://emerge85.io/wp-content/uploads/2017/10/Chinas-Road-to-the-Gulf.pdf.

176. Anjli Raval, "Aramco IPO Puts Saudi Arabia's Grand Vision to the Test," *Financial Times*, 1 May 2018, https://www.ft.com/content/4a1828f6-292f-11e8-9274-2b13fccdc744.

177. Sean Foley, "OBOR and the Dawn of a New Era in Sino-Saudi Ties," in *China's Presence in the Middle East*, edited by Anoushiravan Ehteshami and Niv Horesh (London: Routledge, 2017).

178. Nayla Razzouk, Stephanie Flanders, and Javier Blas, "Saudi Crown Prince Vows Aramco IPO by 2021, Keeps to $2 Trillion," *Bloomberg*, 5 October 2018, https://www.bloomberg.com/news/articles/2018-10-05/saudi-crown-prince-vows-aramco-ipo-by-2021-keeps-to-2-trillion; Cyril Widdershoven, "Is This The End Of The Aramco IPO?" *Oilprice.com*, 20 October 2019, https://oilprice.com/Energy/Energy-General/Is-This-The-End-Of-The-Aramco-IPO.html; David Fickling, "Saudi Aramco Needs to Get Realistic About Its IPO," *Bloomberg*, 21 October 2019, https://www.bloomberg.com/opinion/articles/2019-10-21/saudi-aramco-s-pulled-ipo-shows-it-s-the-wework-of-energy; Rory Jones and Summer Said, "Aramco Emerges Ahead of Apple as World's Most Profitable Company," *Wall Street Journal*, 1 April 2019, https://www.wsj.com/articles/aramco-is-the-most-profitable-company-on-earth-ratings-agencies-say-11554102173; and author conversation with Ali Shihabi, Washington, DC, 30 April 2018.

179. By late 2019, Riyadh announced plans to list the sale in multiple stages, starting with two 1% listings on the Saudi stock exchange and followed by 3% on a foreign exchange. Facing political turmoil in Hong Kong and London, Tokyo emerged as the surprise frontrunner to list Aramco shares outside Saudi Arabia. See Summer Said, Benoit Faucon, Ben Dummett and Julie Steinberg, "Aramco Proposes Two-Stage IPO, Shunning London, Hong Kong," *Wall Street Journal*, 29 August 2019, https://www.wsj.com/articles/aramco-proposes-two-stage-ipo-shunning-london-hong-kong-11567084503.

180. For an example of potential hurdles in New York and London, see Ben Dummett, Summer Said, and Maureen Farrell, "Saudi Aramco IPO Plans Slowed Over Where to List," *Wall Street Journal*, 14 June 2017, https://www.wsj.com/articles/saudi-aramco-ipo-divided-over-where-to-list-1497459211; Anjli Raval, Miles Johnson, and James Fontanella-Khan, "Lawyers Warn

Saudi Aramco of New York IPO Litigation Risks," *Financial Times*, 4 June 2017, https://www.ft.com/content/d25bc250-491e-11e7-919a-1e14ce4af89b.

181. Author conversation with Bernard Haykel, Princeton, New Jersey, 10 May 2018.

182. Mishaal Al Gergawi, "China Is Eyeballing a Major Strategic Investment in Saudi Arabia's Oil," *Foreign Policy*, 26 October 2017, http://foreignpolicy.com/2017/10/26/china-is-eyeballing-a-major-strategic-investment-in-saudi-arabias-oil/.

183. Ellen R. Wald, "5 Ways a Saudi Aramco IPO Could Play Out," *Forbes*, 22 October 2017, https://www.forbes.com/sites/ellenrwald/2017/10/22/5-ways-a-saudi-aramco-ipo-could-play-out/#4df11aeb38a2.

184. See, for instance, al Shihabi, *The Saudi Kingdom*, p. 154; Filkins, "A Saudi Prince's Quest to Remake the Middle East"; Shichor, "Sweet and Sour," in *Sino-US Energy Triangles*, p. 86.

185. For a dramatic example of US "intrusion" in Saudi domestic affairs, see Bruce Riedel's description of how President John F. Kennedy pressured King Faisal to undertake reforms, including the abolition of slavery, in Riedel, *Kings and Presidents*, pp. 40–41.

186. Anand Giridharadas, "Saudi Arabia Pursues a 'Look-East Policy,'" *New York Times*, 26 January 2006, https://www.nytimes.com/2006/01/26/business/worldbusiness/saudi-arabia-pursues-a-lookeast-policy.html.

187. Cited in Riedel, *Kings and Presidents*, p. 148.

188. Vali Nasr, *The Shia Revival* (New York: W. W. Norton, 2007), pp. 34–43.

189. Maloney explains how the Safavids built the bureaucratized religious institutions that would much later serve as a "clerical hierarchy independent of state control" under Khomeini's leadership. See Maloney, *Iran's Political Economy*, pp. 85–86, note 31.

190. Riedel, *Kings and Presidents*, pp. 12–24.

191. Riedel, *Kings and Presidents*, p. 86.

192. Nasr, *The Shia Revival*, p. 24.

193. Iranians trace their national identity to one of the world's oldest civilizations, even as some popularly characterize Saudis as upstart goat-herders. On the other hand, some Saudis—including the country's Grand Mufti in 2016—pejoratively call Iranians "children of Magi," meaning Zoroastrians, in reference to the pre-Islamic religious practices common in the region. See "Saudi-Iran War of Words Escalates over Hajj Row," *Al Jazeera*, 8 September 2016, https://www.aljazeera.com/news/2016/09/saudi-iran-war-words-escalates-hajj-row-160907104137364.html.

194. Nasr writes, "Like many populations that have lived uneasily near each other for a long time, Shias and Sunnis have their stories of common struggles, communal harmony, friendship, and intermarriage. . . . Across the Middle East Shias and Sunnis have often rallied around the same political causes and even fought together in the same trenches, most notably against foreign

occupation, as in Iraq against the British in 1920 and in Lebanon against Israel in the late 1980s. In fact, no cause in modern times has brought the two sides together more than the fight against Israel." See Nasr, *The Shia Revival*, p. 25.

195. Takeyh, *Hidden Iran*, p. 64.

196. See Takeyh, *Hidden Iran*, p. 167 for detail on Iran's view of the Ba'athist regime. The unusual Saudi ambassadorial appointment was helpfully flagged for me by Bruce Riedel in our interview on 8 May 2018. In his book (Riedel, *Kings and Presidents*, p. 125), Riedel cites his source as Maloney, *Iran's Political Economy*, p. 274.

197. Nader Hashemi and Danny Postel make a similar point about the instrumentalization of sectarian identities in Nader Hashemi and Danny Postel, "Iran, Saudi Arabia, and Modern Hatreds," *New York Times*, 15 May 2018, https://www.nytimes.com/2018/05/15/opinion/iran-saudi-arabia-and-modern-hatreds.html as well as their edited volume, Nader Hashemi and Danny Postel, eds., *Sectarianization: Mapping the New Politics of the Middle East* (Oxford: Oxford University Press, 2017).

198. For a sense of Saudi frustration and isolation during this period, see the op-ed by Saudi Arabia's ambassador to Britain, Mohammed bin Abdulaziz al Saud, "Saudi Arabia Will Go It Alone," *New York Times*, 17 December 2013, https://www.nytimes.com/2013/12/18/opinion/saudi-arabia-will-go-it-alone.html. Or see Matthew Kaminski, "Prince Alwaleed bin Talal: An Ally Frets about American Retreat," *Wall Street Journal*, 22 November 2013, https://www.wsj.com/articles/prince-alwaleed-bin-talal-an-ally-frets-about-american-retreat-1385165879.

199. Author conversation with Bernard Haykel, Princeton, New Jersey, 10 May 2018.

200. Vali Nasr, "Iran among the Ruins," *Foreign Affairs*, March/April 2018, https://www.foreignaffairs.com/articles/middle-east/2018-02-13/iran-among-ruins.

201. Nasr, "Iran among the Ruins."

202. On the Nimr incident and its immediate aftermath in Tehran, including the new street name, see Ian Black, "Nimr al-Nimr Street, Tehran: Signpost for Troubled Iran-Saudi Ties," *Guardian*, 2 March 2016, https://www.theguardian.com/world/on-the-middle-east/2016/mar/02/nimr-al-nimr-street-tehran-signpost-for-troubled-iran-saudi-ties. On the wider regional diplomacy, see Ben Hubbard, "Saudi Arabia Cuts Ties with Iran amid Fallout from Cleric's Execution," *New York Times*, 3 January 2016, https://www.nytimes.com/2016/01/04/world/middleeast/iran-saudi-arabia-execution-sheikh-nimr.html.

203. For a video with English subtitles, see "Sheikh Nimr Baqir al-Nimr—about the Oppression in Saudi Arabia and Bahrain (English)," YouTube, 7 October 2011, https://www.youtube.com/watch?v=jSI319UNssc.

204. At least one American expert on Saudi Arabia speculated that the execution of a prominent Shia was most likely motivated by domestic political compulsions

to "show some muscle" against opponents of the Saudi monarchy and, at the same time, to "balance out" the simultaneous and politically divisive execution of dozens of Sunni al Qaeda members. Author conversation with Bernard Haykel, Princeton, New Jersey, 10 May 2018.

205. At least two other US analysts have made the helpful connection between the Nimr episode and China's regional foreign policy. See Shannon Tiezzi, "China's Stake in the Saudi Arabia-Iran Clash," *The Diplomat*, 8 January 2016, https://thediplomat.com/2016/01/chinas-stake-in-the-saudi-arabia-iran-clash/; Gal Luft, "China's New Grand Strategy for the Middle East," *Foreign Policy*, 26 January 2016, http://foreignpolicy.com/2016/01/26/chinas-new-middle-east-grand-strategy-iran-saudi-arabia-oil-xi-jinping/.

206. "China Envoy Calls for Restraint between Saudi and Iran," *Reuters*, 10 January 2016, https://www.reuters.com/article/us-saudi-iran-china-idUSKCN0UP0A220160111.

207. On the Chinese foreign ministry's announcement of the Xi trip, see "Xi to Visit Saudi Arabia, Iran in New Diplomacy Push," *Daily Star*, 16 January 2016, http://www.dailystar.com.lb/News/Middle-East/2016/Jan-16/332228-xi-to-visit-saudi-arabia-iran-in-new-diplomacy-push.ashx.

208. "China has become Iran's least unreliable—not to say most reliable—major power ally and a key pivot for counterbalancing the United States." Kevjn Lim, "Iran Seen from Beijing," Washington Institute for Near East Policy, 11 June 2015, http://www.washingtoninstitute.org/policy-analysis/view/iran-seen-from-beijing.

209. Li Tianyang, "Belt & Road Initiative Expands China-Iran Cooperation," *China Daily*, 25 January 2019, http://www.chinadaily.com.cn/a/201901/25/WS5c4aa81da3106c65c34e6912.html.

210. Dina Esfandiary and Ariane M. Tabatabai, "Will China Undermine Trump's Iran Strategy?" *Foreign Affairs*, 20 July 2018, https://www.foreignaffairs.com/articles/china/2018-07-20/will-china-undermine-trumps-iran-strategy.

211. On European firms that exited Iran, see "How Companies around the World are Reversing Course on Iran Business," Iran Watch, 5 November 2018, https://www.iranwatch.org/our-publications/policy-briefs/how-companies-around-world-are-reversing-course-iran-business. For an example of European rhetoric supporting the deal, see Griff Witte and Michael Birnbaum, "Europe Says It Will Stick with the Iran Deal, Defying a US Demand," *Washington Post*, 15 February 2019, https://www.washingtonpost.com/world/europe/europe-says-it-will-stick-with-the-iran-deal-defying-a-us-demand/2019/02/15/032923ee-2fac-11e9-8781-763619f12cb4_story.html.

212. On the debate over whether the lifting of sanctions would open the door to more Iranian business with Europe or China, see Yitzhak Shichor, "Iran after the Sanctions: The Marginalization of China," Asia Centre, March 2016, p. 4, https://www.researchgate.net/publication/304626756_Iran_after_the_Sanctions_the_Marginalization_of_China; Raz Zimmt, Israel Kanner, Ofek

Ish Maas, and Tal Avidan, "China-Iran Relations Following the Nuclear Agreement and the Lifted Sanctions: Partnership, Inc." *Strategic Assessment*, vol. 20, no. 2 (July 2017): pp. 48–49; Scobell and Nader, *China in the Middle East*, p. 50; Michael Singh, "The Sino-Iranian Tango," *Foreign Affairs*, 21 July 2015, https://www.foreignaffairs.com/articles/china/2015-07-21/sino-iranian-tango.

213. Ehteshami, Horesh, and Xu, "Chinese-Iranian Mutual Strategic Perceptions," p. 6.

214. Ehteshami, Horesh, and Xu, "Chinese-Iranian Mutual Strategic Perceptions," p. 4.

215. Barbara Slavin, "Nixing the Iran Deal Would Be a Boon to China," *Axios*, 3 April 2018, https://www.axios.com/nixing-the-iran-deal-would-be-a-boon-to-china-22fbd552-ce04-4599-8e4a-5220040a8c29.html; Andrew Ward, "China Poised to Profit as Europe Companies Feel Iran Pain," *Financial Times*, 9 May 2018, https://www.ft.com/content/b29aaf7a-5387-11e8-b24e-cad6aa67e23e.

216. In November 2018, CNPC acquired Total's 50.1 percent investment in South Pars' phase 11. Tsvetana Paraskova, "Iran: Chinese CNPC Replaces Total in South Pars Gas Project," OilPrice.com, 26 November 2018, https://oilprice.com/Latest-Energy-News/World-News/Iran-Chinese-CNPC-Replaces-Total-In-South-Pars-Gas-Project.html.

217. CNPC delayed work on the field, likely due to pressure and potential sanctions from the United States. For details on the delayed work, see Bob Tippee, "US Pressure Freezes 11th Phase Work at South Pars Gas Field," *Oil & Gas Journal*, 14 December 2018, https://www.ogj.com/articles/2018/12/us-pressure-freezes-11th-phase-work-at-south-pars-gas-field.html. On October 6, 2019, the Iranian oil ministry announced that CNPC had pulled out of South Pars. See "Iran Says China Has Pulled Out Of South Pars Natural Gas Project," RFE/RL, 6 October 2019, https://www.rferl.org/a/iran-china-south-pars-natural-gas-project-pulled-out/30201771.html.

218. Washington stopped short of sanctioning the parent companies, CNPC or COSCO. See Ian Talley, Costas Paris, and Courtney McBride, "U.S. Sanctions Chinese Firms for Allegedly Shipping Iranian Oil," *Wall Street Journal*, 25 September 2019, https://www.wsj.com/articles/u-s-sanctions-chinese-firms-for-allegedly-shipping-iranian-oil-11569424569.

219. Ehteshami, Horesh, and Xu, "Chinese-Iranian Mutual Strategic Perceptions," p. 10.

220. Ehteshami, Horesh, and Xu, "Chinese-Iranian Mutual Strategic Perceptions," p. 10.

221. "Speaker: No Party Able to Mar Iran-China Relations," *FARS*, 20 February 2019, http://en.farsnews.com/newstext.aspx?nn=13971201000397.

222. Garver makes a similar point. See Garver, "Is China Playing a Dual Game in Iran?," p. 76.

223. John W. Garver, "China and Iran: Expanding Cooperation under Conditions of US Domination," in *Toward Well-Oiled Relations? China's*

Presence in the Middle East following the Arab Spring, edited by Niv Horesh (New York: Palgrave Macmillan, 2016), p. 189.

224. "China's Xi Says Iran Tensions Worrying, Calls for Restraint," *Reuters*, 4 June 2019, https://www.reuters.com/article/us-usa-iran-china/chinas-xi-says-iran-tensions-worrying-calls-for-restraint-idUSKCN1T603R.

225. Kevjn Lim discusses Iran's bid to join the SCO, the strategic value that membership might confer, and Tehran's associated frustrations in Kevjn Lim, "Iran's Shanghai Dream," *Foreign Affairs*, 25 July 2016, https://www.foreignaffairs.com/articles/china/2016-07-25/irans-shanghai-dream.

226. Joshua Kucera, "With Sanctions Lifted, Iran Ready for SCO," *Eurasianet*, 18 January 2016, https://eurasianet.org/s/with-sanctions-lifted-iran-ready-for-sco.

227. Middle East scholar Alex Vatanka emphasizes this point, noting that "Since the Islamic Republic came about in 1979, Iran has repeatedly failed to join any collective bodies that could facilitate diplomatic and economic engagements in any meaningful way. Tehran's experience of costly economic isolation has only increased its appetite for integration." Vatanka, "China Courts Iran."

228. Baris Adibelli, "Sino-Iranian Relations since the Cold War," in *The Emerging Middle East-East Asia Nexus*, p. 116.

229. Javad Heirannia and Maryam Khormaei, "Beijing Supports Full Membership of Iran in Shanghai Cooperation Organization: Ambassador," *Tehran Times*, 28 October 2018, https://www.tehrantimes.com/news/429040/Beijing-supports-full-membership-of-Iran-in-Shanghai-Cooperation.

230. On how Iran perceives the potential of BRI, see Mohsen Shariatinia and Hamidreza Azizi, "Iran-China Cooperation in the Silk Road Economic Belt: From Strategic Understanding to Operational Understanding," *China and the World Economy*, vol. 25, no. 5 (2017): pp. 46–61.

231. "Rouhani Expresses Support for Silk Road Economic Belt," *CCTV News*, 23 May 2014, https://www.youtube.com/watch?v=eZflAnpoIg0.

232. Najmeh Bozorgmehr, "First Freight Trains from China Arrive in Tehran," *Financial Times*, 9 May 2016, https://www.ft.com/content/e964a78e-0bd8-11e6-9456-444ab5211a2f. See also Thomas Erdbrink, "For China's Global Ambitions, 'Iran Is at the Center of Everything,'" *New York Times*, 25 July 2017, https://www.nytimes.com/2017/07/25/world/middleeast/iran-china-business-ties.html.

233. "First Freight Train from China Arrives in Iran in 'Silk Road' Boost: Media," *Reuters*, 16 February 2016, https://www.reuters.com/article/us-china-iran-railway-idUSKCN0VP0W8.

234. Zeynab Sohrabi, "Three Freight Trains Due in Tehran from China This Week," *Financial Tribune*, 9 January 2018, https://financialtribune.com/articles/domestic-economy/79577/three-freight-trains-due-in-tehran-from-china-this-week.

235. Author conversation with Kevjn Lim, Tel Aviv, Israel, 28 June 2017.

236. According to Kevjn Lim, "for Beijing, Iran's geostrategic value is enhanced by its position astride one of China's two overland bridges to the west . . . but Iran arguably presents the more important route because it connects with both Europe and the Gulf." Lim, "Iran Seen from Beijing."

237. Micha'el Tanchum argues that decisions related to Iran's natural gas pipelines could redefine Eurasian gas markets in ways that advantage China over Russia and Western Europe in "A Post-Sanctions Iran and the Eurasian Energy Architecture," The Atlantic Council, 25 September 2015, http://www. atlanticcouncil.org/images/publications/Iran_Energy_Architecture_web_0925. pdf.

238. Mahdi Salami Zavareh and Mehrdad Fallahi Barzoki, "China's Energy Security: I. R. Iran and Saudi Arabia's Role in China's Energy Diplomacy," Iran Economic Review, vol. 22, no. 3 (2018): p. 717. Also, as the US National Defense University's Jeffrey S. Payne writes, "it is Iran's geostrategic position that matters most to Beijing. Of the entire Middle East, the Gulf region is the most important for China. Yet the long-standing relationship between the GCC and Western powers, particularly the United States, makes it difficult for China to develop closer ties. . . . Iran, however, is a Gulf state that has been isolated from much of the West for over 30 years." See Jeffrey S. Payne, "China's Iran Bet," Middle East Institute, 8 June 2015, http://www.mei.edu/ content/map/china%E2%80%99s-iran-bet.

239. Masoud Rezaei and Saeed Vosoughi, "Assessing Iran-China Defensive Relations during the Presidency of Hassan Rouhani," Journal of Strategic Studies of Public Policy, vol. 7, no. 24 (Autumn 2017): pp. 23–47. Translation by Elahe Nezhadhossein. For current arms trade figures, see "Importer/ Exporter TIV Tables," Stockholm International Peace Research Institute, accessed 13 March 2019, http://armstrade.sipri.org/armstrade/page/values. php. A full list of Chinese and Russian exports to Iran can be found by selecting "Russia" and "China" as "Suppliers" and "Iran" as "Recipient(s)" at "Trade Registers," Stockholm International Peace Research Institute, accessed 13 March 2019, http://armstrade.sipri.org/armstrade/page/trade_ register.php.

240. Garver, China & Iran, p. 139.

241. Garver, China & Iran, pp. 143–153.

242. Rezaei and Vosoughi, "Assessing Iran-China Defensive Relations," pp. 23–47.

243. Rezaei and Vosoughi, "Assessing Iran-China Defensive Relations," pp. 23–47.

244. Franz-Stefan Gady, "Iran, China Sign Military Cooperation Agreement," The Diplomat, 15 November 2016, https://thediplomat.com/2016/11/iran-china-sign-military-cooperation-agreement/.

245. Teddy Ng and Kristin Huang, "China and Iran Carry Out Naval Exercise near Strait of Hormuz as US Holds Drill with Qatar," South China Morning Post, 19 June 2017, https://www.scmp.com/news/china/diplomacy-defence/ article/2098898/china-and-iran-carry-out-naval-exercise-near-strait.

246. For example, see Franz-Stefan Gady, "Will Iran Order 150 New Fighter Jets from China?" *The Diplomat*, 4 August 2015, https://thediplomat.com/2015/08/will-iran-order-150-new-fighter-jets-from-china/.

247. Joel Wuthnow, "Posing Problems without an Alliance: China-Iran Relations after the Nuclear Deal," *INSS Strategic Forum*, no. 290 (February 2016), p. 7.

248. See, for example, "Treasury Sanctions Individuals and Entities for Human Rights Abuses and Censorship in Iran, and Support to Sanctioned Weapons Proliferators," US Department of the Treasury, 12 January 2018, https://home.treasury.gov/news/press-releases/sm0250; "Iran Designations, Non-proliferation Designations," US Department of Treasury, 12 January 2018, https://www.treasury.gov/resource-center/sanctions/OFAC-Enforcement/Pages/20180112.aspx; "Treasury Sanctions Supporters of Iran's Ballistic Missile Program and Iran's Islamic Revolutionary Guard Corps—Qods Force," US Department of the Treasury, 3 February 2017, https://www.treasury.gov/press-center/press-releases/Pages/as0004.aspx; "Treasury Targets Persons Supporting Iranian Military and Iran's Islamic Revolutionary Guard Corps," US Department of the Treasury, 18 July 2017, https://www.treasury.gov/press-center/press-releases/Pages/sm0125.aspx.

249. Erik A. Olson, "Iran's Path Dependent Military Doctrine," *Strategic Studies Quarterly* (Summer 2016): pp. 74–77. See also Manochehr Dorraj, "The Future of Sino-Iran Relations," in *Toward Well-Oiled Relations? China's Presence in the Middle East following the Arab Spring*, edited by Niv Horesh (New York: Palgrave Macmillan, 2016), p. 211.

250. Cited in Olson, "Iran's Path Dependent Military Doctrine," p. 69.

251. Iranian analysts trace the development of the Noor, Kosar, Rad, Nasr, Ghader, and Zafar missiles (among others) to Chinese designs and assistance. See Rezaei and Vosoughi, "Assessing Iran-China Defensive Relations," pp. 23–47.

252. On the Houthis, see Emilyn Tuomala, "Houthis," Missile Defense Advocacy Alliance, June 2018, http://missiledefenseadvocacy.org/missile-threat-and-proliferation/todays-missile-threat/non-state-actors/houthis/, and on Hizballah as well as the wider issue of how Chinese missiles have formed the backbone of Iran's anti-access/area denial strategy, see James Brandon Gentry, "China's Role in Iran's Anti-Access/Area Denial Weapons Capability Development," Middle East Institute, 16 April 2013, http://www.mei.edu/content/china's-role-iran's-anti-access-area-denial-weapons-capability-development.

253. Jack Detsch, "Suspected Iranian Strikes Raise US Concerns over Chinese Missile Proliferation," *Al-Monitor*, 17 September 2019, https://www.al-monitor.com/pulse/originals/2019/09/us-concern-china-missile-technology-iran.html.

254. Matt Schroeder and Benjamin King, "Surveying the Battlefield" in *Small Arms Survey 2012: Moving Targets* (Cambridge: Cambridge University Press), p. 327.

255. "Given its financial and defense industrial base, China is likely to have more chances to develop new military technologies than Russia. China's electronics,

composites, advanced materials and shipbuilding industries are all more advanced than those in Russia. The size of the Chinese economy means that it has many more resources and much more manpower to invest in research and development." See Siemon T. Wezeman, "China, Russia, and the Shifting Landscape of Arms Sales," Stockholm International Peace Research Institute, 5 July 2017, https://sipri.org/commentary/topical-backgrounder/2017/china-russia-and-shifting-landscape-arms-sales. See also Robert Farley, "Is Russia's Arms Industry about to Fall off a Cliff?" *The Diplomat*, 4 September 2017, https://thediplomat.com/2017/09/is-russias-arms-industry-about-to-fall-off-a-cliff/.

256. Countries ranked based on net weight, not monetary value. Data for China's oil imports by reporter (China) and top partners (All) can be retrieved at UN Comtrade Database by selecting commodity code 2709, "Petroleum oils and oils obtained from bituminous minerals; crude." See "UN Comtrade Database," United Nations, accessed 17 May 2018, https://comtrade.un.org/data.

257. On the story of how the United States and Saudi Arabia used oil guarantees to get China to abide by international sanctions on Iran, see Shichor, "Sweet and Sour," in *US Energy Triangles*, pp. 82–83.

258. The Trump administration has since worked to ease the sale of armed drones. See Katrina Manson, "Trump Relaxes Conditions over Sale of US Killer Drones," *Financial Times*, 19 April 2018, https://www.ft.com/content/a48b8f56-43e4-11e8-803a-295c97e6fd0b.

259. Minnie Chan, "Chinese Drone Factory in Saudi Arabia First in Middle East," *South China Morning Post*, 26 March 2017, http://www.scmp.com/news/china/diplomacy-defence/article/2081869/chinese-drone-factory-saudi-arabia-first-middle-east; For a full list of Saudi Arabia-China deals, see "Trade Registers," Stockholm International Peace Research Institute, accessed 1 May 2018, http://armstrade.sipri.org/armstrade/page/trade_register.php.

260. For more on the limited extent of Chinese arms sales and military cooperation with Saudi Arabia, see Scobell and Nader, *China in the Middle East*, pp. 39–45.

261. Professor Bernard Haykel also suggests that Saudi leaders have in the past perceived the United States as more invested in the defense of the global economy, including the free flow of Saudi oil, whereas China has been more narrowly mercantilist and self-interested (author conversation with Bernard Haykel, Princeton, New Jersey, 10 May 2018).

262. Author conversation with Ali Shihabi, Washington, DC, 30 April 2018.

263. "Saudi Crown Prince: If Iran Develops Nuclear Bomb, So Will We," *CBS News*, 15 March 2018, https://www.cbsnews.com/news/saudi-crown-prince-mohammed-bin-salman-iran-nuclear-bomb-saudi-arabia/.

264. For an excellent discussion of the Saudi Arabia-Pakistan nuclear nexus, see Christopher Clary and Mara E. Karlin, "The Pak-Saudi Nuke, and How

to Stop It," *The American Interest*, 10 June 2012, https://www.the-american-interest.com/2012/06/10/the-pak-saudi-nuke-and-how-to-stop-it/. For contrary views about the potential for a Pakistani transfer of nuclear capabilities to Saudi Arabia, see Zachary Keck, "Why Pakistan Won't Sell Saudi the Bomb," *The National Interest*, 18 November 2013, http://nationalinterest.org/commentary/why-pakistan-wont-sell-saudi-the-bomb-9416; Colin H. Kahl, Matthew Irvine, and Melissa Dalton, "Atomic Kingdom: If Iran Builds the Bomb, Will Saudi Arabia Be Next?," Center for New American Security, February 2013, https://www.cnas.org/publications/reports/atomic-kingdom-if-iran-builds-the-bomb-will-saudi-arabia-be-next.

265. Simon Henderson, "Chinese-Saudi Cooperation: Oil but Also Missiles," Washington Institute for Near East Policy, 21 April 2006, http://www.washingtoninstitute.org/policy-analysis/view/chinese-saudi-cooperation-oil-but-also-missiles.

266. For a balanced assessment of Sino-Saudi relations, see Yoel Guzansky and Assaf Orion, "Slowly but Surely: Growing Relations between Saudi Arabia and China," Institute for National Security Studies, 29 January 2017, http://www.inss.org.il/publication/slowly-surely-growing-relations-saudi-arabia-china/.

267. Among the relatively small group of analysts who have focused on China's relations in the Middle East, John Garver is unusual for arguing that China actually has a long-term plan to forge "a strategic partnership with Iran that will serve as a major element of Chinese influence in the post-American-dominated West Asia." His argument is plausible, and not entirely at odds with the conclusions in this chapter, but hinges more on still relatively unstated Chinese aims (and competing incentives, especially with respect to the United States) than on a reading of Iran's own policies and agency. See Garver, "China and Iran," in *Toward Well-Oiled Relations?*, pp. 180–205.

Chapter 6

1. For a representative assessment of Mahathir's electoral prospects from January 2018, see Amrita Malhi, "Mahathir Mohamad Crops Up Again in Bid to Lead Malaysia—with Anwar on the Same Side," *The Conversation*, 11 January 2018, http://theconversation.com/mahathir-mohamad-crops-up-again-in-bid-to-lead-malaysia-with-anwar-on-the-same-side-89917.

2. "Mahathir Mohamad Returns to Power as Malaysia's Prime Minister: A Look at the 92-year-old's Political Career," *Firstpost*, 10 May 2018, https://www.firstpost.com/world/mahathir-mohamad-returns-to-power-as-malaysias-prime-minister-a-look-at-the-92-year-olds-political-career-4463699.html.

3. Richard C. Paddock, "In Malaysia, the Old Prime Minister Promises a New Order," *New York Times*, 10 May 2018, https://www.nytimes.com/2018/05/10/world/asia/malaysia-election-mahathir-mohamad.html.

4. Hannah Beech, "'We Cannot Afford This': Malaysia Pushes Back against China's Vision," *New York Times*, 20 August 2018, https://www.nytimes.com/2018/08/20/world/asia/china-malaysia.html.

5. Beech, "'We Cannot Afford This.'"

6. These projects are also noted in Beech, "'We Cannot Afford This.'"

7. Shibani Mahtani, "Fears of a New 'Colonialism,'" *Washington Post*, 11 September 2018, https://www.washingtonpost.com/world/asia_pacific/a-would-be-city-in-the-malaysian-jungle-is-caught-in-a-growing-rift-between-china-and-its-neighbors/2018/09/10/d705cb18-b031-11e8-9a6a-565d92a3585d_story.html.

8. Anisah Shukry and Anuradha Raghu, "Malaysia Nears Deal with China to Revive $20 Billion Rail," *Bloomberg*, 19 February 2019, https://www.bloomberg.com/news/articles/2019-02-19/malaysia-nears-deal-with-china-to-revive-scrapped-rail-project.

9. Bhavan Jaipragas, "Mahathir's Government Agrees to Revive China-Backed Bandar Malaysia Project," *South China Morning Post*, 19 April 2019, https://www.scmp.com/week-asia/politics/article/3006930/mahathirs-government-agrees-revive-china-backed-bandar-malaysia.

10. As Evan Feigenbaum, astutely observes, China's tools of economic statecraft are wide-ranging. He suggests they can be grouped into five types of leverage: passive, active, exclusionary, coercive, and latent. See Feigenbaum, "Is Coercion the New Normal in China's Economic Statecraft?".

11. This history is recounted in Deborah Brautigam, *The Dragon's Gift: The Real Story of China in Africa* (Oxford: Oxford University Press, 2009), p. 60.

12. Brautigam, *The Dragon's Gift*, p. 21.

13. Brian Spegele, "GE Rides the Coattails of China's Global Dream," *Wall Street Journal*, 16 October 2016, https://www.wsj.com/articles/ge-rides-the-coattails-of-chinas-global-dream-1476449185 ; Keith Bradsher, "US Firms Want In on China's Global 'One Belt, One Road' Spending," *New York Times*, 14 May 2017, https://www.nytimes.com/2017/05/14/business/china-one-belt-one-road-us-companies.html; Evelyn Cheng, "Honeywell, Other US Companies Look to Benefit from China's Gigantic 'Belt and Road' Initiative," *CNBC*, 12 March 2018, https://www.cnbc.com/2018/03/12/honeywell-other-us-companies-look-to-benefit-from-chinas-gigantic-belt-and-road-initiative.html.

14. On the lack of a level playing field for US business, see Randall Phillips, "Mercantilism with Chinese Characteristics: Creating Markets and Cultivating Influence," US-China Economic and Security Review Commission, 25 January 2018, www.iberchina.org/files/2018/Phillips_mintz_USCC_Testimony.pdf.

15. On the twenty-first-century backbone infrastructure of the global financial system and its political and strategic implications, see Henry Farrell and Abraham Newman, "Money Moves," *The National Interest* (May/June 2019), pp. 29–38.

16. Rex Tillerson, "Defining Our Relationship with India for the Next Century: An Address by US Secretary of State Rex Tillerson," Center for Strategic and International Studies, 18 October 2017, https://www.csis.org/analysis/defining-our-relationship-india-next-century-address-us-secretary-state-rex-tillerson.

17. Maria Abi-Habib, "How China Got Sri Lanka to Cough Up a Port," *New York Times*, 25 June 2018, https://www.nytimes.com/2018/06/25/world/asia/china-sri-lanka-port.html.

18. "Official Spokesperson's Response to a Query on Participation of India in OBOR/BRI Forum," 13 May 2017, https://mea.gov.in/media-briefings.htm?dtl/28463/Official+Spokespersons+response+to+a+query+on+participation+of+India+in+OBORBRI+Forum.

19. Alexander Cooley, "The League of Authoritarian Gentlemen," *Foreign Policy*, 30 January 2013, https://foreignpolicy.com/2013/01/30/the-league-of-authoritarian-gentlemen/.

20. Paul Mozur, Jonah M. Kessel, and Melissa Chan, "Made in China, Exported to the World: The Surveillance State," *New York Times*, 24 April 2019, https://www.nytimes.com/2019/04/24/technology/ecuador-surveillance-cameras-police-government.html.

21. On this point, see Richard Fontaine and Daniel Kliman, "On China's New Silk Road, Democracy Takes a Toll," *Foreign Policy*, 16 May 2018, https://foreignpolicy.com/2018/05/16/on-chinas-new-silk-road-democracy-pays-a-toll/.

22. On this point, see Ely Ratner, "Geostrategic and Military Drivers and Implications of the Belt and Road Initiative," US-China Economic and Security Review Commission, 25 January 2018, p. 4, https://www.cfr.org/report/geostrategic-and-military-drivers-and-implications-belt-and-road-initiative.

23. Author conversations with Georgian officials and businessmen, Tbilisi, Georgia, 1–3 May 2017.

24. On this point, see Emil Avdaliani, "Growing Chinese Interests in Georgia," *The Central Asia-Caucus Analyst*, 15 March 2018, https://www.cacianalyst.org/publications/analytical-articles/item/13503-growing-chinese-interests-in-georgia.html.

25. Scobell and Nader, *China in the Middle East*, p. 75.

26. Friedberg, "Competing with China," p. 26.

27. Campbell and Ratner, "The China Reckoning: How Beijing Defied American Expectations," p. 60.

28. In the "we told you so" camp is the response from Aaron Friedberg, who notes that a variety of experts were always less optimistic about the US capacity to transform China and more concerned about the security challenge. J. Stapleton Roy and Thomas Christensen take more of the "we never said that" line, suggesting that much of US policy has been intended not to transform or contain China, but to find constructive ways to advance the

American interest in the context of a rising China. Joseph Nye argues that external balancing of Chinese power has always been a component of US strategy, and that it could still work over time. See "Did America Get China Wrong? The Engagement Debate".

29. Swaine, "Chinese Views of Foreign Policy in the 19th Party Congress."

30. As Michael Swaine writes, "perhaps most notable is the effort to contrast China's supposed myriad economic and other successes with the supposed dysfunctionality and destructiveness of . . . the neoliberal model advocated by the Washington Consensus." China is "an alternative to the values and policies of existing democratic, industrialized states, whether in the West or in Asia." See Swaine, "Chinese Views of Foreign Policy in the 19th Party Congress.".

31. Joel Wuthnow, "Chinese Perspectives on the Belt and Road Initiative: Strategic Rationales, Risks, and Implications," *China Strategic Perspectives*, no. 12 (October 2017): p. 18, http://inss.ndu.edu/Portals/68/ Documents/stratperspective/china/ChinaPerspectives-12.pdf.

32. Friedberg, *A Contest for Supremacy*, pp. 39–40; Graham Allison, "The Thucydides Trap: Are the US and China Headed for War?" *The Atlantic*, 24 September 2015, https://www.theatlantic.com/international/archive/2015/09/ united-states-china-war-thucydides-trap/406756/.

33. Paul Heer, "Understanding the Challenge from China," *The Asan Forum*, 3 April 2018, http://www.theasanforum.org/understanding-the-challenge-from-china/.

34. As Friedberg writes, "the current crisis of strategic confidence in the United States and across the West is the product of disturbing developments on a wide range of fronts." See Friedberg, "Competing with China," p. 16.

35. China spent $228 billion on military expenditures, a figure dwarfed by the United States' $610 billion. See "Global Military Spending Remains High at $1.7 Trillion," Stockholm International Peace Research Institute, https://www.sipri.org/media/press-release/2018/ global-military-spending-remains-high-17-trillion.

36. On this point of US-China economic entanglement, see Ashley J. Tellis, *Balancing without Containment: An American Strategy for Managing China* (Washington, DC: Carnegie Endowment for International Peace, 2014), http:// carnegieendowment.org/files/balancing_without_containment.pdf.

37. For an example of this line of argument, see Youwei, "The End of Reform in China," *Foreign Affairs*, vol. 94, no. 3 (May/June 2015), https://www. foreignaffairs.com/articles/china/end-reform-china.

38. As David Shambaugh contends, "a more secure and confident government would not institute such a severe crackdown. It is a symptom of the party leadership's deep anxiety and insecurity." See Shambaugh, "The Coming Chinese Crackup."

39. For video, see "Vice President Mike Pence's Remarks on the Administration's Policy towards China," Hudson Institute, Washington, DC, 4 October

2018, https://www.youtube.com/watch?v=aeVrMniBjSc. For transcript, see "Remarks by Vice President Pence on the Administration's Policy toward China," The White House, 4 October 2018, https://www.whitehouse.gov/briefings-statements/remarks-vice-president-pence-administrations-policy-toward-china/.

40. It is worth recalling that the early Bush administration "concluded that the Pacific Ocean should become the most important focus of US military deployments, with China perceived as the main threat to American global dominance." See Martin Kettle, "US Told to Make China Its No 1 Enemy," *Guardian*, 24 March 2001, https://www.theguardian.com/world/2001/mar/24/china.usa. For its part, the Obama administration "pivoted" or "rebalanced" to Asia. See Hillary Clinton, "America's Pacific Century," *Foreign Policy*, 11 October 2011, https://foreignpolicy.com/2011/10/11/americas-pacific-century/. The Trump administration has, however, taken these concerns to a new level.

41. Author conversation with US State Department official, Washington, DC, 14 August 2018.

42. "Summary of the 2018 National Defense Strategy of the United States of America: Sharpening the American Military's Competitive Edge," Department of Defense of the United States of America, pp. 1, 2.

43. "Summary of the 2018 National Defense Strategy of the United States of America," p. 2.

44. "National Security Strategy of the United States of America," The White House, December 2017, p. 46, https://www.whitehouse.gov/wp-content/uploads/2017/12/NSS-Final-12-18-2017-0905-2.pdf.

45. Tara Copp, "INDOPACOM, It Is: US Pacific Command Gets Renamed," *Military Times*, 30 May 2018, https://www.militarytimes.com/news/your-military/2018/05/30/indo-pacom-it-is-pacific-command-gets-renamed/.

46. Michael R. Pompeo, "Remarks on 'America's Indo-Pacific Economic Vision,' " US Department of State, 30 July 2018, https://www.state.gov/secretary/remarks/2018/07/284722.htm.

47. On the BUILD Act, see George Ingram, "How the BUILD Act Advances Development," Brookings Institution, 10 July 2018, https://www.brookings.edu/blog/future-development/2018/07/10/how-the-build-act-advances-development/; James Roberts and Brett Schaefer, "House and Senate Revisions Have Not Improved the BUILD Act Enough to Warrant Conservative Support," Heritage Foundation, 24 July 2018, https://www.heritage.org/budget-and-spending/report/house-and-senate-revisions-have-not-improved-the-build-act-enough; Josh Zambrun and Siobhan Hughes, "To Counter China, US Looks to Invest Billions More Overseas," *Wall Street Journal*, 31 August 2018, https://www.wsj.com/articles/to-counter-china-u-s-looks-to-invest-billions-more-overseas-1535728206; and Glenn Thrush, "Trump Embraces Foreign Aid to Counter China's Global Influence," *New York Times*, 14 October 2018, https://www.nytimes.com/2018/10/14/world/asia/

donald-trump-foreign-aid-bill.html. On potential pitfalls associated with implementing the new US Development Fincnace Corporation, see Todd Moss and Erin Collinson, "Hidden Daggers Pointed at the Heart of the New USDFC," Center for Global Development, 2 April 2019, https://www.cgdev.org/blog/why-white-house-scuttling-its-biggest-development-win-four-hidden-daggers-pointed-heart-new.

48. In this context, the Trump administration has aligned itself with India's critique of the BRI and Japan's "quality infrastructure" initiatives. For more on these points, see Smith, "China's Belt and Road Initiative: Strategic Implications and International Opposition,".

49. "Summary of the 2018 National Defense Strategy of the United States of America," p. 9.

50. "National Security Strategy of the United States of America," p. 47.

51. Author conversation with longtime US official involved in China policy, Washington, DC, 20 August 2018.

52. Nadège Rolland expertly depicts a "speculative leap into Eurasia's future" circa 2035, by which time China would have created a dense "network of cooperative countries and, even better, like-minded friends" on its way to building a "China-centric" regional order. See Rolland, *China's Eurasian Century?*, p. 152. On the hurdles described in the remainder of this paragraph, see pp. 142–148.

53. On "strongpoint defense" in the Cold War context as George Kennan's preferred containment strategy, Gaddis explains that "the 'strongpoint' concept permitted concentration on areas that were both defensive and vital, without worrying too much about the rest. The assumption was that not all interests were of equal importance; that the United States could tolerate the loss of peripheral areas provided this did not impair its ability to defend those that were vital." See John Lewis Gaddis, *Strategies of Containment* (Oxford: Oxford University Press, 1982), pp. 58–61.

54. Goldstein aims to promote "a modus vivendi built on the principles of negotiation and compromise that will undergird global peace and development in the decades and centuries to come." See Lyle Goldstein, *Meeting China Halfway: How to Defuse the Emerging US-China Rivalry* (Washington, DC: Georgetown University Press, 2015), p. 21.

55. "Washington can afford to take the lead, demonstrating its maturity and taking brave risks for the sake of peace." See Goldstein, *Meeting China Halfway*, p. 20.

56. Schake and Manuel were playing into a wider discussion of the so-called Thucydides Trap. See Allison, "The Thucydides Trap."

57. Kori Schake and Anja Manuel, "How to Manage a Rising Power—or Two," *The Atlantic*, 24 May 2016, https://www.theatlantic.com/international/archive/2016/05/china-india-rising-powers/484106/.

58. On the motives for US-China aid cooperation in Afghanistan, see Denghua Zhang, "A Tango by Two Superpowers: China-US Cooperation

in Trilateral Aid and Implications for Their Bilateral Relations," *Asian Journal of Political Science*, vol. 26, no. 2 (April 2019), https://doi.org/10.1080/02185377.2018.1462218, pp. 181–200.

59. Author conversation with PLA officer at Pakistani National Defense University Conference, Islamabad, Pakistan, 23 February 2016.

60. Gal Luft, "Silk Road 2.0: US Strategy towards China's Belt and Road Initiative," Atlantic Council, October 2017, p. 3, http://www.atlanticcouncil.org/images/US_Strategy_toward_Chinas_BRI_web_1003.pdf.

61. Hal Brands, "China's Master Plan: How the West Can Fight Back," *Bloomberg*, 13 June 2018, https://www.bloomberg.com/view/articles/2018-06-13/china-s-global-master-plan-how-the-west-can-fight-back.

62. For an instructive window into the Trump administration's thinking on this point, see Alex N. Wong, "Briefing on the Indo-Pacific Strategy," US Department of State, 2 April 2018, https://www.state.gov/r/pa/prs/ps/2018/04/280134.htm.

63. Philip S. Davidson, "Advance Policy Questions," US Senate Armed Services Committee, 17 April 2018, https://www.armed-services.senate.gov/download/davidson_apqs_04-17-18.

64. Friedberg, "Competing with China," p. 50.

65. Geoff Wade made this point in greater detail during a presentation to a conference on "China and the Middle East: Current Perspectives," Tel Aviv University, 4 June 2018.

66. See Ely Ratner, "Geostrategic and Military Drivers and Implications of the Belt and Road Initiative," US-China Economic and Security Review Commission, 25 January 2018, https://www.cfr.org/report/geostrategic-and-military-drivers-and-implications-belt-and-road-initiative.

67. Robbie Gramer and Elias Groll, "With New Appointment, State Department Ramps Up War against Foreign Propaganda," *Foreign Policy*, 7 February 2019, https://foreignpolicy.com/2019/02/07/with-new-appointment-state-department-ramps-up-war-against-foreign-propaganda/.

68. For a roundup of US efforts to advance internet freedom overseas, see Patricia Moloney Figliola, "Internet Freedom in China: US Government Activity, Private Sector Initiatives, and Issues of Congressional Interest," Congressional Research Service, May 18, 2018, https://fas.org/sgp/crs/row/R45200.pdf.

69. "Internet Freedom," US Department of State, accessed 21 March 2019, https://www.state.gov/j/drl/internetfreedom/.

70. "Aims and Priorities," Freedom Online Coalition, https://freedomonlinecoalition.com/about-us/about/, accessed 21 March 2019.

71. The strategy advocated by Kliman and Grace offers one good example of this approach. As they write, "the United States in concert with its allies and partners should adopt an approach that seeks to shape the Belt and Road where possible, compete when required, and most critically, advance a positive economic vision." See Daniel Kliman and Abigail Grace, "Power

Play: Addressing China's Belt and Road Strategy," Center for a New American Security, September 2018, p. 2, https://s3.amazonaws.com/files.cnas.org/documents/CNASReport-Power-Play-Addressing-Chinas-Belt-and-Road-Strategy.pdf .

72. Robert D. Blackwill, "Indo-Pacific Strategy in an Era of Geoeconomics," Japan Forum on International Relations, 31 July 2018, https://cfrd8-files.cfr.org/sites/default/files/pdf/8-20%20Tokyo%20Presentation.pdf.

73. Smith, "China's Belt and Road Initiative: Strategic Implications and International Opposition," p. 21.

74. Jeff M. Smith, "China's Belt and Road Initiative: Strategic Implications and International Opposition," Backgrounder No. 3331, Heritage Foundation, 9 August 2018, http://report.heritage.org/bg3331, p. 11.

75. Smith, "China's Belt and Road Initiative," p. 20.

76. Eli Kintisch, "Rooftop Sensors on US Embassies Are Warning the World about 'Crazy Bad' Air Pollution," *Science*, 19 April 2018, https://www.sciencemag.org/news/2018/04/rooftop-sensors-us-embassies-are-warning-world-about-crazy-bad-air-pollution.

77. "The North India Office, US Embassy Collaborates with RTI International to Confront Air Pollution at Its Source," *APN News*, 12 March 2019, https://www.apnnews.com/the-north-india-office-u-s-embassy-collaborates-with-rti-international-to-confront-air-pollution-at-its-source/.

78. Editorial Board, "Xi Jinping's Aggressive Pursuit of Global Power Triggers a Praiseworthy Backlash," *Washington Post*, 30 August 2018, https://www.washingtonpost.com/opinions/global-opinions/xi-jinpings-aggressive-pursuit-of-global-power-triggers-a-praiseworthy-backlash/2018/08/30/aed131b4-a636-11e8-97ce-cc9042272f07_story.html.

79. The Trump administration's $30 million "Infrastructure Transaction and Assistance Network" (ITAN) was launched in 2018 and designed to accomplish similar ends in the Indo-Pacific. If successful, the ITAN's mandate could be expanded into other regions, including Eurasia. See US Department of State, "Advancing a Free and Open Indo-Pacific," Office of the Spokesperson, 30 July 2018, https://www.state.gov/advancing-a-free-and-open-indo-pacific/.

80. Ben Kesling and Jon Emont, "US Goes on the Offensive against China's Empire-Building Funding Plan," *Wall Street Journal*, 9 April 2019, https://www.wsj.com/articles/u-s-goes-on-the-offensive-against-chinas-empire-building-megaplan-11554809402.

81. On how smaller US wireless providers, often in rural America, have purchased from Huawei, which offers equipment at half (or less) the price of American and European alternatives, see Suhauna Hussain and Alice Su, "Trump's Fight and Huawei Could Threaten Internet Access in Rural Areas," *Los Angeles Times*, 22 May 2019, https://www.latimes.com/la-fi-tn-rural-broadband-trump-huawei-sanctions-20190522-story.html. On Huawei's attraction in Europe,

see Ellen Nakashima, "US Pushes Hard for a Ban on Huawei in Europe, but the Firm's 5G Prices Are Nearly Irresistible," *Washington Post*, 29 May 2019, https://www.washingtonpost.com/world/national-security/for-huawei-the-5g-play-is-in-europe--and-the-us-is-pushing-hard-for-a-ban-there/2019/05/28/582a8ff6-78d4-11e9-b7ae-390de4259661_story.html.

82. The authors of a 2019 CSIS task force argue that the United States "cannot allow a single provider to dominate 5G technology, which will become the backbone for tomorrow's digital economy. A winning US strategy for 5G must include a mixture of defensive and offensive measures." They suggest that these should include increasing federal funding for research and development in new digital technologies, among other steps. See Charlene Barshefsky and Stephen J. Hadley, "The Higher Road: Forging a US Strategy for the Global Infrastructure Challenge," Center for Strategic and International Studies, April 2019, https://csis-prod.s3.amazonaws.com/s3fs-public/publication/190423_Hadley%20et%20al_HigherRoads_report_WEB.pdf.

83. Rumer, Sokolsky, Stronski, and Weiss, *Illusions vs Reality*, p. 33.

84. I first heard this term of "elite capture" in a conversation with a US State Department official, who attributed it to a longtime US official involved in China policy, Washington, DC, 14 August 2018.

85. For several examples of China sharing its information control technology, see Smith, "China's Belt and Road Initiative," pp. 7–8.

86. Similar points are made in S. Frederick Starr, "The New Central Asia Nexus," *The American Interest* (July/August 2017), p. 68; also Richard Fontaine and Kara Frederick, "The Autocrat's New Tool Kit," *Wall Street Journal*, 15 March 2019, https://www.wsj.com/articles/the-autocrats-new-tool-kit-11552662637.

INDEX

China International Development
  Cooperation Agency (CIDCA),
  29–30, 31
China Investment Corporation, 26–27
China Merchants Port Holdings, 24
"China Model" of economic
  development, 136, 143,
  167, 179–80
China National Petroleum
  Corporation (CNPC)
  AktobeMunaiGas and, 88–89, 98
  Bank of Kunlun and, 134
  Gazprom's competition in Central
    Asia with, 106
  KazMunaiGas and, 90, 101–2
  oil and gas pipelines in Kazakhstan
    and, 89
  Rosneft and, 109
  South Pars gas field and, 149
China Overseas Security Group, 34
China-Pakistan Economic
  Corridor (CPEC)
  agricultural sector in Pakistan
    and, 52–53
  Belt and Road Initiative and, 48,
    53, 78–79
  China's geostrategic goals
    and, 47–48
  energy sector projects and, 57–58
  Gwadar Port and, 48
  India and, 66, 68, 76–77, 78
  job creation in Pakistan and, 53
  Khan and, 49, 51–52, 53–54,
    57, 59–60
  Pakistan infrastructure projects and,
    47–49, 51, 62
  Pakistan's debt levels and, 60, 65
  Pakistan's domestic economy and,
    51–52, 57
  Pakistan's electoral politics and, 55
  Pakistan's military and, 59, 62
  questions regarding prison labor in
    projects by, 37

security force defending facilities
    of, 166
China-United States Exchange
  Foundation (CUSEF), 38–39
Chinggis Khan, 82–83
CITIC Group, 148
Clinton, Hillary, 116, 165
Cochin (India), 44–45
Cold War
  end of, 15, 108, 119, 124
  Iran and, 122, 123–24, 131–32
  Pakistan and, 45–46, 47
  US-China relations and, 123
  US-Soviet relations during, 172, 176
Collective Security Treaty Organization
  (CSTO), 104, 106, 113
Communist Party of China
  Central Committee of, 35–36
  claims to legitimacy through
    economic growth by, 2–3, 17
  Uighur political internment camps
    and, 13
  United Front Work Department
    and, 39–40
Confucius Institutes, 38
Constantinople, 120–21
Cooley, Alexander, 94, 99, 166–67
Council of Economic and Development
  Affairs (Saudi Arabia), 141
Cruz, Ted, 39
CSS-2 "East Wind" missile,
  126–27, 154
CSS-5 missile, 154
Cyrus the Great, 120

da Gama, Vasco, 83
Dalai Lama, 84
Daqing oil field, 124
Davidson, Philip, 180
Deng Xiaoping, 3, 20–21
DeTrani, Joseph, 10
Ding Hao, 32
DJI (Chinese company), 35

Gwadar (Pakistan) (*cont.*)
  China's role in developing, viii–ix, 4,
    5, 7, 48, 159
  fiberoptics network at, 63
  Frontier Works Organization
    and, 62
  limitations in foreigners'
    access to, 64
  logistical challenges in developing,
    viii–ix
  Musharraf's role in developing, vii,
    viii, 4, 48, 159, 191n4
  Pakistan-India relations and,
    vii–viii, ix, 7
  real estate market and, 5
  terrorist attack (2004) in, viii–ix
  terrorist attack (2019) in, 5–6

Hale, Henry, 99
Hambantota (Sri Lanka), 24, 166
Han Dynasty, 43–44, 81–82
Han ethnic group, 13–14, 83–85, 97
Hansen, Valerie, 81
Haqqani Network, 73
Haykel, Bernard, 146
Heer, Paul, 172
Henderson, Simon, 155
He Yafei, 2
Hezbollah, 132, 153
Ho, Patrick, 8
Honeywell, 165–66
Hormuz Strait, 122, 151, 184
Horn of Africa region, 33
Houthi group (Yemen), 146, 153
Huawei, 3–4, 30–31, 128–29, 138–39,
    164, 186–87
Hui (Chinese Muslim group), 37–38,
    121, 123–24, 130
al-Hujeilan, Saleh, 139
Hu Jintao, 11, 140, 141, 147
Hu Shisheng, 68–69
Hussain, Mushahid, 56
Hussein, Saddam, 144, 145, 154

India
  Afghanistan and, 78
  China and, 11, 22, 44, 45, 46, 47,
    49–50, 66, 68–70, 72–78, 79,
    115, 117, 118, 163, 166, 169,
    174, 175, 184
  Doklam crisis (2017) and, 49–50, 72
  European colonialism in, 45–46
  extremist organizations in, 67
  Five Principles of Peaceful
    Coexistence (Panchsheel) Treaty
    (1954) and, 22
  gross domestic product of, 50
  Hu Jintao's visit (2006) to, 11
  investment from China in, 69–70
  Iran and, 66, 148, 183
  Japan and, 78
  Kargil War (1999) and, viii, 66
  Kashmir and, 67, 68, 69, 71,
    74, 76–77
  Maldives and, 24–25
  military modernization in, 77
  nuclear program in, 66, 76, 187
  oil imports from the Middle East and,
    vii–viii
  Pakistan and, vii–viii, ix, 6–7, 45–46,
    47, 50, 61, 65–69, 71–78, 79, 117,
    118, 161, 163, 169, 183, 187
  Punjab province in, 51, 52–53, 56, 67
  "Quad" security dialogue and, 50
  Russia and, 115
  Saudi Arabia and, 142
  Shanghai Cooperation Organization
    and, 47
  Sino-Indian War (1962) and,
    46, 72–73
  Southeast Asia and, 77–78
  Tibet and, 46
  United States and, 50, 69, 72, 78,
    118, 169, 174, 181–82
Indian Ocean region, ix, 18–19, 43,
    44–45, 77
Indonesia, 45, 78

International Development
Finance Corporation (United
States), 174–75
International Monetary Fund (IMF), 17,
27, 54, 55–56
Inter-Services Intelligence (ISI,
Pakistan), 67, 72–73
Iran
Afghanistan and, 132
Arab Spring (2011) and, 145
Belt and Road Initiative and, 129,
150–51, 155–56
Central Asia transportation links
with, 88
China and, 7, 9, 15, 119–23, 124–25,
127–29, 130–39, 143, 147–54,
155–56, 159, 160, 161, 162–64,
170, 175, 176, 183, 188
Cold War and, 122, 123–24, 131–32
drone warfare and, 128
economic reform proposals
in, 135–36
Green Revolution (2009) in, 138
Hezbollah and, 132
India and, 66, 148, 183
Iraq and, 122–23, 127, 145, 146, 147,
151, 153
Islamic Revolution (1979) in, 122–23,
132, 144
Israel and, 132, 144, 146, 149, 152
Joint Comprehensive Plan of Action
("Iran nuclear deal") and, 128, 131,
133, 140, 146, 147, 148–49, 152,
156, 162–63
missile programs in, 152–53, 170
National Information Network
(censored internet access)
in, 138–39
nuclear program in, 128, 131, 132,
137, 151–52, 155
petroleum industry in, 7, 89, 122,
124–25, 133–35, 134f, 137–38,
148, 149, 153–54, 162–64

repressive nature of government in,
119–20, 122–23, 138–39, 156,
162–63, 167
Russia and, 127, 135, 137–38, 148,
151, 170
Saudi Arabia and, 6–7, 120, 132, 139,
144, 145–48, 149–50, 151, 152–53,
155–56, 163–64
Shanghai Cooperation Organization
and, 150
Shia majority in, 144, 145
Silk Road initiatives and, 150–51
Silkworm anti-ship cruise missiles
and, 128
Soviet Union and, 145
state control of the economy in,
135, 136
Supreme Council of Cyberspace
in, 138
Syria and, 145–46, 147, 148
Turkey and, 146
Turkmenistan and, 91
United Kingdom and, 124–25
United States and, 7, 9, 122, 124–25,
128, 131, 132–35, 137, 145, 146,
148–50, 151–52, 153, 156, 159,
161, 162–64, 170, 178, 183, 188
Xinjiang and, 137
Yemen and, 130–31, 145–46,
147, 153
Iranian Cyber Army, 138
Iranian Revolutionary Guard Corps
(IRGC), 135–36, 138
Iraq
China and, 11–12, 122, 154
Iran and, 122–23, 127, 145, 146, 147,
151, 153
Osirak nuclear reactor bombing
(1981), 127
petroleum industry in, 154
Saudi Arabia and, 144, 145, 147, 154
United States and, 129, 139, 144, 145,
154, 170–71

patronage networks in, 95, 99, 100

petroleum industry in, 80, 88–89, 90, 92–93, 95–96, 98, 99, 101–2, 105–6, 118, 159, 177, 186

repressive nature of government in, 94, 95, 98, 110–11, 118

Russia and, 6–7, 80, 89, 90, 93, 95–96, 97–98, 102–7, 110–11, 114, 117, 118, 162, 163, 188

Shanghai Cooperation Organization and, 19, 92, 96, 113

Silk Road initiatives and, 1, 86

Soviet era in, 81, 89, 96, 99

succession politics in, 94–95, 98–99, 100–3, 104, 117, 162

United States and, 97–98, 103, 104–5, 163, 177, 182–83, 186, 188

uranium reserves in, 89–90

Xi Jinping's visit (2013) to, 1, 43–44, 93, 159

Xinjiang and, 91, 97, 101

Zunghar era in, 84

Kazatomprom, 89–90

KazMunaiGas, 90, 101–2

Kennan, George, 177–78

Khamenei, Ali, 131–32, 138

Khan, Imran

China-Pakistan Economic Corridor (CPEC) and, 49, 51–52, 53–54, 57, 59–60

China's loan to Pakistan (2018) and, 55–56

election (2018) of, 53

foreign nongovernmental organizations and, 64

Karachi consulate attack (2018) and, 65

Orange Line commuter metro rail (Lahore) and, 55

Pakistani military and, 56, 61

Xi Jinping's meeting (2018) with, 53, 55–56

Khashoggi, Jamal, 140, 142, 143

Khatami, Mohammad, 135–36

Khomeini, Ayatollah, 131–32, 144, 145

Khorgos (China), 86–88

Khyber Pakhtunkhwa province (Pakistan), 51, 67

Kissinger, Henry, 46

"KLP" (keeping a low profile strategy), 20–21

Kosnazarov, Daniyar, 93, 95–96

Krepon, Michael, 72

Kublai Khan, 82–83

Kucera, Joshua, 113–14

Kunming knife attack (2014), 13

Kuwait, 144

Kyrgyzstan

Bishkek embassy attack (2016) in, 114–15

China and, 91, 92, 114–15

Collective Security Treaty Organization (CSTO), 104

Shanghai Cooperation Organization, 19, 92, 113

Silk Road of medieval era and, 12

Soviet era in, 81

Tang Dynasty era in, 82

Lahore (Pakistan), 28, 54–55

Lake Balkhash, 105

Lampton, David, 39

Laos, 33–34

Larijani, Ali, 149–50

Lashkar-e-Taiba, 64, 67, 72–73

Latin America, 16, 89, 160, 199n44, 199n46

Lebanon, 145–46, 153

Lee Kwan Yew, 95

Libya, 18–19, 129, 160

Lichtenstein, Natalie, 27–28

Li Keqiang, 158

Lillis, Joanna, 95

Lo, Bobo, 108–9

North Africa, 17*f*, 18–19, 129

North Atlantic Treaty Organization
(NATO), 50, 175

North Korea, 41, 92, 152

North Waziristan, 70

Nuclear Nonproliferation Treaty, 75–76

Nuclear Suppliers Group, 75–76

Nurly Zhol (Kazakhstan's development
program), 86

Nurhaci (Manchurian chieftan), 83–84

Nur-Sultan (Kazakhstan), 80, 87, 95,
97–98, 103

Nusra Front, 114–15

Obama, Barack
Afghanistan and, 10, 11, 178
Central Asia policy and, 107
China and, 10, 21, 173–74, 178
India policy and, 50
Iran policy and, 131, 132, 133, 140
Middle East policy and, 129
"pivot to Asia" by, 21
Saudi Arabia and, 154–55

official development assistance
(ODA), 28–29

Oman, 154

O'Neill, Daniel, 90

Opium Wars, 45

Orange Line commuter metro rail
(Lahore, Pakistan), 28, 54–55

Organization for Security and
Cooperation in Europe, 114–15

Osirak nuclear reactor bombing (Iraq,
1981), 127

Overseas Private Investment
Corporation, 181

Pahlavi, Mohammad Reza Shah (shah of
Iran), 122–23, 145

Pakistan
Afghanistan and, 11–12, 66, 70, 72–73,
94, 169, 183
agricultural sector in, 52–53

Buddhist sites in, 44

China and, vii–ix, 3, 4–6, 7, 9, 14,
28, 33–34, 35, 37, 45–46, 47–49,
50–58, 59–63, 64–65, 66, 68–78,
79, 94, 117, 118, 135, 155, 159,
160, 161, 162, 163, 164, 165, 166,
169, 170, 176, 179, 183–84, 188
(*See also* China-Pakistan Economic
Corridor)

Cold War and, 45–46, 47

corruption in, 55, 57, 59, 60, 118

coup (1999) in, vii, 54

domestic political economy of,
50–53, 62

drone warfare and, 35, 71

election (2013) in, 54

election (2018) in, 53

energy sector in, 57–59

extremist groups in, 14, 64, 66–67,
70, 72–73, 74

foreign nongovernmental
organizations and, 64

IMF loan (2013) to, 54

India and, vii–viii, ix, 6–7, 45–46, 47,
50, 61, 65–69, 71–78, 79, 117, 118,
161, 163, 169, 183, 187

Kargil War (1999) and, viii, 66

Kashmir and, 67, 68, 69, 71,
74, 76–77

military in, 56, 59, 61–65,
71–72, 74, 79

National Highway Authority in, 51

nuclear program in, 66, 75–76, 155, 187

Quadrilateral Cooperation and
Coordination Mechanism (QCCM)
and, 71, 113

repressive nature of government in,
63–64, 79, 113–14, 118, 162, 167

Saudi Arabia and, 142, 155

security operations by China
in, 33–34

Shanghai Cooperation Organization
and, 47

United States
  9/11 terrorist attacks and, 73, 129, 139, 142–43
  Afghanistan and, 10, 11–12, 72–73, 94, 106–7, 132, 169–71, 178, 187
  Agency for International Development (USAID) in, 186
  Belt and Road Initiative and, 25, 165–66, 174
  Canada and, 111–12
  China and, ix, 9, 10–11, 14, 18, 21, 23, 25, 26, 27, 28, 30, 31, 41, 46, 79, 108, 109, 115, 116, 123, 127, 128–29, 133, 134–35, 149, 150, 151–52, 155–56, 160–61, 165–67, 168–69, 170–89
  Cold War and, 172, 176
  drone warfare and, 34–35, 62
  Eurasia integration and, 15
  India and, 50, 69, 72, 78, 118, 169, 174, 181–82
  Iran and, 7, 9, 122, 124–25, 128, 131, 132–35, 137, 145, 146, 148–50, 151–52, 153, 156, 159, 161, 162–64, 170, 178, 183, 188
  Iraq and, 129, 139, 144, 145, 154, 170–71
  Israel and, 132, 152
  Japan and, 181
  Kazakhstan and, 97–98, 103, 104–5, 163, 177, 182–83, 186, 188
  military spending in, 18
  official development assistance (ODA) from, 28–29
  outward foreign direct investment by, 16f, 16
  Pakistan and, 9, 46, 61, 62–63, 69, 70, 71, 72, 73, 74, 94, 165, 169, 170, 179, 183–84, 188
  petroleum industry in, 140
  "Quad" security dialogue and, 50
  Russia and, 107, 108, 109, 115, 117, 118, 170, 174, 183, 186, 188
  Saudi Arabia and, 35, 124–25, 127, 132, 139–40, 142–43, 144, 145–46, 148, 151, 152, 154–55, 165, 170, 186
  Silk Road initiatives and, 165
  State Department in, 165, 180
  Treasury Department in, 134
  universities in, 187
University of Texas at Austin, 39
Uri army base attack (India, 2016), 67–68
Urumqi (Xinjiang), 3, 13
Uzbekistan
  China and, 14, 114
  counterterrorism and, 14
  Islamic Movement of Uzbekistan in, 92
  Islam's arrival in, 82
  Shanghai Cooperation Organization and, 19, 92, 113
  Soviet era in, 81
  succession politics in, 98, 100
  Tang Dynasty era in, 82

Vatanka, Alex, 138
Vietnam, 78, 115, 123
Vision 2030 (Saudi Arabia), 141–42, 170
Voice of China media network, 36

Wade, Geoff, 45
Wahhabi Muslims, 123, 130
Wang Guifang, 32
Wang Xiaotao, 29
Wang Yi, 29, 35–36, 142
Wang Yong, 29
Weitz, Richard, 115
Wing Loong II (CH-4) drones, 62, 93
Wu Bangguo, viii
Wu Bingbing, 128–29
Wu Ding, 43–44, 81
Wu Jianmin, 26

Xenophon, 120
Xian court (Tang dynasty), 44, 121
Xi Jinping

activist foreign policy of, 3, 4, 22, 25, 34, 36, 119, 160, 171, 172
authoritarian nature of regime of, 109, 172
Belt and Road Initiative (BRI), 1, 4, 11, 15–16, 19–20, 25, 26–27, 35–36, 78–79, 129, 150–51
Boao Forum for Asia (2015) and, 2
China International Development Cooperation Agency and, 29
China-Pakistan Economic Corridor (CPEC) and, 4
Chinese Dream philosophy of, 20
consolidation of power at Nineteenth Party Congress (2017) by, 19–20
Egypt visit (2016) by, 130
Kazakhstan visit (2013) by, 1, 43–44, 93, 159
Khan's meeting (2018) with, 53, 55–56
Maldives visit (2014) by, 24
military reform under, 31–32
Modi's meetings with, 50, 69–70
Nazarbayev and, 80, 86, 107
Pakistan and, 4, 74
Putin and, 107, 108, 170
Saudi Arabia and, 141–42, 147–48
"SFA" (striving for achievement) strategy and, 20–22
Silk Road initiatives and, 1, 26–27, 107, 159
United Front Work Department and, 39
United States and, 115
World Economic Forum (2017) and, 36
Xinjiang. *See also* Uighurs
archaeological evidence of ancient Silk Road trade routes from, 81
Beijing government's promotion of Han Chinese settlements in, 13–14
China's economic development policies and, 14
China's security policies in, 3, 12–13, 47, 78–79, 91–92, 130

Han Chinese settlement in, 84–85
Iran and, 137
ISIS and, 130
Kazakhstan and, 91, 97, 101
oil and mineral deposits in, 13
People's Republic of China's consolidation of control over, 84–85
political re-education prisons for Uighurs in, 4, 97
Qing dynasty expansion into, 83–85
surveillance policies in, 13, 34–35
Tang Dynasty era in, 82
Urumqi riots (2009) in, 3
Zunghar era in, 84
Xuanzang (medieval Chinese monk), 44

Yameen, Abdulla, 24–25
Yang Jiechi, 29, 116
Yan Xuetong, 21–22
Yazdgard III (Sasanian emperor), 121
Yazid I, 144
Yemen, 130–31, 145–46, 147, 153
Yinchuan (China), 37–38
Yuan dynasty, 82–83, 122
Yunnan, 34–35

Zaidi, S. Akbar, 63
Zardari, Asif Ali, 55
Zarif, Javad, 149–50
Zenz, Adrian, 13
Zhang Ming, 147
Zhang Qian, 43–44, 81–82, 120
Zhao Lijian, 37
Zheng He, 44–45, 47, 83, 122, 123
Zhongxing Telecommunications Equipment Corporation (ZTE), 128–29, 138
Zhou Enlai, 11
Zhu Rongji, vii
Zimmt, Raz, 139
Zunghar empire, 84–85
Zvyagelskaya, Irina, 112